Simone Fischer-Hübner   Nicholas Hopper (Eds.)

Privacy Enhancing Technologies

11th International Symposium, PETS 2011
Waterloo, ON, Canada, July 27-29, 2011
Proceedings

W0051336

 Springer

Volume Editors

Simone Fischer-Hübner
Karlstad University, Department of Computer Science
Universitetsgatan 1, 65188 Karlstad, Sweden
E-mail: simone.fischer-huebner@kau.se

Nicholas Hopper
University of Minnesota, Department of Computer Science and Engineering
200 Union Street SE, Minneapolis, MN 55455, USA
E-mail: hopper@cs.umn.edu

ISSN 0302-9743   e-ISSN 1611-3349
ISBN 978-3-642-22262-7   ISBN 978-3-642-22263-4 (eBook)
DOI 10.1007/978-3-642-22263-4
Springer Heidelberg Dordrecht London New York

Library of Congress Control Number: 2011930843

CR Subject Classification (1998): K.6.5, D.4.6, C.2, E.3, H.4, J.1

LNCS Sublibrary: SL 4 – Security and Cryptology

Typesetting: Camera-ready by author, data conversion by Scientific Publishing Services, Chennai, India

Printed on acid-free paper

Springer is part of Springer Science+Business Media (www.springer.com)

Lecture Notes in Computer Science   6794

Commenced Publication in 1973
Founding and Former Series Editors:
Gerhard Goos, Juris Hartmanis, and Jan van Leeuwen

Message from the Program Chairs

The 2011 Privacy-Enhancing Technologies Symposium was held at the University of Waterloo in Waterloo, Canada, during July 27-29, 2011. It was the 11th in this series of meetings, and the fourth after the transition from workshop to symposium. PETS remains a premier forum for publishing research on both the theory and the practice of privacy-enhancing technologies, and has a broad scope that includes all facets of the field.

The PETS program this year included a diverse set of 15 peer-reviewed papers, selected from 61 submissions. Each submission was reviewed by at least three members of the Program Committee. This was the fourth year of the popular HotPETs session, designed as a venue to present exciting but still preliminary and evolving ideas, rather than formal and rigorous completed research results. As in past years, there were no published proceedings for HotPETs. PETS also included the traditional "rump session," with brief presentations on a variety of topics, and a panel entitled "On the Ethics of Research on Tor Users."

In addition to the peer-reviewed sessions, PETS 2011 included an invited panel dedicated to the memory of Andreas Pfitzmann, who passed away in September 2010. Andreas was a pioneer in privacy research, and one of the founders of this symposium. As a computer scientist with the rare ability to clearly explain important positions to both scientists and policy makers, he was influential in shaping both German and European technology policy. His absence is a great loss to our community and we dedicated this meeting to his memory.

We are grateful to all of the authors who submitted, to the PETS and Hot-PETs speakers who presented their work selected for the program, and to the rump session participants. We are also grateful to the Program Committee members, and to the external reviewers who assisted them, for their thorough reviews and participation in discussions – they were central to the resulting high-quality program. The following subset of these reviewers gracefully volunteered to continue their work as shepherds helping the authors improve their papers and address the reviewer comments and suggestions: Simson Garfinkel, Gregory Neven, Matthew Wright, Tom Benjamin, and Roger Dingledine. It is also a pleasure to acknowledge the contribution of our General Chairs, Katrina Hanna and Ian Goldberg, and our webmaster since 2007, Jeremy Clark, who did his usual outstanding job at evolving and maintaining the symposium's website. Our gratitude also goes to the HotPETs Chairs, Carmela Troncoso and Julien Freudiger, who put together an outstanding HotPETs program. Finally, we are particularly grateful to Microsoft for its continued sponsorship and support.

May 2011

Simone Fischer-Hübner
Nicholas Hopper

Organization

General Chairs   Ian Goldberg (University of Waterloo, Canada)
      Katrina Hanna (Research in Motion, Canada)

Program Chairs   Simone Fischer-Hübner (Karlstad University,
      Sweden)
      Nicholas Hopper (University of Minnesota,
      USA)

PET Award Chair   Claudia Diaz (K.U. Leuven, Belgium)
Stipends Chair   Roger Dingledine (The Tor Project, USA)
HotPETS Chairs   Julien Freudiger (EPFL, Switzerland)
      Carmela Troncoso (K.U. Leuven, Belgium)

Program Committee

Kevin Bauer	University of Waterloo, Canada
Jean Camp	Indiana University, USA
George Danezis	Microsoft Research, UK
Sabrina De Capitani di Vimercati	Università degli Studi di Milano, Italy
Claudia Diaz	K.U. Leuven, Belgium
Roger Dingledine	The Tor Project, USA
Hannes Federrath	University of Regensburg, Germany
Julien Freudiger	EPFL, Switzerland
Simson Garfinkel	Naval Postgraduate School, USA
Rachel Greenstadt	Drexel University, USA
Thomas S. Benjamin	Cryptocracy LLC, USA
Jean-Pierre Hubaux	EPFL, Switzerland
Aaron Johnson	University of Texas at Austin, USA
Bradley Malin	Vanderbilt University, USA
Damon McCoy	University of California San Diego, USA
Aleecia McDonald	Carnegie Mellon University, USA
David Molnar	Microsoft Research, USA
Steven Murdoch	University of Cambridge, UK
Shishir Nagaraja	IIIT Delhi, India
Arvind Narayanan	Stanford University, USA
Gregory Neven	IBM Research - Zurich, Switzerland
Pierangela Samarati	University of Milan, Italy
Adam Smith	Pennsylvania State University, USA
Carmela Troncoso	K.U. Leuven, Belgium
Matthew Wright	University of Texas at Arlington, USA

External Reviewers

Ero Balsa
Aaron Beach
Igor Bilogrevic
Michael Brennan
Maria Dubovitskaya
Elizabeth Durham
Sara Foresti
Daniel Halperin
Urs Hengartner
Ryan Henry
Victor Heorhiadi
Mathias Humbert
Murtuza Jadliwala
Ravi Jhawar
Zi Lin
Giovanni Livraga

Grigorios Loukides
Nick Mathewson
Stephen McLaughlin
Prateek Mittal
Thomas Ristenpart
Len Sassaman
Stefan Schiffner
Andrei Serjantov
Micah Sherr
Reza Shokri
Paul Syverson
Acar Tamersoy
Eugene Vasserman
Nevena Vratonjic
Nan Zhang

Table of Contents

How Unique and Traceable Are Usernames?

Daniele Perito, Claude Castelluccia, Mohamed Ali Kaafar, and Pere Manils

INRIA Rhone Alpes, Montbonnot, France
{perito,ccastel,kaafar,manils}@inrialpes.fr

Abstract. Usernames are ubiquitously used for identification and authentication purposes on web services and the Internet at large, ranging from the local-part of email addresses to identifiers in social networks. Usernames are generally alphanumerical strings chosen by the users and, by design, are unique within the scope of a single organization or web service. In this paper we investigate the feasibility of using usernames to trace or link multiple profiles across services that belong to the same individual. The intuition is that the probability that two usernames refer to the same physical person strongly depends on the "entropy" of the username string itself. Our experiments, based on usernames gathered from real web services, show that a significant portion of the users' profiles can be linked using their usernames. In collecting the data needed for our study, we also show that users tend to choose a small number of related usernames and use them across many services. To the best of our knowledge, this is the first time that usernames are considered as a source of information when profiling users on the Internet.

1 Introduction

Online profiling is a serious threat to users privacy. In particular, the ability to trace users by linking multiple identities from different public profiles may be of great interest and commercial value to profilers, advertisers and the like. Indeed, it might be possible to gather information from different online services and combine it to sharpen the knowledge of users identities. This knowledge may then be exploited to perform efficient social phishing or targeted spam, and might be as well used by advertisers.

Recent scraping services' activities illustrate well the threats introduced by the ability to match up user's pseudonyms on different social networks [1]. For instance, PeekYou.com has lately applied for a patent for a way to match people's real names to pseudonyms they use on blogs, OSN services and online forums [11]. The methodology relies on public information collected for an user, that might help in matching different online identities. The algorithm empirically assigns weights to each of the collected information to link different identities to the same individual. However, the algorithm is ad-hoc and not robust to false or mismatching information. In light of these recent developments, it is desirable that the research community investigates the capabilities and limits of these profiling techniques. This will, in turn, allow for the design of appropriate countermeasures to protect users' privacy.

S. Fischer-Hübner and N. Hopper (Eds.): PETS 2011, LNCS 6794, pp. 1–17, 2011.

In general, profiling unique identities from multiple public profiles is a challenging task, as information from public profiles is often incorrect, misleading or altogether missing [9]. Techniques designed for the purpose of profiling need to be robust to these occurrences. Recent works [2,3] showed how it is possible to retrieve users information from different online social networks (OSN). All of these works mainly exploit flaws in the OSN's API design (e.g., Facebook friend search). Other approaches [14] use the topology of social network friend graphs to de-anonymize its nodes.

In this paper, we propose a novel methodology that uses usernames — an easy to collect information — to tie user online identities. In this context usernames offer the advantage of being used and publicly accessible on almost all current web services (e.g., Twitter, Facebook, eBay, Skype, etc.). The techniques developed in this work can link different user profiles only knowing their associated usernames and it is widely applicable to all web services that publicly expose usernames. Our purpose is to show that users' pseudonyms allow simple, yet efficient tracking of online activities.

This paper has several contributions. First, we introduce the problem of linking multiple online identities relying only on usernames. This problem is, to the best of our knowledge, novel and has not been exlpored in the literature.

Second, we devise an analytical model to estimate the *uniqueness* of a username, which can in turn be used to assign a probability that a single username, from two different online services, refers to the same user. Our tool can correctly classify a username like `sarah82` as non-identifying, also it can identify the username `dan.perito` as probably identifying. Based on language models and Markov Chain techniques, our model validates an intuitive observation: usernames with low "entropy" (or to be precise *Information Surprisal*) will have higher probabilities of being picked by multiple persons, whereas higher entropy usernames will be very unlikely picked by multiple users and refer in the vast majority of the cases to unique users.

Third, we extend this model to cases when usernames are *different* across many online services . In essence, given two usernames (e.g., `daniele.perito` and `d.perito`) our technique returns the probability that these usernames refer to the same user. We build a classifier upon this probability estimation that, given two usernames, can classify with high accuracy whether the usernames belong to the same individual. This tool could allows to effectively link and trace users identities across multiple web services using their usernames only. These results are tested and validated on real world data, 10 million usernames collected from eBay and Google Profiles.

Fourth, by studying the usernames from our dataset, we discover that users tend to choose their usernames from a small set and re-use them across different services. Also, we discover that users tend to choose usernames that are highly related to each other, like the aforementioned example `daniele.perito` and `d.perito`. These two findings give an explanation of the high accuracy of our tool on the task of linking public profiles using usernames.

We envision several possible uses of these techniques, not all of them malicious. In particular, users might use our tool to test how unique their username is and, therefore, take appropriate decision in case they wish to stay anonymous. To this extent we provide an online tool that can help users choose appropriate usernames by measuring how unique and traceable their usernames are. The tool is available at `http://planete.inrialpes.fr/projects/how-unique-are-your-usernames`. Furthermore, spammers could gather information across the web to send extremely targeted spam, which we dub *E-mail spam 2.0*. For example, by matching a Google profile and an eBay account spammers could send spam emails that mention a recent sale to lure users into a scam. In fact, while eBay profiles do not show much personal information (like real names) they do show recent transactions indexed by username. This would enable very targeted and efficient phishing attacks.

Paper organization. In Section 2, we overview the related work on privacy and introduce the machine learning tools used in our analysis. In Section 3, we introduce our measure to estimate the uniqueness of usernames and in Section 4, we extend our model to compute the probability that two usernames refer to the same person and validate it using the dataset we collected from eBay and Google (Section 2.3). Different techniques are introduced and evaluated. Finally, in Section 5 we discuss potential impact of our proposed techniques and present some possible countermeasures.

2 Related Work and Background

2.1 Related Work

Tracking OSNs users In [9] the authors propose to use what they call the *online social footprint* to profile users on the Internet. This footprint would be the collection of all little pieces of information that each user leaves on web services and OSNs. While the idea is promising this appears to be only a preliminary work and no model, implementation or validation is given.

Similarly in [3], Bilge et al. discuss how to link the membership of users to two different online social networks. Noticing that there might be discrepancies in the information provided by a single user in two social networks, the authors rely on Google search results to decide the equivalence of selected fields of interest (as for assigning uniqueness of a user). Typically, the input of their algorithm is the name and surname of a user, that is augmented by the education/occupation as provided in two different social networks. They use such input to start two separate Google searches, and if both appear in the first top three hits, these are deemed to be equivalent. The corresponding users are consequently identified as a single user on both social networking sites. Bilge et al.'s work illustrates well how challenging the process of identifying users from multiple public profiles is. Despite the usage of customized crawler and parser for each social network, the heterogeneity of information as provided by users (if correct) makes the process hard to deploy, if not unfeasible, at a large scale.

Record linkage. Record linkage (RL)(or alternatively Entity Resolution) [8,4] refers to the task of finding records that refer to the same entity in two or more databases. This is a common task when databases of users records are merged. For example, after two companies merge they might also want to merge their databases and find duplicate entries. Record linkage is needed in this case if there are no unique identifiers available (e.g., social security numbers). In RL terminology two records that have been matched are said to be *linked* (we will use the same term throughout this work). The application of record linkage techniques to link public online user profiles is novel to the best of our knowledge and presents several challenges of its own.

De-anonymizing sparse database and graph data [14] proposes an identification algorithm targeting anonymized social network graphs. The main idea of this work is to de-anonymize online social graph based on information acquired from a secondary social network users are known to belong to as well. Similarity identified in the network topologies of both services allows then to identify users belonging to the anonymized graph.

2.2   Background

Information Surprisal. Self-information or Information Surprisal measures the amount of information associated to a specific outcome of a random variable. If X is a random variable and x one possible outcome, we denote the information surprisal of x as $I(x)$ [5]. Information Surprisal is computed as $I(u) = -\log_2(P(u))$ and hence depends only on the probability of x. The smaller the probability of x the higher is the associated surprisal. Entropy, on the other hand, measures the information associated to a random variable (regardless of any specific outcome), denoted $H(X)$. Entropy and Surprisal are deeply related as entropy can be seen as the expected value of the information surprisal, $H(X) = E(I(X))$. Both are usually measured in bits. Suppose there exists a discrete random variable that models the distribution of usernames in a population, call this variable U. The random variable U follows a probability mass function P_U that associates to each username u a probability $P(u)$. In this context, the information surprisal of $P(u)$ is the amount of identifying information associated to a username u. Every bit of surprisal adds one bit of identifying information and thus allows to cut the population in which u might lie in half.

If we assume that there are w users in a population, then a username u identifies *uniquely* a user in the population if $I(u) > \log_2(w)$. In this sense, information surprisal gives a measure of the "uniqueness" of a username u and it is the measure we are going to use in this work. The challenge lies in estimating the probability $P(u)$, which we will address in Section 3.

Our treatment of information surprisal and its association to privacy is similar to the one recently suggested in [7] in the context of fingerprinting browsers.

2.3   The Dataset

Our study was conducted on several different lists of usernames: (a) a list of 3.5 million usernames gathered from public Google profiles; (b) a list of 6.5 million usernames gathered from eBay accounts; (c) a list of 16000 usernames gathered from our research center LDAP directory; (d) two large username lists found online used in a previous study from Dell'Amico et al. [6]: a "finnish" dataset and a list of usernames collected from Myspace.

The "finnish" dataset comes from a list publicly disclosed in October 2007[1]. The dataset contains usernames, email addresses and passwords of almost 79000 user accounts. This information has been collected from — most likely by hacking — the servers of several Finnish web forums. The MySpace dataset comes from a phishing attack, setting a fake MySpace login web page. This data has been disclosed in October 2006 and it contains more than 30000 unique usernames.

The use we made of these datasets was threefold. First, we used the combined list of 10 million usernames (from eBay and Google) to train our Markov Chain model needed for the probability estimations. Second, we used the information on Google profiles to gather ground truth evidence and test our technique to link multiple public profiles even in case of slightly different usernames (Section 4). Third, we used all the datasets to characterize username uniqueness and depict Surprisal information distributions as seen in the wild.

Notably, a feature of Google Profiles[2], allowed us to build a *ground truth* we used for validation purposes. In fact, users on Google Profiles can optionally decide to provide a list of their other accounts on different OSNs and web services. This provided us with a ground truth, for a subset of all profiles, of linked accounts and usernames. In our experiments we observed that web services differ significantly in their username policies. However, almost all services share a common alphabet of letters and numbers and the dot (.) character. We note that usernames in different alphabets would need a training dataset in the proper alphabet. However, most services enforce strict rules on the username that can only be Latin alphanumerical characters.

3 Estimating Username Uniqueness

As we explained above, we would like to have a measure of username *uniqueness*, which can quantify the amount of identifying information each username carries. Information Surprisal is a measure, expressed in bits, that serves this purpose. However, in order to compute the Information Surprisal associated to usernames, we need a way to estimate the probability $P(u)$ for each username u.

A naive way to estimate $P(u)$, given a dataset of usernames coming from different services, would be to use Maximum Likelihood Estimation (MLE). If we have N usernames then we can estimate the probability of each username u as $\frac{count(u)}{N}$, if u belongs to our dataset, and 0 otherwise. Where $count(u)$ is simply the number of occurrences of u in the sample. In this case we are assigning maximum probability to the observed samples and zero to all the others. This approach has several drawbacks, but the most severe is that it cannot be used

---

[1] http://www.f-secure.com/weblog/archives/00001293.html
[2] http://www.google.com/profiles

to give any estimation for the usernames not in the sample. Furthermore, the estimation given is very coarse.

Instead, we would like to have a probability estimation that allows us to give estimate probabilities for usernames we have never encountered. Markov-Chains have been successfully used to extrapolate knowledge of human language from small corpuses of text. In our case, we apply Markov Chain techniques on usernames to estimate their probability.

3.1   Estimating Username Probabilities with Markov Chains

Markov models are successfully used in many machine learning techniques that need to predict human generated sequences of words, as in speech recognition [12]. In a very common machine learning problem, one is faced with the challenge of predicting the next word in a sentence. If for example the sentence is *"The quick brown fox"*, the word *jumps* would be a more likely candidate than *car*. This problem is usually referred to as *Shannon Game* following Shannon's seminal work on the topic[15]. This task is usually tackled using Markov-Chains and modeling the probability of the word *jumps* depending of a number of words preceding it.

In our scenario, the same technique can be used to estimate the probability of username strings instead of sentences. For example, if one is given the beginning of a username like `sara`, it is possible to predict that the next character in the username will likely be h. Notably Markov-Chain techniques have been successfully used to build password crackers [13] and analyse the strength of passwords [6].

Mathematical treatment with Markov Chains. Without loss of generality, the probability of a given string $c_1, ..., c_n$ can be written as $\Pi_{i=1}^{n} P(c_i|c_1, ..., c_{i-1})$, where the probability of each character is computed based on the occurrence all the characters preceding it. In order to make calculation possible a Markovian assumption is introduced: to compute the probability of the next character, only the previous k characters are considered. This assumption is important because it simplifies the problem of learning the model from a dataset. The probability of any given username can be expressed as:

$$P(c_1, ..., c_n) = \Pi_{i=1}^{n} P(c_i|c_{i-k+1}, ..., c_{i-1})$$

To utilize Markov-Chain for our task we need to estimate, in a learning phase, the model parameters (the conditional probabilities) using a suitable dataset. In our experiments we used the database of approximately 10 million usernames populated by collecting Google public profiles and eBay user accounts (see Section 2.3). In general, the conditional probabilities are computed as:

$$P(c_i|c_{i-k+1}, ..., c_{i-1}) = \frac{count(c_{i-k+1}, ..., c_{i-1}, c_i)}{count(c_{i-k+1}, ..., c_{i-1})}$$

by counting the number of n-grams that contain character c_i and dividing it by the total number of $n - 1$-grams without the character c_i. Where an n-gram is simply a sequence of n characters.

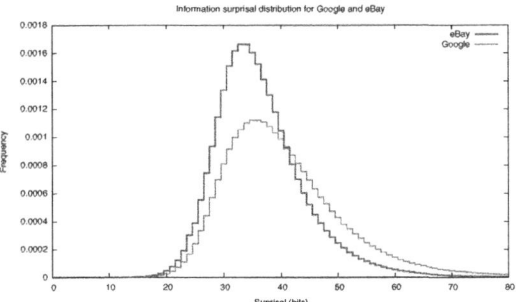

(a) Surprisal distribution for eBay and Google username

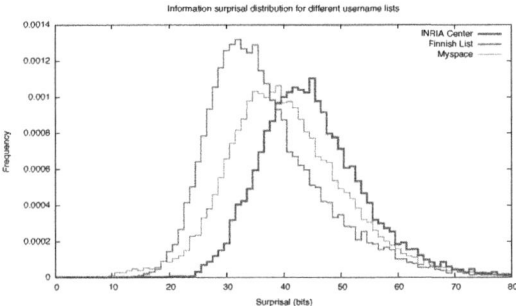

(b) Surprisal distribution for other services

Fig. 1. Information surprisal distribution for all the datasets used

Markov-Chain techniques benefit from the use of longer n-grams, because longer "histories" can be captured. However longer n-grams result into an exponential decrease of the number of samples for each n-gram. In our experiments we used 5-grams for the computation of conditional probabilities. Once we have calculated $P(u)$, we can trivially compute the information surprisal of u as $-\log_2(P(u))$. In Appendix 6 we give a different, yet related, probabilistic explanation of username uniqueness.

3.2 Experiments

We conducted experiments to estimate the surprisal of the usernames in our dataset and hence how unique and identifying they are. As explained above, our Markov-Chain model was trained using the combined 10 million usernames gathered from eBay and Google. The dataset was used for both training and testing by using leave-one-out cross validation. Essentially, when computing the probability of a username u using our Markov-Chain tool, we *excluded* u from the model's occurrence counts. This way, the probability estimation for u depended on all the other usernames but u.

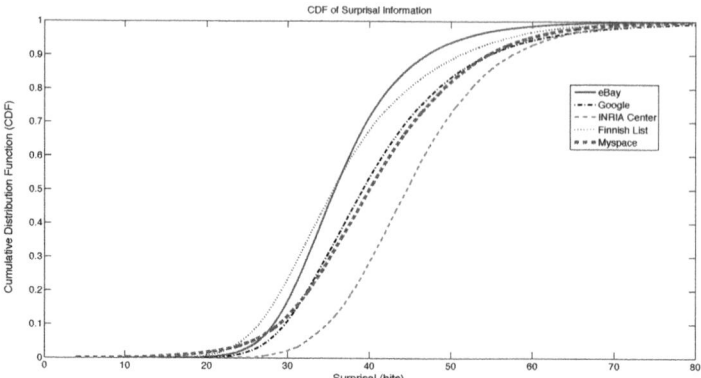

Fig. 2. Cumulative distribution function for the surprisal of all the services

We computed information surprisal for all the usernames in our dataset and the results are shown in Figure 1(a). The entropy of both distributions is higher than 35 bits which would suggest that, on average, usernames are extremely unique identifiers.

Notice the overlap in the distributions that might indicate that our surprisal measure is stable across different services. Notably, the two services have largely different username creation policies, with eBay accepting usernames as short as 3 characters from a wider alphabet and Google giving more restrictions to the users. Also, the account creation interfaces vary greatly across the two services. In fact, Google offers a feature that suggests usernames to new users derived from first and last names. Probably this is the reason why Google usernames have a higher Information Surprisal (see Figure 2). It must also be noted that both services have hundreds of millions of reported users. This raises the entropy of both distributions: as the number of users increases they are forced to choose usernames with higher entropies to find *available* ones. Overall it appears clear that usernames constitute highly identifying piece of information, that can be used to track users across websites.

In Figure 1(b) we plot information surprisal for three datasets gathered from different services. This graph is motivated by our need to understand how much surprisal varies across services. The results are similar to the ones obtained for eBay and Google usernames. The Finnish list is noteworthy, these usernames come from different Finnish forums and most likely belong to Finnish users. However, Suomi (the official language in Finland) shares almost no common roots with Roman or Anglo-Saxon languages. This can be seen as a good representative of the stability of our estimation for different languages.

Furthermore, notice that the dataset coming from our own research center (INRIA) has a higher surprisal than all the other datasets. While there are a possible number of explanations for this, the most likely one comes from the username creation policies in place that require usernames to be the concatenation of first and last name. The high surprisal comes despite the fact that the center has only around 16000 registered usernames and lack of availability does not pressure users to choose more unique usernames.

Comparing the distributions of Information surprisal of our different datasets is enlightening, as illustrated in Figure 2. This confirms that usernames collected from the INRIA center exhibit the highest information surprisal, with almost 75% of usernames with a surprisal higher than 40 bits. We also observe that both Google and MySpace CDF curves closely match. In all cases, it is worth noticing that the maximum (resp. the minimum) fraction of usernames that do exhibit an information surprisal less than 30 bits is 25% (resp. less than 5%). This shows that a vast majority of users from our datasets can be uniquely identified among a population of 1 billion users, relying only on their usernames.

4 Linking Different Username Strings

The technique explained above can only estimate the uniqueness of a single username across multiple web services. However, there are cases in which users, either willingly or forced by availability, decide to change their username. For example, the username dan.perito and daniele.perito likely belong to the same individual. Before embarking in this study, we would like to know whether users change their usernames in any predictable and traceable way. For this purpose, we use a subset of Google Profiles, in which the users explicitly gave information about the usernames of linked accounts.

In Figure 3(a) and 3(b) is plotted the distribution of the Levenshtein (or Edit) Distance for *linked* username couples. In particular, Figure 3(a) depicts the distribution for 10^4 username couples we can verify to belong to single users (we call this set L for *linked*), using our dataset. On the other hand, Figure 3(b) shows the distribution for a sample of random username couples that do not belong to a single user (we call this set NL for *non-linked*). In the first case the mean distance is 4.2 and the standard deviation is 2.2, in the second case the mean Levenshtein distance is 12 and the standard deviation is 3.1.

Clearly, linked usernames are much closer to each other than non linked ones. This suggests that, in many occurrences, users choose usernames that are related. The difference in the two distributions is remarkable and so it might be possible to estimate the probability that two different usernames are used by the same person or, in record linkage terminology, to *link* different usernames.

However, as illustrated in Section 3, and differently from record linkage, an almost perfect username match does not always indicate that the two usernames belong to the same person. The probability that two usernames, e.g. sarah and sarah2, are linked (we call it $P_{same}(sarah, sarah2)$) should depend on: (1) how "unique" is in the common part of the usernames (in this case sarah); and (2) how likely is that a user will change one username into the other (in this case the addition of a 2 at the end).

Our goal is to establish a similarity measure that lies in $[0, 1]$ between two username strings u_1 and u_2, that can then be used to build a classifier to decide whether u_1 and u_2 are linked or not. We will show two different novel approaches

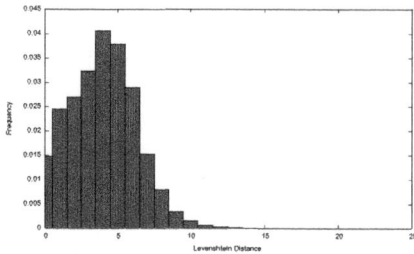
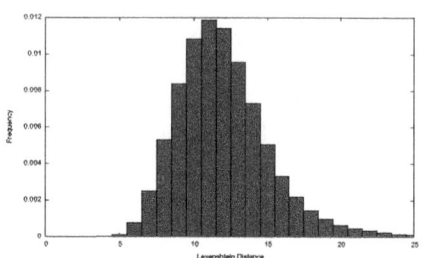
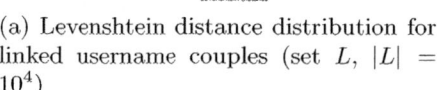

(a) Levenshtein distance distribution for linked username couples (set L, $|L| = 10^4$)

(b) Levenshtein distance distribution for non-linked username couples (set NL, $|NL| = 10^4$)

Fig. 3. Levenshtein distance distribution for username couples gathered from 3.5 million Google profiles. Only couples that different at least in 1 character were considered.

at solving this problem. The first approach uses a combination of Markov Chains and a weighted Levenshtein Distance using probabilities. The second approach makes use of the theory and techniques used for information retrieval in order to compute document similarity, specifically using TF-IDF.

We compare these two techniques to well-known record linkage techniques for a base-line comparison. Specifically we use string-only metrics like the Normalized Levenshtein Distance (NLD) and Jaro distance to link username couples. However, because of lack of space, we will not explain them in detail.

Method 1: Linkage using Markov-Chains. First of all, we need to compute the probability of a certain username u_1 being changed into u_2. We denote this probability as $P(u_2|u_1)$. Going back to our original example, $P(sarah2|sarah)$ is equal to the probability of adding the character 2 at the end of the string $\mathtt{sarah}$. This same principle can be extended to deletion and substitution. In general, if two strings u_1 and u_2 differ by a sequence of basic operations $o_1, o_2, ..., o_n$, we can estimate $P(u_2|u_1) \equiv P(u_1|u_2) = p(o_1) \times p(o_2) \times ... \times p(o_n)$.

In order to estimate the probability that username u_1 and u_2 belong to the same person, we need to consider that there are two different possibilities on how u_1 and u_2 were chosen in the first place. The first possibility is that they were picked independently by two different users. The second possibility is that they were picked by the same user, hence they are not independent.

In the former case we can compute $P(u_1 \wedge u_2)$ as $P(u_1) \times P(u_2)$ since we can assume independence. In the latter, $P(u_1 \wedge u_2)$ equals $P(u_1) \times P(u_2|u_1)$ in case the user is the same. Note that using Markov Chains and the our estimation of $P(u_2|u_1)$, we can compute all the terms involved. Estimating the probability $P_{same}(u_1, u_2)$ is now a matter of estimating and comparing the two probabilities above.

The formula for $P_{same}(u_1, u_2)$ is derived from the probability $P(u_1 \wedge u_2)$ using Bayes' Theorem. In fact, we can rewrite the probability above as $P(u_1 \wedge u_2|S)$ where the random variable S can have values 0 or 1 and it is 1 if u_1 and u_2 belong to the same person and 0 otherwise. Hence without loss of generality:

$$P(S|u_1 \wedge u_2) = \frac{P(u_1 \wedge u_2|S)P(S)}{\sum_{S=0,1}(P(u_1 \wedge u_2|S) * P(S))}$$

which leads to $P(S = 1|u_1 \wedge u_2)$ equal to

$$\frac{P(u_1)P(u_2|u_1)P(S = 1)}{P(u_1)P(u_2)P(S = 0) + P(u_1)P(u_2|u_1)P(S = 1)}$$

where $P(S = 1)$ is the probability of two usernames belonging to the same person, regardless of the usernames. We can estimate this probability to be $\frac{1}{W}$, where W is the population size. Conversely $P(S = 0) = \frac{W-1}{W}$. And so we can rewrite $P_{same}(u_1, u_2)$ as $P(S = 1|u_1 \wedge u_2)$ equal to

$$\frac{P(u_1)P(u_2|u_1)}{W * P(u_1)P(u_2)\frac{W-1}{W} + W * P(u_1)P(u_2|u_1)\frac{1}{W}}$$

Please note that when $u_1 = u_2 = u$ then the formula above becomes

$$P_{same}(u, u) = \frac{1}{(W - 1)P(u) + 1} = P_{uniq}(u)$$

which is the same estimation we devised for the username uniqueness in Appendix.

Method 2: Linkage using TF-IDF. In this case we use a well known information retrieval tool called TF-IDF. However, TF-IDF similarity measures the distance between two documents (or a search query and a document), which are set of words. We need to slightly alter the TF-IDF measure to apply it to username strings instead.

The term frequency-inverse document frequency (TF-IDF) is a weight used to evaluate how important is a word to a document that belongs to a corpus [10]. The weight assigned to a word increases proportionally to the number of times the word appears in the corpus but the importance decreases for common words in the corpus.

If we have a collection of documents D in which each document $d \in D$ is a set of terms, then we can compute the *term frequency* of term $t_i \in d$ as: $tf_{i,j} = \frac{n_{i,j}}{\sum_k n_{k,j}}$ where $n_{i,j}$ is the number of times term t_i appears in document d_j. The *inverse document frequency* of a term t_i in a corpus D is $idf_i = \frac{|D|}{c_i}$ where c_i is the number of documents in the corpus that contain the term t_i. The TF-IDF is computed as $(tf - idf)_{i,j} = tf_{i,j}idf_i$. The TF-IDF is often used to measure the similarity between two documents, say d and d', in the following way: first the TF-IDF is computed over all the term in d and d' and the results are stored in two vectors v and v'; then the similarity between the two vectors is computed, for example using a cosine similarity measure $sim(d, d') = \frac{v \cdot v'}{\|v\| \|v'\|}$.

In our case we need to measure the distance between usernames composed of a single string. The way we solved this problem is pragmatical: we consider all possible substrings, of size q, of a string u to be a document d_u. Where

d_u can be seen as the *building blocks* of the string u. The similarity between username u_1 and u_2 is computed using the similarity measure described above. This similarity measure is referred to in the literature as q-gram similarity [16], however it has been proposed for fuzzy string matching in database applications and its application to online profiling is novel.

4.1   Validation

Our goal is to assess how accurately usernames can be used to link two different accounts. For this purpose we design and build a classifier to separate the two sets L and NL, respectively of *linked* usernames and *non-linked* usernames.

For our tests the ground-truth evidence was gathered from Google Profiles and the size the number of linked username couples $|L|$ is 10000. In order to fairly estimate the performance of the classifier in a real world scenario we also randomly paired 10000 non-linked usernames to generate the NL set. The username couples were separated, shuffled and a list of usernames derived from L and NL was constructed. The task of the classifier is to re-link the usernames in L maximizing the username couples correctly linked while linking as few incorrect couples as possible. In practise for each username in the list our program computed the distance to any other username and kept only the link to the *single* username with highest similarity. If this value is above a threshold then the candidate couple is considered *linked* otherwise *non-linked*.

Measuring the performance of our binary classifier. Binary classifiers are primarily evaluated in terms of *Precision* and *Recall*, where precision is defined in terms of true positives (TP) and false positives (FP) as follows $precision = \frac{TP}{TP+FP}$ and recall takes into account the true positives compared to false negatives $recall = \frac{TP}{TP+FN}$. The recall is the proportion of usernames couples that where correctly classified as linked (TP) out of all linked usernames ($TP + FN$).

In our case, we are interested in finding usernames couples that are actually linked (true positives) while minimizing the number of couples that are linked by mistake (false positives). Precision for us is a measure of exactness or fidelity and higher precision means less profiles linked by mistake. Recall measures how complete our tool is, which is the ratio of linked profiles that are found out of all linked ones. Precision and recall are usually shown together in a precision/recall graph. The reason is that they are often closely related: a classifier with high recall usually has sub-optimal precision while one with high precision has lower recall. An ideal classifier has both a high precision and recall of 1.

Our classifier looks for potentially matching usernames. Once a set of potential matches is identified our scoring algorithms are used to calculate how likely it is that the two usernames represent the same individual. By using our labeled test data, score thresholds can be selected that yield a desired trade-off between recall and precision. Figure 4 shows the precision and recall of the two methods discussed in this paper and known string metrics (Jaro and NLD) at various threshold levels.

In general the metric based on Markov models outperforms the other metrics. Our Markov-Chain method has the advantage of having the highest precision values especially at recalls up 0.71. Remember that a recall of 0.71 means that 71% of all matching username couples have been successfully linked. Depending on the application, one might favor TF-IDF based approach (method 2) which has good precision at higher recalls or the Markov chain approach (method 1) which has the highest precision up to recall 0.7.

Table 1 shows specific examples of the performance of our classifier[3]. The similarity estimation is derived computing P_{same} as described in this Section. Username couples like `johnsmith` and `johnsmith82`, even though very similar, are deemed too common and therefore are correctly not linked by our classifier. Higher "entropy" usernames couples like `daniele.perito` and `d.perito` are correctly classified as likely belonging to the same person, even though there are 6 letters that differ out of 14. Example number 6 shows two slightly different usernames that contain the name Mohamed in them. However, since Mohamed is a very common Arabic first name, the model successfully deems the usernames as common and therefore does not link them.

Table 1. Classifier similarity threshold fixed at $5.6 \times 10{-}4$ to maximize accuracy in the training set. All the username couples with a similarity above this threshold are classified as *linked*, the ones below *non-linked*. I_1 and I_2 stand for information surprisal of username 1 and 2 respectively.

Example #	Username 1	Username 2	Similarity	I_1	I_2	Classifier Decision
1	ladygaga	ladygaga87	9.34×10^{-9}	24.37 bits	34.63 bits	Non-linked
2	johnsmith	john.smith	5.08×10^{-9}	21.87 bits	24.34 bits	Non-linked
3	johnsmith	johnsmith82	2.94×10^{-10}	21.87 bits	30.51 bits	Non-linked
4	mohamed.ali	mohamed.ali.ka	3.28×10^{-7}	28.28 bits	38.23 bits	Non-linked
5	daniele.perito	claude.castelluccia	1.75×10^{-10}	39.76 bits	52.76 bits	Non-linked
6	ccastel	claude.castelluccia	$1.10 \times 10{-}10$	24.76 bits	52.76 bits	Non-linked
7	johnsmith8219	john.smith8219	0.73	37.74 bits	40.21 bits	Linked
8	daniele.perito	d.perito	0.006	39.97 bits	31.79 bits	Linked
9	c.castelluccia	claude.castelluccia	0.046	45.64 bits	52.76 bits	Linked
10	uniquextrxyqm	kswaquniquextrxyqm	0.999	60.09 bits	88.65 bits	Linked
11	uniquextrxyqm	kswaquni1q3u4extrxyqm	0.996	60.09 bits	130.64 bits	Linked

Discussion of Results. Our results show that it is possible, with high precision, to link accounts solely based on usernames. This is due to the high average entropy of usernames and the fact that users tend to choose usernames that are related to each other. Clearly users could completely change their username for each service they use and, in this case, our technique would be rendered useless. However, our analysis shows that users indeed choose similar and high entropy usernames.

This technique might be used by profilers and advertiser trying to link multiple online identities together in order to sharpen their knowledge of the users. By crawling multiple web services and OSNs (a crawl of 100M Facebook profiles

---

[3] These examples are a combination of a set of the authors' usernames and usernames chosen to exemplify common features of the ones in our dataset.

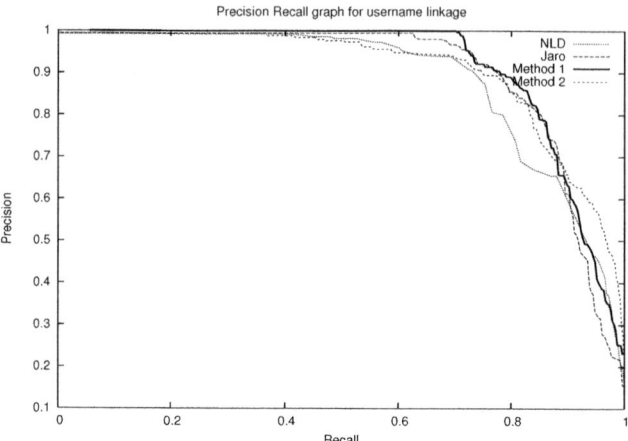

Fig. 4. Precision and recall for username Linkage

has already been made available on BitTorrent) profilers could obtain lists of accounts with their associated usernames. These usernames could be then used to link the accounts using the techniques underlined in the previous section.

Addressing Possible Limitations. The linked username couples we used as ground truth have been gathered from Google Profiles. We have shown how that, in this sample, the users tend to choose related usernames. However, one might argue that this sample might not be sufficiently representative of the whole population. Indeed Google users might be least concerned about privacy and show a preference of being traceable by posting their information on their Profiles.

We were not able to test our tool in linking profiles of certain types of web services in which users are more privacy aware, like dating and medical websites (e.g., WebMD). This was due to the difficulty of gathering ground truth evidence for this class of services. However, even if we assume that users choose completely unrelated usernames for different websites, our tool might still be used. In fact, it might be the case that a user is registered on multiple dating websites with similar usernames. Those profiles might be linked together with our tool and more complete information about the user might be found. For example, a date of birth on a website might be linked with a city of residence and a first name on another, leading to real world identification. A more thorough analysis is left for future work.

Finding linked usernames in a population requires time that is quadratic in the population size, as all possible couples must be tested for similarity. This might be too costly if one has millions of usernames to match. A solution to this problem is to divide the matching task in two phases. First, divide usernames in clusters that are likely be linked. For example, one could choose usernames that share at least one n-gram, thus restricting the number of combinations that need to be tried. Second, test all possible combinations within a cluster.

5 Discussion

This work shows that it is clearly possible to tie digital identities together and, most likely, to real identities in many cases only using ubiquitous usernames. We also showed that, even though users are free to change their usernames at will, they do not do it frequently and, when they do, it is in a predictable way. Our technique might then be used as an additional tool when investigating online crime. It is however also subject to abuse and could result in breaches in privacy. Advertisers could automatically build online profiles of users with high accuracy and minimum effort, without the consent of the users involved.

Spammers could gather information across the web to send extremely targeted spam, which we dub *E-mail spam 2.0*. For example, by matching a Google profile and an eBay account one could send spam emails that mention a recent sale or, by linking with Twitter, recent posts.

Countermeasures for Users. Following this work users might change their username habits and use different usernames on different web services. We released our tool as a web application that users can access to estimate how unique their username is and thus take informed decision on the need to change their usernames when they deem appropriate (`http://planete.inrialpes.fr/projects/how-unique-are-your-usernames`). After its launch and following media coverage [4], our tool has already been used by more than 10000 users.

Countermeasures for Web Services. There are two main features that make our technique possible and exploitable in real case scenarios. First, web services and OSNs allow access to public accounts of their users via their usernames. This can be used to easily check for existence of a given username and to automatically gather information. Some web services like Twitter are built around this particular feature. Second, web services usually allow the user pages to be crawled automatically. While in some cases this might be a necessary evil to allow search engines to access relevant content, in many instances there is no legitimate use of this technique and indeed some OSNs explicitly forbid it in the terms of service agreements, e.g., Facebook.

While preventing automatic abuse of public content can be difficult in general, for example when the attacker has access to a large number of IPs, it is possible to at least throttle access to those resources via CAPTCHAs [17] or similar techniques. For example, in our study we discovered that eBay presents users with a CAPTCHA if too many requests are directed to their servers from the same IP.

6 Conclusion

In this paper we introduced the problem of linking online profiles using only usernames. Our technique has the advantage of being almost always applicable since most web services do not keep usernames secret. Two family of techniques were introduced. The first one estimates the uniqueness of a username to link profiles that have the same username. We gather from language model theory

---

[4] E.g., MIT Technology Review: `http://www.technologyreview.com/web/32326/`

and Markov-Chain techniques to estimate uniqueness. Usernames gathered from multiple services have been shown to have a high entropy and therefore might be easily traceable.

We extend this technique to cope with profiles that are linked but have different usernames and tie our problem to the well known problem of record linkage. All the methods we tried have high precision in linking username couples that belong to the same users. Ultimately we show a new class of profiling techniques that can be exploited to link together and abuse the public information stored on online social networks and web services in general.

Acknowledgments. We would like to thank Jean Baptiste Faddoul, Arvind Narayanan, Emiliano De Cristofaro and Abdelberi Chaabane for their invaluable suggestions and insights. We would also like to thank the reviewers for their insightful comments.

References

1. Scrapers dig deep for data on web, http://online.wsj.com/article/SB10001424052748703358045755443812288117888.html
2. Balduzzi, M., Platzer, C., Holz, T., Kirda, E., Balzarotti, D., Kruegel, C.: Abusing social networks for automated user profiling. In: Jha, S., Sommer, R., Kreibich, C. (eds.) RAID 2010. LNCS, vol. 6307, Springer, Heidelberg (2010)
3. Bilge, L., Strufe, T., Balzarotti, D., Kirda, E.: All your contacts are belong to us: Automated identity theft attacks on social networks. In: 18th International World Wide Web Conference, pp. 551–560 (2009)
4. Cohen, W.W., Ravikumar, P., Fienberg, S.E.: A comparison of string distance metrics for name-matching tasks. In: Proceeding of IJCAI 2003 Workshop on Information Integrtation, pp. 73–78 (August 2003)
5. Cover, T.M., Thomas, J.A.: Elements of information theory. Wiley-Interscience, New York (1991)
6. Dell'Amico, M., Michiardi, P., Roudier, Y.: Measuring password strength: An empirical analysis
7. Eckersley, P.: How unique is your web browser? In: Atallah, M.J., Hopper, N.J. (eds.) PETS 2010. LNCS, vol. 6205, pp. 1–18. Springer, Heidelberg (2010)
8. Elmagarmid, A.K., Ipeirotis, P.G., Verykios, V.S.: Duplicate record detection: A survey. IEEE Transactions on Knowledge and Data Engineering 19, 1–16 (2007)
9. Irani, D., Webb, S., Li, K., Pu, C.: Large online social footprints–an emerging threat. In: CSE 2009: Proceedings of the 2009 International Conference on Computational Science and Engineering, pp. 271–276. IEEE Computer Society Press, Washington, DC, USA (2009)
10. Jones, K.S.: A statistical interpretation of term specificity and its application in retrieval. Journal of Documentation 28, 11–21 (1972)
11. Hussey Jr, M.P., Baranov, P., McArdle, T., Boesenberg, T., Duggal, B.: personal information aggregator. Patent application number 20100010993 (2010), http://www.faqs.org/patents/app/20100010993
12. Manning, C.D., Schuetze, H.: Foundations of Statistical Natural Language Processing, 1st edn. The MIT Press, Cambridge (1999)

13. Narayanan, A.: Fast dictionary attacks on passwords using time-space tradeoff. In: ACM Conference on Computer and Communications Security, pp. 364–372. ACM Press (2005)
14. Narayanan, A., Shmatikov, V.: De-anonymizing social networks, pp. 173–187. IEEE Computer Society Press, Los Alamitos
15. Shannon, C.E.: Prediction and entropy of printed english. Bell Systems Technical Journal 30, 50–64 (1951)
16. Tata, S., Patel, J.M.: Estimating the selectivity of tf-idf based cosine similarity predicates. SIGMOD Rec. 36(6), 7–12 (2007)
17. von Ahn, L., Blum, M., Hopper, N., Langford, J.: Captcha: Using hard ai problems for security. In: Biham, E. (ed.) EUROCRYPT 2003. LNCS, vol. 2656, pp. 646–646. Springer, Heidelberg (2003)

Appendix

Username Uniqueness from a Probabilistic Point of View

We now focus on computing the probability that only *one* users has chosen username u in a population. We refer to this probability as $P_{uniq}(u)$.

Intuitively $P_{uniq}(u)$ should increase with the decrease in likelihood of $P(u)$. However, $P_{uniq}(u)$ also depends on the size of the population in which we are trying to estimate uniqueness. For example, consider the case of first names. Even an uncommon first name does not uniquely identify a person in a very large population, e.g. the US. However, it is very likely to uniquely identify a person in a smaller population, like a classroom.

To achieve this goal we use the $P(u)$ to calculate the expected number of users in the population that would likely choose username u. Let us denote by $n(u)$ the expected number of users that choose string u as a username in a given population W. The value of $n(u)$ is calculated based on $P(u)$ as:

$$n(u) = P(u) * W$$

where W is the total number of users in the population. In our case W is an estimation of the number of users on the Internet: 1.93 billions[5].

In case we are sure there exists *at least one* user that selected the username u (because u is taken on some web service) then the computation of $n(u)$ changes slightly:

$$n(u) = P(u) * (W - 1) + P(u|u) = P(u) * (W - 1) + 1$$

where the addition of 1 comes from the fact that we are sure that there exists *at least* one user that choses u and $W - 1$ is there to account for the person for which we are sure of.

Finally we can estimate the uniqueness of a username u by simply considering the probability that our user is unique in the reference set determined by $n(u)$, hence:

$$P_{uniq}(u) = \frac{1}{n(u)}$$

---

[5] http://www.internetworldstats.com/stats.htm

Text Classification for Data Loss Prevention

Michael Hart[1], Pratyusa Manadhata[2], and Rob Johnson[1]

[1] Computer Science Department, Stony Brook University
{mhart,rob}@cs.stonybrook.edu
[2] HP Labs
manadhata@cmu.edu

Abstract. Businesses, governments, and individuals leak confidential information, both accidentally and maliciously, at tremendous cost in money, privacy, national security, and reputation. Several security software vendors now offer "data loss prevention" (DLP) solutions that use simple algorithms, such as keyword lists and hashing, which are too coarse to capture the features what makes sensitive documents secret. In this paper, we present automatic text classification algorithms for classifying enterprise documents as either sensitive or non-sensitive. We also introduce a novel training strategy, *supplement and adjust*, to create a classifier that has a low false discovery rate, even when presented with documents unrelated to the enterprise. We evaluated our algorithm on several corpora that we assembled from confidential documents published on WikiLeaks and other archives. Our classifier had a false negative rate of less than 3.0% and a false discovery rate of less than 1.0% on all our tests (i.e, in a real deployment, the classifier can identify more than 97% of information leaks while raising at most 1 false alarm every 100th time).

1 Introduction

Modern enterprises increasingly depend on data sharing, both inside and outside their organizations. Increased sharing has led to an increasing number of *data breaches*, i.e., malicious or inadvertent disclosures of confidential and sensitive information, such as social security numbers (SSN), medical records, trade secrets, and enterprise financial information, to unintended parties. The consequences of data breach can also be severe: violation of customers' privacy, loss of competitive advantage, loss of customers and reputation, punitive fines, and tangible monetary loss. The Ponemon Institute's 2009 *Cost of a Data Breach Study* found that a data breach costs an average of $6.6 million to an organization [26]. The Privacy Rights Clearinghouse lists almost 500 million records that have been leaked in data breaches since 2005 [11].

Security vendors have begun to offer a raft of "Data Loss Prevention" (DLP) products designed to help businesses avoid data breaches [37,50,53,46,45]. DLP systems identify confidential data on network storage servers, monitor network traffic and output channels to peripheral devices such as USB ports, and either enforce data control policies or generate reports that administrators can use to investigate potential breaches.

S. Fischer-Hübner and N. Hopper (Eds.): PETS 2011, LNCS 6794, pp. 18–37, 2011.

Although existing DLP solutions are quite sophisticated in detecting, capturing and assembling information flows, they are currently limited in their capability to recognize sensitive information. Many vendors offer solutions that rely on keywords, regular expressions and fingerprinting, but these techniques alone cannot fully capture the organization's secrets when it is re-phrased or re-formatted. More elaborate and comprehensive human annotations and access control will not solve the problem because they rely on users to encode in a machine-readable form the sensitive contents of the message. This is simply infeasible for certain types of data, too time consuming and too error prone. Security vendors now recognize[50] the need for DLP systems to learn and automatically classify sensitive materials.

In this paper we develop practical, accurate, and efficient machine learning algorithms to learn what is sensitive and classify both structured and unstructured enterprise documents as either public or private. Our scheme is practical because enterprise administrators need only provide an initial set of public and private documents. Our system trains a classifier using these documents, and then uses the resulting classifier to distinguish public and private documents. System administrators do not have to develop and maintain keyword lists, and our classifier can recognize private information, even in documents that do not have a substantial overlap with previously-observed private documents.

We summarize the results of our classifier on 5 testing corpora in Section 5 and compare the results with a baseline off-the-shelf classifier (Section 3). Our classifier achieves an average false positive rate of 0.46% and an average false negative rate of 1.6% on our testing corpora. The classifier also achieves a much lower false discovery rate (FDR), i.e., the percentage of false alarms defined as:

$$FDR = \frac{FP}{TP + FP}$$

raised by the classifier, than the baseline classifier. A low FDR is essential since users will ignore a system that frequently raises false alarms. If we assume a typical enterprise network (Section 5), then our classifier has an average FDR rate of 0.47% compared to the baseline classifier's average FDR rate of 16.65%. These results demonstrate that our classifier can meet the demanding needs of enterprise administrators.

In summary, this paper makes the following key contributions to the field of enterprise data loss prevention.

- We demonstrate that simply training a classifier combining enterprise data, both public and private, yields prohibitively high false positive rates on non-enterprise data, indicating that it will not perform well in real networks.
- We present a new algorithm for classifying sensitive enterprise documents with low false negative rates and false positive rates. This algorithm employs a new training technique, supplement and adjust, to better distinguish between sensitive, public and non-enterprise documents. Our algorithm scales to real time enterprise network traffic and does not rely on any metadata.
- We construct the first publicly available corpora for evaluating DLP systems.

The rest of the paper is organized as follows. We briefly describe a typical DLP system in Section 2 and discuss how our classifier fits into a DLP system. We introduce our classification algorithms in Section 3 and describe our test corpora in Section 4. We discuss our classification results in Sections 5 and 6. In Section 7, we compare our work with related work. We conclude with a summary and possible avenues of future work in Section 8.

2 Data Loss Prevention Systems

In this section, we describe a typical DLP system's building blocks and discuss how our proposed approach fits into the system. A DLP system aims to protect three types of data in an enterprise: *data-at-rest*, *data-in-motion*, and *data-in-use*. Data-at-rest is static data stored on enterprise devices such as document management systems, email servers, file servers, networked-attached storage, personal computers, and storage area networks. Data-in-motion is enterprise data contained in outbound network traffic such as emails, instant messages, and web traffic. Data-in-use is data being "used" by the enterprise's employees on end point devices, e.g., a file being copied to a USB drive.

Let us consider the definition of confidential for an organization. There certainly exist certain types of data such as Personally Identifiable Information, e.g., names, credit cards, social security numbers, that should be confidential regardless of the organization. The definition becomes more difficult to articulate, however, when we consider trade secrets and internal communications, which may be unstructured. Broadly, we define secret as information generated within the organization that is either not generally known, e.g., facts that can be found in an encyclopedia or industry magazines, or contained in public materials from the company. A DLP system will include some functionality to identify sensitive information in one or more of the aforementioned data types.

A DLP system performs three broad steps to prevent enterprise data loss. First, the system discovers the three types of enterprise data by scanning storage devices, intercepting network traffic in real time, and monitoring user actions on end point devices. Second, the system identifies confidential enterprise data from the data discovered in the first step. Third, the system enforces enterprise policies on confidential data. For example, the system may encrypt confidential data-at-rest to prevent unauthorized use; the system may block confidential data-in-motion from leaving the enterprise and may prevent confidential data from being copied to a USB device.

A DLP system faces two operational challenges: performance and accuracy. In an enterprise setting, the system should scan terabytes of data-at-rest, monitor hundreds of megabytes of real time network traffic, and monitor user actions on thousands of end point devices. The system should identify confidential data accurately in a scalable manner without producing many false positives or false negatives.

Current DLP products identify confidential data in three ways: regular expressions, keywords, and hashing. Regular expressions are used primarily to recognize data by type, e.g., social security numbers, telephone numbers, addresses, and other data that has a significant amount of structure. Keyword matching is appropriate when a small number of known keywords can identify private data. For example, medical or financial records may meet this criteria. For less structured data, DLP products use hash fingerprinting. The DLP system takes as input a set of private documents and computes a database of hashes of substrings of those documents. The system considers a new document private if it contains a substring with a matching hash in the database. Regular expressions are good for detecting well-structured data, but keyword lists can be difficult to maintain and fingerprint-based methods can miss confidential information if it is reformatted or rephrased for different contexts such as email or social networks.

It is also unlikely that more sophisticated access controls and additional user annotation will necessarily improve DLP products. First, it is likely that most sensitive materials contain a fair amount of public knowledge. Former analysts of the C.I.A. have noted that only 5% of intelligence was captured through covert actions, meaning that 95% of information in these reports is derived from public sources[24]. Therefore, assigning the privacy level to text copied and pasted from such a document is not guaranteed be the correct action. Relying on the users themselves to better identify and police sensitive materials poses several complications. Users may find encoding sensitive material to not be trivial. Even if the user has the ability to sufficiently define what is confidential in this system, it is possible for the user to forget or make a mistake. Lastly, it may not be feasible to expect that all users annotate their content consistently.

In this paper, we propose automatic document classification techniques to identify confidential data in a scalable and accurate manner. In our approach, the enterprise IT administrator provides a labeled training set of secret and non-secret documents to the DLP system instead of keywords and regular expression. We *learn* a classifier from the training set; the classifier can accurately label both structured and unstructured content as confidential and non-confidential. The DLP system will use the classifier to identify confidential data stored on the enterprise devices or sent through the network.

Our approach builds on a well-studied machine learning technique, Support Vector Machines (SVMs), that scales well to large data sets [30]. The classifier can meet an enterprise's needs ranging from a small collection of a user's sensitive material to a large enterprise-wide corpus of documents. We assume that the DLP system cannot access meta-data associated with documents, e.g., author, location, time of creation, and type. We also assume that administrators will only provide the document classifier with examples of confidential and non-confidential materials. Employees and managers, therefore, can provide confidential documents directly to the classifier, alleviating the burden of collecting a training set on IT administrators and minimizing their exposure to confidential information.

The major drawback of confidential data identification schemes used in DLP systems, including ours, is the inability of these systems to classify data they do not "understand." Encrypted data and multimedia content are examples of such data. Loss of confidential data via encryption is relatively rare in practice, only

1 out of more than 200 data breaches use encryption [54]. Hence we leave the challenges of identifying confidential data in encrypted content and multimedia content as future work.

3   Text Classifiers for DLP

This section will discuss present our approach for building text classifiers for Data Loss Prevention. We will begin by discussing the types of data a text classifier will encounter with respect to prominence and privacy. We will then describe our baseline approach for performance comparison. We will conclude the section with our approach to building text classsifiers for DLP.

Enterprise networks and computers handle three types of data: public enterprise data, private enterprise data, and non-enterprise data. Public enterprise data (*public*) includes public web pages, emails to customers and other external entities, public relations blog posts, etc. Private enterprise data (*secret*) may include internal policy manuals, legal agreements, financial records, private customer data, source code or other trade secrets. Non-enterprise data (*NE*) is everything else, and so cannot be described succinctly, but is likely to include personal emails, Facebook pages, news articles, and web pages from other organizations, some of which may be topically related to the business of the enterprise. We consider private documents to be confidential and require protection whereas *NE* and *public* documents do not. From this high-level description, we can draw several conclusions:

– Enterprise public and private documents are likely to be relatively similar since they discuss different aspects of the same underlying topics.
– Many non-enterprise documents will share almost no features with enterprise documents.
– Some non-enterprise documents may be quite similar to enterprise public documents. For example, non-enterprise documents may include news articles about the enterprise or web pages from related organizations.

A DLP text classifier is thus faced with two contradictory requirements: it must be finely tuned to enterprise documents so that it can make the subtle distinction between public and private documents that discuss the same topic, but it must not overfit the data so that it can correctly mark non-enterprise documents as public. As explained below, our solution uses a two-step classifier to solve this problem. The first step eliminates most non-enterprise documents that have little in common with enterprise documents, and the second step uses a classifier focused on documents related to the enterprise to make the finer distinction between enterprise public and private documents.

3.1   Baseline Approach

We are not aware of any previously published results on text classification for DLP. We also could not test our solution against existing DLP solutions because we could not verify if the software adhered to the constraints our classifier abides to (e.g. no meta-data is associated with documents). We first developed a baseline classifier to provide a basis for comparison and to garner insight into the structure of the DLP text classification problem.

We performed a brute search evaluating multiple machine learning algorithms and feature spaces known for their text classification performance for our baseline classifier, including SVMs [28], Naive Bayesian classifiers [35], and Rocchio classifiers [35] from the the WEKA toolkit [20] to determine the best classifier across all the datasets. We found that a support vector machine with a linear kernel performed the best on our test corpora (described in Section 4). The best performing feature space across all corpora is unigrams, i.e. single words, with binary weights. We eliminated stop words, common words such as "is" and "the", and limited the total number of features to 20,000. If a corpus contained more than 20,000 unique non-stop words, we choose the 20,000 most frequently-occurring non-stop words as our features. We use this configuration as our baseline classifier for all experiments reported in Section 5.

An SVM trained on enterprise documents achieves reasonable performance on enterprise documents, but has an unacceptably high false positive rate on non-enterprise (NE) documents. The poor performance can be explained by identifying weaknesses in the training approach. First, for two of our corpora, the classifier was biased towards the secret class, e.g., its initial expectation was most documents to be secret. And since many NE documents share very few features in common with secret documents, the classifier mislabeled these instances because it had too little information to contradict its a priori expectation. The second issue arose from overfitting of features. The public documents could not alone capture the behavior of these features for non-secret documents. It will, therefore, overweight certain features; we noticed common words like "policy" and "procedure" being instrumental in the misclassification of NE documents.

3.2   Supplement and Adjust

To remedy overfitting and overweighting common features, we *supplement* the classifier by adding training data from non-enterprise collections such as Wikipedia [16], Reuters[33], or other public corpora. As we will show in Section 5, our supplemental corpus does not need to be comprehensive. The presence of supplementary data does not train the classifier to recognize NE documents, but prevents it from overfitting the enterprise data.

We use 10,000 randomly-selected Wikipedia articles and a 1,100 document set featuring documents on finance, law and sport as our supplementary data set. We labeled the supplementary articles as *public* during training. The supplement classifier uses the same feature set as the baseline classifier and does not include features found in the supplemental data set. This prevents the classifier from using words from the supplemental data set to learn to distinguish enterprise and non-enterprise documents.

Adding supplemental training data will likely introduce a new problem: class imbalance. Supplemental instances will bias the classifier towards *public* documents because the size of this class will overwhelm the size of *secret* documents. This will result in a high false-negative rate on *secret* documents. Therefore, we need to adjust the decision boundary towards *public* instances. This will reduce the false negative rate while increasing the false positive rate. For our classifier, we measure the distance between the decision boundary and the closest, correctly classified *public* instance (either NE or *public*) and move the boundary $x\%$ of the distance towards it, for some value of x. We chose $x = 90\%$, although we show in Appendix A that our classifier is robust and performs well when $50\% \leq x \leq 90\%$.

The supplement and adjustment technique can be applied to train classifiers tailored to both *public* and *secret* documents, with the supplemental instances in both cases drawing from the same source, e.g., Wikipedia. Therefore, we denote a supplement and adjust classifier as SA_{class} where class is either *public* or *secret*. When training an SA_{secret} classifier, we combine *public* and NE documents and adjust the boundary to the closest, correctly classified *public* or NE. An SA_{public} classifier is constructed by combining *secret* and NE documents and adjust the boundary to the closest, correctly classified *secret* or NE document. We employ an SA_{secret} classifier as the first stage of our DLP text classification system.

3.3   Meta-space Classification

The first-level classifier significantly reduces the number of false positives generated by NE documents, but not completely. These documents tend to contain salient features of the *secret* class, but upon further inspection, clearly unrelated topically to confidential documents. Also, the number of false positives for *public* documents increases. Therefore, we apply a second step to eliminate false positives from documents labeled *secret* by the first step.

We address these remaining false positives in three ways. First, for a target document, we will measure how similar it is to either the *secret* or *public* set of documents. Second, we build classifiers specifically tailored for the *public* class. *Secret* and *public* documents will likely overlap in content since they are topically related and may even discuss the same entities employing similar language. Therefore, our system will attempt to learn what combination of features make these documents *public* rather than *secret*. We can use the output of this classifier in conjunction with the first step to better gauge if a document should be labeled *secret* or not. Lastly, we classify the target document based on the output of the similarity measures and classifiers (hence why we refer to this classifier as a "meta-space" classifier). We use three classes (*public*, NE, *secret*) instead of two classes (*secret*, ¬*secret*) for this step. Three classes assist the classification of *secret* documents because NE false positives exhibit different behaviors than *public* false positives for these features, making classification much more difficult if we group NE and *public* together.

To address the problem of topically unrelated documents being labeled as *secret*, we created two attributes, $xtra.info_{secret}$ and $xtra.info_{public}$, that measure the percentage of words in a document that do not appear in any document from the *secret* and *public* training corpora, respectively. These features are intended to measure the overall dissimilarity of a document, d, to documents in the *public* and *secret* corpora. For example, if d has a large value for $xtra.info_{public}$, then it is very different from documents in the *public* training corpus. We can improve the $xtra.info$ features by ignoring words that occur commonly in English and hence convey little contextual information. We compute for each word w an estimate, df_w of how often w occurs in "general" English documents. We can then ignore all words that have a high df_w value. We used 400,000 randomly-selected Wikipedia articles to estimate df_w for all words across all our training sets. If a word in our training set never occurred in Wikipedia, we assigned it a frequency of $1/400,000$. We then computed

$$xtra.info_c(d) = \frac{\left| d_{df} \setminus \bigcup_{d' \in c} d' \right|}{|d_{df}|}$$

where $d_{df} = \{w \in d | df_w \leq df\}$. In our experiments, we used $df = 0.5\%$.

The $xtra.info_{secret}$ attribute aides the classifier by giving some context information about the document being classified. If the test document is truly *secret*, than we expect it to be similar to existing *secret* documents with respect to non-trivial language (enforced by the df threshold). Table 4 shows that for *NE* examples from the Wikipedia Test corpus, the $xtra.info_{secret}$ is quite high and enables a second classifier to easily separate these documents from true *secret* documents.

To better differentiate between *public* and *secret* documents, we train a SA_{public} classifier. By combining *secret* and *NE* documents, the classifier will better recognize which features correlate with *public* documents. On it's own, the output of the classifier will not necessarily exceed the performance of the SA_{secret} classifier. But when combined with the output of SA_{secret}, $xtra.info_{public}$ and $xtra.info_{secret}$, the classifier better discriminates between *public* and *secret* enterprise documents.

The usage of this meta-space classification is improved by using three classes instead two (i.e. *secret* or $\neg secret$). Combining *public* and *NE* is not optimal because we expect much different behavior for each of the attributes. *NE* documents will most likely have higher $xtra.info_{private}$ and $xtra.info_{public}$ scores than *public* documents and be classified $\neg public$ by SA_{public}. This will negatively affect classification for these attributes because the separability of these values is diminished by grouping them together. Our SVM uses Hastie et al [21] pairwise coupling algorithm for multiclass classification.

In summary, our meta-space classifier is trained four features: the outputs of SA_{public} and SA_{secret} classifiers, $xtra.info_{public}$ and $xtra.info_{secret}$. We train the classifier on the *NE*, *public*, and *secret* documents that were misclassified by SA_{public}. *NE* and *public* documents are not combined together as in the $SA_{private}$ classifier, but rather, assigned to one of three classes (*NE*, *public* and *secret*) based on its prominence. To classify a new document, d, we first compute $SA_{secret}(d)$. If this classifier indicates that d is not *secret*, we mark d as *public*. Otherwise, we compute $SA_{public}(d)$ and $xtra.info_{public}$ and $xtra.info_{secret}$ for d and apply the meta-space classifier to obtain a final decision.

4   DLP Corpora

We have created five corpora for training and evaluating DLP classification algorithms. To our knowledge, these are the first publicly-available corpora for evaluating DLP systems. Constructing DLP corpora is challenging because they should contain private information from some enterprise, but private information is, by definition, difficult to obtain.

Three of our corpora – DynCorp, TM, and Mormon – contain private documents leaked from these organizations to WikiLeaks and public documents taken from the organizations' public web sites. We collected 23 documents from DynCorp, a military contractor, from their field manual for operatives. We obtained 174 web pages from their website [15]. WikiLeaks hosts 102 documents from Transcendental Meditation, a religious organization, that include workshop instructions written by high-ranking members of the organization. We obtained 120 public materials from various TM affiliated websites [38]. The Mormon corpus includes a Mormon handbook that is not to be distributed outside of its members. We split the handbook into 1000 character-long pieces and added two other smaller supplemental organizational documents from the church available through WikiLeaks. We split the document into smaller chunks since the handbook is the main document we could obtain from this organization, but it is also one of the most sensitive documents the organization possesses. We took an arbitrary split of 1000 characters since it should provide enough textual information for classification. We gathered 277 webpages from the Church of Jesus Christ of Latter Day Saints website [42]. Note that our inclusion of texts from religious organizations is not intended to denigrate these faiths, but because they are documents that these organizations tried to keep secret.

Our Enron corpus contains emails released during the Federal Energy Regulatory Commission labeled by Hearst et al. [23]. Our data set only includes "business-related" emails. Since Enron is now defunct, we used the Internet Archive to obtain documents from its public website [3]. We were able to obtain 581 web pages.

The Google private document dataset consists of 1119 posts by Google employees to software-development blogs. Google collaborates with many open-source software projects, so much of its software development discussions take place in public. If these same projects were conducted as closed source development, then these blog posts would be private, internal documents, so we treat them as such in our dataset. 1481 public documents were taken from PR-related blogs.

Finally, we include several corpora that are intended to represent non-enterprise documents. We sampled 10K randomly selected Wikipedia articles and denote it as the Wikipedia Test corpus. We also test the robustness of our classifier on the Brown [2] (500 samples) and Reuters [33] corpora (10788).

5   Evaluation

A successful DLP classifier must meet several evaluation criteria. It must have a low false negative rate (i.e. misclassifying *secret* documents) and low false positive rate for any non-*secret* document. It should also achieve a low false discovery rate. Furthermore, we need to show that our classifier is robust with respect to its training parameters, in particular: the choice of the supplemental corpus, the size of the supplemental corpus, and the degree of adjustment used in the supplement and adjust classifier.

We present the results of our training strategy against a baseline classifier. For all our classifiers, we tokenize all our datasets and use unigrams for features. For a baseline classifier, we only train the classifier on enterprise documents using the binary weighting scheme. For the results presented in Tables 1 and 2, we supplement the classifiers with 10000 Wikipedia articles and 1100 topical articles and adjust the classifier to move the decision boundary 90% of the distance between the decision boundary and the closest correctly labeled *public* instance. We use a document frequency of 0.5% to compute $xtra.info_{secret}$ and $xtra.info_{public}$. We compute the false negative and false positive rates by performing a 10-fold cross validation on each of the corpora, and then determine the false positive rate for NE documents by training the classifier on the entire enterprise dataset and then classifying our Wikipedia false positive corpus.

The results of our classification tests show that our training strategy maintains low false negative and false positive rates on enterprise documents while

Table 1. The false positive (FP) and false negative (FN) rates on the enterprise corpora for each of our classification strategies. 11,100 instances and an adjustment of 90% are used.

Classifier	DynCorp		TM		Enron		Mormon		Google	
	FP	FN	FP	FN	FP	FN	FP	FN	FP	FN
Baseline	0.0%	0.0%	2.5%	0.98%	0.87%	0.0%	0.72%	1.4%	1.8%	1.9%
Supplement	0.0%	8.0%	0.0%	11.0%	0.0%	5.0%	0.0%	0.3%	0.0%	3.7%
Supplement and Adjust	2.0%	0.0%	28.3%	0.0%	4.1%	1.2%	4.6%	0.0%	15.9%	0.3%
Two-step	0.0%	0.0%	0.0%	0.98%	0.87%	3.0%	0.36%	1.4%	1.0%	2.1%

Table 2. The false positive rates on our Wikipedia false positive corpus for each of the classification strategies

Classifier	Non-enterprise False Positive Rate				
	DynCorp	Enron	Mormon	Google	TM
Baseline	4.7%	87.2%	0.16%	7.9%	25.1%
Supplement	0.0%	0.01%	0.06%	0.0%	0.0%
Supplement and Adjust	0.26%	2.5%	0.1%	2.8%	0.93%
Two-step	0.0%	0.05%	0.0%	0.06%	0.01%

Table 3. The False Discovery Rate of the baseline approach far exceeds our classifier, implying that the baseline approach would fare poorly in real world networks whereas ours would not raise much fewer alarms

Dataset	Baseline FDR	Our classifier FDR
DynCorp	4.49%	**0.00%**
Enron	47.05%	**0.92%**
Google	8.99%	**1.06%**
Mormon	0.88%	**0.36%**
TM	22.06%	**0.01%**

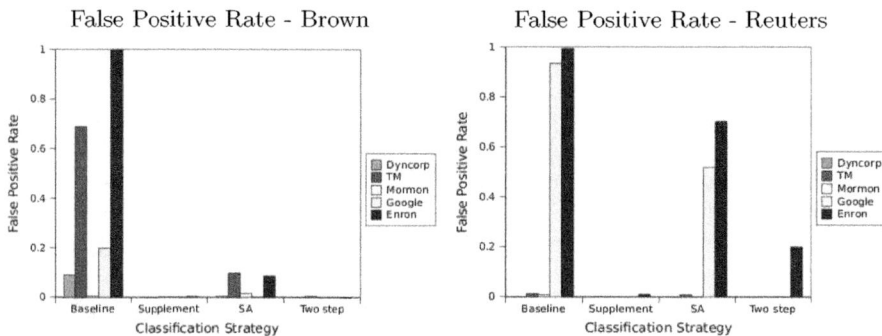

Fig. 1. The false positive rates for each classification strategy. The two-step classifier is able to maintain a low false positive rate across all the different corpora for each *non-enterprise* corpora.

dramatically improving the false positive rate on NE documents. The baseline approach would be unusable in practice because of its high false positive rate on NE documents.

In our results shown in Table 3, we assume the following traffic composition in a typical enterprise network: 25% enterprise secret documents, 25% enterprise public documents, and 50% non-enterprise documents. We believe that our approach will not engender "alarm fatigue", whereas the baseline approach is likely to overwhelm operators with false alarms.

The supplement and adjust classifier achieves a low false positive rate on NE documents for several reasons. The supplement and adjustment classifier did not rely on finding features that were strongly indicative of the *public* class. This is a crucial benefit because the NE document set's size is so large that it would be impossible to create a set of features that were *strongly indicative* of all possible *public* documents. In addition to relying less on features that were indicative of *public* documents, the supplement and adjustment classifier moves the expectation further towards the *public* class, which is in line with our expectation of the problem outlined in the problem description. And by performing an adjustment to the decision boundary, the classifier reduces the false negative rate without increasing the false positive rate, when combined with the second level classifier.

5.1   Effective Training Parameters

Figure 1 demonstrates that our classifier is robust with respect to the choice of the supplemental corpus. Our supplemental corpus consisted solely of Wikipedia documents but, as Figure 1 shows, the resulting two-step classifier has a low false positive rate on NE documents drawn from drastically different corpora, such as the Brown or Reuters news corpora. Thus, we can build a standard non-enterprise corpus that is used by all enterprises to train their DLP systems. The corpus will not need to be customized for each enterprise or for each new form of Internet traffic.

As expected, a larger supplemental corpus decreases the false positive rate but increases the false negative rate as the classifier becomes more biased towards *public* documents (see Appendix A for details). Note that Google is a clear outlier in this evaluation. We suspect that this may be because the Google corpus is the only artificial corpus in our data set. Recall that all the Google documents, including the "private" ones, are in reality *public* documents, unlike our other corpora which contain genuine private enterprise documents. The second step of our approach remedies the errors made on *public* enterprise documents. We also conclude that the supplemental corpus does not need to be too large – about 10,000 documents suffice.

We also investigated the effect of the adjustment value on the classifier. According to the graphs in Appendix A, an adjustment value of 0.5 provides a good trade-off between increased false positives and false negatives in the supplement and adjust classifier. However, since we added a second-level classifier that can filter out many false positives, we chose an adjustment value of 0.9 in order to achieve a slightly lower false negative rate.

6   Discussion

The algorithm presented in this paper should prevent accidental leakages of information, but how will it fare against intentional leakages? According to Proof-Point [44], most data leakages are accidental. The most common intentional leakage occurs when employees download sensitive information upon termination of employment. Our method coupled with the DLP system's ability to recognize data flow from a trusted to an untrusted device should prevent these type of leakages. If the data were encrypted or re-encoded, this would exceed the capability of our classifier. These more sophisticated attacks, fortunately, only account for 1 in 200 data breaches [54].

It is instructive to highlight key differences between our solution and existing semi-supervised and class imbalance solutions. Our algorithm is a supervised learning approach: all examples are labeled. During training, the classifier will know if the enterprise document is confidential or not. Since supplemental training instances do not come from the enterprise, these instances are labeled opposite from the class we wish to train on, e.g., for the $SA_{private}$ classifier, these supplemental instances are labeled as *public*. For the purposes of our algorithm, we focus on recognizing sensitive information that either it has either seen before or is similar to an existing confidential document. In the future, we hope to explore how the system can infer if a document is sensitive if it has zero training data to support this decision (possibly relying on metadata).

Our study demonstrates that DLP systems face an inherent class imbalance issue: nearly all documents that exist are outside the organization and are not sensitive. To train a classifier on this class is simply infeasible because of its size. Our key insight into this problem is recognizing that our classifiers needed to be trained to effectively learn what is *secret*, and not rely too heavily upon features that were correlated with non-*secret* documents. The problem of class imbalance has been studied and work in this area is discussed in Section 7. Once we recognized that class imbalance would be an issue for achieving maximal performance, we tried many of the approaches listed in the Section 7, but found that they were ineffectual on this specific problem.

Our approach is unique from other class imbalance techniques because we attempt to better determine which features correlate with sensitive information by adding additional samples that express a diverse usage of language. We cannot say how well this technique will extrapolate to other machine learning problems, but it is applicable to our specific problem of generating a classifier robust enough to perform well in the presence of many unrelated documents. To the best of our knowledge, using supplemental data (not synthetically generated) to generate negative examples has not been applied to the class imbalance for text classification.

An important design decision in this algorithm was to restrict the vector space to features included only in *secret* and *public* documents. The reasoning behind this decision is related to the class imbalance aspect of this problem. Since the number of non-*secret* documents is so large, adding additional features to the vector space would have resulted in overfitting because those features would factor prominently into classifying NE documents in the training step. The classifier may not accurately reweight features that *secret* documents share with non-*secret* documents. And since it would be impossible to provide the classifier with training representative of everything that is NE, the classifier would be more likely to generate false positives.

The *xtra.info* attribute performs exceedingly well in maximizing separability between NE and *secret* documents, as shown in Table 4. Contextual information is quite important because we have limited our vector space to only enterprise documents, which these terms are assumed to be related to the knowledge domain of the enterprise. Using a unigram vector space, we lose contextual information that may help counteract the effect of polysemy that contributes to the misclassification of NE documents. Our *xtra.info* attribute is effective in the second level of classification in providing contextual information to disambiguate between *secret* and NE classes and is easily computable.

The techniques of our algorithm performed well for many different different types of media and organizations. One limitation in creating our DLP corpora is that it the documents for each organization do not represent the entirety of its

Table 4. This table presents the means for the $xtra.info_{secret}$ attribute for each of our private corpora and the document classes *secret* and *NE*. The significant differences between the means for these classes suggest that this attribute will aide the classifier in distinguishing *NE* documents from *secret*.

Mean $xtra.info_{secret}$	Dyncorp	Enron	Google	Mormon	TM
Secret documents	0.54 (0.10)	0.83 (0.09)	0.70 (0.15)	0.49 (0.15)	0.66 (0.11)
NE documents	0.96 (0.03)	0.99 (0.02)	0.98 (0.04)	0.95 (0.08)	0.99 (0.02)

operations. It was not feasible to either find or build a corpus of this nature because of the risk for corporations assembling and releasing this data. We believe, however, that since our algorithm performed well in many different instances, it will perform well enterprise wide. Depending on the size and structure of the organization, multiple classifiers can be built for each of the different departments and group. Text clustering can also assist in building cogent collections of documents to train and build classifiers. And since the classification techniques we use are not computationally expensive, the penalty for evaluating multiple classifiers is not prohibitively greater.

The system described in this paper will most likely be part of a larger enforcement framework that will defend the network from intrusions and malware. Administrators will need to provide instances of *secret* and *public* documents because the training of our system is supervised. This collection of samples, however, should not be difficult to obtain because it can be automated and does not require further annotations. Employees can designate folders on storage devices that contain either *secret* or *public* documents or manually submit examples through a collection facility, e.g, email or web-based system. Depending on the enterprise policy enforcement guidelines, messages that the classifier suspects to be *secret* may prompt the sender to reconsider, queue the message for an administrator to review, or simply block the transaction. The toolkit we implemented will be made available from the author's website.

7 Related Work

Automated document classification is a well studied research area. Research in the document classification field dates back to 1960s [36,6]. The use of machine learning in text classification, however, became popular in the last two decades. Sebastiani provides an excellent overview of the area: he describes various text categorization algorithms, approaches to evaluate the algorithms, and various application of automated text categorization [48]. The proliferation of digital documents and the explosion of the web has given rise to many applications of document classification, e.g., automatic document indexing for information retrieval systems [18], classification of news stories [22], email filtering to classify emails into categories [12], spam filtering to identify spam from legitimate email messages [1], automatic categorization of web pages [4,8], and product review classification [51]. The research community has explored many different machine learning approaches for text categorization, e.g., Bayesian classifiers [1,34,32], decision trees [7], k-nearest neighbors [14], neural networks [41], regression models [17], and support vector machines [29]. Researchers have also experimented with the idea of combining multiple classifiers to increase efficacy, most notable being Schapire et al.'s *boosting* approach [47].

We utilize Support Vector Machines, a powerful margin-based classification and regression technique introduced by Cortes and Vapnik, in our classifier [13]. Joachims applied SVMs to the text classification task [28] and identified properties of text categorization that makes SVMs suitable for the task. For example, text categorization has to deal with large numbers of features, as words present in a document are considered the document's features. Feature selection is a traditional approach to select a few *relevant* features from many. In the case of text, however, most features are relevant. Hence a good text classifier should be able to handle many features. SVMs can handle large numbers of features due to overfitting protection. Also, SVMs are good *linear* classifiers and many text categorization tasks are linearly separable.

Text classification for DLP presents difficulties that standard classifiers cannot solve because of the lack of a proper training set. It is difficult to supply the classifier with an adequate representation of what should be *public* (i.e., not *secret*). Therefore, this paper addresses the precise problem of an unrepresentative dataset for text classification with the techniques of supplement and adjust, *xtra.info*, and utilizing a two-step classifier. Other research has focused on related topics.

Accurate text classification in the case of limited training examples is a challenging task. Joachims used a transductive approach to handle the problem [31]; his approach focuses on improving the classification accuracy of SVMs for a given test set. Blum and Mitchell introduced a co-training approach to categorize web pages [5]. They improved classification accuracy by adding a larger number of unlabeled examples to a smaller set of labeled examples. Toutanova et al. demonstrated the use of hierarchical mixture models in the presence of many text categories [52].

Researchers have also investigated mitigating the effect of class imbalance on classification performance [10]. Both oversampling and undersampling classes in the training instances has been widely investigated. The sampling can be random or directed. Synthetic generation of examples for underrepresented classes has also been explored and combined with under and over sampling [9]. One class learning classifiers have been proposed to improve classification for target classes where examples are relatively scarce compared to other classes [27]. An instance is compared with training examples in terms of similarity to determine whether the instance is a member of the target class. Lastly, feature selection techniques can improve classification of underrepresented classes because high dimensional data may overfit or be biased towards the majority classes [40].

Several projects have used Wikipedia to enhance text classification, particularly where context is unavailable due to the brevity of the text to be classified [19,43,25,39]. Gabrilovich et al. [19] first proposed transforming a document into its representation in Wikipedia topic space. Others have modified this basic idea by including topic hyponomy and synonymy [25] or performing LSA on this topic space [39]. Others have investigated using Wikipedia to determine relatedness between texts, particularly short texts [49]. To our knowledge, no one has investigated using Wikipedia explicitly to augment their training corpus.

8   Conclusion and Future Work

This paper presents a simple, efficient, and effective way to train classifiers and perform classification for Data Loss Prevention. In doing so, it presents the first corpora for the DLP task. Our results indicate a naive approach to training a classifier, solely on documents from the enterprise, will lead to a high false positive rate on unrelated documents, indicating poor real world performance. The paper presents a novel technique, supplement and adjust, which reduced the false positive rate for documents unrelated to the core business function.

We plan to further study the efficacy of our text classification approach by deploying it on existing private, enterprise and governmental networks. We will also look to expand our approach to include encrypted and multimedia content. In this work, we only consider the content of a document to render a decision. We would like to investigate what meta data associated with the content could be used to improve classification.

Lastly, not all secret documents in the world are written in English. We will hope to expand our private corpus in the future to include non-English sources. Our intuition is that many language processing techniques developed to handle language specific obstacles should be applied to the processing of these documents. We will also have to adjust our supplemental corpus accordingly to provide realistic behavior for NE feature behavior.

References

1. Androutsopoulos, I., Koutsias, J., Chandrinos, K.V., Spyropoulos, C.D.: An experimental comparison of naive bayesian and keyword-based anti-spam filtering with personal e-mail messages. In: SIGIR 2000: Proceedings of the 23rd annual international ACM SIGIR Conference on Research and Development in Information Retrieval, pp. 160–167. ACM, New York (2000)
2. Internet Archive. Brown corpus, http://www.archive.org/details/BrownCorpus
3. Internet Archive. Wayback machine, http://www.archive.org/web/web.php
4. Attardi, G., Gull, A., Sebastiani, F.: Automatic web page categorization by link and context analysis. In: Proceedings of THAI 1999, 1st European Symposium on Telematics, Hypermedia and Artificial Intelligence (1999)
5. Blum, A., Mitchell, T.: Combining labeled and unlabeled data with co-training. In: COLT 1998: Proceedings of the eleventh annual conference on Computational learning theory, pp. 92–100. ACM, New York (1998)
6. Borko, H., Bernick, M.: Automatic document classification. J. ACM 10(2), 151–162 (1963)

7. Breiman, L., Friedman, J., Olshen, R., Stone, C.: Classification and Regression Trees. Wadsworth, Belmont (1984)
8. Chakrabarti, S., Dom, B., Agrawal, R., Raghavan, P.: Scalable feature selection, classification and signature generation for organizing large text databases into hierarchical topic taxonomies. The VLDB Journal 7(3), 163–178 (1998)
9. Chawla, N.V., Bowyer, K.W., Hall, L.O., Kegelmeyer, W.P.: Smote: synthetic minority over-sampling technique. Journal of Artificial Inteligence Research 16, 321–357 (2002)
10. Chawla, N.V., Japkowicz, N., Kolcz, A.: Editorial: Special issue on learning from imbalanced data sets. SIGKDD Explorer Newsletter 6(1) (2004)
11. Privacy Rights Clearinghouse. Chronology of data breaches: Security breaches 2005–present (August 2010), http://www.privacyrights.org/data-breach
12. Cohen, W.W.: Learning rules that classify e-mail. In: In Papers from the AAAI Spring Symposium on Machine Learning in Information Access, pp. 18–25. AAAI Press, Menlo Park (1996)
13. Cortes, C., Vapnik, V.: Support-vector networks. Machine Learning, 273–297 (1995)
14. Cover, T., Hart, P.: Nearest neighbor pattern classification. IEEE Transactions on Information Theory 13(1) (1967)
15. Dyncorp. Dyncorp website, http://www.dyncorp.com
16. Wikimedia Foundation. Wikipedia, http://en.wikipedia.org/
17. Freedman, D.: Statistical Models: Theory and Practice. Cambridge University Press, New York (2005)
18. Fuhr, N., Knorz, G.E.: Retrieval test evaluation of a rule based automatic indexing (air/phys). In: Proc. of the Third Joint BCS and ACM Symposium on Research and Development in Information Retrieval, pp. 391–408. Cambridge University Press, Cambridge (1984)
19. Gabrilovich, E., Markovitch, S.: Computing semantic relatedness using wikipedia-based explicit semantic analysis. In: Proceedings of the 20th International Joint Conference on Artifical Intelligence, pp. 1606–1611. Morgan Kaufmann Publishers Inc, San Francisco (2007)
20. Hall, M., Frank, E., Holmes, G., Pfahringer, B., Reutemann, P., Witten, I.H.: The weka data mining software: an update. SIGKDD Explor. Newsl. 11(1), 10–18 (2009)
21. Hastie, T., Tibshirani, R.: Classification by pairwise coupling. In: Proceedings of the 1997 Conference on Advances in Neural Information Processing Systems 10. NIPS 1997, pp. 507–513. MIT Press, Cambridge (1997)
22. Hayes, P.J., Weinstein, S.P.: Construe/tis: A system for content-based indexing of a database of news stories. In: IAAI 1990: Proceedings of the The Second Conference on Innovative Applications of Artificial Intelligence, pp. 49–64. AAAI Press, Menlo Park (1991)
23. Hearst, M.: Teaching applied natural language processing: triumphs and tribulations. In: TeachNLP 2005: Proceedings of the Second ACL Workshop on Effective Tools and Methodologies for Teaching Natural Language Processing and Computational Linguistics. Association for Computational Linguistics, Morristown, NJ, USA (2005)
24. Hitz, F.: Why Spy?: Espionage in an Age of Uncertainty. Thomas Dunne Books (2008)
25. Hu, J., Fang, L., Cao, Y., Zeng, H.-J., Li, H., Yang, Q., Chen, Z.: Enhancing text clustering by leveraging wikipedia semantics. In: Proceedings of the 31st Annual International ACM SIGIR Conference on Research and Development in Information Retrieval. SIGIR 2008, pp. 179–186. ACM, New York (2008)

26. Poneman Institute. Fourth annual us cost of data breach study (January 2009), http://www.ponemon.org/local/upload/fckjail/generalcontent/18/file/2008-2009USCostofDataBreachReportFinal.pdf
27. Japkowicz, N.: Supervised versus unsupervised binary-learning by feedforward neural networks. Machine Learning 42, 97–122 (2001)
28. Joachims, T.: Text categorization with support vector machines: Learning with many relevant features. In: Nédellec, C., Rouveirol, C. (eds.) ECML 1998. LNCS, vol. 1398, pp. 137–142. Springer, Heidelberg (1998)
29. Joachims, T.: Learning to Classify Text Using Support Vector Machines – Methods, Theory, and Algorithms. Springer, Kluwer (2002)
30. Joachims, T.: Making large-scale support vector machine learning practical. MIT Press, Cambridge (1999)
31. Joachims, T.: Transductive inference for text classification using support vector machines. In: International Conference on Machine Learning (ICML), Bled, Slowenien, pp. 200–209 (1999)
32. Koller, D., Lerner, U., Angelov, D.: A general algorithm for approximate inference and its application to hybrid bayes nets. In: Proceedings of the Fifteenth Annual Conference on Uncertainty in Artificial Intelligence (1999)
33. Lewis, D.: Reuters 21578, http://www.daviddlewis.com/resources/testcollections/reuters21578/
34. Li, X., Liu, B.: Learning to classify texts using positive and unlabeled data. In: IJCAI 2003: Proceedings of the 18th International Joint Conference on Artificial Intelligence, pp. 587–592. Morgan Kaufmann Publishers Inc, San Francisco (2003)
35. Manning, C.D., Raghavan, P., Schtze, H.: Introduction to Information Retrieval. Cambridge University Press, New York (2008)
36. Maron, M.E.: Automatic indexing: An experimental inquiry. J. ACM 8(3), 404–417 (1961)
37. McAfee. Data loss prevention, http://www.mcafee.com/us/enterprise/products/data_loss_prevention/
38. Transcendental Meditation. Transcendental meditation websites, http://www.alltm.org, http://www.alltm.org
39. Minier, Z., Bodo, Z., Csato, L.: Wikipedia-based kernels for text categorization. In: Proceedings of the Ninth International Symposium on Symbolic and Numeric Algorithms for Scientific Computing, pp. 157–164. IEEE Computer Society Press, Los Alamitos (2007)
40. Mladenic, D., Grobelnik, M.: Feature selection for unbalanced class distribution and naive bayes. In: Proceedings of the Sixteenth International Conference on Machine Learning. ICML 1999, pp. 258–267. Morgan Kaufmann, San Francisco (1999)
41. Ng, K.: A comparative study of the practical characteristics of neural network and conventional pattern classifiers. Technical report (1990)
42. Church of Jesus Christ of Latter Day Saints. Church of jesus christ of latter day saints website, http://lds.org
43. Phan, X.-H., Nguyen, L.-M., Horiguchi, S.: Learning to classify short and sparse text & web with hidden topics from large-scale data collections. In: Proceeding of the 17th International Conference on World Wide Web (WWW 2008), pp. 91–100. ACM, New York (2008)
44. Proofpoint. Outbound email security and data loss prevention, http://www.proofpoint.com/id/outbound/index.php

45. proofpoint. Unified email security, email archiving, data loss prevention and encryption, http://www.proofpoint.com/products/

46. RSA Data Loss Prevention, http://www.rsa.com/node.aspx?id=1130

47. Schapire, R.E.: Theoretical Views of Boosting and Applications. In: Watanabe, O., Yokomori, T. (eds.) ALT 1999. LNCS (LNAI), vol. 1720, pp. 13–25. Springer, Heidelberg (1999)

48. Sebastiani, F.: Machine learning in automated text categorization. ACM Comput. Surv. 34(1), 1–47 (2002)

49. Strube, M., Ponzetto, S.P.: Wikirelate! computing semantic relatedness using wikipedia. In: Proceedings of the 21st National Conference on Artificial Intelligence, vol. 2, pp. 1419–1424. AAAI Press, Menlo Park (2006)

50. Symantec. Data Loss Prevention Products & Services, http://www.symantec.com/business/theme.jsp?themeid=vontu

51. Thet, T.T., Na, J.-C., Khoo, C.S.G.: Filtering product reviews from web search results. In: DocEng 2007: Proceedings of the 2007 ACM symposium on Document engineering, pp. 196–198. ACM, New York (2007)

52. Toutanova, K., Chen, F., Popat, K., Hofmann, T.: Text classification in a hierarchical mixture model for small training sets. In: CIKM 2001: Proceedings of the Tenth International Conference on Information and Knowledge Management, pp. 105–113. ACM, New York (2001)

53. Trend Micro. Trend Micro Data Loss Prevention, http://us.trendmicro.com/us/products/enterprise/data-loss-prevention/

54. Trustwave. Global security report 2010 (February 2010), https://www.trustwave.com/whitePapers.php

A   Effects of Supplement and Adjustment

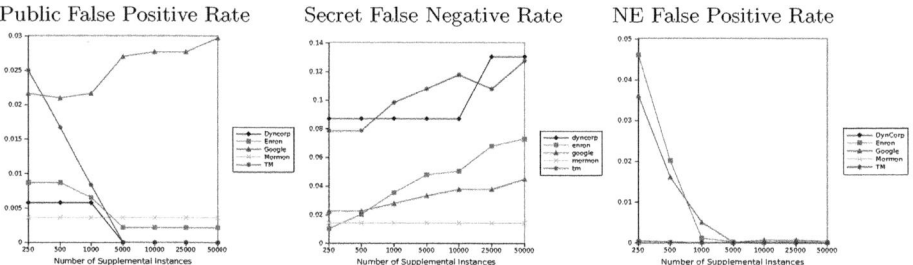

The effect on the false negative and false positive rates for our corpora when supplementing the training instances with Wikipedia examples. For the Mormon corpus, the effect of adding any supplemental instances seems to affect the classification of the same documents.

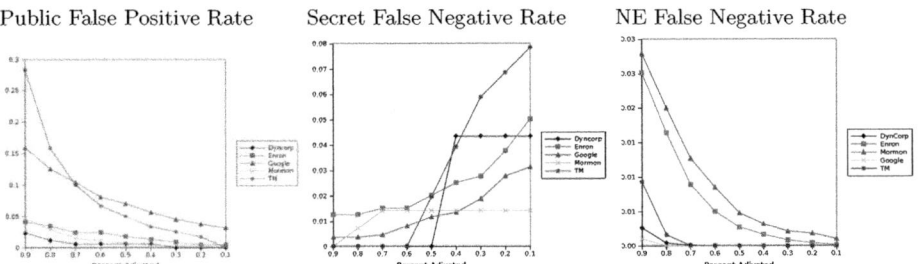

The false positive and false negative rates on enterprise documents after applying the supplement and adjust classifier.

P3CA: Private Anomaly Detection Across ISP Networks*

Shishir Nagaraja[1], Virajith Jalaparti[2], Matthew Caesar[2], and Nikita Borisov[2]

[1] IIIT Delhi
nagaraja@iiitd.ac.in
[2] University of Illinois at Urbana-Champaign
{jalapar1,caesar,nikita}@illinois.edu

Abstract. Detection of malicious traffic in the Internet would be much easier if ISP networks shared their traffic traces. Unfortunately, state-of-the-art anomaly detection algorithms require detailed traffic information which is considered extremely private by operators. To address this, we propose an algorithm that allows ISPs to cooperatively detect anomalies without requiring them to reveal private traffic information. We leverage secure multiparty computation to design a privacy-preserving variant of *principal component analysis* (PCA) that limits information propagation across domains. PCA is a well-proven technique for isolating anomalies on network traffic and we target a design that retains its scalability and accuracy. To validate our approach, we evaluate an implementation of our design against traces from the Abilene Internet2 IP backbone network as well as synthetic traces, show that it performs *efficiently* to support an online anomaly detection system and and conclude that privacy-preserving anomaly detection shows promise as a key element of a wider network anomaly detection framework. In the presence of increasingly serious threats from modern networked malware, our work provides a first step towards enabling larger-scale cooperation across ISPs in the presence of privacy concerns.

1 Introduction

A serious threat to Internet users is the increasingly advanced set of attacks employed by malware to remotely compromise their resources. Compromised machines are used to propagate spam, worms and viruses and participate in DoS attacks. The tremendous scale and complexity of network traffic makes detection of malicious behavior in network traffic an extremely hard problem.

The seriousness of this problem has led network operators to pursue *in-network* solutions to detect and localize malicious traffic. Modern ISPs run monitoring systems to localize malicious traffic, and some offer "scrubbing" services to customers to remove malicious traffic before delivery to the customer [31]. While several approaches have been proposed for detecting malicious traffic, the

---

* This research was supported in part by the National Science Foundation grants: CNS 08–31488 and CNS 10–53781 and the IBM X10 innovation award.

S. Fischer-Hübner and N. Hopper (Eds.): PETS 2011, LNCS 6794, pp. 38–56, 2011.

use of *principal component analysis* (PCA) stands out. An array of techniques based on PCA have been recently proposed [17,25,27] to detect statistical anomalies in volume or other characteristics of traffic flowing across networks. These schemes rely on monitoring protocols employed at routers to sample traffic (e.g., NetFlow [8] and SNMP counters), aggregate these observations across routers and perform anomaly detection on the aggregate. PCA enables scaling to large datasets by reducing the dimensionality of the traffic and has been shown in the literature to perform well on a variety of workloads and topologies to detect malicious traffic, performance problems, and other forms of outages and hard-to-detect failures.

Performance of these techniques improves with increasing number of vantage (monitoring) points. In addition to providing visibility into a larger number of inter-host paths, additional vantage points increase the likelihood that a given malicious traffic flow is "exposed" due to different statistical mixes of traffic appearing on each observed link. For example, it has been shown that if neighboring ISPs were to cooperate by sharing traffic measurements, anomaly detection could be done with much higher accuracy and anomalies that cannot be detected by each of the ISPs individually could be detected [30]. However, anomaly detection today is unfortunately constrained to operate within a single ISP network as ISPs are highly reluctant to reveal the topology and traffic information necessary for these algorithms to run since they are extremely confidential business information.

Contributions: In our work, we leverage work in secure multiparty computation (SMC) and propose *Privacy-Preserving PCA* (P3CA), a mechanism which supports cooperation among ISPs, allowing them to perform anomaly detection jointly with other ISPs without requiring them to reveal their private information. P3CA retains the desirable properties of PCA, including its accuracy and robustness. One challenge with using SMC-based approaches is scalability, as we target designing a system that can handle collaborations across the large workloads of several core ISP networks (millions of flows, hundreds of routers, tens of collaborating ISPs). To address this, we develop efficient algorithms that scale *linearly* with the number of observations per ISP. We also support incremental anomaly detection to speed up processing by updating the previously computed principal components when new data is obtained. Unlike previous work on preventing information leakage in data mining algorithms [13,23], we target algorithms in the context of anomaly detection in large-scale networks. In addition, unlike some schemes [13], P3CA *does not publish the dominant principal components* (i.e., their plain text values) allowing privacy of the network traffic and topology to be retained. At the end of P3CA, each of the participating ISP finds the anomalies in its own network and these are not revealed to the others. Our evaluation results show that P3CA (and its incremental version) perform quite efficiently at the scale of large networks. We note that P3CA extends PCA for multiple ISPs and thus, like PCA, can be used only to find the anomalies in a network and not the end hosts responsible for these. Further mechanisms (e.g., [28]) are required to perform root cause analysis and are out of the scope of this paper.

2   System Overview

The Internet is made up of a set of *Internet Service Providers* (ISPs) connected by peering links. Each ISP is a network owned and operated by a single administrative entity (e.g., a campus/enterprise network). To discover routes across ISPs, the Border Gateway Protocol (BGP) [3] is run across peering links. BGP routing advertisements carry information such as the reachable destination prefix and do not reveal the details of the ISP's internals such as topology, traffic (for e.g., set of communicating IP addresses, the load on the ISP's links) as they are considered highly private. Revealing such information can make an ISP subject to directed attacks along with revealing confidential information. ISPs also have economic reasons to hide this information as it may reveal shortcomings of their own deployments to competitors. For example, in one recently publicized case, a tier-1 ISP published information about their internal failure patterns in a technical paper and a second ISP re-published that information in their marketing literature to convince customers to use the second ISP's own services [4]. Therefore, to enable PCA-based anomaly detection across ISPs, we must ensure the privacy of data regarding internal traffic information.

To address this problem, we design for the target architecture shown in Figure 1. Each ISP runs a Secure Exchange Point (SEP) that collects information about its traffic and coordinates with SEPs located in other collaborating ISPs to diagnose anomalies together. To simplify deployment, the SEP runs on a separate server infrastructure and communicates with routers using existing protocols (SNMP and NetFlow to learn traffic information and the IGP to learn topology information). SEPs may be configured into arbitrary topologies following the trust relationships between ISPs (the inter-SEP connections may traverse multiple intermediate ISPs, if the two collaborators are not directly adjacent). ISPs often already run dedicated infrastructures to detect anomalies and our design can be incorporated into such existing deployments to reduce need for new infrastructure.

2.1   Threat Model

Adversarial model: In our work, we assume that adversaries are *semi-honest* (also referred to as *honest but curious*), as defined in [14]. In this model, all

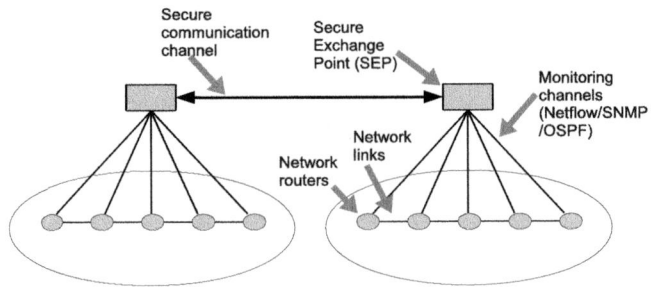

Fig. 1. P3CA system architecture

participants correctly follow the protocol but may observe and record arbitrary information from protocol message exchanges. We believe this model is appropriate for inter-ISP collaborations. ISPs enter into contracts that require them to follow the protocol as well as perform periodic audits to verify its correct operation. However, any private data that is revealed directly to another ISP (for e.g., through accidental misconfiguration) is difficult to contain. Thus, our goal is to limit the amount of private data that can be obtained by any ISP following the protocol.

Privacy goals: Our aim is to develop an privacy preserving scheme where several ISPs can jointly perform PCA on their private traffic observation datasets and detect anomalies in their networks while revealing no further information. In particular, there are three main sources of information about ISPs and we aim to reduce the amount of information revealed about each of them:

1. *Topology:* Each ISP consists of a set of routers and links organized into a graph. We would like to avoid revealing any information about this graph, including its size and topology.
2. *Workload:* Each ISP forwards data traffic between its routers. We would like to avoid revealing information about the set of inter-communicating hosts, packet headers and the volume of traffic.
3. *Monitoring infrastructure:* Each ISP runs a monitoring infrastructure to monitor and collect information about traffic for anomaly detection. We would like to avoid revealing information about the structure, size and visibility of this infrastructure, including the number of vantage points and their placement within the network.

2.2   Protocol Overview

We build upon several key features of previous work [20,21] and provide P3CA, a protocol the allows ISPs to detect anomalies in their networks by computing the principal components of their aggregated data in a privacy preserving manner. In our model, p ISPs collaborate to jointly perform PCA over a distributed traffic matrix Y. Y is a $t \times l$ non-symmetric dense matrix with $l = m \cdot p$, the total number of vantage points at p ISPs, each running (up to) m vantage points internally. Y can be represented as $Y = [Y_1|Y_2| \ldots |Y_p]$ where each Y_i $(i = 1 \ldots p)$ is an $t \times m$ matrix supplied (i.e., *owned*) by ISP i and '|' indicates column-wise concatenation. Each column of matrix Y_i corresponds to the traffic values collected by ISP i from a specific vantage point and each row corresponds to the traffic values collected over one time interval from all vantage points. The specific mechanism by which Y is measured may be selected independently by the participants.

Given a $t \times l$ matrix Y distributed across p ISPs as described above, we wish to privately compute the principal components of Y. The SEPs of the collaborating ISPs execute the following protocol to find the principal components of the combined traffic matrix Y:

1. All ISPs jointly select two special parties, the *Coordinator* and the *Keyholder*. The Coordinator collects encrypted data from all ISPs and all data is encrypted with the Keyholder's public key using the Paillier homomorphic encryption scheme [24] (described in Appendix A.1). The Coordinator uses the Keyholder to perform computations on the encrypted data after blinding it. In this way, neither the Coordinator nor the Keyholder are trusted with the plaintext content of actual traffic data. We note that the Coordinator and the Keyholder are unique for the entire protocol and are elected before each execution of the protocol. To minimize the threat of a compromised Coordinator, the computation may be repeated by multiple Coordinators, with simple voting to resolve conflicts. Likewise, the Keyholder key may be replaced by one generated in a distributed fashion by all the ISPs; queries to the Keyholder could then be replaced by distributed encryption [12].
2. All ISPs execute the semi-centralized procedure P3CA (Algorithm 1) to obtain the encrypted set of n principal components $\{Enc(x_i)\}_{i=1}^{n}$ of the matrix Y. n is chosen apriori and is typically between 5-8 [20,21].
3. Each ISP i now uses these encrypted principal components to verify if its traffic matrix Y_i has any anomalies. This is done by calculating the residual traffic matrix $Enc(R_i) = (I - Enc(P)Enc(P)^T)Y_i$ where $Enc(P) = [Enc(x_1)|Enc(x_2)|\ldots|Enc(x_n)]$. $Enc(R_i)$ is blinded by multiplying with a random rotation matrix R (an orthogonal matrix) and a random number r similar to the procedure described in Section 3.3, decrypted with the help of the Keyholder and unblinded by multiplying it with R^T (the inverse of R) and dividing by r. ISP i then uses statistical methods like Q-statistic [18] over R_i to detect the anomalies in its own network.

3   The P3CA Algorithm

In this section we present the Privacy Preserving PCA (P3CA) algorithm, which enables multiple cooperating ISPs to calculate the principal components of their combined traffic matrix without revealing their private values to others. We start by describing the core P3CA algorithm (Section 3.1). We then describe three subroutines used in P3CA (Sections 3.2–3.4). We further give extensions to P3CA to support *incremental* computation by leveraging previously-computed results to speed up processing of incoming updates to the traffic matrix (Section 3.5).

3.1   P3CA Overview

P3CA computes the principal components of the traffic matrix Y distributed across p parties (ISPs), with each party holding one or more columns of data. This translates to the computation of the top n eigenvectors of the corresponding covariance matrix YY^T such that none of the participants learn any information about the principal components of the matrix. However, calculating the entire covariance matrix is fairly expensive, requiring $O(l^2 t)$ operations. To reduce computation overhead, P3CA uses a modified version of the *power method* (original method described in Appendix A.2), reducing computational costs to $O(lt)$, and reducing communication costs from $O(t^2)$ to $O(t)$. Algorithm 3 (pseudo-code given in Appendix) provides a centralized version of our scheme for plaintext input.

Algorithm 1 presents P3CA, a *semi-centralized privacy preserving* version of Algorithm 3 in which a set of p collaborating ISPs privately compute the top n principal components of the $t \times l$ traffic matrix Y. For this, we introduce secure linear algebra primitives later in this section which are used as building blocks. These include efficient privacy preserving matrix-vector multiplication: *MULR* and *MULC* (Section 3.2), privacy preserving vector normalization: *VECNORM* (Section 3.3) and privacy preserving number comparison: *INTCMP* (Section 3.4).

Input: P is the set of ISPs contributing data including the Coordinator but excluding the Keyholder and $|P| = p$. ISP i has its traffic matrix Y_i

Output: Top n-eigenpairs of YY^T namely encrypted principal component matrix $P = (Enc(\boldsymbol{x}_1), Enc(\boldsymbol{x}_2), \dots, Enc(\boldsymbol{x}_n))$ and corresponding eigenvalues $\lambda_1, \dots, \lambda_n$ are known to all ISPs

Notation:

1. $A \Rightarrow B : M$ denotes a network communication of M from party A to party B;

2. $A \Longleftrightarrow B : r = f(\cdot)$ indicates that parties A and B compute $f(\cdot)$ in a multi-step protocol ending with party A holding the result r.

3. In $F()$ $[[text]]$, *text* is the corresponding plain text equivalent of $F()$.

4. $\oplus$ and $\otimes$ denotes addition and multiplication on ciphertext as illustrated in Appendix A.1

foreach *Eigenpair* $(\lambda_q, \boldsymbol{x}_q)$ *for* $q = 1, \dots, n$ *to be calculated* **do**

> **Coordinator**: $v = random\_vector()$; $S \leftarrow t \times t$ zeros matrix; $\delta \leftarrow Enc(1)$, $\lambda_q \leftarrow 0$;
>
> **while** $INTCMP(Enc(\delta), Enc(\tau|\lambda_q|))$ *is* **TRUE** $[[While \ \delta \geq \tau|\lambda_q|]]$ **do**
>
> > **Coordinator** $\Longleftrightarrow$ **Keyholder**: $Enc(\hat{v}) = VECNORM(v)$ $[[\ \hat{v} = \frac{v}{||v||}$
> > $]]$;
> >
> > $\forall i \in P$ **Party** i: $Enc(v'_i) = MULR(Y^T_{i*}, Enc(\hat{v}_i))$ $[[\ v' = Y^T \hat{v}]]$;
> >
> > $\forall i \in P$ **Party** i $\Longleftrightarrow$ **Coordinator**:
> >
> > $w = MULC(Enc(Y), [Enc(v')_1|Enc(v')_2|\dots|Enc(v')_p])$ $[[w = Yv']]$;
> >
> > **Coordinator**: $Enc(v) = w - S \otimes Enc(\hat{v})$ $[[v = w - S\hat{v}]]$;
> >
> > **Coordinator** $\Longleftrightarrow$ **Keyholder**: $Enc(\lambda_q) = MULC(Enc(\hat{v}^T), Enc(v))$ $[[\lambda_q = \hat{v}^Y v]]$;
> >
> > **Coordinator**: $Enc(\delta) = v - Enc(\hat{v}\lambda_q)$ $[[\delta = v - \hat{v}\lambda_q]]$;
>
> **end**
>
> **Coordinator**: generates a random value a;
>
> **Coordinator** $\Rightarrow$ **Keyholder**: $Enc(a') = a \otimes Enc(\lambda)$ $[[a' = a + \lambda]]$;
>
> **Keyholder** $\Rightarrow$ **Coordinator**: a' (decryption);
>
> **Coordinator**: $\lambda_q = a' - a$, $Enc(\boldsymbol{x}_q) = Enc(v)$ $[[\boldsymbol{x}_q = v]]$;
>
> $S = S + \lambda_q * (\hat{v}^T \hat{v})$ $[[S = S + \lambda_q(\hat{v}^T \hat{v})]]$;

end

Algorithm 1. P3CA: Privacy Preserving PCA

Handling fixed point computation and negative numbers: The inputs in our traffic matrix Y are floating point numbers. To perform real arithmetic over a finite field, we represent floating point numbers as fixed point numbers by multiplying them by a fixed base. By ensuring that the modulus N is large enough, we can obtain the necessary precision our application requires. Further, N of the field used for encryption is chosen to prevent overflow: for a core router with 10Gbps bandwidth (2^{35} values) and 5 minute time bins (2^7 values), a 42-bit key is sufficient. We use 1024-bit keys in our implementation because this is necessary to achieve an acceptable security level in Paillier encryption. In our experiments (see Section 4), we use a base of 10^6. Negative numbers are represented by subtracting them from the modulus; so $-x$ is represented as $N - x$.

Security: The security of the P3CA algorithm results from the security of the individual steps, as described in the following sections. Further, we use existing methods to ensure that malicious inputs to P3CA do not affect the accuracy of our method. The details of this are discussed in Appendix B.

3.2   Private Matrix-Vector Multiplication

The P3CA algorithm performs computations, iteratively, on the combined traffic matrix Y containing different columns belonging to different ISPs. All ISPs are collectively required to first compute the product $YY^T Enc(v)$ where v holds the current estimate of a principal component of Y. Since the matrix is distributed across multiple ISPs, we require a scheme to securely multiply a matrix with a vector, without leaking information about the contents of either the matrix or the vector. We implement this step in a distributed fashion, with all the ISPs participating. Private matrix-vector computation algorithms proposed in the past [19] are designed for a two-party model and would be computationally inefficient due to the fact that they require the entire matrix Y to be encrypted and assembled at the Coordinator.

In P3CA, the matrix Y is column-wise distributed among the p ISPs . Correspondingly, Y^T is distributed row-wise. We, thus, perform the computation $YY^T Enc(v)$ in two steps; first we compute $v' = Y^T v$ and then $v = Y v'$ These steps are computed using the *MULR* and *MULC* primitives (described below) which satisfy the following privacy goals:

Privacy goals: Given the vector $Enc(v)$ and matrix Y, the *MULR* and *MULC* protocols should ensure the privacy of the length ($\|v\|$) and direction of the vector v and the length and direction of the columns of Y.

Matrix-vector multiplication with row ownership ($MULR$): Given the $l \times t$ matrix Y^T, we would like to calculate $v' = Y^T v$. Each party owns one or more rows Y_{i*}^T of Y^T and has access to $Enc(v)$. This means that each party can locally compute a part of $Enc(v')$ without having to exchange the values of $Y_{i,*}^T$ with others. To compute $Y^T v$, the ISP which owns the row Y_{i*}^T of the matrix Y^T

(corresponds to owning column i on matrix Y) computes encrypted value of the ith element of $\boldsymbol{v}'$ i.e. $\boldsymbol{v}'_i$, using $Enc(\boldsymbol{v}'_i) = ((Enc(\boldsymbol{v}_1) \otimes Y^T_{i1}) \oplus \ldots \oplus (Enc(\boldsymbol{v}_t) \otimes Y^T_{it}))$ (Notation $\oplus$ and $\otimes$ given in Appendix A.1).

Matrix-vector multiplication with column ownership ($MULC$): Now the second step of computing $\boldsymbol{v} = Y\boldsymbol{v}'$ uses the result of $MULR$. The party which owns the ith column of matrix Y i.e. Y_{*i} also has access to $Enc(\boldsymbol{v}'_i)$, the ciphertext of the ith element of $\boldsymbol{v}'$ from MULR. The party owning column i in Y computes $Enc(Y'_{ji}) = Enc(\boldsymbol{v}_i) \otimes Y_{ji}$ for $j = 1 \ldots t$, and forwards $Enc(Y'_{ji})$ to the Coordinator. This step requires $O(t)$ exponentiations and $O(t)$ communication. The Coordinator then computes the encrypted j^{th} element (for $j = 1 \ldots t$) of the new estimate of $\boldsymbol{v}$, i.e. $Enc(\boldsymbol{v}_j)$ using $Enc(\boldsymbol{v}_j) = Enc(Y'_{j1}) \oplus \ldots \oplus Enc(Y'_{jl})$ which finally gives the ciphertext of the result of $YY^T\boldsymbol{v}$. This step requires $O(l)$ multiplications and $O(t)$ communication.

Security: Note that each party transmits values encrypted under the Keyholder's public key, and no party involved in this protocol has a copy of the secret key. The Paillier encryption scheme is known to be CPA-secure [24]; thus these protocols reveal no information about the vector or matrix in the honest-but-curious setting.

3.3   Private Vector Normalization

In P3CA computation, we have a vector $\boldsymbol{v}$ which is an estimate of the principal component of the traffic matrix Y. Part of the P3CA computation involves normalizing $\boldsymbol{v}$, which is done to speed up the convergence of the power method in practice. Since different parts of $\boldsymbol{v}$ contain information from different ISPs, we need some way to normalize the vector in a privacy-preserving way. We now describe a technique to perform this efficiently.

Given an input vector $\boldsymbol{v}$, the normalization of $\boldsymbol{v}$ is simply another vector $\hat{\boldsymbol{v}}$ in the same direction as $\boldsymbol{v}$ but of unit length (or norm). The Coordinator holds the encryption of vector $\boldsymbol{v}$, i.e. $Enc(\boldsymbol{v})$ (as a result of $MULC$ described above) to be normalized while the Keyholder holds the corresponding decryption key. At the end of the private vector normalization protocol $VECNORM$, the Coordinator holds the encryption of the normalized vector $Enc(\hat{\boldsymbol{v}})$ whilst neither of them gains any information about the input vector.

Privacy goals: Given input vector $\boldsymbol{v}$, the $VECNORM$ protocol ensures that both length $||\boldsymbol{v}||$ of the vector and its direction are not revealed.

Vector normalization ($VECNORM$): In order to secure vector normalization, the Coordinator rotates the encrypted input vector $Enc(\boldsymbol{v})$ to hide its direction and multiplies the result with an random integer to hide the length of the vector. It then sends this modified vector to the Keyholder who decrypts it, normalizes it and returns the result. The Coordinator then derives the normalization of the input vector, $Enc(\hat{\boldsymbol{v}})$, using the Keyholder's result. The protocol can be summarized as follows:

1. *Blinding direction:* In this step, the Coordinator generates a $t \times t$ transformation matrix R that maps a given vector $\boldsymbol{v}$ to a randomly chosen vector $\boldsymbol{w}$ on a c-dimensional sphere, S^c, of radius $||\boldsymbol{v}||$. Here $c + 1 \leq t$ is a security parameter chosen such that the security of the scheme is the same as that of the finite field used by the cryptosystem; i.e., $|S^c| \geq N$. For $i = 1 \ldots (c+1)$, the Coordinator generates an orthogonal rotation matrix R_i using 3 parameters: (θ_i, p_i, q_i), where (p_i, q_i) are selected from $1, \ldots, t(t-1)/2$ uniformly at random without replacement and θ_i is chosen uniformly at random from $-\pi$ to π. R_i can be represented as:

$$
R_i = \begin{bmatrix}
 & & & \text{col. } p_i & & \text{col. } q_i & \\
 & & & \downarrow & & \downarrow & \\
 & & 1 \ldots & 0 & \ldots & 0 & \ldots 0 \\
 & & 0 \ldots & 0 & \ldots & 0 & \ldots 0 \\
\text{row } p_i \rightarrow & 0 \ldots & \cos(\theta_i) & \ldots & -\sin(\theta_i) & \ldots 0 \\
 & & \vdots & & \ddots & & \vdots \\
\text{row } q_i \rightarrow & & \ldots \sin(\theta_i) & \ldots & \cos(\theta_i) & \ldots 0 \\
 & & 0 \ldots & 0 & \ldots & 0 & \ldots 0 \\
 & & 0 \ldots & 0 & \ldots & 0 & \ldots 1
\end{bmatrix}
$$

The Coordinator then multiplies all the R_i's to obtain a single transformation matrix R using $R = R_{c+1} * R_c * \ldots * R_1$. and applies the rotation transformation R on $Enc(\boldsymbol{v})$ to get $Enc(\boldsymbol{v}_{rot}) = Enc(\boldsymbol{v}) \otimes R$.

2. *Blinding length:* the Coordinator generates a random blinding factor r and computes $Enc(\boldsymbol{v}'_{rot}) = Enc(\boldsymbol{v}_{rot}) \otimes r$ to blind the length $||\boldsymbol{v}||$ of the vector $\boldsymbol{v}$. Note that both blinding and rotation are required so that no information about $\boldsymbol{v}$ is leaked.

3. The Coordinator sends $Enc(\boldsymbol{v}'_{rot})$ to the Keyholder. The Keyholder then decrypts $Enc(\boldsymbol{v}'_{rot})$ to obtain $\boldsymbol{v}'_{rot}$, computes $\hat{\boldsymbol{v}}'_{rot} = \frac{\boldsymbol{v}'_{rot}}{||\boldsymbol{v}'_{rot}||}$ and sends $Enc(\hat{\boldsymbol{v}}'_{rot})$ to the Coordinator.

4. The Coordinator obtains the normalization of $\boldsymbol{v}$ by applying the inverse of the earlier transformation: $Enc(\hat{\boldsymbol{v}}) = Enc(\hat{\boldsymbol{v}}'_{rot}) \otimes R^T$ to obtain the normalization of $\boldsymbol{v}$. R^T is the inverse of R as it is an orthogonal matrix.

Security: The two blinding steps serve to hide the value of the original vector. Due to the fixed-point representation of the vector values, this hiding is imperfect, as we select a random discretized rotation matrix, rather than a random rotation matrix in general. We have tried to estimate how much uncertainty the Keyholder has about the original vector, given the blinded one. In other words, we computed the conditional entropy $H(O|B)$, where O and B are random variables that represent the original and blinded vector, respectively. To do this, we performed an exhaustive search of the state space, enumerating all possibilities for random choices of rotation matrices and the blinding factor. Of course, we were only able to do this for very small parameter sizes: 2-dimensional vectors and 3- and 4-bit fixed-point representation. Even in this situation, we found that there was between 4 and 5.5 bits of uncertainty, depending on the fixed-point size (out of a total 6–8 bits). Extrapolating from this (albeit limited) data set, we expect that for larger fixed-point sizes, it is possible to introduce 10–15 bits of uncertainty per vector.

This estimate is an information-theoretic upper bound on the success of a possible attack; a computationally bounded adversary would not be able to perform such a brute-force state exploration. A successful attack would have to exploit some algebraic structure of the integers used to represent the fixed-point numbers; we leave the exploration of such attacks to future work and recommend that conservative parameters (i.e., large fixed-point bases with randomized lower bits) be used in practice.

3.4 Private Number Comparison

P3CA uses an iterative process (the *while* loop in Algorithm 1) to determine each eigenvector of YY^T. In particular, an initial estimate v_i of the eigenvector x_i is chosen, it is checked to see if $\delta_i = Yv_i - \lambda_i v_i$ is within a threshold, τ times the correct eigenvalue λ_i and if not the loop is repeated. Since the contents of Y and hence δ_i are private, we need some way to securely compare $||\delta_i||$ and $\tau\lambda_i$ without revealing their contents. Since the L^2 norm is difficult to compute for encrypted vectors, we approximate it by using the L^∞ norm. To see if $||\delta_i||_\infty$ is less than $\tau\lambda_i$, the Coordinator executes the *INTCMP* protocol to see if $|(\delta_i)_j| > \tau\lambda_i$ for any j; if so, the power method is continued for another round.

Given encrypted real numbers $Enc(a)$ and $Enc(b)$, *INTCMP* allows the holder of these encryptions to learn if $a > b$ using the Keyholder. The Coordinator learns if $a > b$ and nothing more while the Keyholder learns nothing. The protocol can be summarized as follows:

1. The Coordinator knows $Enc(a)$ and $Enc(b)$. It picks a random r_1 while ensuring that $ar_1, br_1 < 2^{1024}$.
2. The Coordinator sends $Enc((a - b) * r_1)$ to the Keyholder. The Keyholder returns ">" if the decrypted value is > 0, "$\leq$" otherwise.

Note that to compute whether $|a| > b$, we must first run *INTCMP* to see if $a < 0$ and then compute $a > b$ or $(-a) > b$ depending on the answer. To ensure privacy from the Keyholder, the Coordinator should randomly swap a and b during the *INTCMP* protocol.

Security: As in the previous protocol, blinding does not provide perfect hiding; in particular, if the Keyholder can estimate the maximum values for $a - b$, and r_1, he can learn some information when the values are in fact close to the limit. However, we can pick r_1 from a very large range (e.g., $[1, 2^{500}]$), thus reducing the chance that we will pick values close to the maximum. Note that the semi-honest model is essential for security in this step, as otherwise the Coordinator could decrypt an arbitrary number by performing a binary search with *INTCMP* [26].

3.5 Incremental Private PCA Computation

So far, the P3CA algorithm we discussed requires the entire set of inputs from all the parties to be available before finding the principal components of the input dataset (Y). However in the context of ISPs jointly computing PCA, an anomaly detection system needs to function as new traffic data arrives. To further reduce computation overhead, we describe how to modify our approach to enable the result to be incrementally updated rather than performing the entire computation from scratch when new information arrives. This allows principal components to be incrementally derived for a long stream of incoming network traffic, thereby speeding up their computation.

Several techniques have been proposed in the image processing literature to address this requirement. Our scheme for incremental private PCA computation is based on the popular and rigorously analyzed CCIPCA [32] (Candid Covariance-free Incremental PCA) algorithm, which provides an iterative method for updating the principal components when new data arrives. In Algorithm 2, we extend CCIPCA to privately compute the principal components of the traffic matrix of p cooperating ISPs. Consider the traffic matrix Y for time intervals $1, \ldots, t-1$ containing rows $\boldsymbol{u}_1, \ldots, \boldsymbol{u}_{t-1}$ (recall each $\boldsymbol{u}_i$ is distributed across ISPs). Now suppose a new traffic vector $\boldsymbol{u}_t$ is generated for time interval t. The new eigenpair for this modified traffic matrix (with u_t included) is estimated as: $\boldsymbol{x}_t = \frac{1}{t} \sum_{i=1}^{t-1} \boldsymbol{u}_i \boldsymbol{u}_i^T \boldsymbol{x}_i$. The idea is to update Y with a covariance matrix estimate using the new distributed vector $\boldsymbol{u}_t$ and $\boldsymbol{x}_{i-1}$ is set as $\boldsymbol{x}_i$ which is the eigenvector estimate obtained using the P3CA method. Note that the entire covariance matrix is not recalculated from scratch.

Input: Eigenpairs $(\lambda_1, \boldsymbol{x}_1) \ldots (\lambda_n, \boldsymbol{x}_n))$ over traffic vectors $\boldsymbol{u}_1 \ldots \boldsymbol{u}_{t-1}$, and $\boldsymbol{u}_{i,t}$;
$\quad\quad$ P be the set of collaborating ISPs
Output: Top n-eigenpairs of traffic vectors $\boldsymbol{u}_1 \ldots \boldsymbol{u}_t$ namely
$\quad\quad\quad$ $(\lambda_1, \boldsymbol{x}_1), \ldots, (\lambda_k, \boldsymbol{x}_n)$ are known to all ISPs
foreach *eigenvector required* $i = 1, 2, \ldots, n$ **do**
$\quad$ **foreach** $p \in P$ **do**
$\quad\quad$ $\boldsymbol{u}_{p,t}^i = \boldsymbol{u}_{p,t}$;
$\quad\quad$ **Party** $p \Rightarrow$ **party** $q \in P \setminus p$: $Enc(\boldsymbol{u}_{p,t}^i)$;
$\quad\quad$ $Enc(\boldsymbol{a}_p) = (Enc(\boldsymbol{u}_{p,t}^i) \otimes Enc(\boldsymbol{u}_{1,t}^i), \ldots, Enc(\boldsymbol{u}_{p,t}^i) \otimes Enc(\boldsymbol{u}_{|P|,t}^i))$;
$\quad\quad$ $Enc(\boldsymbol{b}_p) = \frac{(t-1-l)}{t} * (\lambda_i \boldsymbol{x}_i) + Enc(\boldsymbol{a}_p) \otimes \frac{1+l}{n} \frac{\lambda_i \boldsymbol{x}_i}{||\lambda_i \boldsymbol{x}_i||}$;
$\quad\quad$ // except $\boldsymbol{a}_p$ all other inputs are plaintext and known to all ISPs
$\quad$ **end**
$\quad$ **Party** $p \Rightarrow$ **party** $q \in P \setminus p$: $Enc(\boldsymbol{b}_p)$;
$\quad$ $\boldsymbol{u}_{p,t} = \boldsymbol{u}_{p,t-1} - \boldsymbol{u}_{p,t-1} \otimes VECNORM(\boldsymbol{b})_p$;
$\quad$ //Remove any component in the direction of the new eigenvector to ensure
$\quad$ orthogonality of eigenvectors
end

Algorithm 2. Incremental P3CA extensions

---

4   Evaluation

Our design enables ISPs to collaborate to detect anomalies. However, our design also comes at some cost. First, it incurs additional computation overhead since it requires encryption and multi-round exchanges between nodes. Second, the use of fixed point operations in our design can lead to a loss of precision resulting in the calculation of principal components that are potentially different compared to those calculated by PCA. To quantify the affect of these, we evaluate the computational overhead of our design (Section 4.1) and compare the detection probability using PCA with that using our algorithm (Section 4.2).

To measure these costs, we constructed an implementation of our design. Our design is implemented in roughly 1000 lines of C++. We use the GMP library for large numbers (bignums), OpenMP library for parallelization and the libpaillier library for the Paillier cryptosystem [1]. All encryptions use a 1024-bit key. To evaluate performance over realistic workloads, we leveraged traces from the Abilene Internet2 IP backbone [2]. In particular, we used NetFlow traces to determine traffic volumes between source/destination IP addresses, and used OSPF and BGP traces to map the flows onto the underlying physical topology.

4.1 Scalability

To evaluate the computational overhead of P3CA, we measured the amount of time it takes for our implementation to finish running on its input data set. To characterize performance, we would ideally like to run our design on varying network topology sizes. However, due to the privacy of traffic information, acquiring traces from a number of different-sized ISPs represents a substantial challenge. Hence, to study scalability for different network sizes, we extrapolated a traffic model from the Abilene dataset and used that to construct synthetic traces for larger networks. Extrapolation of traffic traces is itself a challenging research problem and beyond the scope of this paper. We use a fairly simple extrapolation procedure: we generate a random network topology, randomly select flows contained in the Abilene data set, and map their ingress/egress to random pairs of routers contained in the generated topology. We then take this graph and divide it up into a set of ten constituent ISPs. We do this by picking ten random points in the graph, and performing breadth-first search to select nearby regions to form the ISP (repeating this process until ten connected ISPs are created).

Table 1a shows run time of a single run of our algorithm as a function of topology size, where we vary (i) the total number of monitored links in all ISPs (l), and (ii) the total number of time bins (each lasting 10 minutes) used for traffic history when computing principal components (t). These experiments were performed on an 3.07GHz Intel Core i7 processor with 6GB memory. As a comparison, we note that large networks only monitor a subset of links (e.g.,the tier-1 ISP network used for PCA in [21] had $l = 41$, as monitoring a subset of core links is sufficient to observe most traffic in the network) and t is often set to small values to speed reaction and adapt to recent changes. Table 1b shows the run time for incrementally refreshing current PCA results with new traffic observations using Algorithm 2.

We find that P3CA requires only a few minutes to run, even for relatively large numbers of monitored links. P3CA requires only around 10 minutes to process data for 320 minutes, making it an *efficient online algorithm* for anomaly detection. Further, the advantages of using incremental P3CA are clearly evident (as seen in Table 1b): incremental updates are processed within 6 seconds even for large networks with a total of 320 links for a data spanning 320 minutes.

This makes incremental P3CA as efficient as PCA on raw data. To investigate the source of computational bottlenecks, we instrumented our code with timing functions to collect the microbenchmarks shown in Table 2a. Our design can be trivially parallelized across a cluster of machines or CPU cores to further reduce overhead, as shown in Table 2b. While the Coordinator requires additional computation, this additional work may be distributed across several machines to accelerate computation and improve resilience.

Table 1. Performance and scalability of original and incremental P3CA with increasing # of links l and # of bins t for 5 eigenpairs on 4 processors

(a) P3CA

l	t	Party i (secs)	Coordinator (secs)
20	2	0.525	2.183
40	4	1.376	6.472
80	8	3.529	14.134
160	16	52.999	194.175
320	32	194.126	637.649

(b) Incremental P3CA

l	t	time (secs)
20	2	3.56
40	4	3.72
80	8	4.03
160	16	4.66
320	32	5.91

Table 2. Microbenchmarks and evaluation of parallelization of P3CA for 5 eigenvectors

(a) Microbenchmarks. The first three and the last two rows represent two different breakdown of operations.

Percent of time	Operation
39.6%	multiplying cipher and plain texts
36.6%	adding cipher texts
18.2%	decryption
16.5%	private vector normalization
82.5%	private matrix-vector multiplication and subtractions

(b) Performance of P3CA with increasing numbers of processors r for l links, t bins

l	t	r	Party i (secs)	Coordinator (secs)
320	32	8	194.1	637.6 (10m 37s)
640	64	8	6649.6	20823.4 (5h 47m)
320	32	32	48.5	151.4 (2m 31s)
640	64	32	1662.4	5205.8 (1h 27m)
320	32	64	24.2	75.7
640	64	64	881.2	2602.9 (43m 22s)

4.2 Precision

The performance of PCA algorithms in general has been widely evaluated in previous work. Our approach performs essentially the same computation as PCA, but might potentially lose some precision due to the use of fixed point numbers. We note that some implementations of PCA intentionally round to filter minor traffic fluctuations. To evaluate how the precision of our algorithm affects the results, we must use a more realistic topology and traffic information. We use the real Abilene dataset and topology here (but do not investigate sensitivity to network size), and run PCA and P3CA to detect traffic volume anomalies. To investigate sensitivity to anomaly type, we also inject synthetic anomalies with different characteristics. To do this, we randomly choose time bins, and insert a constant amount of extra traffic on a randomly chosen subset of 1 to 5 links.

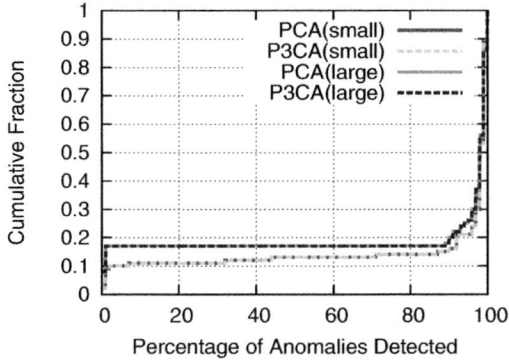

Fig. 2. Comparison in precision between PCA and P3CA

We ran the experiment 100 times with different random seeds, for two different kinds of injected anomalies: *small* corresponds to the case in which the volume of the injected anomalies is twice the volume of the background traffic on the link, and *large* corresponds to the case in which the anomalies have a volume which is ten times larger than the background traffic in the link. We use the Q-statistic test [18] for detecting abnormal variations in the traffic at a 99.9% confidence level. Figure 2 plots the CDF of the anomaly detection percentage of PCA and P3CA. The cumulative fraction is over the multiple runs we performed. We find that in every run, P3CA and PCA computed nearly the same result (detected the same set of anomalies).

5   Related Work

To our knowledge, our work is the first attempt to perform scalable privacy-preserving traffic anomaly detection. Our work builds upon two key areas of previous results:

Anomaly detection in ISP networks: Given the increasing severity of DoS, scanning, and other malicious traffic, traffic anomaly detection in large networks is gaining increased attention. Lakhina et. al. [20,21] showed that PCA has much potential in uncovering anomalies by leveraging traffic matrices constructed using summarizations of traffic feature distributions. While there are alternatives to PCA (for e.g., [35]), PCA-based approaches remain a state-of-the-art technique due to its robustness to noise and high efficiency on limited data. Extensions to PCA make it robust to attacks such as variance-injection [33], and enable PCA to be used for other goals, such as diagnosing network disruptions [17].

Further, accuracy of anomaly detection is improved with more visibility of traffic. If ISPs cooperated to share data, accuracy of anomaly detection could be substantially improved. Soule et. al. [30] show that by jointly analyzing the data of peering ISPs more anomalies were detected, especially those anomalies that transited the two ISPs they studied. However, traditional anomaly detection requires sharing of detailed traffic traces, which are considered highly private by network providers. Our work extends PCA to multiple parties, preserving the privacy of participants' data. By extending PCA, our approach computes the same result as this well-proven technique, retains the desirable properties mentioned above and enables more widespread cooperation of ISPs to counter the increasing threat of malicious traffic.

Secure multiparty computation: Secure multiparty computation (SMC) techniques allow a collection of participants to compute a public function F without revealing their private inputs to F. Generic SMC techniques date back to Yao [34] and Goldreich et. al. [15] and have been well studied in cryptography literature [6,16]. Recent years have seen some improvements in efficiency [11,7]. However from the viewpoint of the systems designer, the generic schemes are only of theoretical interest. For the scale of computation required for mining anomalies in Internet traffic, privacy and security must be added with manageable costs. Developing a practical, scalable way of computing PCA in a privacy-preserving way is the main focus of our work.

P4P [13] presents a generic scheme for private computation of statistical functions that can be represented as an iterated matrix-vector product. When used to compute PCA, the privacy goal of P4P and several other schemes is to reveal no more information apart from the principal components themselves. However, given the eigenvectors and eigenvalues of a matrix it is possible to reconstruct the matrix itself. When used by ISPs, this scheme would reveal the eigenvectors of $Y^T Y$ but not YY^T for traffic matrix Y. In the context of the concrete problem of anomaly detection, this does not constitute privacy preservation at all since $Y^T Y$ can be reconstituted to a close approximation from its eigenvectors and eigenvalues (end result of the P4P scheme section 6 of [13]). $Y^T Y$ can then be used to infer Y (the input distributed matrix) which is supposed to be private. This can be done as follows: suppose Y_{ij} (traffic volume) is a real number between 1 and N. Y_{ij} is the dot product of columns Y_{*i} and Y_{*j}. When the elements of column Y_{*i} and Y_{*j} are close to N then $Y^T Y_{ij}$ will be close to maximal. Similarly, close to minimal values in Y_{*i} and Y_{*j} leads to a close to minimal $Y^T Y_{ij}$. Therefore $Y^T Y_{ij}$ can be used to construct Y to a close approximation. In contrast with P4P, our scheme presents an advancement in that we only reveal the variance of a projected traffic data point Y_{*j}, namely $||PR_i||^2$ where P the eigenvector matrix of YY^T itself is never revealed.

6   Conclusions

The increasingly distributed nature of malicious attacks renders their identification and localization a difficult task. The ability to identify traffic anomalies across multiple ISPs could be a significant step forward towards this goal. P3CA represents an important step, by allowing a set of ISPs to collectively identify anomalous traffic while limiting information propagation across them. P3CA scales to large and high-bandwidth networks addressing the need for refreshing current results with fresh traffic observations, yet retains the accuracy and precision of PCA-based approaches. We envision our work as an important step towards enabling larger-scale cooperation across ISPs to counter the increasingly serious threats posed by modern networked malware.

References

1. http://acsc.cs.utexas.edu/libpaillier/
2. http://www.internet2.edu/network/
3. A Border Gateway Protocol 4 (BGP-4). RFC 4271
4. Private communication, employee of tier-1 ISP (2006)
5. Aggarwal, G., Mishra, N., Pinkas, B.: Secure computation of the kth-ranked element. In: Eurocyrpt (2004)
6. Beaver, D., Goldwasser, S.: Multiparty computation with faulty majority. In: Brassard, G. (ed.) CRYPTO 1989. LNCS, vol. 435, Springer, Heidelberg (1990)
7. Chen, H., Cramer, R.: Algebraic geometric secret sharing schemes and secure multiparty computations over small fields. In: Dwork, C. (ed.) CRYPTO 2006. LNCS, vol. 4117, pp. 521–536. Springer, Heidelberg (2006)
8. Claise, B.: Cisco Systems NetFlow Services Export Version 9, RFC 3954 (October 2004)
9. Croux, C., Filzmoser, P., Oliveira, M.: Algorithms for projection-pursuit robust principal component analysis. In: Chemometrics and Intelligent Laboratory Systems (2007)
10. Croux, C., Haesbroeck, G.: Principal component analysis based on robust estimators of the covariance or correlation matrix: Influence functions and efficiencies. In: BIOMETRIKA (2000)
11. Damgård, I., Ishai, Y., Krøigaard, M., Nielsen, J.B., Smith, A.: Scalable multiparty computation with nearly optimal work and resilience. In: Wagner, D. (ed.) CRYPTO 2008. LNCS, vol. 5157, pp. 241–261. Springer, Heidelberg (2008)
12. Damgard, I., Jurik, M.: A generalisation, a simplification and some applications of Paillier's probabilistic public-key system. In: Public Key Cryptography, Springer, Heidelberg (2001)
13. Duan, Y., Youdao, N., Canny, J., Zhan, J.: P4P: Practical large-scale privacy-preserving distributed computation robust against malicious users
14. Goldreich, O.: Secure multi-party computation. Theory of Cryptography Library (1999), http://philby.ucsb.edu/cryptolib/BOOKS
15. Goldreich, O., Micali, S., Wigderson, A.: How to play any mental game. In: ACM Symposium on Theory of Computing (1987)
16. Goldwasser, S., Levin, L.: Fair computation of general functions in presence of immoral majority. In: Feigenbaum, J. (ed.) CRYPTO 1991. LNCS, vol. 576. Springer, Heidelberg (1992)
17. Huang, Y., Feamster, N., Lakhina, A., Xu, J.: Diagnosing network disruptions with network-wide analysis. SIGMETRICS (2007)
18. Edward Jackson, J., Mudholkar, G.S.: Control procedures for residuals associated with principal component analysis. Technometrics 21, 341–349 (1979)
19. Kiltz, E., Mohassel, P., Weinreb, E., Franklin, M.K.: Secure linear algebra using linearly recurrent sequences. In: Vadhan, S.P. (ed.) TCC 2007. LNCS, vol. 4392, pp. 291–310. Springer, Heidelberg (2007)
20. Lakhina, A., Crovella, M., Diot, C.: Diagnosing network-wide traffic anomalies. ACM SIGCOMM, pp. 219–230 (2004)

21. Lakhina, A., Crovella, M., Diot, C.: Mining anomalies using traffic feature distributions. ACM SIGCOMM, pp. 217–228 (2005)
22. Lehoucq, R.B., Sorensen, D.C.: Deflation techniques for an implicitly restarted arnoldi iteration. SIAM J. Matrix Anal. Appl. (1996)
23. Lindell, Y., Pinkas, B.: Secure multiparty computation for privacy-preserving data mining (2008), http://eprint.iacr.org/
24. Paillier, P.: Public-key cryptosystems based on composite degree residuosity classes. In: Fumy, W. (ed.) EUROCRYPT 1997. LNCS, vol. 1233, pp. 223–238. Springer, Heidelberg (1997)
25. Ringberg, H., Soule, A., Rexford, J., Diot, C.: Sensitivity of pca for traffic anomaly detection. SIGMETRICS (June 2007)
26. Rivest, R.L., Adleman, L., Dertouzos, M.L.: On data banks and privacy homomorphisms. Foundations of Secure Computation (1978)
27. Rubenstein, B., Nelson, B., Huang, L., Joseph, A., Lau, S., Rao, S., Taft, N., Tygar, D.: Antidote: Understanding and defending against poisoning of anomaly detectors. In: Tavangarian, D., Kirste, T., Timmermann, D., Lucke, U., Versick, D. (eds.) IMC 2009. Communications in Computer and Information Science, vol. 53, Springer, Heidelberg (2009)
28. Silveira, F., Diot, C.: Urca: pulling out anomalies by their root causes. INFOCOM (March 2010)
29. Sleijpen, G.L.G., der Vorst, H.A.V.: A jacobi–davidson iteration method for linear eigenvalue problems. SIAM Rev. (2000)
30. Soule, A., Ringberg, H., Silveira, F., Rexford, J., Diot, C.: Detectability of traffic anomalies in two adjacent networks (2007)
31. Vasudevan, R., Mao, Z., Spatscheck, O., Van der Merwe, J.: Reval: A tool for real-time evaluation of DDoS mitigation strategies. In: USENIX ATC (2006)
32. Weng, J., Zhang, Y., Hwang, W.: Candid covariance-free incremental principal component analysis. IEEE Trans. on Pattern Analysis and Machine Intelligence (2003)
33. Xu, W., Huang, L., Fox, A., Patterson, D., Jordan, M.: Detecting large-scale system problems by mining console logs. In: SOSP (2009)
34. Yao, A.: Protocols for secure computations (extended abstract). In: FOCS (1982)
35. Zhang, Y., Ge, Z., Greenberg, A., Roughan, M.: Network animography. In: IMC (2005)

A   Appendix: Background

In this section, we describe two existing techniques we build upon in our design: *homomorphic encryption* and the *power method*.

A.1   Homomorphic Encryption

A homomorphic cryptosystem allows operations to be performed on plaintext by performing a corresponding operation on its ciphertext. In our scheme participants only have access to the encrypted data of others. They can perform computations over it without knowing its unencrypted value hence protecting the privacy of the party supplying the data. To protect privacy, we use the Paillier encryption [24] to perform computation on encrypted values. We now briefly describe the operation of the Paillier cryptosystem. The original cryptosystem is defined over scalars, but we present its natural extension to encrypted vectors. (They can be readily extended to handle matrices).

Given a public key (N, g) produced by a key-generation algorithm, a random number $r \in \mathbb{Z}_N$ and a k-dimensional vector $\boldsymbol{u} = (u_1, \dots, u_k) \in \mathbb{Z}_N^k$, its encryption, $Enc(\boldsymbol{u})$, is given by: $Enc(\boldsymbol{u}) = (g^{u_1} r^N \bmod N^2, \dots, g^{u_k} r^N \bmod N^2)$

Suppose we are given two vectors $\boldsymbol{u} = (u_1, \dots, u_k)$ and $\boldsymbol{v} = (v_1, \dots, v_k)$ in $\mathbb{Z}_N^k$. The Paillier encryption scheme provides us the two following properties which we use to perform various arithmetic operations on ciphertexts in P3CA:

1. We can compute the encrypted value of the sum of $\boldsymbol{u}$ and $\boldsymbol{v}$ by multiplying their corresponding ciphertexts: $Enc(\boldsymbol{u} + \boldsymbol{v}) = Enc(\boldsymbol{u}) \oplus Enc(\boldsymbol{v}) = (Enc(u_1) * Enc(v_1) \bmod N^2, \dots, Enc(u_k) * Enc(v_k) \bmod N^2)$

2. We can compute of the encrypted value of the product $\boldsymbol{u}$ and $\boldsymbol{v}$ by multiply the ciphertext of $\boldsymbol{u}$ i.e. $Enc(\boldsymbol{u})$ and the plain text value of $\boldsymbol{v}$: $Enc(\boldsymbol{u} * \boldsymbol{v}) = Enc(\boldsymbol{u}) \otimes \boldsymbol{v} = (Enc(u_1)^{v_1} \bmod N^2, \dots, Enc(u_k)^{v_k} \bmod N^2)$

A.2   The Power Method

To use principal component analysis, we are required to find the n largest principal components of the traffic matrix Y. This translates to finding the n largest eigenpairs of its covariance matrix $COV = YY^T$. The *power method* [29] is one of the appropriate candidate techniques when n is much smaller than the rank (sum total of traffic observations) of the covariance matrix. Indeed, previous studies [20,21] indicate that five to eight principal components capture most of the variance within ISP traffic. Based on this, we believe that the power-method is the most appropriate technique for PCA, which we briefly describe below. To calculate the principal components of Y, we replace Y by COV in the following.

The power method first computes the dominant eigenvector, x_1, of a matrix Y by simply choosing a random vector $v_0^1 \in \mathbb{R}^l$ and iteratively multiplying v_0^1 by powers of Y until the resulting vector converges to x_1. This is ensured as long as the starting vector v_0 has a non-zero component along x_1. A single iteration is given by:

$$v_j^1 = \frac{Y v_{j-1}^1}{||Y v_{j-1}^1||}; j = j + 1 \qquad (1)$$

This process is repeated until $j = s$, the smallest value for which $||Y v_j^1 - v_j^1 \lambda_1|| \leq \tau |\lambda_1|$. The corresponding eigenvalue is computed using $\lambda_1 = \frac{v_s^{1T} Y v_s^1}{v_s^{1T} v_s^1}$.

To obtain the next largest eigenvector the power method uses a well known deflation technique [22]. Once the ith eigenpair (x_i, λ_i) (x_i is the ith eigenvector and λ_i is the ith eigenvalue) is computed, a transformation is applied on the matrix Y to move λ_i to the center of the eigenspectrum. To compute the $i + 1^{th}$ largest eigenvector the power method applies the following transformation on Y_i, where Y_i is the matrix used for computing the ith dominant eigenvector of Y: $Y_{i+1} = Y_i - \lambda_i \frac{x_i x_i^T}{x_i^T x_i}$ with $Y_1 = Y$.

This process is repeated until n eigenpairs have been found. The parameter n need not be decided beforehand. Instead, n is simply specified in terms of the smallest eigenvalue of the eigenpair we are interested in. Upon uncovering eigenpair (λ_i, x_i), if $\lambda_i \leq \epsilon$, the eigenpair is discarded and the algorithm terminates. ϵ can be interpreted as the accuracy required for representing column vectors of Y as a linear combination of its eigenvectors.

Input: $t \times l$ matrix Y; τ, the convergence parameter
Output: Top n-eigenpairs of YY^T namely $(\lambda_1, \boldsymbol{x_1}), \ldots, (\lambda_n, \boldsymbol{x_n})$
foreach *Eigenpair* $(\lambda_{q \leq n}, \boldsymbol{x_{q \leq n}})$ *to be calculated* **do**
  $\quad \delta \leftarrow 1; \boldsymbol{v} \leftarrow random\_vector(); S \leftarrow t \times t$ zeros; $\lambda_q \leftarrow 0;$
  $\quad$ **while** $\delta \geq \tau |\lambda_q|$ **do**
  $\quad\quad \hat{\boldsymbol{v}} = \frac{\boldsymbol{v}}{||\boldsymbol{v}||};$
  $\quad\quad \boldsymbol{v}' = Y^T \hat{\boldsymbol{v}};$
  $\quad\quad \boldsymbol{w} = Y\boldsymbol{v}';$
  $\quad\quad \boldsymbol{v} = \boldsymbol{w} - S\hat{\boldsymbol{v}};$
  $\quad\quad \lambda_q = \hat{\boldsymbol{v}}^T \boldsymbol{v};$
  $\quad\quad \delta = \boldsymbol{v} - \hat{\boldsymbol{v}}\lambda_q;$
  $\quad$ **end**
  $\quad \boldsymbol{x_q} = \boldsymbol{v};$
  $\quad S = S + \lambda_q(\hat{\boldsymbol{v}}^T \hat{\boldsymbol{v}});$
end

Algorithm 3. Algorithm for computing principal components of a matrix

B   Handling Malicious Inputs

PCA is an excellent example of how machine learning techniques can assist in anomaly detection. However in its basic form it is fairly vulnerable in that a small fraction of false inputs can significantly change the final result. To address this problem, Croux published a series of papers [10,9] showing that PCA could be made more robust by centering input data over the median instead of the mean. In ANTIDOTE [27], Rubenstein et al. study the malice resistance modifications proposed by Croux in the context of anomaly detection in AS networks. They show that the modifications are of significant help in defending against malicious inputs that could, for instance, enable a participant to hide the presence of a DDoS attack.

P3CA readily supports the modifications proposed by Croux and verified by Rubenstein et al. In particular, along with the primitives we discussed above, we need a privacy-preserving method of computing the median over the entire dataset and centering the data over the median. This requirement is met by the scheme of Aggarwal et al. [5] which computes the median of a distributed dataset among N parties in the honest-but-curious threat model. Its complexity is $O(N(\log M)^2)$ where $\log M$ is the number of bits needed to describe each (unencrypted) scalar input.

Quantifying Location Privacy:
The Case of Sporadic Location Exposure

Reza Shokri[1], George Theodorakopoulos[1], George Danezis[2],
Jean-Pierre Hubaux[1], and Jean-Yves Le Boudec[1]

[1] LCA, EPFL, Lausanne, Switzerland
firstname.lastname@epfl.ch
[2] Microsoft Research, Cambridge, UK
gdane@microsoft.com

Abstract. Mobile users expose their location to potentially untrusted entities by using location-based services. Based on the frequency of location exposure in these applications, we divide them into two main types: *Continuous* and *Sporadic*. These two location exposure types lead to different threats. For example, in the continuous case, the adversary can track users over time and space, whereas in the sporadic case, his focus is more on localizing users at certain points in time. We propose a systematic way to quantify users' location privacy by modeling both the location-based applications and the location-privacy preserving mechanisms (LPPMs), and by considering a well-defined adversary model. This framework enables us to customize the LPPMs to the employed location-based application, in order to provide higher location privacy for the users. In this paper, we formalize *localization* attacks for the case of sporadic location exposure, using Bayesian inference for Hidden Markov Processes. We also quantify user location privacy with respect to the adversaries with two different forms of background knowledge: Those who only know the geographical distribution of users over the considered regions, and those who also know how users move between the regions (i.e., their mobility pattern). Using the Location-Privacy Meter tool, we examine the effectiveness of the following techniques in increasing the expected error of the adversary in the localization attack: Location obfuscation and fake location injection mechanisms for anonymous traces.

1   Introduction

Mobile devices equipped with various positioning systems have paved the way for the emergence of numerous interesting location-based services. Unfortunately, this phenomenon has opened the door to many new threats to users' privacy, as untrusted entities (including the service providers themselves) can track users' locations and activities over time by observing their location-based queries.

Location-based applications, in effect, expose over time some of the locations of users to curious observers (adversaries) who might collect this information for various monetary or malicious purposes. In most of such applications, users share/expose their location in a *sporadic* manner as opposed to a *continuous*

S. Fischer-Hübner and N. Hopper (Eds.): PETS 2011, LNCS 6794, pp. 57–76, 2011.

manner. Widely used location-based services (LBSs), such as local search applications for finding nearby points-of-interests or nearby friends, are good examples of this type of applications.

To protect users' location privacy, location-privacy preserving mechanisms (LPPMs) can be used as a filter between the location-based applications and the potentially adversarial observers. Many interesting LPPMs have been proposed for sporadic applications. Anonymization and obfuscation of users' location events (e.g., LBS queries) are the most popular techniques.

However, so far there is no theoretical framework to both formalize the effectiveness of various location-privacy preserving mechanisms, and to take into account the characteristics of the underlying location-based application. To fill this gap, we leverage on the framework that we have proposed and used in our previous contributions [17,18,19]. More specifically, in this paper we make three major contributions. First, we formalize the location exposure in location-based services, particularly their location-exposure pattern, and add it to the framework. Second, we build upon this formalization to quantitatively evaluate the effectiveness of various LPPMs, notably the *fake-location injection* as a mechanism to protect location privacy of users. Third, we provide an analytical model, based on Hidden Markov Processes, for localization attacks. We extend the Location-Privacy Meter tool [1] to support these new features. We use the incorrectness of the adversary (i.e., his expected estimation error) [19] in localizing users over time as the location-privacy metric. We also implement some example location-based applications in our evaluation tool and assess the effectiveness of various LPPMs.

It is noteworthy that we do not address the problem of quality-of-service degradation in location-based services due to the usage of a location-privacy preserving mechanism. This issue is orthogonal to our objective in this paper, which is to provide methods to accurately assess the loss of location privacy.

The rest of the paper is organized as follows. In Section 2, we describe our framework. In Section 3, we detail the localization attack, based on Bayesian analysis. In Section 4, we evaluate the approach on a concrete example. We provide the related work in Section 5, and conclude the paper in Section 6.

2   Framework

2.1   Mobile Users

We consider $\mathcal{U} = \{u_1, u_2, \ldots, u_N\}$ a set of N mobile users who move within an area that is partitioned into M distinct regions (locations) $\mathcal{R} = \{r_1, r_2, \ldots, r_M\}$. Time is considered to be discrete, and the set of time instants when the location of users may be observed is $\mathcal{T} = \{1, \ldots, T\}$. The precision at which we want to represent the user mobility determines the granularity of the space and time. For example, regions can be of a city/block size, and two successive time instants can be a day/hour apart, if the mobility is supposed to have a low/high precision.

The spatiotemporal position of users is modeled through events and traces. An *event* is defined as a triplet $\langle u, r, t \rangle$, where $u \in \mathcal{U}$, $r \in \mathcal{R}$, $t \in \mathcal{T}$. A *trace* of user u is a T-size vector of events $a_u = (a_u(1), a_u(2), \dots, a_u(T))$. The set of all traces that may belong to user u is denoted by $\mathcal{A}_u$. Notice that, of all the traces in $\mathcal{A}_u$, exactly one is the true trace that user u created in the time period of interest $(t = 1 \dots T)$; the true trace, denoted by a_u, is called the *actual trace* of user u, and its events are called the *actual events* of user u. The set of all possible traces of all users is denoted by $\mathcal{A} = \mathcal{A}_{u_1} \times \mathcal{A}_{u_2} \times \dots \times \mathcal{A}_{u_N}$; the member of $\mathcal{A}$ that is actually created by the N users is denoted by a and it is equal to $(a_{u_1}, a_{u_2}, \dots, a_{u_N})$. The vector of actual traces a is in fact a sample from the random variable $\boldsymbol{A}$ that is distributed according to $p(\cdot) = \Pr\{\boldsymbol{A} = \cdot\}$. The distribution p reflects the joint mobility pattern of the users. We refer to each marginal distribution p_u as the *mobility profile* of user u, that is $a_u \sim p_u(\cdot) = \Pr\{\boldsymbol{A_u} = \cdot\}$.

In this paper, we assume that the users' profiles are independent of each other, i.e., $p(\cdot) = \prod_u p_u(\cdot)$. In other words, the location of a user is independent of others, *given* the user's profile (i.e., there is a conditional independence between the users' locations). As users tend to have different mobility patterns at different *time periods* (e.g., morning vs. afternoon, or weekday vs. weekend), we assume the users' profiles to be time-period dependent. The set of time instants in $\mathcal{T}$ is partitioned by the time periods. Notice that the independence of user profiles means that we are ignoring social correlations among users, e.g., we ignore information about friendships among users; this is outside the scope of this paper. However, because of the time dependence, we do take into account indirect correlation among the users' locations, for instance traffic jams in the morning and in the evening.

Further, we assume that the mobility of a user is modeled as a Markov chain on the set of regions. So, for user u, the distribution p_u of actual traces can be computed using the transition matrix of its Markov chain. Each state of the Markov chain represents a region and a time period. We use $p_u^\tau(r, s)$ to indicate the probability of a transition from region r to s by user u in time period τ. We also use $\pi_u^\tau(r)$ to indicate the probability that user u is in region r in time period τ, according to the stationary probability distribution of p_u^τ.

Thus, we illustrate the mobility profile of users using a first-order Markov chain model which is dependent on time (periods). It is worth noting that the Markov chain model can be turned into a more powerful (yet more complex) model depending on how the states of the chain are defined. If states represent complex previous location behaviors (past n location, or locations in past day), then the model can become arbitrarily accurate.

2.2   Location-Based Applications

We differentiate among the location-based applications according to the frequency at which the users' locations are exposed. On one end of the spectrum, users' locations are continuously exposed through the application, whereas on the other end, there are applications using which users expose their location in a rather sporadic manner. In a nutshell, an application is considered to be *sporadic* if the exposed locations from the users are sparsely distributed over time, and it is considered *continuous* otherwise.

In this paper, we focus on the sporadic case (for some examples of the continuous case see [9,11]). Examples for this type of systems are (i) location-based services where users make location-stamped queries concerning their nearby points of interest in order to receive contextual information, and (ii) location-sharing applications by which users can share their location with their friends, or with people-centric sensing servers, e.g., when they report about a social event.

Let $x_u \in \{0,1\}^T$ be a vector that shows which actual events of user u are exposed through the application. In effect, x_u acts as a bit-mask, for example, if $x_u(t) = 1$, then $a_u(t)$ is exposed.

We define a location-based application as a function that maps actual traces $a \in \mathcal{A}$ to a random variable X that takes values in the set $\mathcal{X} = \{0,1\}^{N \times T}$. The corresponding probability distribution function $\Pr\{X = x | A = a, p\}$ can be computed as follows, considering that mobile users usually make use of the location-based applications independently at each time instant:

$$\Pr\{X = x | A = a, p\} = \prod_u \prod_t \Pr\{X_u(t) = x_u(t) | A_u(t) = a_u(t), p\} \quad (1)$$

where p is the set of all users' actual mobility profiles.

2.3   Location-Privacy Preserving Mechanisms

The service provider, or any other entity that can access to the users' locations through some location-based applications, is considered as the adversary (or the observer) in this paper. Such an entity can indeed de-anonymize the users' traces and eventually localize users over time by relying on its background knowledge about users (e.g., their home/work address, their mobility patterns). We denote the background knowledge of the adversary about users by $\mathcal{K}$.

In order to thwart such threats, the users distort their exposed locations before an untrusted entity can see them. Location-privacy preserving mechanisms (LPPMs) are put in place to perform this distortion. LPPMs can be implemented both in a centralized architecture, by means of a trusted third party, and in a distributed architecture, i.e., an independent installation on each of the mobile devices. We abstract away these details and provide a generic model: the LPPMs act on the set of exposed traces and produce a set of traces that are observed by the untrusted entities. The LPPM is assumed to modify the set of exposed events using anonymization and obfuscation techniques. We now describe each of these in turn.

In the anonymization process, the username part of each trace is replaced by a *user pseudonym* in the set $\mathcal{U}' = \{1, ..., N\}$. The *anonymization* mechanism that we consider is the random permutation. That is, a permutation of the users is chosen uniformly at random among all $N!$ permutations and each user's pseudonym is her position in the permutation. More formally, the anonymization mechanism selects, independent of everything else, a permutation σ according to the probability distribution function $\Pr\{\Sigma = \sigma\} = \frac{1}{N!}$, and each user's pseudonym is $\sigma(u) \in \mathcal{U}'$.

Notice that the pseudonym of a user remains the same for the whole time period $t = 1, \ldots, T$. The larger the value of T, the easier it is, in general, for the adversary to de-anonymize the users. In this paper, we do not study changing pseudonyms. However, we do study the effect of T on the privacy, and in particular the anonymity, of users (Section 4). Knowing the relation between T and user privacy is useful for deciding when to change a pseudonym, for example, when user privacy drops below a certain threshold.

In the obfuscation process, three event/trace transformations can happen:

- The location part of each exposed event can be replaced by a *location pseudonym* in the set $\mathcal{R}' = \mathcal{P}(R) = \{r'_1, \ldots, r'_{2^M}\}$. Each location pseudonym corresponds to a subset of regions in $\mathcal{R}$. Notice that each region can be obfuscated to a different location pseudonym each time it is encountered in a trace, whereas each user is always anonymized to the same user pseudonym.[1]
- Fake location-pseudonyms can be injected at times that the user does not expose anything (it is equivalent to say that the LPPM selects a fake location and then obfuscates it).
- Some of the exposed events can be removed (become hidden).

The LPPM, as the combination of the two processes, probabilistically maps exposed traces $(a, x) \in \mathcal{A} \times \mathcal{X}$ to obfuscated and anonymized traces. The output is a random variable O that takes values in the set $\mathcal{O}$, which is the set of all possible obfuscated and anonymized traces of all users. Such a trace is composed of T events of the form $o_{u'}(t) = \langle u', r', t \rangle$, where $u' \in \mathcal{U}'$, $r' \in \mathcal{R}'$, for $t = \{1, 2, \cdots, T\}$. A complete trace is denoted by $o_{u'}$.

In this paper, we study the case where each exposed event of a user is obfuscated independently of other events which belong to that user or other users. The mobility profiles of all users are used by the LPPM in the process of obfuscating users' locations. This knowledge of the users' profiles enables us to design strong LPPMs against the adversary who also relies on this type of information. The probability of a given output o is then computed as follows:

$$\Pr\{O = o | X = x, A = a, p\} =$$
$$= \sum_{\sigma} \prod_{u'} \prod_{t} \underbrace{\Pr\{O_{u'}(t) = o_{u'}(t) | \Sigma = \sigma, X = x, A = a, p\}}_{\text{Obfuscation mechanism}}$$
$$\cdot \underbrace{\Pr\{\Sigma = \sigma | X = x, A = a, p\}}_{\text{Anonymization mechanism}} \tag{2}$$

Notice that, in general, employing an LPPM reduces the quality of the information provided to the location-based service. Consequently, the quality of

---

[1] In this paper, we do not consider the obfuscation of the events' time-stamps, and leave it for future work.

service that the user receives is also reduced. Therefore, there exists a tradeoff between the effectiveness of the LPPM and the quality of service for the user. Addressing this tradeoff is beyond the scope of this paper. Our objective is to evaluate the privacy that a given LPPM provides to the users.

2.4   Attacker

The adversary observes o, and by relying on his background knowledge $\mathcal{K}$, tries to infer the actual location of users. The adversary is assumed to be aware of the type and the characteristics of the location-based application, and also the location-privacy preserving mechanism. In order to infer the location of users, the adversary has to reverse the two mechanisms. The adversary's ultimate goal is then formally defined as calculating the following probability distribution function:

$$h_o(\hat{a}) = \Pr\{A = \hat{a}|O = o, \mathcal{K}\} \tag{3}$$

2.5   Location-Privacy Metric

We quantify the location privacy of users as the error of the adversary in estimating the actual location of users. The metric is justified in [19], and its superiority to other metrics, such as k-anonymity and entropy, is shown qualitatively and quantitatively. According to the expected-estimation-error metric, the users' location privacy is computed as follows:

$$\text{LP} = \sum_{\hat{a} \in \mathcal{A}} h_o(\hat{a}) \Delta(a, \hat{a}) \tag{4}$$

where $\Delta(a, \hat{a})$ is a distortion function that determines the distance between actual traces a and hypothesized traces $\hat{a}$. In this paper, we use the following distortion function:

$$\Delta(a, \hat{a}) = \frac{1}{N \cdot T} \sum_u \sum_t 1_{a_u(t) \neq \hat{a}_u(t)} \tag{5}$$

which makes LP the average probability of error of the adversary in estimating the actual location of users over time. Note that, the location privacy of each user can be computed separately in the same way.

3   Localization Attack

We define the goal of the adversary to be the localization of users over time: That is, for a given user at a given time instant, the adversary computes the probability distribution over regions where the user might be at that specific time instant, considering the observed traces. More formally, the adversary computes $\Pr\{A_u(t) = \langle u, t, r\rangle|o, \mathcal{K}\}$ for user u at time instant t for all regions $r \in \mathcal{R}$. We call this the *localization attack*.

As an aside, more general objectives can be imagined for the attacker. The most general one is to recover all traces of all users, i.e., to compute the probability $\Pr\{A = \cdot | O = o, \mathcal{K}\}$ as in (3).

Monte Carlo methods can be used to compute any desired probability in our framework. At its base, a Monte Carlo method uses repeated sampling from an appropriate distribution to estimate the desired probability. In our case, sampling from the distribution that is appropriate for the most general objective, $\Pr\{A = \cdot | O = o, \mathcal{K}\}$, is computationally inefficient for large user populations and long time intervals. Even for the localization attack, the space from which the Monte Carlo method needs to sample includes all the $N!$ permutations of user-pseudonym assignments. Therefore, we choose a different method, which can be applied more generally.

We split the localization attack into two parts: de-anonymization, and de-obfuscation. In the first step, we find the most likely assignments between users and pseudonyms. Formally, we compute

$$\sigma^* = \underbrace{\arg\max_\sigma \Pr\{\Sigma = \sigma | o, \mathcal{K}\}}_{\text{de-anonymization}}. \tag{6}$$

Then, given this assignment, we compute the probability distribution of the given user's location at the given time instant.

$$\Pr\{A_u(t) = \langle u, t, r\rangle | o, \mathcal{K}\} \approx \underbrace{\Pr\{A_u(t) = \langle u, t, r\rangle | \Sigma = \sigma^*, o, \mathcal{K}\}}_{\text{de-obfuscation}} \tag{7}$$

We use Bayesian inference in order to perform both the de-anonymization and the de-obfuscation. Both steps have polynomial-time complexity (in N and T), so they are computationally efficient even for large problem sizes.

Notice that this computation is an approximation of the a-posteriori probability $\Pr\{A_u(t) = \langle u, t, r\rangle | o, \mathcal{K}\}$, which can be written as a weighted sum as follows (we omit, but still imply the existence of, $\mathcal{K}$):

$$\Pr\{A_u(t) = \langle u, t, r\rangle | o\} = \sum_\sigma \Pr\{A_u(t) = \langle u, t, r\rangle, \sigma | o\}$$

$$= \sum_\sigma \Pr\{A_u(t) = \langle u, t, r\rangle | \sigma, o\} \Pr\{\sigma | o\} \tag{8}$$

In effect, our approximation replaces the weighted sum with the probability $\Pr\{A_u(t) = \langle u, t, r\rangle | \sigma^*, o\}$. We call this the *zeroth-order* approximation.

Our approximation can be made arbitrarily precise, at the cost of extra computations, in the following way. The basic idea is to separate the permutations, over which the summation is done, into N groups according to the pseudonym that they assign to user u (group 1 assigns pseudonym u_1' to user u, group 2 assigns pseudonym u_2', etc.). Without loss of generality, we assume that u is u_1.

$$\Pr\{\boldsymbol{A_u}(t) = \langle u, t, r\rangle | o\} = \sum_{\sigma} \Pr\{\boldsymbol{A_u}(t) = \langle u, t, r\rangle, \sigma | o\} =$$

$$= \sum_{u_1' \in \mathcal{U}'} \sum_{\sigma:\sigma(u_1)=u_1'} \Pr\{\boldsymbol{A_u}(t) = \langle u, t, r\rangle, \sigma | o\}$$

$$= \sum_{u_1' \in \mathcal{U}'} \sum_{\sigma:\sigma(u_1)=u_1'} \Pr\{\boldsymbol{A_u}(t) = \langle u, t, r\rangle | \sigma(u_1) = u_1', o_{u_1'}\} \Pr\{\sigma | o\}$$

$$= \sum_{u_1' \in \mathcal{U}'} \left(\Pr\{\boldsymbol{A_u}(t) = \langle u, t, r\rangle | \sigma(u_1) = u_1', o_{u_1'}\} \sum_{\sigma:\sigma(u_1)=u_1'} \Pr\{\sigma | o\} \right) \quad (9)$$

It is computationally infeasible to compute the second sum explicitly. So, we can do the *first-order* approximation: we replace the sum with the maximum of the quantity $\Pr\{\boldsymbol{\Sigma} = \sigma | o\}$ over all indicated permutations $\sigma : \sigma(u_1) = u_1'$. That is, for each $u_1' \in \mathcal{U}'$ we compute the maximum $\Pr\{\boldsymbol{\Sigma} = \sigma | o\}$ over all permutations that assign the pseudonym u_1' to user u_1. Then, in the first sum, we use this maximum as the weight for the probability $\Pr\{\boldsymbol{A_u}(t) = \langle u, t, r\rangle | \sigma(u_1) = u_1', o_{u_1'}\}$. Finding the maximum is a Maximum Assignment Problem, which is solvable in polynomial time; we need to find N such maxima, one for each value of $u_1' \in \mathcal{U}'$. Therefore, the whole computation is still polynomial, although longer than our original approximation.

However, the successive approximation need not stop at the first order. Instead of computing the maximum $\Pr\{\boldsymbol{\Sigma} = \sigma | o\}$ over all permutations that assign the pseudonym u_1' to user u_1, we can expand the second sum as follows:

$$\sum_{\sigma:\sigma(u_1)=u_1'} \Pr\{\boldsymbol{\Sigma} = \sigma | o\} = \sum_{u_2' \in \mathcal{U}' \setminus \{u_1'\}} \sum_{\substack{\sigma:\sigma(u_1)=u_1', \\ \sigma(u_2)=u_2'}} \Pr\{\boldsymbol{\Sigma} = \sigma | o\} \quad (10)$$

Now, as before, we can approximate the second sum by a maximum over the indicated permutations, and use the computed maxima (one for each value of u_2') as weights to compute the weighted sum. Alternatively, we can keep improving the approximation by considering user u_3, and so on. If we do this for all users, then we will have computed the exact value of $\Pr\{\boldsymbol{\Sigma} = \sigma | o\}$. In this paper, we stay at the zeroth-order approximation, as it is shown in (6) and (7).

De-anonymization: In order to obtain the σ^* of (6), we need to maximize the probability

$$\Pr\{\boldsymbol{\Sigma} = \sigma | o, \mathcal{K}\} = \Pr\{o | \boldsymbol{\Sigma} = \sigma, \mathcal{K}\} \cdot \underbrace{\frac{\Pr\{\boldsymbol{\Sigma} = \sigma | \mathcal{K}\} \equiv \frac{1}{N!}}{\Pr\{o | \mathcal{K}\}}}_{\text{constant}},$$

where $\Pr\{o | \boldsymbol{\Sigma} = \sigma, \mathcal{K}\} = \prod_{u'} \Pr\{o_{u'} | \boldsymbol{\Sigma} = \sigma, \mathcal{K}\}.$ \quad (11)

Thus, $\sigma^* = \arg\max_\sigma \Pr\{\Sigma = \sigma|o, \mathcal{K}\} = \arg\max_\sigma \prod_{u'} \Pr\{o_{u'}|\Sigma = \sigma, \mathcal{K}\}$. Notice that, given the assignment of a user u to the pseudonym u', the probability $\Pr\{o_{u'}|\Sigma = \sigma, \mathcal{K}\}$ is independent of all other user-pseudonym assignments. So, to find the most likely assignment σ^*, we first compute $\Pr\{o_{u'}|\sigma(u) = u', \mathcal{K}\}$ for all pairs of $u \in \mathcal{U}$ and $u' \in \mathcal{U}'$. Then, we construct a complete weighted bipartite graph whose disjoint sets of vertices are $\mathcal{U}$ and $\mathcal{U}'$ and the weight on the edge between given vertices u and u' is the likelihood $\Pr\{o_{u'}|\sigma(u) = u', \mathcal{K}\}$. In order to obtain σ^*, we then solve the maximum weight assignment problem for this graph (see also [21]). In our simulation, we use the Hungarian algorithm in order to solve this problem, which is a special case of a linear program.

De-obfuscation: Given the most likely user-pseudonym assignment σ^*, we perform the de-obfuscation (7) as follows:

$$
\begin{aligned}
\Pr\{A_u(t) &= \langle u, t, r\rangle | \Sigma = \sigma^*, o, \mathcal{K}\} = \\
&= \Pr\{A_u(t) = \langle u, t, r\rangle | o_{u'}, \sigma^*(u) = u', \mathcal{K}\} \\
&= \frac{\Pr\{A_u(t) = \langle u, t, r\rangle, o_{u'} | \sigma^*(u) = u', \mathcal{K}\}}{\sum_{s \in \mathcal{R}} \Pr\{A_u(t) = \langle u, t, s\rangle, o_{u'} | \sigma^*(u) = u', \mathcal{K}\}}
\end{aligned}
\tag{12}
$$

The distribution over all regions r is obtained by computing the probability $\Pr\{A_u(t) = \langle u, t, r\rangle, o_{u'} | \sigma^*(u) = u', \mathcal{K}\}$ for all $r \in \mathcal{R}$.

Adversary Knowledge: The de-anonymization and the de-obfuscation processes have been reduced, as seen in (11) and (12), to the computation of the probabilities $\Pr\{o_{u'}|\sigma(u) = u', \mathcal{K}\}$ and $\Pr\{A_u(t) = \langle u, t, r\rangle, o_{u'} | \sigma^*(u) = u', \mathcal{K}\}$.

These probabilities should be computed appropriately according to the background knowledge $\mathcal{K}$ that we consider for the adversary. In the next subsections, we compute these probabilities for two adversaries with different background knowledge:

- Adversary (I) whose knowledge of users' mobility is their geographical distribution over the regions, i.e., $\mathcal{K} \equiv \hat{\pi}$.
- Adversary (II) who is a stronger adversary and knows the users' probability of transition between the regions, i.e., $\mathcal{K} \equiv \hat{p}$.

We construct $\hat{\pi}$ and $\hat{p}$ from the users' actual traces. The element $\hat{\pi}_u(r)$ of $\hat{\pi}$ is calculated as the fraction of time instants when user u is in region r. The element $\hat{p}_u(r_i, r_j)$ of $\hat{p}$ is calculated as the fraction of transitions of user u to r_j over all time instants when u is in region r_i.

We perform analytic probability calculations, where we also use the conditional independence of observed events, given the actual events. In effect, we decompose the desired probability into basic parts that can be computed from known functions. As these calculations are made by the adversary in performing the attack, the basic parts need to be computable from functions known to the adversary.

3.1   Adversary (I)

De-anonymization

$$\Pr\left\{o_{u'}|\sigma(u)=u',\hat{\pi}\right\}=$$

$$=\prod_t\left(\sum_{r\in\mathcal{R}}\sum_{x\in\{0,1\}}\underbrace{\Pr\left\{o_{u'}(t)|\boldsymbol{X_u}(t)=x,\boldsymbol{A_u}(t)=\langle u,t,r\rangle,\sigma(u)=u',\hat{\pi}\right\}}_{\text{LPPM - Obfuscation mechanism}}\right.$$

$$\cdot\underbrace{\Pr\left\{\boldsymbol{X_u}(t)=x|\boldsymbol{A_u}(t)=\langle u,t,r\rangle,\hat{\pi}\right\}}_{\text{Application}}$$

$$\left.\cdot\underbrace{\Pr\left\{\boldsymbol{A_u}(t)=\langle u,t,r\rangle|\hat{\pi}\right\}\equiv\hat{\pi}_u^\tau(r),t\in\tau}_{\text{Background Knowledge of the Adversary}}\right) \qquad (13)$$

De-obfuscation

$$\Pr\left\{\boldsymbol{A_u}(t)=\langle u,t,r\rangle,o_{u'}(t)|\sigma^*(u)=u',\hat{\pi}\right\}=$$

$$=\Pr\left\{o_{u'}(t)|\boldsymbol{A_u}(t)=\langle u,t,r\rangle,\sigma^*(u)=u',\hat{\pi}\right\}$$
$$\cdot\Pr\left\{\boldsymbol{A_u}(t)=\langle u,t,r\rangle|\hat{\pi}\right\}$$

$$=\left(\sum_{x\in\{0,1\}}\underbrace{\Pr\left\{o_{u'}(t)|\boldsymbol{X_u}(t)=x,\boldsymbol{A_u}(t)=\langle u,t,r\rangle,\sigma^*(u)=u',\hat{\pi}\right\}}_{\text{LPPM - Obfuscation mechanism}}\right.$$

$$\left.\cdot\underbrace{\Pr\left\{\boldsymbol{X_u}(t)=x|\boldsymbol{A_u}(t)=\langle u,t,r\rangle,\hat{\pi}\right\}}_{\text{Application}}\right)$$

$$\cdot\underbrace{\Pr\left\{\boldsymbol{A_u}(t)=\langle u,t,r\rangle|\hat{\pi}\right\}\equiv\hat{\pi}_u^\tau(r),t\in\tau}_{\text{Background Knowledge of the Adversary}} \qquad (14)$$

3.2   Adversary (II)

In this case, the calculations can be simplified if we use two helper functions α and β, as defined below. In effect, the problem that the attacker faces is equivalent to estimating the hidden state of a Hidden Markov Process. In the context of Hidden Markov Processes, the functions α and β are the forward-backward variables [16].

$$\alpha_t^{u,u'}(r) \equiv \Pr\left\{A_u(t) = \langle u, t, r \rangle, o_{u'}(1), \cdots, o_{u'}(t) | \sigma(u) = u', \hat{p}\right\} \tag{15}$$

$$\beta_t^{u,u'}(r) \equiv \Pr\left\{o_{u'}(t+1), \cdots, o_{u'}(T) | A_u(t) = \langle u, t, r \rangle, \sigma(u) = u', \hat{p}\right\} \tag{16}$$

In Appendix B, we show how to calculate these two functions in our case. Having calculated them for all $t \in \mathcal{T}$ and $r \in \mathcal{R}$, we can use them to compute the probabilities of interest.

De-anonymization

$$\Pr\left\{o_{u'} | \sigma(u) = u', \hat{p}\right\} = \sum_{r \in \mathcal{R}} \alpha_T^{u,u'}(r) \tag{17}$$

De-obfuscation

$$\Pr\left\{A_u(t) = \langle u, t, r \rangle, o_{u'} | \sigma^*(u) = u', \hat{p}\right\} = \alpha_t^{u,u'}(r) \cdot \beta_t^{u,u'}(r) \tag{18}$$

where we compute α and β given σ^*.

4   Evaluation

In this section, we present the effectiveness of some location-privacy preserving mechanisms in protecting users' location privacy while they expose their location through some location-based applications. We evaluate the location privacy of users with respect to the two adversary types we introduced in the previous sections. We have extended the *Location-Privacy Meter* tool [19] by adding the location-based applications, implementing new LPPMs, and new localization attacks for sporadic applications, as described in the paper.

4.1   Simulation Setting

The location traces that we use in our simulation belong to $N = 20$ randomly chosen mobile users (vehicles) from the epfl/mobility dataset at CRAWDAD [15]. The area within which users move (the San Francisco bay area) is divided into $M = 40$ regions forming a 5×8 grid.

We evaluate various LPPMs that operate on top of two kinds of applications. The first type of application is the *once-in-a-while* application, which also serves as a baseline for comparison. In this type of application, events are exposed independently at random with the same probability θ. That is,

$$\Pr\left\{X_u(t) = 1 | A_u(t) = \langle u, t, r \rangle\right\} = \Pr\left\{X_u(t) = 1\right\} = \theta. \tag{19}$$

The second type of application is the *local search* application. In this application, users make queries, thus exposing their location, when they find themselves in unfamiliar places (which are the places that the user does not visit often, and hence needs more information about). We model this application as exposing the events of user u at location r independently at random with probability that is a decreasing function of $\pi_u(r)$. In particular,

$$\Pr\{X_u(t) = 1 | A_u(t) = \langle u, t, r \rangle, \pi\} = \theta(1 - \pi_u(r)). \tag{20}$$

where θ here determines the upper-bound on the probability of location exposure.

We refer to the application simply by using its parameter θ, and its type (o: once-in-a-while application, and s: local search). For example a local search application with exposure rate 0.1 is denoted by APP(0.1, s).

For our considered LPPMs, we have to define two modes of behavior, according to whether the application exposes or hides the location. When the application exposes the user's location, the LPPM obfuscates it by removing some low-order bits/digits of the location-stamp of the event. We refer to the number of removed bits as the *obfuscation level* ρ of the LPPM. When the application hides the location, the LPPM chooses, with some probability ϕ, to create a fake location and then obfuscates it (as it does for the actual locations). We consider two ways in which the LPPM can create a fake location: The first way is to create a fake location uniformly at random among all locations $r \in \mathcal{R}$, and the second way is to create it according to the aggregate user geographical distribution $\bar{\pi} = \frac{1}{N} \sum_{u \in \mathcal{U}} \pi_u$ (i.e., the average mobility profile). We refer to an LPPM using its parameters ϕ and ρ, and its type (u: uniform selection, g: selection according to the average mobility profile). For example LPPM(0.3, 2, u) injects a fake location (uniformly selected at random) with probability 0.3 if there is no location exposure, and obfuscated the (both fake and actual) locations by dropping their 2 low-order bits.

The metric that we use to evaluate the LPPMs is the expected error, as described in Section 2.5. We evaluate the effect of the application and LPPM parameters that we listed above (obfuscation level, probability ϕ of injecting a fake location) as well as the effect of the different application types and of the different ways of creating fake locations.

We are also interested in the effect of the pseudonym lifetime on the privacy of users. In our model, we consider that all users keep their pseudonyms from time 1 to T. By attacking at time T, we can compare the privacy achieved by users for various values of T.

4.2   Simulation Results

We run the simulator for all combinations of the following parameters: APP(0.1, {o, s}), LPPM({0, 0.3, 0.6}, {0, 2, 4}, {u, g}), and pseudonym lifetimes {31, 71, 141, 281}. We then perform the de-anonymization and localization attacks (for both (I) weak, and (II) strong adversaries) that are described in the previous section. The results are averaged over 20 simulation runs. Hereafter, we present some of the results that we obtain regarding the anonymity and location-privacy of users.

In Figure 1, we plot user anonymity as a function of pseudonym lifetime. The anonymity is quantified as the percentage of users that are incorrectly de-anonymized by the attacker. Notice that we do not yet plot the location privacy

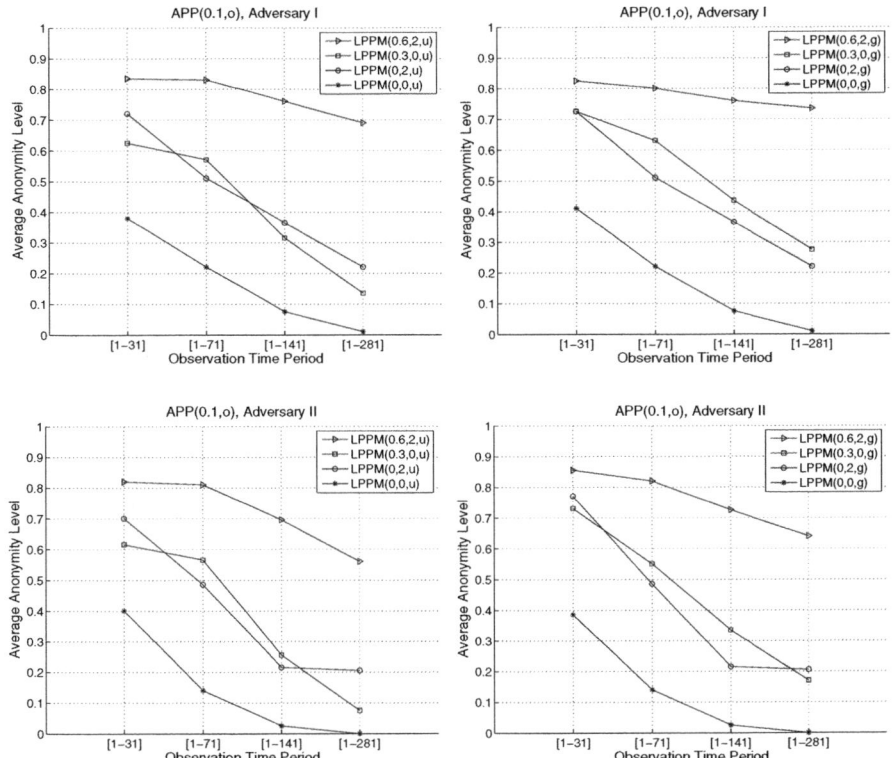

Fig. 1. User anonymity versus pseudonym lifetime in location-based application APP(0.1, o). The anonymity is quantified as the percentage of users that are incorrectly de-anonymized by the attacker. In the top two sub-figures, we consider the weak adversary (I), whereas in the bottom two, we consider the strong one (II). The left column considers the uniform (u) LPPM type, whereas the right column considers the LPPM type g. Each line in a sub-figure corresponds to different combinations of obfuscation levels {0, 2} and fake-location injection rates {0, 0.3, 0.6}.

of users, just their anonymity as defined. Each of the four sub-figures corresponds to each of the four combinations of adversary type (I-weak, II-strong) and LPPM type (u, g). Each line in a sub-figure corresponds to different combinations of obfuscation level and probability of injecting a fake location.

We observe that the anonymity decreases as the pseudonym lifetime (the size of the observation period) increases. The same trend is seen in all four sub-figures, for all combination parameters. By comparing the results that are obtained from different LPPMs, we observe the following interesting phenomenon, regarding the effect of stronger LPPM parameters, in particular when both the obfuscation level and the fake injection probability are non-zero: By jointly increasing the protection level of the two mechanisms, not only the absolute value of anonymity gets higher, but also the robustness to longer pseudonym lifetimes becomes better. That is, the level of anonymity drops with a slower rate as

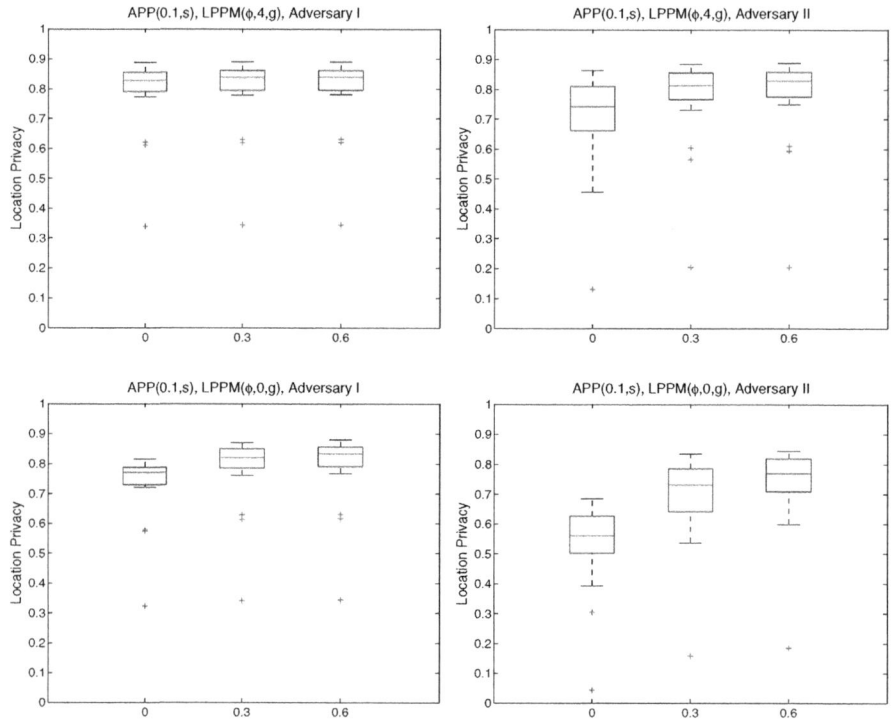

Fig. 2. Users' location privacy in location-based application APP(0.1, s), using various LPPMs, with respect to localization attack performed by two adversaries (I-weak: left column, and II-strong: right column). The x-axis shows the fake-location injection rate ϕ. The sub-figures corresponds to LPPM with obfuscation level 4 (for the top two), and 0 (for the bottom two). Each box-and-whisker diagram (boxplot) shows all location-privacy values (hence, system-level), where the bottom and top of a box show the 25th and 75th percentiles, and the central mark shows the median. The ends of the whiskers represent the most extreme data points not considered as outliers, and the outliers are plotted individually.

the pseudonym lifetime increases. This shows the relation between the effects of obfuscation and anonymization techniques. The LPPM designer can choose appropriately the parameters to achieve a desired level of anonymity; or alternatively, the pseudonym should be changed when the desired level of anonymity is no longer achieved.

In Figure 2, we show the location privacy of users who (i) sporadically expose their location with exposure rate 0.1 in a *local search* application, and (ii) use LPPM that adds fake locations to their observed trace according to the *aggregate user geographical distribution*. As it is expected, the users' location privacy increases when the level of location-obfuscation or fake-location injection increases. However, the main finding of our result is that, in sporadic applications, the fake-location injection can dominate the obfuscation method, in preserving users' location-privacy, when the injection rate is higher. Moreover, adding fake location has a high impact on misleading the stronger adversary, as it reduces his success down to that of weaker adversary (compare the location-privacy improvement obtained by injecting fake-locations with rate 0.3 in the bottom sub-figures).

5   Related Work

The work related to our paper is threefold: (i) The papers that evaluate the risk of exposing locations through location-based services (which are mainly sporadic), (ii) The papers that aim at protecting users' location privacy for sporadic applications, and (iii) The papers that provide a framework for location privacy and describe possible threats and protections mechanisms as well as the location-privacy metrics.

The risk of location disclosure in mobile networks is evaluated in multiple papers. The authors use different attacks to de-anonymize the users' exposed traces (which are exposed in a sporadic manner). Ma et al. [14] make use of maximum likelihood estimation to identify the users from which the adversary has obtained some noisy past traces. Freudiger et al. [5] assume the adversary has access to the users' home and work addresses and performs the de-anonymization attack on the observed traces using some clustering algorithms. Similar de-anonymization of mobile users through identifying their home and work addresses have been performed by various researchers. Golle and Partridge [7], Beresford and Stajano [2], Hoh et al. [10], and Krumm [12] use different techniques to show that users can be identified by inferring where they spend most of their time (notably their home and workplace). De Mulder et al. [3] also present some statistical inference attacks on users' traces in GSM cellular networks. The authors show how easily the adversary can identify users if he has access to their location pattern (i.e., how they are distributed throughout the cells) in such setting. Compared to this set of contributions, in this paper we take two more major steps: We not only formalize the location-based application, but also the protection mechanisms that can be used to preserve users' location-privacy. Moreover, besides the de-anonymization, we evaluate the success of the adversary in finding the location of users over time. We provide a systematic formal framework that can be used to model the combination of a variety of LBSs and LPPMs.

Protecting location privacy of users in location-based services has received a tremendous attention from researchers in different disciplines such as database, and ubiquitous computing. A majority of the protection mechanisms revolve around combination of anonymization and location obfuscation. Duckham and Kulik [4] propose a formal model for location obfuscation techniques such as adding inaccuracy, imprecision, and vagueness. Krumm [12] shows that the effects of spatial cloaking algorithms and adding Gaussian noise, or discretizing the location (i.e., reducing granularity) can degrade the identification success of the adversary. Gruteser and Grunwald [8] propose spatial and temporal cloaking methods to increase the adversary's uncertainty in identifying the users. The privacy of users is quantified according to k-anonymity. Gedik *et al.* [6] propose an architecture and some algorithms to protect location privacy using personalized k-anonymity. A majority of the location-obfuscation techniques revolve around k-anonymity. The interested reader is referred to [20] for a more in depth overview of k-anonymity-based obfuscation techniques, and also to [19] for a quantitative analysis of k-anonymity metric for location privacy. As it is shown in [19,20] these interesting approaches still lack an appropriate evaluation mechanism and metric that we provide in this paper. In addition to the obfuscation techniques, we also formalize and evaluate fake-location injection (adding dummy events) as another powerful method.

Krumm [13] provides a literature survey of computational location privacy. Shokri *et al.* [17] also provide a unified framework for location privacy, which is extended and more formalized in [19]. We have built up our system model on top of these frameworks by extending them in such a way that location-based services and new LPPMs can be defined and analyzed with respect to the localization attack.

6   Conclusion

We propose, to the best of our knowledge, the first formal framework for quantifying location privacy in the case where users expose their location sporadically. We formalize sporadic location-based applications. Using this formalization, we model various location-privacy preserving mechanisms, such as location obfuscation and fake-location injection. Formalizing both location-based applications and location-privacy preserving mechanisms in the same framework enables us to design more effective protection mechanisms that are appropriately tailored to each location-based service. We also establish an analytical framework, based on Bayesian inference in Hidden Markov Processes, to perform localization attacks on anonymized traces (for adversaries with different background knowledge). The results obtained from the simulations of the attacks on mobility traces unveil the potential of various mechanisms, such as the location obfuscation, the fake-location injection, and anonymization, in preserving location-privacy of mobile users.

Acknowledgements

The authors would like to thank Ehsan Kazemi for his valuable comments on the submitted manuscript, and also Vincent Bindschaedler for his effective contribution to the development of the Location-Privacy Meter.

References

1. Location-Privacy Meter tool, (2011), `http://people.epfl.ch/reza.shokri`
2. Beresford, A.R., Stajano, F.: Location privacy in pervasive computing. IEEE Pervasive Computing 2(1), 46–55 (2003)
3. De Mulder, Y., Danezis, G., Batina, L., Preneel, B.: Identification via location-profiling in gsm networks. In: WPES 2008: Proceedings of the 7th ACM Workshop on Privacy in the Electronic Society, pp. 23–32. ACM Press, New York (2008)
4. Duckham, M., Kulik, L.: A formal model of obfuscation and negotiation for location privacy. In: Gellersen, H.-W., Want, R., Schmidt, A. (eds.) PERVASIVE 2005. LNCS, vol. 3468, Springer, Heidelberg (2005)
5. Freudiger, J., Shokri, R., Hubaux, J.-P.: Evaluating the privacy risk of location-based services. In: Financial Cryptography and Data Security, FC (2011)
6. Gedik, B., Liu, L.: Protecting location privacy with personalized k-anonymity: Architecture and algorithms. IEEE Transactions on Mobile Computing 7(1), 1–18 (2008)
7. Golle, P., Partridge, K.: On the anonymity of home/work location pairs. In: Pervasive 2009: Proceedings of the 7th International Conference on Pervasive Computing, pp. 390–397. Springer, Berlin (2009)
8. Gruteser, M., Grunwald, D.: Anonymous usage of location-based services through spatial and temporal cloaking. In: MobiSys 2003: Proceedings of the 1st International Conference on Mobile Systems, Applications and Services, pp. 31–42. ACM Press, New York (2003)
9. Hoh, B., Gruteser, M.: Protecting location privacy through path confusion. In: SECURECOMM 2005: Proceedings of the First International Conference on Security and Privacy for Emerging Areas in Communications Networks, pp. 194–205. IEEE Computer Society Press, Washington (2005)
10. Hoh, B., Gruteser, M., Xiong, H., Alrabady, A.: Enhancing security and privacy in traffic-monitoring systems. IEEE Pervasive Computing 5(4), 38–46 (2006)
11. Hoh, B., Gruteser, M., Xiong, H., Alrabady, A.: Preserving privacy in gps traces via uncertainty-aware path cloaking. In: CCS 2007: Proceedings of the 14th ACM Conference on Computer and Communications Security, pp. 161–171. ACM Press, New York (2007)
12. Krumm, J.: Inference attacks on location tracks. In: LaMarca, A., Langheinrich, M., Truong, K.N. (eds.) Pervasive 2007. LNCS, vol. 4480, pp. 127–143. Springer, Heidelberg (2007)
13. Krumm, J.: A survey of computational location privacy. Personal Ubiquitous Comput. 13(6), 391–399 (2009)
14. Ma, C.Y., Yau, D.K., Yip, N.K., Rao, N.S.: Privacy vulnerability of published anonymous mobility traces. In: Proceedings of the sixteenth annual international conference on Mobile computing and networking. MobiCom 2010, pp. 185–196. ACM Press, New York (2010)
15. Piorkowski, M., Sarafijanovic-Djukic, N., Grossglauser, M.: CRAWDAD data set epfl/mobility (v. 2009-02-24) (February 2009),
    `http://crawdad.cs.dartmouth.edu/epfl/mobility`
16. Rabiner, L.: A tutorial on hidden Markov models and selected applications in speech recognition. Proceedings of the IEEE 77(2), 257–286 (1989)
17. Shokri, R., Freudiger, J., Hubaux, J.-P.: A unified framework for location privacy. Technical Report EPFL-REPORT-148708, EPFL, Switzerland (2010)

18. Shokri, R., Freudiger, J., Jadliwala, M., Hubaux, J.-P.: A distortion-based metric for location privacy. In: WPES 2009: Proceedings of the 8th ACM workshop on Privacy in the electronic society, pp. 21–30. ACM Press, New York (2009)
19. Shokri, R., Theodorakopoulos, G., Boudec, J.-Y.L., Hubaux, J.-P.: Quantifying location privacy. In: IEEE Symposium on Security and Privacy, Oakland, CA, USA (2011)
20. Shokri, R., Troncoso, C., Diaz, C., Freudiger, J., Hubaux, J.-P.: Unraveling an old cloak: k-anonymity for location privacy. In: Proceedings of the 9th Annual ACM Workshop on Privacy in the Electronic Society. WPES 2010, pp. 115–118. ACM Press, New York (2010)
21. Troncoso, C., Gierlichs, B., Preneel, B., Verbauwhede, I.: Perfect matching disclosure attacks. In: Borisov, N., Goldberg, I. (eds.) PETS 2008. LNCS, vol. 5134, pp. 2–23. Springer, Heidelberg (2008)

A Notations

Throughout the paper, we use bold capital letters to denote random variables, lower case letters to denote realizations of random variables, and script letters to denote sets within which the random variables take values. For example, a random variable X takes values x in $\mathcal{X}$.

Table 1. Notations

$\mathcal{U}$	set of mobile users
$\mathcal{R}$	set of regions that partition the whole area
$\mathcal{T}$	time period under consideration
$\mathcal{A}$	set of all possible actual traces
$\mathcal{X}$	set of all possible exposed-locations bit-masks
$\mathcal{O}$	set of all observable traces
$\mathcal{U}'$	set of user pseudonyms
$\mathcal{R}'$	set of location pseudonyms (it is equivalent to $\mathcal{P}(R)$)
N	number of users
M	number of regions
T	number of considered time instants (length of $\mathcal{T}$)
a_u	actual trace of user u
x_u	exposed trace-bit-mask of user u
$o_{u'}$	observed trace of a user with pseudonym $u' \in \mathcal{U}'$
$\Delta(.,.)$	distortion (distance) function
p_u	actual mobility profile of user u
$\hat{p}_u$	profile of user u estimated by the adversary
π_u	geographical distribution of user u's location
$\hat{\pi}_u$	estimation of π_u by the adversary
$\mathcal{K}$	background knowledge of the adversary about users
$APP(\theta, \text{type})$	LBS application with location exposure rate θ, and types: o (once-in-a-while), and s (local search).
$LPPM(\phi, \rho, \text{type})$	LPPM with fake-location injection rate ϕ, obfuscation level ρ, and types: u (uniform selection of fake locations), and g (selecting the fake location from the aggregated geographical distribution of users).

B   Computing α and β

The computations of α (15) and β (16) are done recursively as follows.

$$\alpha_1^{u,u'}(r) = \Pr\left\{\boldsymbol{A_u(1)} = \langle u,1,r \rangle, o_{u'}(1) | \sigma(u) = u', \hat{p}\right\} =$$

$$= \sum_{x \in \{0,1\}} \underbrace{\Pr\left\{o_{u'}(1) | \boldsymbol{A_u(1)} = \langle u,1,r \rangle, \boldsymbol{X_u(1)} = x, \sigma(u) = u', \hat{p}\right\}}_{\text{LPPM - Obfuscation mechanism}}$$

$$\cdot \underbrace{\Pr\left\{\boldsymbol{X_u(1)} = x | \boldsymbol{A_u(1)} = \langle u,1,r \rangle, \hat{p}\right\}}_{\text{Application}}$$

$$\cdot \underbrace{\Pr\left\{\boldsymbol{A_u(1)} = \langle u,1,r \rangle | \hat{p}\right\} \equiv \hat{\pi}_u^\tau(r), t \in \tau}_{\text{Background Knowledge of the Adversary}} \tag{21}$$

$$\alpha_{t+1}^{u,u'}(r) = \Pr\left\{\boldsymbol{A_u(t+1)} = \langle u,t+1,r \rangle, o_{u'}(1), \cdots, o_{u'}(t+1) | \sigma(u) = u', \hat{p}\right\} =$$

$$= \sum_{x \in \{0,1\}} \underbrace{\Pr\left\{o_{u'}(t+1) | \boldsymbol{X_u(t+1)} = x, \boldsymbol{A_u(t+1)} = \langle u,t+1,r \rangle, \sigma(u) = u', \hat{p}\right\}}_{\text{LPPM - Obfuscation mechanism}}$$

$$\cdot \underbrace{\Pr\left\{\boldsymbol{X_u(t+1)} = x | \boldsymbol{A_u(t+1)} = \langle u,t+1,r \rangle, \hat{p}\right\}}_{\text{Application}}$$

$$\cdot \sum_{s \in \mathcal{R}} \underbrace{\Pr\left\{\boldsymbol{A_u(t+1)} = \langle u,t+1,r \rangle | \boldsymbol{A_u(t)} = \langle u,t,s \rangle, \hat{p}\right\} \equiv \hat{p}_u^{\tau_1,\tau_2}(s,r)}_{\text{Background Knowledge of the Adversary}}$$

$$\cdot \underbrace{\Pr\left\{\boldsymbol{A_u(t)} = \langle u,t,s \rangle, o_{u'}(1), \cdots, o_{u'}(t) | \sigma(u) = u', \hat{p}\right\}}_{\equiv \alpha_t^{u,u'}(s)} \tag{22}$$

$$\beta_T^{u,u'}(r) = 1, \quad \forall r \in \mathcal{R} \tag{23}$$

$$\beta_t^{u,u'}(r) = \Pr\left\{o_{u'}(t+1), \cdots, o_{u'}(T) | \boldsymbol{A_u(t)} = \langle u,t,r \rangle, \sigma(u) = u', \hat{p}\right\} =$$

$$= \sum_{s \in \mathcal{R}} \underbrace{\Pr\left\{o_{u'}(t+2), \cdots, o_{u'}(T) | \boldsymbol{A_u(t+1)} = \langle u,t+1,s \rangle, \sigma(u) = u', \hat{p}\right\}}_{\equiv \beta_{t+1}^{u,u'}(s)}$$

$$\cdot \sum_{x \in \{0,1\}} \underbrace{\Pr\left\{o_{u'}(t+1) | \boldsymbol{X_u(t+1)} = x, \boldsymbol{A_u(t+1)} = \langle u,t+1,s \rangle, \sigma(u) = u', \hat{p}\right\}}_{\text{LPPM - Obfuscation mechanism}}$$

$$\cdot \underbrace{\Pr\left\{\boldsymbol{X_u(t+1)} = x | \boldsymbol{A_u(t+1)} = \langle u,t+1,s \rangle, \hat{p}\right\}}_{\text{Application}}$$

$$\cdot \underbrace{\Pr\left\{\boldsymbol{A_u(t+1)} = \langle u,t+1,s \rangle | \boldsymbol{A_u(t)} = \langle u,t,r \rangle, \hat{p}\right\} \equiv \hat{p}_u^{\tau_1,\tau_2}(r,s)}_{\text{Background Knowledge of the Adversary}}$$

$$\tag{24}$$

where $t \in \tau_1$ and $t+1 \in \tau_2$.

Privacy in Mobile Computing for Location-Sharing-Based Services

Igor Bilogrevic[1], Murtuza Jadliwala[1], Kübra Kalkan[2], Jean-Pierre Hubaux[1], and Imad Aad[3]

[1] Laboratory for Communications and Applications,
EPFL, Lausanne, Switzerland
[2] Faculty of Engineering and Natural Sciences,
Sabanci University, Istanbul, Turkey
[3] Nokia Research Center,
Lausanne, Switzerland
`firstname.lastname@{epfl.ch,nokia.com}`,
`kubrakalkan@sabanciuniv.edu`

Abstract. Location-Sharing-Based Services (LSBS) complement Location-Based Services by using locations from a group of users, and not just individuals, to provide some contextualized service based on the locations in the group. However, there are growing concerns about the misuse of location data by third-parties, which fuels the need for more privacy controls in such services. We address the relevant problem of privacy in LSBSs by providing practical and effective solutions to the privacy problem in one such service, namely the fair rendez-vous point (FRVP) determination service. The privacy preserving FRVP (PPFRVP) problem is general enough and nicely captures the computations and privacy requirements in LSBSs. In this paper, we propose two privacy-preserving algorithms for the FRVP problem and analytically evaluate their privacy in both passive and active adversarial scenarios. We study the practical feasibility and performance of the proposed approaches by implementing them on Nokia mobile devices. By means of a targeted user-study, we attempt to gain further understanding of the popularity, the privacy and acceptance of the proposed solutions.

1 Introduction

From Google to Facebook, online service providers are increasingly proposing sophisticated context-aware services in order to attract new customers and improve the user-experience of existing ones. Location-based services (LBS), offered by such providers and used by millions of mobile subscribers every day [8], have proven to be very effective in this respect.

Place check-ins and location-sharing are two popular features. By checking into a place, users share their current location with their families or friends, and the ones who do it frequently may also obtain special deals, provided by the nearby businesses, as incentives for sharing their locations [9]. Facebook, for instance, recently launched such a service by which users who want to check-in can

S. Fischer-Hübner and N. Hopper (Eds.): PETS 2011, LNCS 6794, pp. 77–96, 2011.

look for on-the-spot discounts and deals [7]. Services based on *location-sharing*, already used by almost 20% of mobile users [18], are undoubtedly becoming popular. For instance, one recently announced application that exploits location data from different users is a taxi-sharing application, offered by a global telecom operator [19]. In order to share a taxi, users have to reveal their departure and destination points to the server.

Determining a suitable *location* for a set of users is a relevant issue. Several providers already offer variants of this service either as on-line web applications ([16,17]) or as stand-alone applications for mobile devices [17]. Not only is such a feature desirable, but it also optimizes the trade-off between convenience and cost for the involved parties.

However, there are growing concerns about how private information is used and processed by these providers. We conducted a study on privacy in location-sharing-based services (LSBS) with 35 participants (college students and non-scientific personnel), and according to the results 88% of them believe it is important to protect their location privacy from unauthorized uses. Similar results have been obtained in a different study on location-based services (LBS) [18]. Without effective protection, even sparse location information has been shown to provide reliable information about a user's private sphere, which could have severe consequences on the users' social, financial and private life [12]. For instance, a web service [21] has shown how thieves may misuse users' location updates (from a popular online social network) in order to rob their residences while they are not at home. In the taxi-sharing application, if the server is not fully trusted by all users, revealing sensitive locations (such as users home/work addresses) could pave the way for inference attacks by third-parties. Thus, the disclosure of location data to potentially untrusted third-parties and peers must be limited in any location-sharing-based service.

In this paper, we highlight the privacy issues in LSBS by studying one practical and relevant instance of such a general scenario, which is the determination of a *fair rendez-vous point (FRVP)* in a privacy-preserving way, given a set of user-provided locations. This is a novel and potentially useful problem for LSBS applications, which captures the essence of the computations that are generally required in any LSBS, and mitigates their inherent and important privacy issues. Our user-study indicates that 51% of the respondents would be very interested in such a service based on location-sharing.

Our contributions are as follows. First, we present the results of our targeted user-study on location-sharing and privacy in mobile services. Second, motivated by the results of this study and the need for privacy in LSBSs, we design and analyze two practical solutions to the FRVP problem, which do not reveal any additional information to third parties or other peers. The proposed solutions are independent of any underlying service or network provider, and can be included in existing location-sharing-based services. Third, we evaluate the robustness and resilience of our schemes to both passive and active attacks through a privacy analysis of the proposed solutions. Fourth, by implementing our proposed algorithms on a testbed of real mobile devices, we show that their performance in computing the rendez-vous point is acceptable, and that users do not incur in significant additional overhead due to the inherent privacy features.

2 Background and User Study

Background. Novel LSB services, such as deals and check-ins, are offered by large service providers such as Google and Facebook. In order to assess users' opinions about the potential and challenges of such services, we conducted a targeted user study on 35 respondents, sampling a population of technology-savvy college students (in the age group of 20-30 years) and non-scientific personnel. The questionnaires are based on the privacy and usability guidelines from [5,13].

User-Study. The entire study consisted of three phases; the goal of Phase 1, during which respondents answered a first set of 22 questions without knowing the subject of the study, was to assess the participants' level of adoption of mobile LSBS and their sensitivity to privacy issues in such services. The answers to these questions are either "Yes" or "No", or on a 4-point Lickert scale (where 1 means *Disagree*, 4 is *Agree*). In Phase 2, the respondents were instructed to use our prototype mobile FRVP application. Finally, in Phase 3, the participants answered the second set of 12 questions, choosing from a 4-point Lickert scale, after having used our application. The goal of this phase was to obtain feedback on the usability and privacy features of our prototype. The results of Phase 1 are described next, whereas Phase 2 and 3 are discussed in Section 7.2.

Phase 1 Results. The majority of the respondents are males in the 20-25 year-age. Around 86% of them use social networks, and 74% browse the Internet with a mobile device. Although only 14% are aware of existing LSBS, 51% would be very or quite interested in using a LSBS such as the FRVP. However, people are sensitive to privacy (98%) and anonymity (74%) in their online interactions, especially with respect to the potential misuse of their private information by non-specified third-parties (88%). Due to space constraints, we are unable to include here the full details of the study.

These results indicate that, although rare at the moment, LSBSs are perceived as interesting by the majority of the sampled population, which is also the most likely to adopt LBS technologies [18]. With respect to privacy, people agree that it is crucial for the acceptability of such services, and thus LSBS should work properly by requiring a minimum amount of personal information.

In the next sections, we introduce the system architecture, the FRVP problem and our two solutions for computing the FRVP in a privacy-preserving way.

3 System Architecture

We consider a system which is composed of two main entities: (i) a set of users[1] (or mobile devices) $\mathbb{U} = \{u_1, \ldots, u_N\}$ and (ii) a third-party service provider,

---

[1] Throughout this paper, we use the words *users* and *devices* interchangeably. The meaning is clear from the context, unless stated otherwise.

called *Location Determination Server (LDS)*. The N users want to determine the fair rendez-vous location that is computed by the LDS.

Each user's mobile device is assumed to be able to establish communication with the LDS either in a P2P fashion or through a fixed infrastructure-based Internet connection. The mobile devices are able to perform public-key cryptographic operations, and each user u_i has means of determining the position $L_i = (x_i, y_i) \in \mathbb{N}^2$ of his preferred rendez-vous location (or his own location) by using a common coordinate system. We consider a two-dimensional position coordinates system, but the proposed schemes are general enough and can easily be extended to other practical coordinate systems. For instance, such definition of L_i can be made fully compliant with the UTM coordinate system [27], which is a plane coordinate system where points are represented as a 2-tuple of positive values (distances in meters from a given reference point).

We define the set of the preferred rendez-vous locations of all users as $\mathbb{L} = \{L_i\}_{i=1}^N$. For the sake of simplicity, we assume a flat-Earth model and we consider line-of-sight Euclidian distances between preferred rendez-vous locations. Even though the actual real-world distance (road, railway, boat, etc.) between two locations is at least as large as their Euclidian distance, the proportion between distances in the real world is assumed to be correlated with the proportion of the respective Euclidian distances. Location priorities, which are not discussed in this paper, can be used for isolated or unsuitable locations.

We assume that each of the N users has his own public/private key pair $(K_P^{u_i}, K_s^{u_i})$, certified by a trusted CA, which is used to digitally sign the messages that are sent to the LDS. Moreover, we assume that the N users share a common secret that is utilized to generate a shared public/private key pair $(K_P^{M_v}, K_s^{M_v})$ in an online fashion for each meeting setup instance v. The private key $K_s^{M_v}$ generated in this way is known only to all meeting participants, whereas the public key $K_P^{M_v}$ is known to everyone including the LDS. This could be achieved through a secure credential establishment protocol such as in [3,4,15].

The LDS executes the FRVP algorithm on the inputs it receives by the users in order to compute the FRV location. The LDS is also able to perform public-key cryptographic functions. For instance, a common public-key infrastructure using the RSA cryptosystem [22] could be employed. Let K_P^{LDS} be the public key, certified by a trusted CA, and K_s^{LDS} the corresponding private key of the LDS. K_P^{LDS} is publicly known and users encrypt their input to the FRVP algorithm using this key; the encrypted input can be decrypted by the LDS using its private key K_s^{LDS}. This ensures message confidentiality and integrity for all the messages exchanged between users and the LDS. For simplicity of exposition, in our protocols we do not explicitly show these cryptographic operations involving LDS's public/private key.

3.1 Threat Model

Location Determination Server. The LDS is assumed to execute the algorithms correctly, i.e., take all the inputs and produce the output according to the algorithm. However, the LDS may try to learn information about users' location preferences from the received inputs, the intermediate results and the produced outputs. This type of adversarial behavior is usually referred to as *honest-but-curious* adversary (or semi-honest) [11]. In most practical settings, where service providers have a commercial interest in providing a faithful service to their customers, the assumption of a semi-honest LDS is generally sufficient. **Users.** The participating users also want to learn the private location preferences of other users from the output of the algorithm they receive from the LDS. We refer to such attacks as passive attacks. As user inputs are encrypted with the LDS's public key K_P^{LDS}, there is a confidentiality guarantee against basic eavesdropping by participants and non participants. In addition to these attacks, participating users may also attempt to actively attack the protocol by colluding with other users or manipulating their own inputs to learn the output.

4   The *Rendez-vous* Problem

In this work, we consider the problem of finding, in a privacy-preserving way, the rendez-vous point among a set of user-proposed locations, such that (i) the rendez-vous point is a point that is *fair* (as defined in Section 5.1) with respect to the given locations, (ii) each of the users gets to know only the final rendez-vous location and (iii) no participating user or third-party server learns private location information about any other user involved in the computations. We refer to an algorithm that solves this problem as *Privacy-Preserving Fair Rendez-Vous Point (PPFRVP)* algorithm. In general, any PPFRVP algorithm A should accept the inputs and produce the outputs, as described below.

- *Input*: a transformation f of private locations L_i: $f(L_1)||f(L_2)||\ldots||f(L_N)$. where f is a one-way public function (based on secret key) such that it is hard (success with only a negligible probability) to determine the input L_i without knowing the secret key, by just observing $f(L_i)$.
- *Output*: an output $f(L_{fair}) = g(f(L_1),\ldots,f(L_N))$, where g is a fairness function and $L_{fair} = (x_l, y_l) \in \mathbb{N}^2$ is the fair rendez-vous location that has been selected for this particular set of users, such that it is hard for the LDS to determine L_{fair} by just observing $f(L_{fair})$. Given $f(L_{fair})$, each user is able to compute $L_{fair} = f^{-1}(f(L_{fair}))$ using his local data.

The fairness function g can be defined in several ways, depending on the preferences of users or policies. For instance, users might prefer to meet in locations that are close to their offices, and their employers might prefer a place that is closest to their clients. In Section 5.1 we describe one such fairness function that minimizes the maximum displacement of any user to all other locations. Such function is globally fair and general enough, as it captures the essential computations required for optimization It can be extended to include more complex constraints and parameters.

5   Proposed Solutions and Analysis

In this section, we present our solution to the PPFRVP. First, we discuss the mathematical tools that we use in order to model the fairness function g and the transformation functions f. In order to achieve the integration between resource-constrained mobile devices and the client-server network paradigm, our solutions have to be efficient in terms of computations and communication complexities.

In order to separate the optimization part of the PPFRVP algorithm A from its implementation using cryptographic primitives, we first discuss the fairness function g and then the transformation function f.

5.1   Fairness Function g

In this work, we consider the fairness criterion that has been widely used in operations research to solve the *k-center* problem. In the k-center problem, the goal is to find $L_1, \ldots, L_k$ locations among N given possible places, in order to optimally place k facilities, such that the maximum distance from any place to its closest facility is minimized. For a two dimensional coordinate system, the Euclidian distance metric is usually employed.

As the PPFRVP problem consists in determining the fair rendez-vous location from a set of user-desired locations, we focus on the *k-center* formulation of the problem with $k = 1$. This choice is also grounded on the fact that not choosing L_{fair} from one of the location preferences $L_1, \ldots, L_N$ might potentially result in a location L_{fair} that is not suited for the kind of meeting that the participants require. The solution can easily be extended or integrated with mapping applications (on the users' devices) so that POIs around L_{fair} are automatically suggested for the meeting. Figure 1 shows an example PPFRVP scenario modeled as a k-center problem, where four users want to determine the fair rendez-vous location L_{fair}.

The k-center formulation considers the Euclidian distances, but it does not encompass other fairness parameters, such as accessibility of a place and the means of transportation. In this work, we focus on the pure k-center formulation as the essential building block of a more complete model, which can be extended when such an application is to be deployed in existing services.

Let $d_{ij} \geq 0$ be the Euclidian distance between two points $L_i, L_j \in \mathbb{N}^2$, and $D_i^M = \max_{j \neq i} d_{ij}$ be the maximum distance from L_i to any other point L_j. Then, the PPFRVP problem can be formally defined as follows.

Definition 1. *The PPFRVP problem is to determine a location $L_{fair} \in \mathbb{L} = \{L_1, \ldots, L_N\}$, where $fair = arg \min_i D_i^M$*

A solution for the PPFRVP problem finds, in a privacy-preserving way, the fair rendez-vous location among the set of proposed (and user-desired) locations, such that the distance of the furthest desired location to the fair one is minimized.

There are two important steps involved in the computation of the fair location L_{fair}. The first step is to compute the pairwise distances d_{ij} among all users $i, j \in \{1, \ldots, N\}$ participating in the PPFRVP algorithm. The second step requires the computations of the maximum and minimum values of such distances.

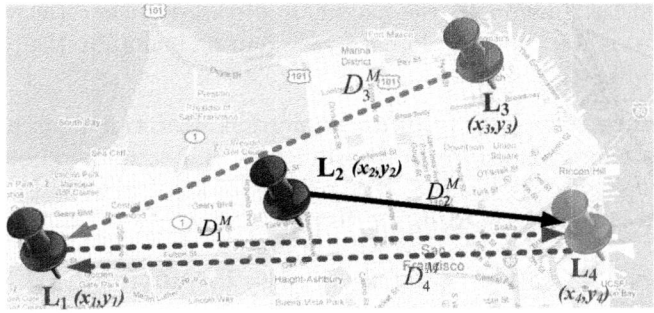

Fig. 1. PPFRVP scenario, where the fairness function is $g = \mathrm{argmin}_i(D_i^M)$. The dashed arrows represent the maximum distance D_i^M from each user u_i to any user $j \neq i$, whereas the solid line is the minimum of all such maximum distances. The fair rendez-vous location is $L_{fair} = L_2 = (x_2, y_2)$.

5.2 Transformation Functions f

The fairness function g requires the computation of two functions on the private user-desired locations L_i: (i) the distance between any two locations $L_i \neq L_j$ and (ii) the minimum of the maximum of these distances. In order to achieve the final result and to preserve the privacy of the personal information, we rely on computationally secure cryptographic functions. In our protocol, we consider three such schemes: the *Boneh-Goh-Nissim* (BGN) [2], the *ElGamal* [6] and the *Paillier* [20] public-key encryption schemes.

What makes these schemes useful are their homomorphic encryption properties. Given two plaintexts m_1, m_2 with their respective encryptions $E(m_1), E(m_2)$, the multiplicative property (possessed by the ElGamal and partially by the BGN schemes) states that $E(m_1) \odot E(m_2) = E(m_1 \cdot m_2)$, where $\odot$ is an arithmetic operation in the encrypted domain that is equivalent to the usual multiplication operation in the plaintext domain. The additive homomorphic property (possessed by the BGN and the Paillier schemes) states that $E(m_1) \oplus E(m_2) = E(m_1 + m_2)$, where $\oplus$ is an arithmetic operation in the encrypted domain which is equivalent to the usual sum operation in the plaintext domain. Details about the initialization, operation and security of the encryption schemes can be found in [6,2,20].

Based on the three aforementioned encryption schemes, we now describe the distance computation algorithms that are used in our solution.

5.3 Distance Computations

In order to determine the fair rendez-vous location, we need to find the location L_{fair}, where $fair \in \{1, \ldots, N\}$, that minimizes the maximum distance between any user-desired location and L_{fair}. In our algorithms, we work with the *square* of the distances, as they are much easier to compute in an oblivious fashion using the homomorphic properties of the cryptographic schemes. The problem of finding the argument that minimizes the maximum distance is equivalent to finding the argument that minimizes the maximum distance *squared* (provided that all distances are greater than 1). Moreover, as squaring maintains the relative order, the algorithm is still correct.

BGN-distance. Our first distance computation algorithm is based on the BGN encryption scheme. This novel protocol requires only one round of communication between each user and the LDS, and it works as follows. In Step 1, each user u_i, $\forall i \in \{1, \ldots, N\}$, creates the vectors

$$E_i(a) =< a_{i1}|\ldots|a_{i6} >=< E(x_i^2)|E(T - 2x_i)|E(1)|E(T - 2y_i)|E(y_i^2)|E(1) >$$
$$E_i(b) =< b_{i1}|\ldots|b_{i6} >=< E(1)|E(x_i)|E(x_i^2)|E(y_i)|E(1)|E(y_i^2) >$$

where $E(.)$ is the encryption of $(.)$ using the BGN scheme and $L_i = (x_i, y_i)$ is the desired rendez-vous location of user u_i. Afterwards, each user sends the two vectors $E_i(a)$, $E_i(b)$ over a secure channel to the LDS. In Step 2, the LDS computes the scalar product of the received vectors by first applying the multiplicative and then the additive homomorphic property of the BGN scheme.

Paillier-ElGamal-distance. An alternative scheme for the distance computation is based on both the Paillier and ElGamal encryption schemes, as shown in Figure 2. As neither Paillier or ElGamal possess both multiplicative and additive properties, the resulting algorithm requires one extra step in order to achieve the same result as the BGN-based scheme, i.e., obliviously computing the pairwise distances d_{ij}^2. The distances are computed as follows. In Step 1, each user u_i, $\forall i \in \{1, \ldots, N\}$, creates the vector

$$E_i(a) =< a_{i1}|\ldots|a_{i4} >=< Pai(x_i^2)|ElG(x_i)|Pai(y_i^2)|ElG(y_i) >$$

where $Pai(.)$ and $ElG(.)$ refer to the encryption of $(.)$ using the Paillier or ElGamal encryption schemes, respectively. Afterwards, each user u_i sends the vector $E_i(a)$ to the LDS, encrypted with LDS's public key. In the following steps of the protocol, the LDS computes the scalar products of the second and fourth elements of the received vectors (Step 2.1), randomizes (in an order-preserving fashion) the results and send a different set of values back to each user (Step 2.2). In Step 3, the users re-encrypt the values with the Paillier scheme and send it to the LDS, which then obliviously computes the pairwise distances (Step 4.1).

5.4   The *PPFRVP* Protocol

We now describe our protocol for the PPFRVP problem, as shown in Figure 3. The protocol has three main modules: (A) the distance computation module, (B) the MAX module and (C) the ARGMIN MAX module.

Distance computations. The first module (distance computation) uses one of the two protocols defined in the previous subsection (BGN-distance or Paillier-ElGamal-distance). We note that modules (B) and (C) use the same encryption scheme as the one used in module (A). In other words, $E(.)$ of Figure 3 refers to the encryption of $(.)$ using either the BGN or the Paillier encryption scheme.

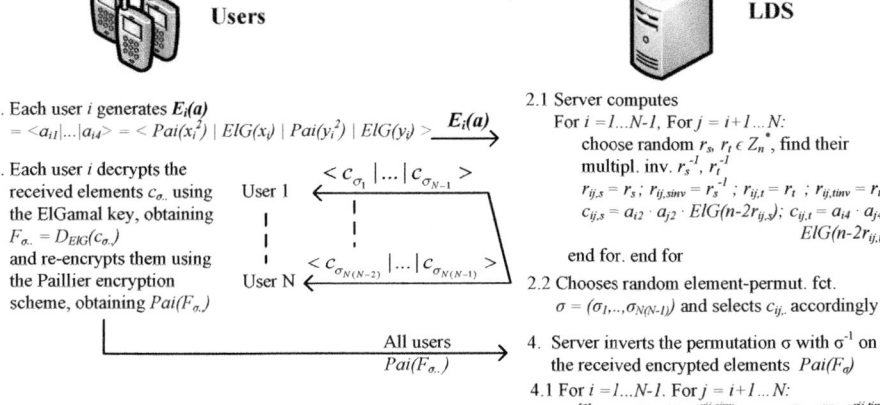

Fig. 2. Distance computation protocol based on the ElGamal and Paillier encryption schemes

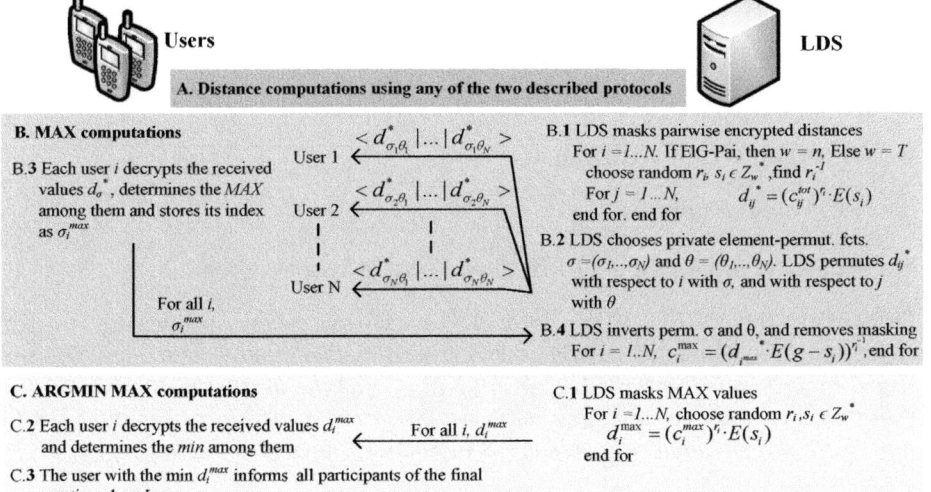

Fig. 3. Privacy-Preserving Fair Rendez-Vous Point (PPFRVP) protocol

MAX computations. In Step B.1, the LDS needs to obliviously hide the values within the encrypted elements (i.e., the pairwise distances computed earlier), before sending them to the users, in order to avoid leaking any kind of private information such as the pairwise distance or desired locations to any user.[2] In order to obliviously mask such values, for each index i the LDS generates two random values r_i, s_i that are used to scale and shift the c_{ij}^{tot} (the encrypted square distance between L_i, L_j) for all j, obtaining d_{ij}^*. This is done in order to (i) ensure privacy of real pairwise distances, (ii) be resilient in case of collusion among users and (iii) preserve the internal order (the inequalities) among the pairwise distance from each user to all other users. Afterwards, in Step B.2 the LDS chooses two private element-permutation functions σ (for i) and θ (for j) and permutes d_{ij}^*, obtaining the permuted values $d_{\sigma_i \theta_j}^*$, where $i, j \in \{1, \ldots, N\}$. The LDS sends N such distinct elements to each user. In Step B.3, each user decrypts the received values, determines their maximum and sends the index σ_i^{max} of the maximum value to the LDS. In Step B.4 of the MAX module (B), the LDS inverts the permutation functions σ, θ and removes the masking from the received indexes corresponding to the maximum distance values.

ARGMIN MAX computations. In Step C.1, the LDS masks the true maximum distances by scaling and shifting them by the same random amount, such that their order (the inequalities among them) is preserved. Then the LDS sends to each user all the masked maximum distances. In Step C.2 each user decrypts the received masked (randomly scaled and shifted) maximum values, and determines the minimum among all maxima. In Step C.3, each user knows which identifier corresponds to himself, and the user with the minimum distance sends to all other users his desired rendez-vous location in an anonymous way.

After the last step, each user receives the final fair rendez-vous location, but no other information regarding non-fair locations or distances is leaked.

6   Analytical Evaluation

6.1   Privacy Analysis

We define the privacy of a PPFRVP protocol as follows.

Definition 2. *A PPFRVP protocol A is* execution privacy-preserving *if a participating user cannot determine (with a non-negligible probability) (i) the preferred rendez-vous locations L_i (except L_{fair}), (ii) the mutual distances and (iii) coordinate relations of any user, after an execution of A. Moreover, the LDS (or any third-party) should not be able to infer any information about L_{fair}.*

---

[2] After the distance computation module (A), the LDS possesses all encrypted pairwise distances. This encryption is made with the public key of the participants and thus the LDS cannot decrypt the distances without the corresponding private key. The oblivious (and order-preserving) masking performed by the LDS at Step B.1 is used in order to hide the pairwise distances from the users themselves, as otherwise they would be able to obtain these distances and violate the privacy of the users.

In our analysis, we consider two types of adversaries: Passive (honest-but-curious) and active adversaries. The passive try to learn as much information as possible from their inputs, the execution of the PPFRVP protocol and its output, without maliciously injecting or modifying data. The active adversaries, on the contrary, try on purpose to manipulate the data in order to obtain private information.

The aforementioned definition captures the privacy requirements of a single execution of a PPFRVP algorithm. By repeated interactions among a stable set of users, L_{fair} could be used to infer possible L_i of other users. The issue of *learning* from repeated interaction is inherent to any algorithm that, based on a set of private inputs, chooses one of them in particular, based on some criterion. For this reason, in this work we consider privacy for a single execution of the PPFRVP algorithm, or for repeated executions but with different sets of users.

Passive Adversary. Under the passive adversary model, we have the following.

Proposition 1. *The BGN and ElGamal-Paillier based PPFRVP protocols are execution privacy-preserving.*

In simple words, Proposition 1 states that both proposed algorithms correctly compute the fair rendez-vous location, given the received inputs, and that they do not reveal any users' preferred rendez-vous locations to any other user, except the fair rendez-vous location L_{fair}. Moreover, the LDS does not learn any information about any user-preferred locations. In the Appendix we prove the proposition by considering a standard challenger-adversary game methodology that is usually employed for privacy proofs in cryptographic schemes.

Active Adversary. We consider three main categories of active attacks against PPFRVP protocols, namely (i) the collusion among users and/or LDS, (ii) the fake user generation and/or replay attacks and (iii) unfair rendez-vous location.

Collusion. Regardless of the protocol used or the encryption methods, in the case when users collude among themselves the published fair result (together with the additional information malicious users may get from colluders) can be used to construct exclusion zones, based on the set of equations and known parameters. An exclusion zone is a region that does not contain any location preferences, and the number of such exclusion zones increases with the number of colluders. We are currently working on quantifying this impact on our optimization and encryption methods. However, in the unlikely case of collusion between the LDS and the participants, the latter will be able to obtain other participants' preferences. In order to mitigate such a threat, the invited participants could agree on establishing a shared secret by using techniques from threshold cryptography [25]. The LDS should then collude with at least a given number of participants in order to obtain the shared secret and learn L_i.

Fake Users. In case the LDS generates fake users, it would not be able to obtain the secret that is shared among the honest users and which is used to derive the secret key $K_s^{M_v}$ for each session v. This attack is more dangerous if a legitimate participant creates a fake, because the legitimate participant knows the shared secret. In this scenario, however, the LDS knows the list of meeting participants (as it computes the fair rendez-vous location) and therefore it would accept only messages digitally signed by each one of them. Here we rely on the fact that fake users will not be able to get their public keys signed by a CA. Replay attacks could be thwarted by adding and verifying an individually signed *nonce*, derived using the shared secret, in each user's meeting message.

Unfair RV. The last type of active attack could lead to the determination of an unfair rendez-vous location. Maliciously modifying or untruthfully reporting the maximum masked values (Step B.3 of Figure 3) could deceive the LDS to accept the false received index as the maximum value, and therefore potentially lead to the determination of a subfair rendez-vous location. However, this is rather unlikely to happen in practice. For instance, even if in Step B.3 a user falsely reports one of his values to be the maximum when actually it is not, this would cause the algorithm to select a subfair rendez-vous location if and only if no other user selected a smaller value as the maximum distance.

6.2   Complexity Analysis

Table 1 summarizes the complexity results for our two protocols, both for the client devices and for the LDS. As it can be seen, the client complexity is in general $O(N)$, where N is the number of users. However, there is a notable exception for the BGN-based scheme; the number of exponentiation required for a single decryption is $O(\sqrt{T})$ [2], where T is the order of the plaintext domain. In Section 7 we show how this charateristic impacts the decryption performance.

Table 1. Asymptotic complexity of the proposed PPFRVP protocols, where N is the number of participants. The *Distance* protocol is the one used in the module A of Figure 3, whereas PPFRVP includes modules A,B and C.

CLIENT	PROTOCOL	BGN (mod n)	ELGAMAL-PAILLIER (mod n^2)	LDS	BGN (mod n)	ELGAMAL-PAILLIER (mod n^2)
Mult.	Distance / PPFRVP	O(1)	O(N)	**Mult. Exp.**	O(N^2)	O(N^2)
Exp.	Distance / PPFRVP	O(1) / O(N$\sqrt{T}$)	O(N)	**Bilinear mapping**	O(N^2)	-------
Memory	Distance / PPFRVP	O(1) / O(N)	O(N)	**Memory**	O(N^2)	O(N^2)
Comm.	Distance / PPFRVP	O(1) / O(N)	O(N)	**Comm.**	O(N) / O(N^2)	O(N^2)

The LDS complexity for both protocols is in general $O(N^2)$, with the notable exception of BGN, where in addition to multiplications and exponentiations the schemes requires additional $O(N^2)$ bilinear mappings. These operations are required in order to support the multiplicative property of the BGN scheme.

7   Implementation Performance and User-Experience

In this section, we discuss the results of the performance measurements using implementations of the proposed algorithms on Nokia devices, and we present the related results of Phase 3 of our user-study on the prototype application.

7.1   Performance Measurements

The tests were conducted on a testbed of Nokia N810 mobile devices (ARM 400 MHz CPU, Figure 4), and the LDS on a Linux machine (2 GHz CPU, 3 GB RAM). For the elliptic curve BGN-based PPFRVP protocol, we measured the performance using both a 160-bit and a 256-bit secret key, whereas for the ElGamal-Paillier-based one we used 1024-bit secret keys. As BGN is an elliptic curve-based scheme, much shorter keys can be used compared to ElGamal and RSA. A 160-bit key in elliptic curve cryptosystems is generally believed to provide equivalent security as a 1024-bit key in RSA and ElGamal [23].

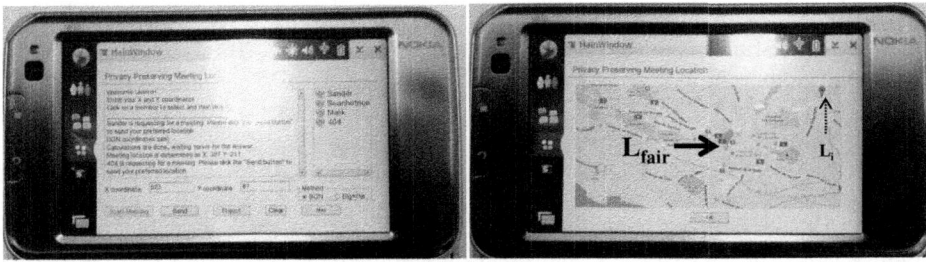

Fig. 4. Prototype PPFRVP application running on a Nokia N810 mobile device. The image on the left is the main window, where users add the desired meeting participants. The image on the right is the map that shows the fair rendez-vous location (green pin) and the user-desired rendez-vous location (red pin).

LDS performance. Figure 5(a), 5(b) and 5(c) show the computation time required by the LDS. We can see that such time increases with the number of users, and that the ElGamal-Paillier algorithm is the most efficient across all computations, requiring 4 seconds to execute the PPFRVP protocol with 10 participants. The two BGN-based algorithms are less efficient, but are still practical enough (9 seconds). The CPU-intensive bilinear mappings in BGN are certainly one important reason for such delays.

Client performance. Figure 5(d) and 5(e) show the different computation times on the Nokia N810 mobile device. As it can be seen, thanks to the efficient use of the homomorphic properties of our BGN-based algorithm, this protocol is the most efficient for the distance computations, requiring only 0.3 seconds, independently of the number of users. On the contrary, the alternative protocol needs 4 seconds with 10 participants. However, the subsequent phases reverse such results, as the BGN protocol makes intensive use of bilinear mappings.

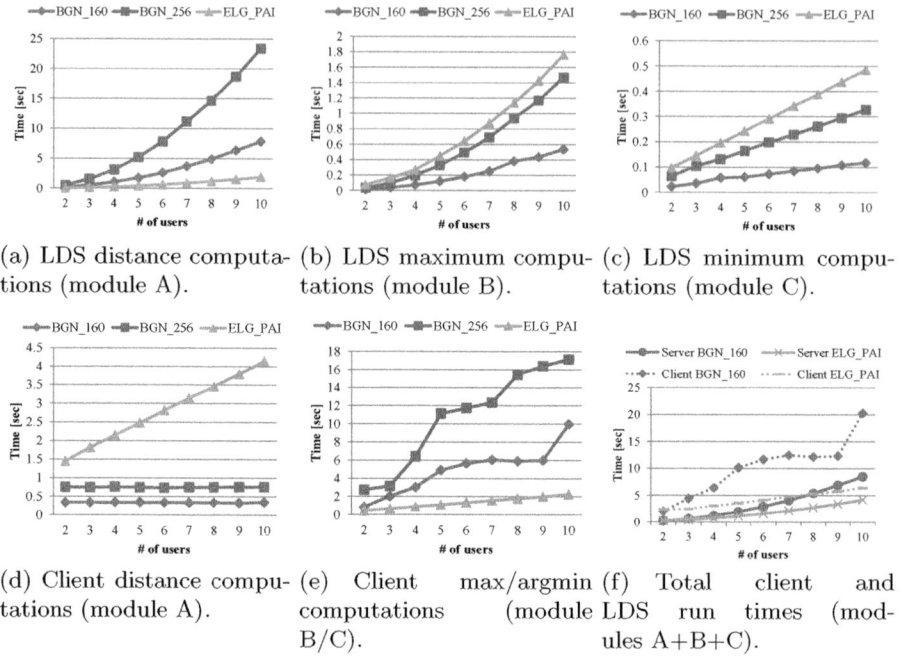

(a) LDS distance computations (module A).

(b) LDS maximum computations (module B).

(c) LDS minimum computations (module C).

(d) Client distance computations (module A).

(e) Client max/argmin computations (module B/C).

(f) Total client and LDS run times (modules A+B+C).

Fig. 5. Performance measurements

Overall, we can see that the ElGamal-Paillier protocol has a better performance than the BGN-based one, both on the client and on the LDS. Nevertheless, both schemes are practical enough and have acceptable time requirements in order to be implemented on current generations of mobile devices.

7.2   User-Experience

We present the PPFRVP application-related results of our user study introduced in Section 2. After using our application, all participants tend to agree (34%) or agree (66%) that our application was easy to use, and that they could quickly compute the task (97%). More than 71% appreciated that their preferred rendez-vous point was not revealed to other participants, and only 8% do not care about the privacy of their rendez-vous location preference. 26% of the respondents were able to identify to whom the FRVP location belonged to, which is expected. The users run our application in groups of 5 during the experimentation, and therefore there was always one person out of five that knew that the FRVP location was his preferred location.

From a software developer standpoint, this means that both ease of use and privacy need to be taken into account from the beginning of the application development process. In particular, the privacy mechanisms should be implemented in a way that does not significantly affect the usability or performance.

The acceptance of LSBS applications is highly influenced by the availability of effective and intuitive privacy features.

8 Related Work

Hereafter, we present some works in the literature that address, without protecting privacy, strategies to determine the fair rendez-vous location. To the best of our knowledge, this is the first work to address such a problem in a privacy-preserving way.

Santos and Vaughn [1] present a survey of existing literature on meeting-location algorithms, and propose a more comprehensive solution for such a problem. Although considering aspects such as user preferences and constraints, their work (or the surveyed papers) does not address any security or privacy issues. Similarly, Berger et. al [24] propose an efficient meeting-location algorithm that considers the time in-between two consecutive meetings. However, all private information about users is public.

In the domain of Secure Multiparty Computation (SMC), several authors have addressed privacy issues related to the computation of the distance between two routes [10] or points [14,26]. Frikken and Atallah [10] propose SMC protocols for securely computing the distance between a point and a line segment, the distance between two moving points and the distance between two line segments. Zhong et al. [28] design and implement three distributed privacy-preserving protocols for nearby friend discovery, and they show how to cryptographically compute the distance between a pair of users. However, due to the fully distributed nature of the aforementioned approaches, the computational and communication complexities increase significantly with the size of the participants and inputs. Moreover, all parties involved in the computations need to be online and synchronized.

As both our protocols are centralized, most of the cryptographic operations are performed by the LDS and not by the mobile devices. Additionally, the proposed solutions do not require all users to be online at the same time, and they necessitate only minimal synchronization among the mobile devices.

9 Conclusion and Future Work

In this work, we address the problem of privacy in LSBS by providing practical and effective solutions to one such popular and relevant service. The PPFRVP problem captures the essential computational and privacy building blocks present in any LSBS offered on mobile devices. We designed, implemented on real mobile devices and evaluated the performance of our privacy-preserving protocols for the fair rendez-vous problem. Our solutions are effective in terms of privacy, have acceptable performance, and do not create additional overhead for the users. Moreover, our user-study showed that the proposed privacy features are crucial for the adoption of any such application, which reinforces the need for further exploration in privacy of LSB services. To the best of our knowledge, this is the first such effort in this direction.

Acknowledgment

We would like to thank Mathias Humbert for helping improving the quality of this work, as well as the Nokia Research Center for supporting this project.

References

1. Berger, F., Klein, R., Nussbaum, D., Sack, J.-R., Yi, J.: A meeting scheduling problem respecting time and space. GeoInformatica (2009)
2. Boneh, D., Goh, E.-J., Nissim, K.: Evaluating 2-DNF formulas on ciphertexts. In: Kilian, J. (ed.) TCC 2005. LNCS, vol. 3378, pp. 325–341. Springer, Heidelberg (2005)
3. Cachin, C., Strobl, R.: Asynchronous group key exchange with failures. In: ACM PODC 2004 (2004)
4. Chen, C.-H.O., Chen, C.-W., Kuo, C., Lai, Y.-H., McCune, J.M., Studer, A., Perrig, A., Yang, B.-Y., Wu, T.-C.: Gangs: Gather, authenticate 'n group securely. In: ACM MobiCom 2008 (2008)
5. Chignell, M., Quan-Haase, A., Gwizdka, J.: The privacy attitudes questionnaire (paq): initial development and validation. In: Human Factors and Ergonomics Society Annual Meeting Proceedings (2003)
6. ElGamal, T.: A public key cryptosystem and a signature scheme based on discrete logarithms. IEEE Transactions on Information Theory 31 (1985)
7. Facebook Deals, http://www.facebook.com/deals/
8. Facebook Statistics, http://www.facebook.com/press/info.php?statistics
9. Foursquare for Business, http://foursquare.com/business/ (last visited February 04, 2011)
10. Frikken, K.B., Atallah, M.J.: Privacy preserving route planning. In: WPES 2004 (2004)
11. Goldreich, O.: Foundations of cryptography: Basic applications. Cambridge University Press, Cambridge (2004)
12. Krumm, J.: A survey of computational location privacy. Personal and Ubiquitous Computing 13(6), 391–399 (2009)
13. Lewis, J.: IBM computer usability satisfaction questionnaires: psychometric evaluation and instructions for use. International Journal of Human-Computer Interaction 7 (1995)
14. Li, S.-D., Dai, Y.-Q.: Secure two-party computational geometry. Journal of Computer Science and Technology 20 (2005)
15. Lin, Y.-H., Studer, A., Hsiao, H.-C., McCune, J.M., Wang, K.-H., Krohn, M., Lin, P.-L., Perrig, A., Sun, H.-M., Yang, B.-Y.: Spate: Small-group PKI-less authenticated trust establishment. In: MobiSys 2009 (2009)
16. MeetWays, http://www.meetways.com/
17. Mezzoman, http://www.mezzoman.com/
18. Microsoft survey on LBS (2011), http://go.microsoft.com/?linkid=9758039
19. Orange Taxi sharing app, http://event.orange.com/default/EN/all/mondial_auto_en/taxi_partage.htm
20. Paillier, P.: Public-key cryptosystems based on composite degree residuosity classes. In: Stern, J. (ed.) EUROCRYPT 1999. LNCS, vol. 1592, p. 223. Springer, Heidelberg (1999)
21. Please Rob Me, http://pleaserobme.com/

22. Rivest, R., Shamir, A., Adleman, L.: A method for obtaining digital signatures and public-key cryptosystems. Communications of the ACM 21 (1978)
23. Robshaw, M., Yin, Y.: Elliptic curve cryptosystems. An RSA Laboratories Technical Note (1997)
24. Santos, P., Vaughn, H.: Where shall we meet? Proposing optimal locations for meetings. In: MapISNet 2007 (2007)
25. Schoenmakers, B.: A simple publicly verifiable secret sharing scheme and its application to electronic voting. In: Wiener, M. (ed.) CRYPTO 1999. LNCS, vol. 1666, p. 148. Springer, Heidelberg (1999)
26. Solanas, A., Martínez-Ballesté, A.: Privacy protection in location-based services through a public-key privacy homomorphism. In: Public Key Infrastructure (2007)
27. UTM coordinate system, https://www.e-education.psu.edu/natureofgeoinfo/c2_p21.html
28. Zhong, G., Goldberg, I., Hengartner, U.: Louis, lester and pierre: Three protocols for location privacy. In: Privacy Enhancing Technologies, pp. 62–76 (2007)

Proof of Proposition 1

We express the privacy in terms of three probabilistic advantages that an adversary u_a (a user or a third-party) gains after an execution of a PPFRVP algorithm A. First, we measure the *identifiability advantage*, which is the probabilistic advantage of u_a in correctly guessing the preferred location L_i of any user $u_i \neq u_a$. We denote it as $Adv_a^{IDT}(A)$. Second, the *distance-linkability advantage* is the probabilistic advantage of u_a in correctly guessing whether the distance d_{ij} between any two users $u_i \neq u_j$ is greater than a given parameter s, without necessarily knowing any users' preferred locations L_i, L_j. We denote it as Adv_a^{d-LNK}. Finally, the *coordinate-linkability advantage* is the probabilistic advantage of u_a in correctly guessing whether a given coordinate x_i (or y_i) of a user u_i is greater than the corresponding coordinate(s) of another user $u_j \neq u_i$, i.e., x_j (or y_j), without necessarily knowing any users' preferred locations L_i, L_j. We denote it as Adv_a^{c-LNK}.

Challenger-Adversary Games

We describe hereafter the challenger-adversary game for the identifiability advantage $Adv_a^{IDT}(A)$ of any user u_a, $a \in \{1, \ldots, N\}$, after executing the PPFRVP algorithm A:

1. Initialization: Challenger privately collects $\mathbb{L} = \{L_i\}_{i=1}^N$, where $L_i = (x_i, y_i)$ is the preferred rendez-vous location of user u_i, and $f(L_i)$, $\forall i \in \{1, \ldots, N\}$.
2. PPFRVP algorithm: Challenger executes the PPFRVP algorithm A and computes $f(L_{fair}) = g(f(L_1), \ldots, f(L_N))$. It then sends $f(L_{fair})$ to each user $u_i, \forall i \in \{1, \ldots, N\}$.
3. Challenger randomly chooses a user u_a, $a \in \{1, \ldots, N\}$, as the adversary.
4. u_a chooses $u_j \neq u_a$ and sends j to the challenger.
5. Challenge: Challenger chooses a random $k \in \{1, \ldots, N\}$ and sends L_k to the adversary. The challenge is to correctly guess whether $L_k = L_j$.

6. The adversary sends L_j^* to the challenger. If the adversary thinks that L_k is the preferred rendez-vous location of user u_j, i.e., if $L_k = L_j$ then the adversary sets $L_j^* = 1$. If the adversary thinks that L_k is not the preferred rendez-vous location of user u_j, then he sets $L_j^* = 0$. If $L_j^* = L_k$ the adversary wins the game, otherwise he loses.

The challenger-adversary game for the distance-linkability advantage $Adv_a^{d-LNK}(A)$ of any user u_a is defined as follows.

1. Initialization: Challenger privately collects $\mathbb{L} = \{L_i\}_{i=1}^N$, where $L_i = (x_i, y_i)$ is the preferred rendez-vous location of user u_i, and $f(L_i)$, $\forall i \in \{1, \ldots, N\}$.
2. PPFRVP algorithm: Challenger executes the PPFRVP algorithm A and computes $f(L_{fair}) = g(f(L_1), \ldots, f(L_N))$. It then sends $f(L_{fair})$ to each user $u_i, \forall i \in \{1, \ldots, N\}$.
3. Challenger randomly chooses a user u_a, $a \in \{1, \ldots, N\}$, as the adversary.
4. u_a chooses $u_j, u_k \neq u_a$ and sends (j, k) to the challenger.
5. Challenge: Challenger computes a value s, such as the average Euclidian distance $d = \sum_{n=1}^{N-1} \sum_{m=n+1}^{N} d_{nm}/(2N(N-1))$ between any two users $u_n \neq u_m$, and sends (j, k, s) to the adversary. The challenge is to correctly guess whether $d_{jk} < s$.
6. The adversary sends d^* to the challenger. If the adversary thinks that $d_{jk} < s$ then he sets $d^* = 1$, otherwise $d^* = 0$. The adversary wins the game if: (i) $d^* = 1 \wedge d_{jk} < s$ or (ii) $d^* = 0 \wedge d_{jk} \geq s$. Otherwise, the adversary loses.

The challenger-adversary game for the coordinate-linkability advantage $Adv_a^{c-LNK}(A)$ of any user u_a is defined as follows.

1. Initialization: Challenger privately collects $\mathbb{L} = \{L_i\}_{i=1}^N$, where $L_i = (x_i, y_i)$ is the preferred rendez-vous location of user u_i, and $f(L_i)$, $\forall i \in \{1, \ldots, N\}$.
2. PPFRVP algorithm: Challenger executes the PPFRVP algorithm A and computes $f(L_{fair}) = g(f(L_1), \ldots, f(L_N))$. It then sends $f(L_{fair})$ to each user $u_i, \forall i \in \{1, \ldots, N\}$.
3. Challenger randomly chooses a user u_a, $a \in \{1, \ldots, N\}$, as the adversary.
4. u_a chooses $u_j, u_k \neq u_i$ and sends (j, k) to the challenger.
5. Challenge: Challenger chooses a coordinate axis $c \in \{x, y\}$ and sends (j, k, c) to the adversary. The challenge is to correctly guess whether $c_j < c_k$.
6. The adversary sends c^* to the challenger. If the adversary thinks that $c_j < c_k$ then he sets $c^* = 1$, otherwise $c^* = 0$. The adversary wins the game if: (i) $c^* = 1 \wedge c_j < c_k$ or (ii) $c^* = 0 \wedge c_j \geq c_k$. Otherwise, the adversary loses.

For the third-party (LDS) adversary, the game definitions are similar to those of the user adversary. However, as mentioned, the third-party shall not be able to infer (with a non-negligible probability) the L_{fair}, in addition to any L_i.

Proofs

Correctness. Given the encrypted set of user-preferred locations $f(L_1), \ldots, f(L_N)$, the proposed PPFRVP algorithms compute the pairwise distance between each pair of users d_{ij}, $\forall i, j \in \{1, \ldots, N\}$, according to the schemes of the respective distance computation algorithms. Following the sequence of steps for such computation, one can easily verify that the ElGamal-Paillier based distance computation algorithm computes

$$Pai(d_{ij}^2) = Pai(x_i^2) \cdot Pai(-2x_i x_j) \cdot Pai(y_j^2) \cdot Pai(y_i^2) \cdot Pai(-2y_i y_j) \cdot Pai(y_j^2)$$
$$= Pai(x_i^2 - 2x_i x_j + x_j^2 + y_i^2 - 2y_i y_j + y_j^2)$$

which is the same result that is achieved by the BGN-based distance algorithm.

After the pairwise distance computations, the PPFRVP algorithm computes the masking of these pairwise distances by scaling and shifting operations. The scaling operation is achieved by exponentiating the encrypted element to the power of r_i, where $r_i \in \mathbb{Z}_w^*$ is a random integer and r_i^{-1} is its multiplicative inverse. The shifting operation is done by multiplying the encrypted element with the encryption (using the public key of the users) of another random integer s_i privately chosen by the LDS. These two algebraic operations mask the values d_{ij}^2 (within the encrypted elements), such that the true d_{ij}^2 are hidden from the users. Nevertheless, thanks to the homomorphic properties of the encryption schemes, the LDS is still able to remove the masking (after the users have identified the maximum value) and correctly re-mask all maxima, such that each user is able to correctly find the minimum of all maxima.

In the end, each user is able to determine L_{fair} where $fair = \mathrm{argmin}_i \max_j d_{ij}^2$ from the outputs of the PPFRVP algorithm, and therefore the PPFRVP algorithms are correct.

User Identifiability Advantage. Using the previously defined challenger-adversary games, we define the identifiability advantage of an attacker u_a as

$$Adv_a^{IDT}(A) = \left| Pr[L_j^* = L_k] - 1/N \right|$$

where $Pr[L_j^* = L_k]$ is the probability of user u_a winning the game by correctly answering the challenge, computed over the coin tosses of the challenger, and $R(\mathbb{K}/N$ is the probability of a random guess over the N possible user-preferred locations. Now, at the end of the PPFRVP protocol, the attacker knows L_{fair} and its own preferred location $L_a = (x_a, y_a) \in \mathbb{N}^2$. Assuming that all users other than u_a have executed the protocol correctly, u_a does not know any preferred location L_i, for $i \neq a$. Hence, the probability $Pr[L_j^* = L_k]$ of him making a correct guess j^* about the preferred rendez-vous location L_k of user u_k equals the probability of a random guess, which in this case is $1/N - 1$. Thus, the identifiability advantage of the attacker u_a is negligible.

User Distance-Linkability Advantage. The distance-linkability of an attacker u_a is defined as

$$Adv_a^{d-LNK}(A) = \left| Pr[(d^* = 1] \wedge d_{jk} < s) \vee (d^* = 0 \wedge d_{jk} \geq s)] - \frac{1}{2} \right|$$

where $Pr[.]$ is the probability of the adversary u_a winning the game by correctly answering the challenge, computed over the coin tosses of the challenger, d^* is the guess of the adversary, d_{jk} is the distance between L_j, L_k and s is a parameter chosen by the challenger. In this case, the attacker has to guess whether the distance d_{jk} between two users j, k is greater than s, and clearly if he at some point in the protocol obtains any pairwise distance d_{jk}, his advantage is non-negligible. However, as explained in the correctness proof, each user gets to know only N masked (and anonymized) values of the squares of pairwise distances. Thus, the attacker wants to solve the following system of linear equations:

$$\begin{cases} C_{\sigma_a,\theta_1} & = r_a \cdot d^2_{\sigma_1,\theta_1} + s_a \\ & \vdots \\ C_{\sigma_a,\theta_N} & = r_a \cdot d^2_{\sigma_1,\theta_N} + s_a \end{cases}$$

where C_{ij} is the received masked value of the pairwise distances and r_a, s_a are random integers privately chosen by the LDS. Hence, possessing only the knowledge of his own preferred location and the fair fair rendez-vous location, the attacker cannot uniquely solve this system of equation, because it is still under-determined. Therefore, the distance-linkability advantage of u_a is negligible.

User Coordinate-Linkability Advantage. In order to have non-negligible coordinate-linkability advantage, an attacker u_a needs to have additional information regarding at least one of the two coordinates of any other user's preferred rendez-vous location. As discussed in the identifiability and distance linkability advantage proofs, after a private execution of the PPFRVP algorithm A, the attacker does not gain any additional information about any other user's locations. Therefore, not knowing any other user's coordinate, an attacker does not gain any probabilistic advantage on correctly guessing the relationship between their spatial coordinates. Hence, the coordinate-linkability advantage is negligible.

Third-party Advantages. All elements that are received and processed by the LDS have previously been encrypted by the users with their common public key. In order to efficiently decrypt such elements, the LDS would need to have access to the private key that has been generated with the public key used for the encryption. As explained in Section 3, in most practical settings, where service providers have a commercial interest in providing a faithful service to their customers, the LDS would not try to maliciously obtain the secret key. Therefore, all the LDS does in the PPFRVP algorithm is to obliviously execute algebraic operation on encrypted elements, without knowing the values within the encrypted elements. Hence, the PPFRVP algorithms do not disclose any information the a third-party, such as the LDS, during or after its execution.

On the Practicality of UHF RFID Fingerprinting: How Real is the RFID Tracking Problem?

Davide Zanetti, Pascal Sachs, and Srdjan Capkun

Department of Computer Science,
ETHZ, Zurich, Switzerland
{zanettid,sachsp,capkuns}@inf.ethz.ch

Abstract. In this work, we demonstrate the practicality of people tracking by means of physical-layer fingerprints of RFID tags that they carry. We build a portable low-cost USRP-based RFID fingerprinter and we show, over a set of 210 EPC C1G2 tags, that this fingerprinter enables reliable identification of individual tags from varying distances and across different tag placements (wallet, shopping bag, etc.). We further investigate the use of this setup for clandestine people tracking in an example Shopping Mall scenario and show that in this scenario the mobility traces of people can be reconstructed with a high accuracy.

Keywords: RFID, physical-layer identification, fingerprinting, tracking, privacy.

1 Introduction

Radio Frequency IDentification (RFID) technology has raised a number of privacy concerns in many different applications, especially when considering consumer privacy [17]. A person carrying several tags – attached to various objects like books, passports, medicines, medical devices, and clothes – can be subject to clandestine tracking by any reader in the read range of those tags; it has been shown that the read range of RFID tags can be extended up to 50 m [19]. Even if some objects are only temporarily with a person (e.g., a shopping bag), they will enable tracking of a person's behavior for shorter periods (e.g., during a morning or during a visit to a shopping mall). Other objects, such as wallets, personal bags, and medical devices will be frequently or permanently carried by people, thus allowing people being tracked over wider time periods.

Solutions that prevent a (clandestine) reader to communicate with tags were proposed on a logical level, and typically rely on the use of pseudonyms and access control mechanisms [1, 4, 8, 9, 20, 31]. Although effective on the logical level, these solutions do not prevent physical-layer identification of RFID tags. A number of features have been identified that allow physical-layer identification of RFID tags of different manufacturers, but also of individual RFID tags from the same manufacturer and model [6, 21–23, 27, 28, 34]. So far, physical-layer identification has been demonstrated in laboratory conditions, using high-sampling oscilloscopes and low-noise peripherals. This equipment can be costly and is rather impractical for real world tracking.

In this work, we present a low-cost, USRP-based RFID fingerprinter and show that physical-layer fingerprinting of RFID tags is feasible even with this portable setup. For

S. Fischer-Hübner and N. Hopper (Eds.): PETS 2011, LNCS 6794, pp. 97–116, 2011.

tag identification, we use timing features that rely on the extraction of tags backscatter frequencies [23, 34]. We tested our setup on a tag population composed of 210 EPC class-1 generation-2 (C1G2) RFID tags [11] of 12 different models and 3 manufacturers. EPC C1G2 tags are the *de facto* standard passive UHF tags and the most present in the current market. Our results show that this setup and features enable reliable identification of individual tags from varying distances and across different tag placements (wallet, jacket, shopping bag, backpack). The used feature allows the extraction of $\lfloor 2^{5.4} \rfloor$ RFID tag fingerprints independently of the population size (i.e., this feature results in approx. 5.4 bits of entropy). Since people will typically carry several tags, this will allow the creation of a large number of composite fingerprints, thus enabling, in a number of scenarios, highly precise people tracking (e.g., a set of 5 tags provides approx. 22 bits of entropy).

We investigate the use of our setup for clandestine people tracking in an example Shopping Mall scenario and show that in this scenario the mobility traces of people can be reconstructed with a high accuracy.

Although solutions that prevent a (clandestine) reader to communicate with tags at the physical layer exist (e.g., tag kill and sleep functions, Faraday cages, active jammers, and "clipped" tags [18]), the provided privacy comes at the price of tag functionality (e.g., the kill function permanently disables tags and therefore possible after-sales services or long-term deployments) or requires additional efforts (e.g., user interaction or extra hardware) that could make those solutions impractical and unattractive.

Therefore, the proposed setup and feature break people's privacy by enabling the tracking and mobility trace reconstruction of people carrying RFID tags. This privacy breach occurs disregarding of the RFID tag content (e.g., serial number) and with no need for interpreting the information transmitted by the RFID tags (which could be protected, e.g., encrypted, by logical-level mechanisms). People's privacy could be further compromised by means of side-channel information (e.g., a priori knowledge about target people) that builds the associations between tag fingerprints and objects to which they are attached, and between composite fingerprints and people's identities.

The rest of this paper is organized as follows. In Section 2, we define the people tracking scenario and our problem statement. In Section 3, we introduce the considered RFID tag population and physical-layer identification technique. In Section 4, we present our low-cost RFID fingerprinter, while in Section 5 we detail the performed experiments and summarize the collected data. We present the evaluation results in terms of tag distinguishability and fingerprint stability of our fingerprinter in Section 6, while we discuss their implications on tag holders' privacy in Section 7. We make an overview of background and related work in Section 8 and conclude the paper in Section 9.

2   Scenario and Problem Statement

In our study, we consider a scenario in which an attacker aims at tracking people carrying several passive UHF RFID tags over a limited period of time and within a bounded area (e.g., a mall). We assume that the attacker has the ability to position several physical-layer identification devices, i.e., *fingerprinters*, at strategic locations in the considered area. A fingerprinter profiles a person by (i) collecting RF signals from the set of tags assumed to be on a person, (ii) extracting the fingerprints for each tag in the set based on specific RF signal characteristics, or *features*, and finally, (iii) creating a profile, which is the collection of all tag fingerprints for the considered set of tags. The created profiles are then used for people tracking, which can reveal information about people's behavior (e.g., people are likely to visit shop A after they have visited shop B).

A number of works considered the threat of RFID-based tracking real [1, 8, 9, 17, 20]; however, some reservations still remain as to whether tracking is practical or confined only to laboratory environments. In this work we investigate how feasible and practical is RFID-based tracking in real-world scenarios. We consider that tracking will be practical if people's profiles (i.e., RFID fingerprints) can be reliably extracted in dynamic settings (i.e., when tags are on people, in wallets, bags, pockets, and when people are moving), if the fingerprinters can be built as compact, possibly low-cost devices, and if the profiles allow people's traces to be reconstructed with high accuracy. In the rest of the paper we will show that with the proposed fingerprinter setup and with the used features these three conditions are fulfilled.

3   RFID Tags, Signal Features and Tag Fingerprints

In our work, we evaluate the feasibility of people tracking by using our low-cost fingerprinter (Section 4) on a tag population composed of 210 EPC class-1 generation-2 (C1G2) RFID tags [11] of 12 different models and 3 manufacturers. EPC C1G2 tags are the *de facto* standard passive UHF tags and the most present in the current market. Those tags are mainly conceived for item- and pallet-level barcode replacement, which (especially for item-level tagging) makes them pervasive into everyday life.

3.1   EPC C1G2 Background

The communication between RFID readers and tags is half-duplex. A reader transmits commands and data to a tag by modulating an RF signal. The tag replies using a backscattered signal modulated by modifying the reflection coefficient of its antenna. Readers use pulse-interval encoding (PIE) and phase-reversal amplitude shift keying (PR-ASK) modulation to transmit data and commands to tags. Tags backscatter information by modulating an RF signal using ASK and/or PSK modulation and either FM0 baseband or Miller modulation as data encoding. The frequency range of RF signals is defined from 860 to 960 MHz. Readers transmit data at a maximum rate between 40 and 160 kbps. The tag backscatter link frequency (BLF, i.e., the tag data rate) is selected by the readers; the EPC C1G2 specification defines a BLF range between 40 and 640 kHz.

The communication sequence between a reader and a tag during the tag inventorying process with no collisions is shown in Figure 1. The reader challenges the tag with a set of commands to select a particular tag population (*Select*), to initiate an inventory round (*Query*), and to request the transmission of the tag's identification (EPC) number (*Ack*). The tag replies first with an RN16 packet[1] (after the reader's Query) and then with an EPC packet (after the reader's Ack) containing the identification number.

---

[1] RN16 packets are sent as a part of the anti-collision protocol used during tag inventorying.

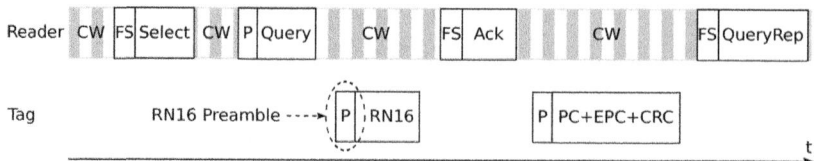

Fig. 1. EPC tag inventory sequence. P, FS, and CW stand for preamble, frame-sync, and continuous wave respectively.

3.2 Signal Features and Tag Fingerprints

Physical-layer device identification relies on random hardware impairments in the analog circuitry components introduced at the manufacturing process. Those impairments then manifest in the transmitted signals making them measurable.

To facilitate the adoption of RFID tags on a large-scale, tag manufacturers tend to optimize both the tag manufacturing process and the size of tag embedded integrated circuits in a effort to reduce the overall tag cost. Although the RFID tag market has been growing in the past years, high-speed processes and low-complexity integrated circuits may increase the possibility of finding tags' internal components affected by hardware impairments, as well as of finding impairments which create measurable and substantial differences between tags.

In our study, we consider random hardware impairments in the tags' local oscillator. According to the EPC C1G2 specification, the backscatter link frequency (BLF) at which tags communicate is defined within a range between 40 and 640 kHz with a frequency tolerance between ±4% and ±22% depending on the selected BLF. As shown by Periaswamy et al. [23] and Zanetti et al. [34], the relatively large BLF tolerances allowed by the EPC specification can represent a distinguishing factor between different tags of the same model and manufacturer. Additionally, it has been shown [34] that the BLF is not affected by the tag-reader distance and mutual position; this can allow tag distinguishability disregarding tags' location and position. Therefore, the signal feature we consider for tag identification is the backscatter link frequency at which each tag transmits data. We extract this signal feature from the fixed preamble of the RN16 packets sent by tags during tag inventorying. This is done not to introduce any data-dependent bias in our evaluation, since the RN16 preamble is fixed for all tags. Tag fingerprints are built from N acquired RN16 preambles, i.e., a tag fingerprint is a one-dimensional value corresponding to the average BLF over N RN16 preambles collected for a certain tag.

4   Low-Cost RFID Fingerprinter

In our study, we build and deploy a compact and low-cost fingerprinter that challenges tags to initiate an EPC C1G2 inventory round, collects tags' responses, i.e., RN16 packets, and builds tag fingerprints based on the backscatter link frequency (BLF) that it extracts from the RN16 preambles. Our fingerprinter is composed of a Universal Software Radio Peripheral 2 (USRP2) platform and an RFX900 daughterboard by Ettus

Research [2], as well as of a host PC providing signal processing through the GNU Radio toolkit [3]. The block diagram of our low-cost fingerprinter is shown in Figure 6 (Appendix A).

Our fingerprinter consists of a transmitter, a receiver and a feature extraction module. It uses a bistatic antenna configuration to minimize the leakage from the transmitter to the receiver. The chosen antennas are circularly polarized, which allows our fingerprinter to power up (and then communicate with) a tag thus minimizing the impact of the tag orientation. The transmitter outputs commands and data at the baseband frequency according to the pulse-interval encoding (PIE) and phase-reversal amplitude shift keying (PR-ASK) modulation (as defined in the EPC C1G2 specification [11]). The carrier frequency that is used for upmixing the baseband signal is 866.7 MHz[2] and, after the final amplification stage, the nominal transmission power is 29.5 dBm (including the antenna gain). The receiver is based on a direct-conversion I/Q demodulator[3]. After quadrature downmixing, the tag backscatter baseband signal is first converted into the digital domain with a nominal sampling rate of 10 MS/s (for each of the I and Q channels) and 14-bit resolution, and then low-pass filtered. For each channel, the feature extraction module processes the baseband tag signal to extract the BLF from the RN16 preambles. The extraction is a streaming-like process: the module continuously monitors the incoming signal for RN16 packets. When one is detected, the length of the preamble is measured and the BLF is computed and recorded.

5   Performed Experiments and Collected Data

We base our experiments on the interaction between a reader and a tag population that is used for inventorying purposes as defined in the EPC C1G2 specification [11]. We use our fingerprinter to challenge RFID tags (i.e., to initiate an inventory round), collect tags' replies (i.e., RN16 packets), and extract the specified signal feature (i.e., the backscatter link frequency, BLF) to obtain tag fingerprints.

Our tag population is composed of 210 EPC C1G2 RFID tags of 12 different models and 3 manufacturers: Alien Technology ALN9540, ALN9562, ALN9640 and ALN9654, Avery Dennison AD821, AD833, AD224 and AD824, and UPM Raflatac Dogbone (3 different integrated circuit models) and ShortDipole. The selected tag models present different characteristics in terms of antenna size and material, embedded integrated circuit, and application. Table 5 (Appendix B) summarizes the considered models and their main characteristics.

In order to increase the possibility of finding the largest distinguishing characteristic, for all experiments we select the BLF which, according to the EPC C1G2 specification, presents the largest allowed frequency tolerance. The selected nominal BLF is thus equal to 426 kHz and presents a maximal allowed frequency tolerance equal to $\pm 22\%$.

---

[2] The chosen carrier frequency corresponds to channel 6, band 2, of the ETSI EN 302 208 regulations [12], which define 10 channels of 200 KHz @ 2W ERP between 865.6 and 867.6 MHz.

[3] The phase of the tag backscatter signal is not predictable or controllable, as it varies with the distance to the tag; the I/Q demodulator allows the reception of a backscatter signal regardless of the distance to the tag.

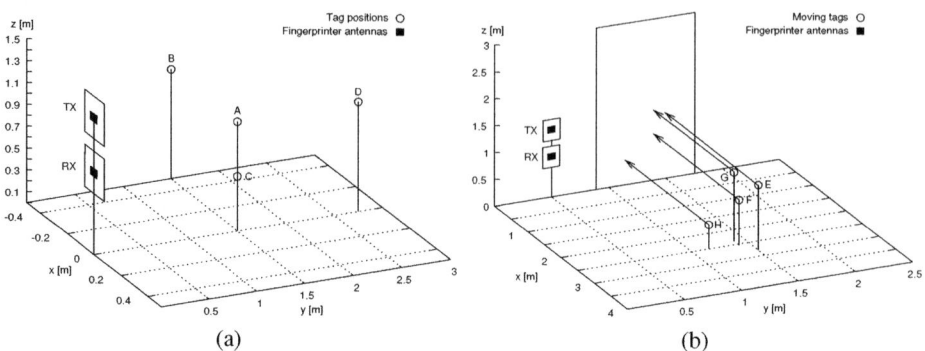

(a)   (b)

Fig. 2. Considered positions of the fingerprinter antennas and of the tags. In our experiments, fingerprinter antennas (TX and RX) are fixed, while tag responses are acquired (a) from different fixed locations (A-D, Table 1) and (b) when tags are moving (E-H, Table 2).

5.1   Performed Experiments

For all the tags in our population, we use our fingerprinter to initiate an inventory round and extract the BLF while tags are at a fixed location (on a stand). Figure 2(a) shows the considered positions of the fingerprinter transmitting (TX) and receiving (RX) antennas and of the tags (position A). Table 1 – configuration 3 summarizes the fingerprinter and tag settings for this experiment.

For a subset of tags in our population placed on a stand, we use our fingerprinter to extract the BLF under 16 different configurations of tag and antenna positions, acquisition sampling rate, tag temperature, transmission power, and fingerprinter hardware. The different configurations are summarized in Table 1 (configurations 1 to 16). The considered positions of the fingerprinter TX and RX antennas and of the tags are shown in Figure 2(a). In terms of tag position, we explore different tag distances to the fingerprinter antennas (up to 2.75 m), as well as different tag vertical and lateral positions. We also explore 3 different transmission powers (from 17.5 to 23 dBm), 3 different acquisition sampling rates (from 5 to 20 MS/s), and 5 different temperatures (from 10 to 50°C). Additionally, we consider 3 different fingerprinter hardware configurations (changing USRP2 platform, USRP daughterboard, antennas, and host PC) and swap the position of the TX and RX antennas. Finally, we explore time effects by acquiring RN16 preambles and extracting BLF one month after the beginning of this experiment.

For a subset of tags in our population, we use our fingerprinter to extract the BLF while tags are carried by a person. For this experiment, we investigate 6 different configurations of tag location (backpack, wallet, jacket, shopping bag), tag holder's activity (standing, walking), and number of carried tags (from 1 to 5). The fingerprinter is configured as detailed in Table 1 – configurations 17-22, while the different tag configurations are summarized in Table 2. The considered positions of the fingerprinter TX and RX antennas and of the tags are shown in Figure 2(b).

Table 1. Varied parameters for the different configurations - tags placed on a stand

Config.	Fig. 2(a)	Tag position (x,y,z)-axis [m]	Antennas position (TX,RX) [m]	TX power[1] [dBm]	Temp.[2] [°C]	Sampling rate [MS/s]	Fingerprinter hardware set[3]
1	A	(0, 1.5, 1.0)	(1.25, 0.75)	21	22	5	1
2	‖	‖	‖	‖	‖	20	‖
3	‖	‖	‖	‖	‖	10	‖
4[4]	‖	‖	‖	‖	‖	‖	‖
5	‖	‖	(0.75, 1.25)	‖	‖	‖	‖
6	B	(-0.5, 1.5, 1.0)	(1.25, 0.75)	‖	‖	‖	‖
7	C	(0, 1.5, 0.5)	‖	‖	‖	‖	‖
8	D	(0, 2.75, 1.0)	‖	23	‖	‖	‖
9	A	(0, 1.5, 1.0)	‖	17.5	‖	‖	‖
10	‖	‖	‖	23	‖	‖	‖
11	‖	‖	‖	21	‖	‖	2
12	‖	‖	‖	‖	‖	‖	3
13	‖	‖	‖	‖	10	‖	1
14	‖	‖	‖	‖	30	‖	‖
15	‖	‖	‖	‖	40	‖	‖
16	‖	‖	‖	‖	50	‖	‖
17-22	Tag on a person, see Table 2		‖	23	22	‖	‖

[1] Power before the TX antenna. For fingerprinter sets 1 and 3, the TX antenna has a gain of 8.5 dBi, while for set 2 this is equal to 6 dBi.
[2] Temperature variations of $\pm 2°$C.
[3] Set 2: same host PC as set 1, but different USRP, USRP daughterboard and antennas.
  Set 3: same USRP, USRP daughterboard and antennas as set 1, but different host PC.
[4] Same as configuration 3, but fingerprints obtained from RN16 preambles collected 1 month after the RN16 preambles collected for configuration 3.

Table 2. Varied parameters for the different configurations - tags on a person

Configuration	Tag location Fig. 2(b)		Tag holder's activity	# of tags during acquisition
17	E	Backpack	walking away from TX/RX antennas	1
18	F	Wallet	‖	‖
19	G	Jacket	walking towards TX/RX antennas	‖
20	H	Shopping bag	‖	‖
21	‖	‖	standing in front of TX/RX antennas	5
22	‖	‖	walking towards TX/RX antennas	‖

5.2   Collected Data

Using our fingerprinter, we performed the experiments described in Section 5.1. Table 3 summarizes the data that we collected, represented in a form of datasets.

Data collection was performed over one month, one tag at the time (unless otherwise indicated, i.e., for data collection under configurations 21 and 22 – Table 2), 200 extracted BLFs in a row, in an indoor, RF noisy environment with active Wi-Fi and GSM networks. The nominal environment temperature was approx. 22°C. We increased the tag temperature by means of a heat gun, while we lowered it by decreasing the overall environment temperature. Temperatures were measured with an infrared thermometer[4]. We note a $\pm 2°$C variations for the given temperatures. We sped up the acquisition process by adjusting the aforementioned EPC inventory sequence (Figure 1) in a way to collect several RN16 packets in the same inventory round and by not requesting the tag's identification (EPC) number[5]. Giving the considered acquisition sequence, the theoretical upper bound for BLF acquisition is approx. 1250 extracted BLFs per second (we discuss the fingerprinter acquisition speed in Section 7.3).

6   Evaluation of Tag Distinguishability and Fingerprint Stability

In this section, we first review the metrics that we used to evaluate the tag distinguishability and the fingerprint stability. Then, we present the results for those evaluations obtained by the proposed signal feature over the considered tag population.

6.1   Evaluation Metrics

To evaluate the tag distinguishability and the fingerprint stability, we compute the entropy of the probability distribution of the tag fingerprints given the selected signal feature. For each tag and configuration, fingerprints are built from N extracted BLFs. Table 4 summarizes the computed entropies for the different analysis we performed.

We compute the entropy of the fingerprint probability distribution in order to show how many bits of information are contained within that distribution. To compute the entropy, we consider bins of width equal to the double of the average standard deviation of the signal feature in the dataset and count the number of fingerprints that fall into the different bins. We then apply the standard entropy formula [29].

Additionally, for each performed analysis, we define an entropy upper bound[6] by computing its theoretical maximum given the EPC C1G2 specification [11], i.e., the maximum number of information bits that could be learned from the BLF feature considering the maximal allowed frequency tolerance as defined in the EPC specification ($\pm 22\%$ around the nominal BLF) and giving the bin width of the considered analysis.

---

[4] Temperature was measured on the tag front surface. Tags were heated up from the back surface and, for each considered temperature, for at least 5 minutes before data acquisition.

[5] This procedure is also valid for multiple-tag acquisitions. For each tag, several RN16 packets are collected before moving to the next tag. This also provides the association between extracted BLFs and tags.

[6] The entropy upper bound is computed by assuming the fingerprint distribution as uniform [13].

Table 3. Collected data

Dataset	Model	# tags	# extracted BLFs per tag	Conf. (Table 1)	Total # extracted BLFs per tag
1	ALN9640	100	200	3	200
2[1]	ALN{9540, 9562, 9640[2], 9654}	40	200	3	200
	AD{224, 821, 824, 833}	||	||	||	||
	ShortDipole, Dogbone[3]	||	||	||	||
3	ALN9640[2]	10	200	3-22	4000
4	ALN9640	100	200	1,2	400

[1] For each model, 10 tags are considered.
[2] Tags randomly selected among the 100 used in datasets 1 and 4.
[3] For Dogbone tags, 3 different integrated circuit models are considered.

6.2   Tag Distinguishability

In this section, we analyze the tag distinguishability of the proposed feature based on the fingerprint probability distribution of two datasets: dataset 1, which contains 20,000 extracted BLFs for 100 same-model (and same-manufacturer) tags, and dataset 2, which contains 24,000 extracted BLFs for 120 tags of 12 different models.

Figure 3(a) and 3(b) show the computed fingerprints for the 100 same-model and the 120 different-model tags respectively. Each fingerprint is obtained by averaging 5 extracted BLFs ($N = 5$), resulting in 40 fingerprints per tag. Tag distinguishability depends only on the variations of the BLF within each tag and between different tags. For both sets of tags, we can observe a certain degree of distinguishability. First, the fingerprint variations within each tag are relatively small (average standard deviation of approx. 120 and 196 Hz for the 100 same-model and the 120 different-model tags respectively). Second, fingerprints of different tags are located in different frequency areas. However, we note that (i) fingerprints of different tags also overlap (i.e., different tags present a similar BLF), which reduces the possibility, or even prevent to distinguish those tags, and (ii) that the overall frequency range is less than the maximal frequency range allowed by the EPC C1G2 specification (between 332 and 520 kHz given the $\pm 22\%$ tolerance around the nominal BLF), which indicates that the actual fingerprint entropy will not correspond to its potential upper bound. Additionally, we note that different tag models could also be distinguished, in particular when considering tags embedding Impinj Monza IC.

Figure 3(c) and 3(d) show the empirical fingerprint distributions for the 100 same-model and the 120 different-model tags respectively. The entropy result based on the empirical distribution of 120 different-model tags suggests that we could learn 6.78 bits of information about a single UHF RFID tag. For the 100 same-model tags, this value is equal to 6.32 bits. The difference between these two results simply lies in the larger frequency range exploited by several models with respect to one single model. The entropy upper bound considering the maximal allowed BLF tolerance is, for same-model tags, equal to 9.45 bits and, for different-model tags, to 9.38 bits.

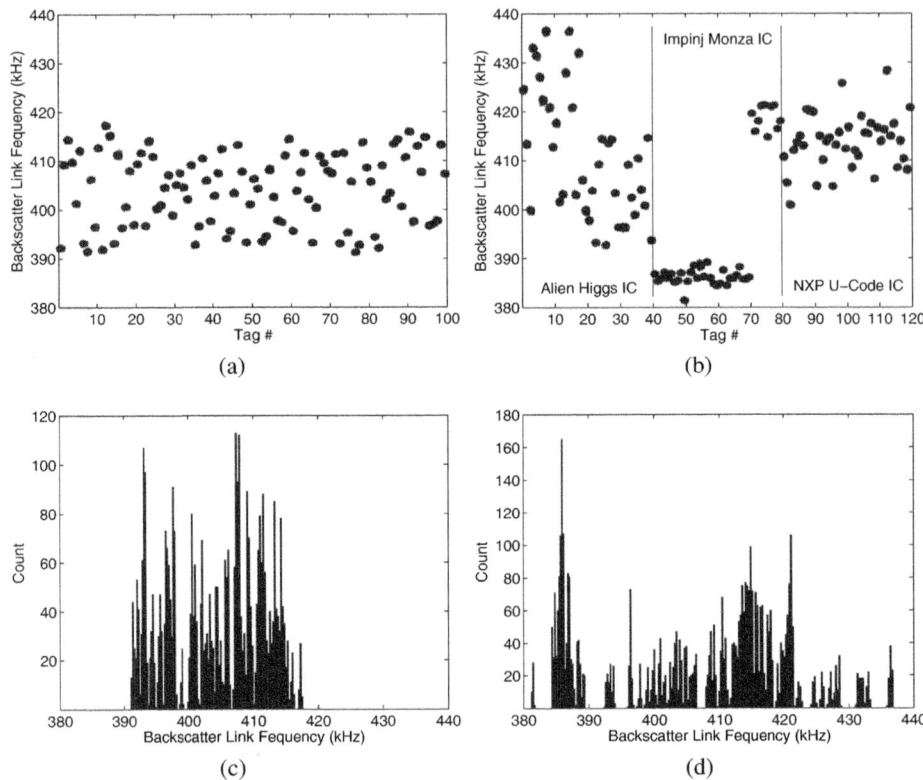

Fig. 3. Fingerprints for (a) 100 same-model tags and (b) 120 tags of 12 different models. Fingerprint distribution for (c) 100 same-model tags and (d) 120 tags of 12 different models. For each tag, 40 fingerprints are considered ($N = 5$).

We evaluate the impact of the number N of extracted BLFs over which we average to obtain the tag fingerprints by computing the entropy based on the empirical distribution of the 100 same-model tags obtained for different values of N. The results of the analysis for $N = 1, 2, 5, 10, 20$ are 5.39, 5.81, 6.32, 6.67, and 6.97 bits respectively.

6.3   Fingerprint Stability

In the previous section, we have analyzed the tag distinguishability under a fixed configuration of fingerprinter and tag settings. In this section, we evaluate the stability of the proposed signal feature under different settings, i.e., we analyze the impact of different settings on the tag distinguishability. More specifically, we evaluate:

1. The entropy of the proposed feature under 16 different configurations of tag position (with respect to the fingerprinter antennas) and location (on a stand, on a person), antenna position, transmission power, fingerprinter hardware, and, when tags are carried by a person, tag holder's activity (walking, standing) and the number of carried tags (Table 1 – configurations 3-12 and 17-22, and Table 2).

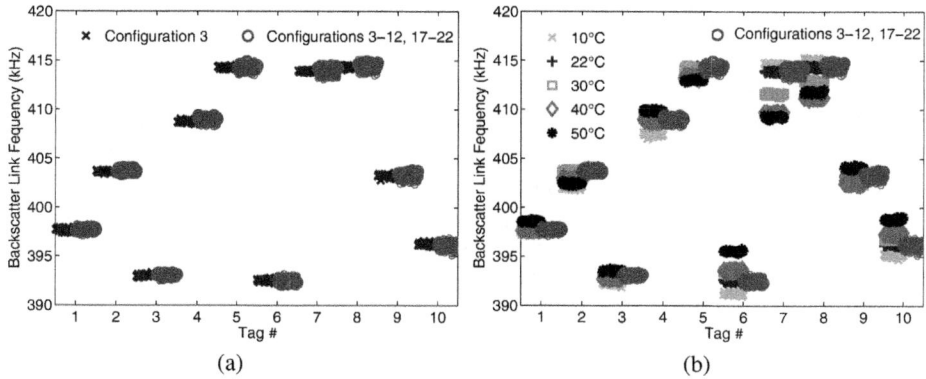

Fig. 4. Fingerprint visualization for 10 randomly selected ALN9640 tags and different settings ($N = 5$). For each tag in (a), the set of fingerprints on the left is composed of 40 fingerprints of 1 fixed configuration, while the set on the right of 640 fingerprints of 16 different configurations. For each tag in (b), the set of fingerprints on the left is composed of 200 fingerprints of 5 different temperatures, while the set on the right of 640 fingerprints of 16 different configurations.

2. The entropy of the proposed feature given different acquisition sampling rates (Table 1 – configurations 1-3).
3. The effect of temperature on tag fingerprints (Table 1 – configurations 3, 13-16).

Figure 4(a) shows the fingerprints of the selected 10 tags under 16 different configurations of fingerprinter and tag settings ($N = 5$, 40 fingerprints for each tag and configuration). For each tag, two sets of fingerprints are shown: 40 fingerprints (the set on the left) obtained under one single configuration (Table 1 – configuration 3) and 640 fingerprints (the set on the right) obtained under 16 different configurations of fingerprinter and tag settings (Table 1 – configurations 3-12 and 17-22). We observe an increase on the BLF variation within each tag when comparing those two sets: the average standard deviation within each tag increases from approx. 120 to 150 Hz. Although this increase (less than 30 Hz) seems relatively small when compared to the considered frequency range (approx. 30 kHz for the 100 same-model tags), the entropy for the 100 same-model tag decreases from 6.32 (Section 6.2) to 5.39 bits[7]. Similarly, the entropy upper bound decreases from 9.45 to 8.41 bits.

In order to evaluate the impact of the acquisition sampling rate, we compute the entropy based on the empirical distribution of the 100 same-model tags obtained for RN16 preambles acquired at different rates. The results of the analysis for 5, 10, and 20 MS/s are 6.19, 6.32, and 6.49 bits respectively.

Figure 4(b) shows the fingerprints of the selected 10 tags under 20 different configurations ($N = 5$, 40 fingerprints for each tag and configuration). For each tag, two sets of fingerprints are shown: 200 fingerprints (the set on the left) obtained under 5 different temperatures (Table 1 – configurations 3, 13-16) and 640 fingerprints (the set

---

[7] We compute this entropy over dataset 1 (100 tags, 1 configuration), but considering the standard deviation under the stability analysis of dataset 3 (10 tags, 16 configurations), i.e., 150 Hz. This allows us to compare entropies and evaluate the effect of different configurations.

Table 4. Computed entropies (with 95% confidence interval) for the performed analysis

Dataset	Sampling rate [MS/s]	N	Config. (Table 1)	Standard deviation [Hz]	Entropy (empirical dist.) [bits]	Entropy (upper bound) [bits]
1	10	1	3	273.32 (270.14;275.99)	5.39 (5.38;5.42)	8.27 (8.25;8.29)
II	II	2	II	192.63 (189.89;195.19)	5.81 (5.78;5.83)	8.77 (8.75;8.79)
II	II	5	II	120.21 (117.05;123.31)	6.32 (6.29;6.35)	9.45 (9.42;9.49)
II	II	10	II	83.45 (81.14;86.02)	6.67 (6.62;6.71)	9.97 (9.94;10.02)
II	II	20	II	56.58 (54.06;58.99)	6.97 (6.91;7.02)	10.54 (10.48;10.60)
2	10	5	3	196.05 (180.38;211.80)	6.78 (6.75;6.80)	9.38 (9.35;9.41)
3	10	5	3-12,17-22	149.57 (140.42;159.72)	5.39[1] (5.37;5.42)	8.41[1] (8.41;8.41)
4	5	5	1	134.12 (129.78;138.40)	6.19 (6.14;6.24)	9.29 (9.24;9.34)
II	20	II	2	109.35 (106.44;112.65)	6.49 (6.45;6.52)	9.59 (9.55;9.63)

[1] Computed for dataset 1 (100 tags) given the standard deviation of dataset 3 (10 tags).

on the right) obtained under 16 different configurations of fingerprinter and tag settings (Table 1 – configurations 3-12 and 17-22). Differently from the previous results, temperature seems to have a relatively large impact on the BLF variation within each tag, especially when considering the limit temperatures in our analysis (10 and 50°C). We note that tags are not equally affected by temperature and that we could not observe any common trend (i.e., a relation between temperature and BLF variation) that would facilitate the mitigation of the temperature effect on tag fingerprints.

7   Implications on Tag Holders' Privacy

In this section, we first discuss the implications on people's privacy given the obtained results, in particular with respect to people tracking. Then, we discuss possible countermeasures against clandestine tracking and fingerprinter requirements for practical tracking.

7.1   People Tracking: Breaking Tag Holders' Privacy

The results of our work show that we can learn 5.39 bits of information about a single RFID tag by only observing the data rate at which it transmits[8]. This information can be extracted independently of the tag position and location, fingerprinter hardware and antennas position, transmission power, tag holder's activity, and number of carried tags.

The relatively low distinguishability (per tag) can be improved when considering sets of tags. Our fingerprinter extracts $b = 5.39$ bits of information for each tag, i.e, when individually considered, a maximum of $n = \lfloor 2^b \rfloor$ tags can be uniquely distinguished.

---

[8] The amount of information could be further increased by considering sets of tags composed of different tag models and manufacturers, an higher acquisition sampling rate, and a larger number of acquired signals over which the tag fingerprints are obtained.

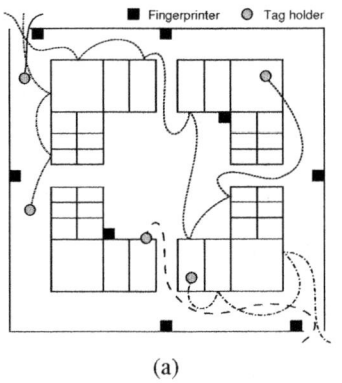
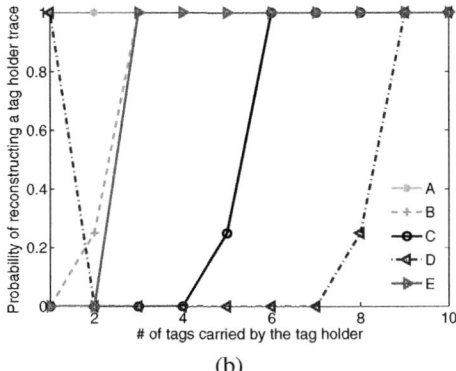

(a)   (b)

Fig. 5. (a) A possible shopping mall scenario and (b) the upper bound probability of reconstructing a tag holder's trace as a function of the number of tags carried by that tag holder. Curve A represents a population size of $P = 3000$, where $p_T = \mathcal{N}(5, 1)$, the tag entropy $b = 5.39$, and each tag holder has been profiled once, i.e., $E_H = 1$. Curves B, C, D, and E are similar to A, but they consider $p_T = \mathcal{N}(2, 1)$, $P = 5,000,000$, $b = 1$, and $E_H = 10$ respectively.

As a consequence, a set S composed of T tags can be uniquely distinguished among other $S_T = \binom{n+T-1}{T} = \frac{(n+T-1)!}{T!(n-1)!}$ sets. For example, a set composed of 5 tags can be uniquely distinguished among other 1.2 million sets of 5 tags. Larger sets provide more information (for $T = 5$, approx. 22 bits) and lead to a larger distinguishability of people carrying several tags, even with relatively low distinguishability per tag.

To show the impact of our technique on tag holders' privacy, we evaluate the probability that the attacker can correctly reconstruct a customer's path in a shopping mall. Reconstructed paths, or traces, can be used to derive customers' behavior and trend and, ultimately, to optimize the location of shops and facilities in the mall.

We consider a scenario in which several fingerprinters are disseminated in a shopping mall (Figure 5(a)). Tag holders, i.e., customers carrying tags, are subject to profiling when passing near the fingerprinters. Each profile is composed of the profiling time and location, and of the set of fingerprints obtained from the carried tags. A tag holder's trace is composed of all the profiles built by the disseminated fingerprinters that relate to that tag holder over a period of interest. We note that the number of tags carried by a customer may increase over time, i.e., the more he/she buys, the more tags he/she carries. Considering this scenario, we evaluate the probability of entirely reconstructing a tag holder's trace given all profiles built over the period of interest. We define as P the size of the customer population which has been profiled over the considered period.

The anonymity set $k_{S,T}$ represents how many tag holders within a population of size P carry the same set S of T tags (fingerprints). $k_{S,T}$ depends on the population size P, the distribution p_T of the number of carried tags per customer within P, the number of carried tag T, the distribution p_S of the possible tag sets, and the tag entropy b. An anonymity set $k_{S,T} = 2$ means that each profile referring to a specific set S of T tags could be potentially related to 2 different tag holders. It is possible to derive the minimal population size in order to find at least 2 customers carrying the same set S of T tags. For example, giving $p_T = \mathcal{N}(5, 1)$, $p_S = \mathcal{U}(1, S_T)$, and $b = 5.39$ bits, the minimal population size necessary to find at least 2 customers carrying the same set S of T tags is 149,480, 3.2 million, and 66 billion for $T = 2, 5, 8$ tags respectively.

For a tag holder carrying a set S of T tags and having an anonymity set of $k_{S,T}$, the probability p_R of reconstructing that tag holder's trace is computed as $(k_{S,T})^{-E}$, where E is the total number of profiles referring to the considered set of tags S (i.e., all the profiles built for all the customers carrying that set S). Figure 5(b) shows the upper bound probability[9] $\overline{p_R}$ of reconstructing a tag holder's trace as a function of the number of tags T carried by that tag holder (curve A) and for a different distribution of the number of carried tags p_T (curve B), population size P (curve C), tag entropy b (curve D), and number of profiles built for each tag holder in the considered population E_H (curve E). Since p_R is derived from the anonymity set, this is affected by the tag entropy, the population size, the distribution of the number of carried tags within that population, and the number of carried tags by the consider tag holder. In general, for the same b, P, p_T, and E_H, increasing the number of carried tags T increases p_R: the more shopping, the less anonymity[10]. Differently, increasing the population size, decreasing the tag entropy, or having a population with a smaller number of carried tags per customer increases the anonymity set and therefore reduces p_R. Additionally, p_R is also affected by the total number of profiles built for all the customers carrying the same set of tags: the more profiles, the larger the number of possible profile combinations that a certain tag holder's trace could match, and therefore, the less p_R. Finally, we note that p_R could be increased by considering information like spatial and temporal correlation of profiles.

Therefore, our fingerprinter and selected signal feature allow, in fact, people profiling and clandestine tracking. Temperature effects on tag fingerprints can be neglected when tags maintain a similar temperature over the different profilings, for example, like in a shopping mall where temperature control is used.

7.2 Countermeasures: How to Preserve Tag Holders' Privacy

Countermeasures against physical-layer identification can be categorized into solutions that prevent tag-reader communication or that prevent physical-layer identification.

Tag kill and sleep functions, Faraday cages, and active jammers [17] are solutions that prevent any reader[11] to communicate with a tag, thus eliminating any possible physical-layer identification. Permanently killing tags will guarantee privacy, but at the price of tag functionality. Sleep functions and active jammers will preserve long-term tag functionality, but the required additional measures in order to guarantee privacy (e.g., user interaction, tag access control, or extra hardware) could make those solutions unattractive (especially given the deployment model of RFID tags, in particular when considering item-level tagging). Faraday cages are the most simple and effective

---

[9] The upper bound probability is computed by assuming p_S as uniform.

[10] Exceptions can occur depending on the size of the group of all customers carrying T tags and the entropy b. As shown in Figure 5(b) - curve D, $\overline{p_R}$ decreases when increasing T from 1 to 2, since the small size of the group of all customers carrying 1 tag allows to reconstruct all traces, while the bigger size of the group of all customers carrying 2 tags provides some anonymity.

[11] Preventing only clandestine readers will not provide any benefit, since the communication between a tag and a legitimate reader can be easily eavesdropped.

solutions to guarantee privacy by temporarily preventing tag-reader communication, but, although shielded wallets and shopping bags could be easily deployed, other RFID-enabled devices (e.g., medical devices) may require additional efforts that could make those solutions impractical.

Solutions that prevent physical-layer identification aim at removing or reducing the effect of the random hardware impairments in the analog circuitry components introduced at the manufacturing process that make physical-layer identification possible. Although very effective, those solutions require first the (possibly hard) task to identify the components that make devices identifiable, and then to adjust the manufacturing process accordingly, which may introduce additional costs that could make those solutions unattractive. In addition, such solutions do not guarantee that a new discriminant feature will never be exploited in future.

Achieving effective and practical countermeasures against unauthorized physical-layer identifications remains an open issue that needs to be addressed.

7.3 RFID Fingerprinter Requirements

Besides tag distinguishability, requirements for a practical use of an RFID fingerprinter for people tracking include acquisition speed, system cost, read range, and size.

Giving the acquisition sequence as detailed in Section 5.2 and the selected EPC C1G2 settings (nominal BLF equal to 426 kHz and 4-subcarrier Miller encoding [11]), the theoretical upper bound for the BLF acquisition speed is approx. 1250 BLFs per second. Besides the well-known factors affecting the tag read rate like tag position, orientation, surrounding material, etc., the communication and computation capabilities of our fingerprinter also influence the actual acquisition speed. If for a sampling rate of 5 MS/s the acquisition speed is close to the theoretical upper bound (approx. 1220 BLF/s), for higher sampling rates the larger amount of data to transmit and process reduces the actual acquisition speed. For 10 and 20 MS/s, the acquisition speed is reduced to approx. 390 and 75 BLF/s respectively[12]. We note that, since tags share the same medium, the EPC C1G2 specification provides a medium access control mechanism to limit tag collisions, which, in fact, reduces the overall acquisition speed. Although for 10 MS/s and 5 tags we find a relatively low acquisition speed equal to approx. 85 BLF/s, this was enough to acquire the necessary tag signals in all our experiments.

The system cost relates to the quality of the obtained fingerprints and the acquisition speed. With our fingerprinter, we were able to obtain reliable fingerprints for people tracking at a relatively low-cost: the overall cost of our fingerprinter (USRP2, USRP daughterboard, host PC, and antennas) is less than USD3200.

During our experiments, we tested tag-reader distances of up to 2.75 m. Although we did not evaluate larger distances (for this, an external amplifier increasing the fingerprinter transmission power would have been necessary), given the exploited signal feature and the obtained results, we can extend the tag distinguishability range to the actual tag read range (which can reach up to 50 m [19]).

---

[12] Those values could be increased by tuning some of the EPC C1G2 settings (e.g., by increasing the nominal BLF or using FM0 as data encoding scheme) and by optimizing the fingerprinter blocks having the highest demand of computational power (e.g., the signal filtering processes).

In terms of size, our fingerprinter fits in a briefcase: the USRP2 platform has sizes 21x17x5 cm, while a laptop can be used as host PC. We deployed planar antennas of sizes 37x37x4 cm (smaller could be used), which can be easily hidden in wall panels.

8   Related Work

Physical-layer fingerprinting (identification) of UHF RFID tags has been investigated in several works [21–23, 34]. Periaswamy et al. [22] studied physical-layer identification of UHF RFID tags as a mechanism to detect counterfeit tags. The authors used the tag minimum power response measured at multiple frequencies as discriminant feature. The authors considered a set of 100 tags from 2 manufacturers and collected tag signals with a middle/high-range acquisition setup in a clean environment (anechoic chamber). The results showed that same-model tags can be distinguished, but fingerprint stability was not considered. The same authors also proposed a method to enable ownership transfer of UHF RFID tags based on the same discriminant feature [21]. Timing characteristics (packet length) of the tag-to-reader communication are used by Periaswamy, Thompson and Romero [23] to identify (classify) UHF RFID tag. The authors considered a set of 30 tags from 3 manufacturers and collected tag signals with a high-range acquisition setup in a noisy environment (lab room). Results showed that tags can be correctly classified, depending on the considered model, with an accuracy between approx. 32 and 98%. Fingerprint stability was not considered. Zanetti et al. [34] studied physical-layer identification of UHF RFID tags using timing and spectral characteristics of tag signals. The authors considered a set of 70 tags from 3 manufacturers and collected tag signals with a high-range acquisition setup in a noisy environment (lab room). The results showed the existence of stable physical-layer fingerprints for distinguishing UHF RFID tags. The authors also evaluated the implications of the proposed fingerprinting techniques on users' privacy and as cloning detection mechanism.

In comparison to the above works, our work is the first to evaluate the practicality of UHF RFID fingerprinting for people tracking. More specifically, we deployed low-cost fingerprinters to challenge tags, collect tags' responses, and build fingerprints in a tracking-like scenario, i.e., in which tags are carried by people moving into a bounded area. In our study, we considered a larger tag population of 210 tags of 12 models and 3 manufacturers and a more complete fingerprint stability evaluation.

Besides the mentioned works on UHF RFID tags, physical-layer fingerprinting has been explored on different platforms such as VHF [10, 30, 32], Bluetooth [15], IEEE 802.11 [5, 14, 16, 33], IEEE 802.15.4 (ZigBee) [7, 24], and GSM [25, 26]. Physical-layer identification has also been considered for inductive coupled HF RFID devices [6, 27, 28], especially for detecting cloned or counterfeit HF RFID smart cards and electronic passports. The results showed that the proposed techniques enable identification of same model and manufacturer HF RFID devices, but at a very close proximity.

9   Conclusion

In this work, we investigated the practicality of people tracking by means of physical-layer fingerprints of RFID tags that they carry. We have constructed a compact

USRP-based RFID fingerprinter and have shown that using this fingerprinter people's RFID profiles (i.e., RFID fingerprints) can be reliably extracted in dynamic settings (i.e., when tags are on people, in wallets, bags, pockets, and when people are moving). We have further shown, in a representative mall scenario, that these profiles allow people's traces to be reconstructed with high accuracy. Effective and practical countermeasures against unauthorized physical-layer fingerprinting remain an open problem.

References

1. http://www.avoine.net/rfid/index.html
2. http://www.ettus.com/
3. http://www.gnu.org/software/gnuradio/
4. Berbain, C., Billet, O., Etrog, J., Gilbert, H.: An efficient forward private RFID protocol. In: Proc. ACM Conference on Computer and Communications Security, pp. 43–53 (2009)
5. Brik, V., Banerjee, S., Gruteser, M., Oh, S.: Wireless device identification with radiometric signatures. In: Proc. ACM International Conference on Mobile Computing and Networking (2008)
6. Danev, B., Heydt-Benjamin, T.S., Čapkun, S.: Physical-layer identification of RFID devices. In: Proc. USENIX Security Symposium (2009)
7. Danev, B., Čapkun, S.: Transient-based identification of wireless sensor nodes. In: Proc. ACM/IEEE Conference on Information Processing in Sensor Networks (2009)
8. Dimitriou, T.: A lightweight RFID protocol to protect against traceability and cloning attacks. In: Proc. International ICST Conference on Security and Privacy in Communication Networks (2005)
9. Duc, D.N., Park, J., Lee, H., Kim, K.: Enhancing security of EPCglobal Gen-2 RFID tag against traceability and cloning. In: Proc. Symposium on Cryptography and Information Security (2006)
10. Ellis, K., Serinken, N.: Characteristics of radio transmitter fingerprints. Radio Science 36, 585–597 (2001)
11. EPCglobal: UHF Class 1 Gen 2 Standard v. 1.2.0. Standard (2008)
12. ETSI: ETSI EN 302 208-1 (2006)
13. Guiasu, S., Shenitzer, A.: The principle of maximum entropy. The Mathematical Intelligencer 7, 42–48 (1985)
14. Hall, J., Barbeau, M., Kranakis, E.: Enhancing intrusion detection in wireless networks using radio frequency fingerprinting. In: Proc. Communications, Internet, and Information Technology (2004)
15. Hall, J., Barbeau, M., Kranakis, E.: Detecting rogue devices in Bluetooth networks using radio frequency fingerprinting. In: Proc. IASTED International Conference on Communications and Computer Networks (2006)
16. Jana, S., Kasera, S.K.: On fast and accurate detection of unauthorized wireless access points using clock skews. In: Proc. ACM International Conference on Mobile Computing and Networking (2008)
17. Juels, A.: RFID security and privacy: A research survey. IEEE Journal on Selected Areas in Communications 24(2) (2006)
18. Karjoth, G., Moskowitz, P.A.: Disabling RFID tags with visible confirmation: clipped tags are silenced. In: Proc. ACM Workshop on Privacy in the Electronic Society (2005)
19. Koscher, K., Juels, A., Kohno, T., Brajkovic, V.: EPC RFID tag security weaknesses and defenses: Passport cards, enhanced drivers licenses, and beyond. In: Proc. ACM Conference on Computer and Communications Security (2009)

20. Lee, Y.K., Batina, L., Singelée, D., Verbauwhede, I.: Low-cost untraceable authentication protocols for RFID. In: Proc. ACM Conference on Wireless Network Security (2010)
21. Periaswamy, S.C.G., Thompson, D.R., Di, J.: Ownership transfer of RFID tags based on electronic fingerprint. In: Proc. International Conference on Security and Management (2008)
22. Periaswamy, S.C.G., Thompson, D.R., Di, J.: Fingerprinting RFID tags. IEEE Transactions on Dependable and Secure Computing PrePrints (99) (2010)
23. Periaswamy, S.C.G., Thompson, D.R., Romero, H.P., Di, J.: Fingerprinting radio frequency identification tags using timing characteristics. In: Proc. Workshop on RFID Security - RFIDsec Asia (2010)
24. Rasmussen, K., Čapkun, S.: Implications of radio fingerprinting on the security of sensor networks. In: Proc. International ICST Conference on Security and Privacy in Communication Networks (2007)
25. Reising, D.R., Temple, M.A., Mendenhall, M.J.: Improved wireless security for GMSK-based devices using RF fingerprinting. International Journal of Electronic Security and Digital Forensics 3, 41–59 (2010)
26. Reising, D.R., Temple, M.A., Mendenhall, M.J.: Improving intra-cellular security using air monitoring with RF fingerprints. In: Proc. IEEE Wireless Communications and Networking Conference (2010)
27. Romero, H.P., Remley, K.A., Williams, D.F., Wang, C.M.: Electromagnetic measurements for counterfeit detection of radio frequency identification cards. IEEE Transactions on Microwave Theory and Techniques 57(5), 1383–1387 (2009)
28. Romero, H.P., Remley, K.A., Williams, D.F., Wang, C.M., Brown, T.X.: Identifying RF identification cards from measurements of resonance and carrier harmonics. IEEE Transactions on Microwave Theory and Techniques 58(7), 1758–1765 (2010)
29. Shannon, C.: A mathematical theory of communication. The Bell System Technical Journal 27, 379–423 (1948)
30. Shaw, D., Kinsner, W.: Multifractal modeling of radio transmitter transients for classification. In: Proc. IEEE Conference on Communications, Power and Computing (1997)
31. Spiekermann, S., Evdokimov, S.: Privacy enhancing technologies for RFID - A critical investigation of state of the art research. In: Proc. IEEE Privacy and Security (2009)
32. Ureten, O., Serinken, N.: Detection of radio transmitter turn-on transients. Electronic Letters 35, 1996–1997 (2007)
33. Ureten, O., Serinken, N.: Wireless security through RF fingerprinting. Canadian Journal of Electrical and Computer Engineering 32(1) (Winder 2007)
34. Zanetti, D., Danev, B., Čapkun, S.: Physical-layer identification of UHF RFID tags. In: Proc. ACM Conference on Mobile Computing and Networking (2010)

Appendix A: Low-Cost Fingerprinter Block Diagram

The block diagram of our low-cost fingerprinter is shown in Figure 6.

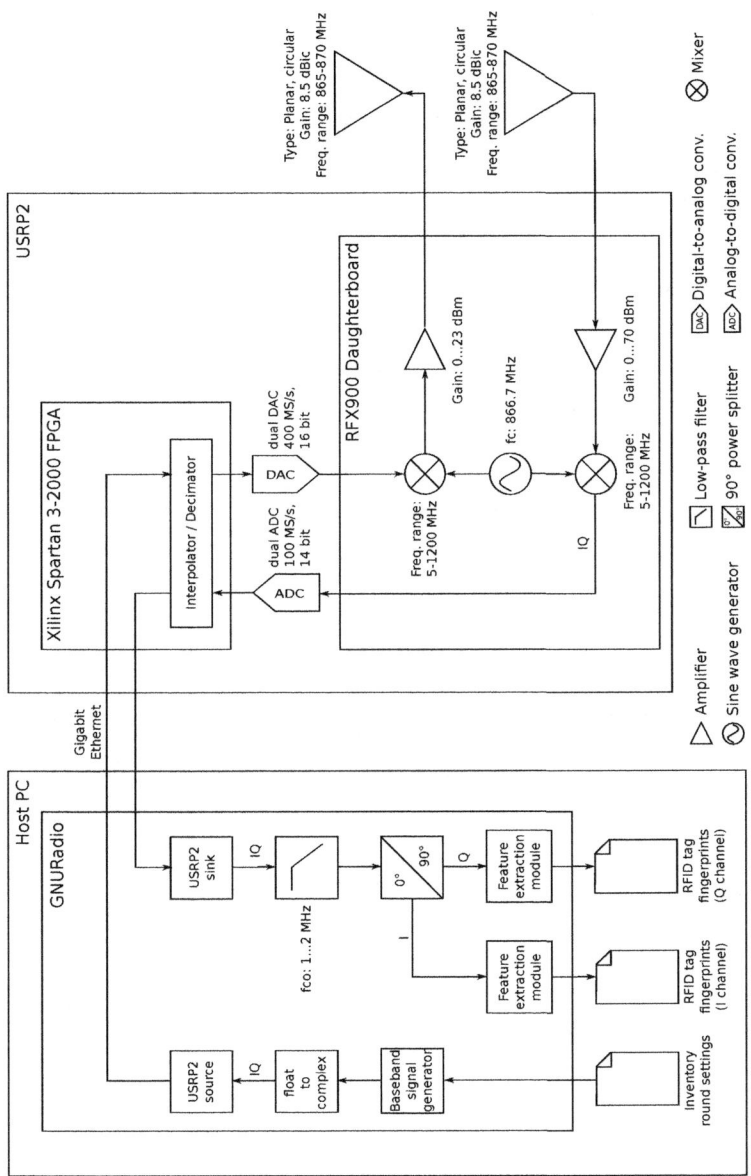

Fig. 6. Block diagram of our low-cost fingerprinter

Appendix B: Considered Tag Models

In our study, we consider a tag population composed of 210 EPC C1G2 RFID tags of 12 different models and 3 manufacturers. Table 5 summarizes the considered models and their main characteristics.

Table 5. Considered tag models and their main characteristics

Model	Manufacturer	IC	IC characteristics	Antenna size [mm]	Antenna material	Application (tagging)
ALN9540	Alien Technology	Alien Higgs-2	96-bit EPC num.	94.8 x 8.1	Cu	Cartoon, pallet
ALN9562	‖	‖	‖	70 x 19	‖	‖
ALN9640	‖	Alien Higgs-3	96/480-bit EPC num. 512-bit user memory	94.8 x 8.1	‖	‖
ALN9654	‖	‖	‖	93 x 19	‖	‖
AD821	Avery Dennison	Impinj Monza1	96-bit EPC num.	72 x 30	Al	Item, carton, pallet
AD833	‖	Impinj Monza3	‖	38 x 93.5	‖	‖
AD224	‖	NXP U-Code Gen2 XM	96/240-bit EPC num 512-bit user memory	95 x 7.4	‖	‖
AD824	‖	‖	‖	30 x 50	‖	Item
Dogbone	UPM Raflatac	Impinj Monza2	96-bit EPC num.	93 x 23	Al	Item, carton, pallet
Dogbone	‖	Impinj Monza4	128/480-bit EPC num. 512-bit user memory	86 x 24	‖	‖
Dogbone	‖	NXP U-Code Gen2 XM	96/240-bit EPC num 512-bit user memory	93 x 23	‖	‖
ShortDipole	‖	‖	‖	92 x 11	‖	‖

An Accurate System-Wide Anonymity Metric for Probabilistic Attacks

Rajiv Bagai, Huabo Lu, Rong Li, and Bin Tang

Department of Electrical Engineering and Computer Science
Wichita State University, Wichita, KS 67260-0083, USA
{rajiv.bagai,hxlu,rxli1,bin.tang}@wichita.edu

Abstract. We give a critical analysis of the system-wide anonymity metric of Edman et al. [3], which is based on the permanent value of a doubly-stochastic matrix. By providing an intuitive understanding of the permanent of such a matrix, we show that a metric that looks no further than this composite value is at best a rough indicator of anonymity. We identify situations where its inaccuracy is acute, and reveal a better anonymity indicator. Also, by constructing an information-preserving embedding of a smaller class of attacks into the wider class for which this metric was proposed, we show that this metric fails to possess desirable generalization properties. Finally, we present a new anonymity metric that does not exhibit these shortcomings. Our new metric is accurate as well as general.

Keywords: System-wide anonymity metric, Probabilistic attacks, Combinatorial matrix theory.

1 Introduction

Measuring the amount of anonymity that remains in an anonymity system in the aftermath of an attack has been a concern ever since a need for web anonymity systems was first recognized. Much of the work on anonymity metrics, such as that of Serjantov and Danezis [1] or of Diaz, Seys, Claessens and Preneel [2], has focused on measuring anonymity from the point of view of a single message or user. In contrast, Edman, Sivrikaya and Yener [3] proposed a *system-wide* metric for measuring an attacker's uncertainty in linking each input message of a system with the corresponding output message it exited the system as. They employ the framework of a complete bipartite graph between the system's input and output messages. Any perfect matching between nodes of this graph is a possible message communication pattern of the system. Anonymity in this framework is measured as the extent to which the single perfect matching reflecting the system's true communication pattern is hidden, after an attack, among all perfect matchings in the graph.

Edman et al. [3] gave metrics for measuring anonymity after two kinds of attacks, which we name as *infeasibility* and *probabilistic* attacks. Infeasibility attacks determine infeasibility of some edges in the system's complete bipartite

S. Fischer-Hübner and N. Hopper (Eds.): PETS 2011, LNCS 6794, pp. 117–133, 2011.

graph and arrive at a reduced graph by removing such edges. Probabilistic attacks, on the other hand, arrive at probabilities for each edge in the complete bipartite graph of being the actual communication pattern. Both metrics of [3] are based upon *permanent* values of certain underlying matrices.

Contributions of our paper are two-fold. We first demonstrate that while the metric given in [3] for infeasibility attacks is sound, the one for probabilistic attacks has two major shortcomings. We then propose a new, unified anonymity metric for both classes of attacks that overcomes these shortcomings.

By presenting an intuitive understanding of the permanent of a matrix for probabilistic attacks, we show that the first shortcoming of the metric in [3] for such attacks is that the permanent, which is a composite value, is at best a rough indicator of the system's anonymity level. We highlight situations in which the permanent is especially inadequate, and show that a better anonymity indicator is the breakdown of the permanent as a probability distribution on the graph's perfect matchings.

The second shortcoming shown of the metric in [3] for probabilistic attacks is that it is not a generalization of their metric for infeasibility attacks. We present an information-preserving embedding of infeasibility attacks into the wider class of probabilistic attacks to show that the former are just special cases of the latter, a relationship ideally reflected in the metrics of [3], but is not.

The rest of this paper is organized as follows. Section 2 contains an overview of the two metrics proposed by Edman et al. [3], namely for infeasibility and probabilistic attacks. Section 3 analyzes the metric of [3] for probabilistic attacks and exposes two shortcomings of it. The inadequacy of permanent as an indicator of anonymity is explained in Section 3.1, and its failure to correctly generalize infeasibility attacks in Section 3.2. These sections also develop much of the mathematical framework that is used to construct our new, unified metric, which is then presented in Section 4. Finally, Section 5 concludes our work and mentions some directions for future work.

2   Overview of a System-Wide Metric

In this section we give an overview of the anonymity metrics proposed by Edman, Sivrikaya, and Yener [3]. Their metrics give a *system-wide* measure of the anonymity provided to the messages sent via an anonymity system, rather than to any *single* message going through it.

Let S be the set of n input messages observed by an attacker having entered an anonymity system, and T be the set of output messages observed by the attacker having exited from that system. It is assumed that every input message eventually appears at the output, i.e. $|S| = |T| = n$. The anonymity system attempts to hide from the attacker which input message in S exited the system as which output message in T. It may employ a number of techniques to this end, such as outputting messages in an order other than the one in which they arrived to prevent sequence number association, or modifying message encoding by encryption/decryption to prevent message bit-pattern comparison, etc. The

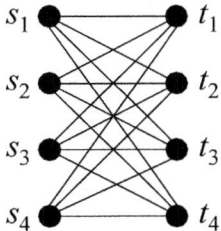

Fig. 1. Complete anonymity, when all edges in the complete bipartite graph between the system's input and output messages are equally likely

maximum anonymity this system can strive to achieve is when for any particular input message in S, each of the output messages in T is equally likely to be the one that input message in S exited the system as. This situation is depicted by the complete bipartite graph $K_{n,n}$ between S and T, as shown in Fig. 1 for $n = 4$. Any edge $\langle s_i, t_j \rangle$ in this graph indicates that the incoming message s_i could possibly have been the outgoing message t_j. All edges in the graph are considered equally likely.

Edman et al. in [3] consider two different classes of attacks. The first class is of attacks that label some of the edges (i.e. input-output pairings) in the above complete bipartite graph as infeasible. Removal by the attacker of these infeasible edges from the graph results in decreased anonymity. The latency-based attack of [3] and the route length attack of Serjantov and Danezis [1] are examples of such attacks. The second class considered in [3] is of attacks that arrive at probabilities for the edges in the graph of Fig. 1 of being the actual communication pattern. This also reduces the anonymity provided by the system, and an example of such a probabilistic attack is given in [3] as well.

For both of these classes of attacks, Edman et al. [3] propose anonymity metrics to reflect the level of anonymity remaining in the system in the aftermath of an attack. While our work in this paper is an improvement of just the second metric of [3], namely for probabilistic attacks, here we give an overview of both metrics of [3] as they are related.

2.1   A Metric for Infeasibility Attacks

An infeasibility attack removes from the system's complete bipartite graph, like the one shown in Fig. 1, edges that are determined by the attack to be infeasible due to some attacker's observation.

Edman et al. [3] give an example of such an attack that notes the times at which messages enter and exit the system, and uses its knowledge of the minimum and/or maximum latency of messages in the system. In this example, suppose each message entering the system always comes out after a delay of between 1 and 4 time units, and this characteristic of the system is known to the attacker. If 4 messages enter and exit this system at times shown in Fig. 2(a), then s_1 must be either t_1 or t_2, because the other outgoing messages, namely t_3

Entry times	Exit times
$s_1 = 1$	$t_1 = 4$
$s_2 = 2$	$t_2 = 5$
$s_3 = 4$	$t_3 = 7$
$s_4 = 5$	$t_4 = 8$

(a)

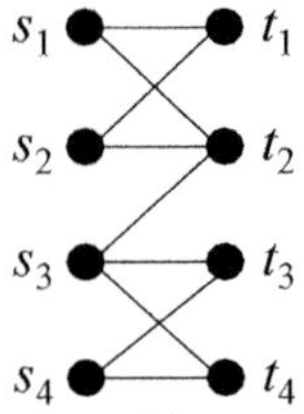

(b)

	t_1	t_2	t_3	t_4
s_1	1	1	0	0
s_2	1	1	0	0
s_3	0	1	1	1
s_4	0	0	1	1

(c)

Fig. 2. (a) Message entry and exit times observed by attacker. (b) Graph resulting from the attack, which removed edges it determined to be infeasible from system's complete bipartite graph. (c) Biadjacency matrix of this graph.

and t_4, are outside the possible latency window of s_1. Similar reasoning can be performed on all other messages to arrive at the reduced graph produced by this attack, shown in Fig. 2(b). Note that in this graph s_1 is connected to only t_1 and t_2, and not to t_3 or t_4, since the edges $\langle s_1, t_3 \rangle$ and $\langle s_1, t_4 \rangle$ were determined by the attack to be infeasible. The *biadjacency matrix* of this graph, a 0-1 matrix with a row for each input message and a column for each output message, is given in Fig. 2(c).

The number of perfect matchings between the system's input and output messages allowed by the bipartite graph resulting from such an attack is a good indication of the level of anonymity left in the system after the attack. It is well known (see, for example, Asratian et al. [4]) that this number is the same as the permanent of the biadjacency matrix of that graph. The *permanent* of any $n \times n$ matrix $M = [m_{ij}]$ of real numbers is defined as:

$$\text{per}(M) = \sum_{\pi \in S_n} m_{1\pi(1)} m_{2\pi(2)} \cdots m_{n\pi(n)},$$

where S_n is the set of all permutations of the set $\{1, 2, \ldots, n\}$. It can be seen that the graph of Fig. 2(b) allows 4 perfect matchings, and that is also the permanent of its biadjacency matrix in Fig. 2(c).

Given any n by n bipartite graph G resulting from an attack, it is assumed that G contains at least one perfect matching between the input and output messages, the one that corresponds to the true communication pattern. The minimum value of the permanent of its biadjacency matrix A is thus 1, when A contains exactly one 1 in each of its rows and columns. In this case, the system is considered to provide no anonymity as the attacker has identified the actual perfect matching, by ruling out all others. The largest number of perfect matchings in G is $n!$, when G is the complete bipartite graph $K_{n,n}$. Therefore, the maximum value of $\text{per}(A)$ is $n!$, when all entries in A are 1. In this case, the system is considered to provide maximum anonymity as the attacker has been unable to rule out any perfect matching as being the actual one.

Definition 1 (Infeasibility Attacks Metric). *Edman et al. [3] define a system's degree of anonymity after an infeasibility attack that results in an $n \times n$ biadjacency matrix A as:*

$$d(A) = \begin{cases} 0 & \text{if } n = 1, \\ \dfrac{log(per(A))}{log(n!)} & \text{otherwise.} \end{cases}$$

The above anonymity metric is reasonable as it compares the number of perfect matchings deemed feasible by the attack with their maximum number. Note that $0 \le d(A) \le 1$. Also, $d(A) = 0$ iff A has just one perfect matching, i.e. the system provides no anonymity, and $d(A) = 1$ iff $n > 1$ and A has $n!$ perfect matchings, i.e. full anonymity.

The matrix of Fig. 2(c) contains 4 perfect matchings out of the 24 maximum possible. By the above metric, the system's degree of anonymity after that attack is $log(4) / log(24) \approx 0.436$.

2.2 A Metric for Probabilistic Attacks

Unlike infeasibility attacks, that simply label edges of the system's complete bipartite graph as being feasible or infeasible, probabilistic attacks assign to each edge of the graph a real value between 0 and 1 as that edge's probability of being a part of the actual communication pattern.

As an example of this attack, consider the simple mix network shown in Fig. 3(a), with two mix nodes, M_1 and M_2, and four input as well as output messages. The message from mix M_1 to M_2 is internal to the network. As dis-

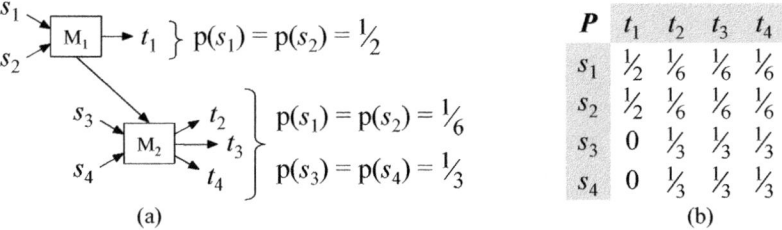

(a)   (b)

Fig. 3. (a) Message flow via a mix network, observed by attacker to arrive at probabilities of input-output message pairings. (b) Probability matrix of this network.

cussed in Serjantov and Danezis [1], suppose each mix node randomly shuffles all its input messages before sending them out, i.e. a message entering any mix node is equally likely to appear as any of that node's output messages. If this characteristic of mix nodes is known to the attacker, and the entire message flow pattern of the network (including internal messages) is visible to the attacker, the attacker can arrive at probabilities for each input-output message pairing of the system, as shown next to the output messages in Fig. 3(a). These probabilities are essentially labels produced by the attack on edges of the system's complete bipartite graph, and can be arranged as a *probability matrix* $P = [p_{ij}]$, as shown in Fig. 3(b). Any entry p_{ij} in this matrix contains the probability that the system's input message s_i appeared as its output message t_j. Real values from the closed interval $[0, 1]$ are used for probabilities.

A probability matrix produced by an attack is *doubly-stochastic*, i.e. the sum of all values in any of its rows or columns is 1. This follows from the assumption that each input message must appear as some output message, and each output message must have been one of the input messages. The maximum value of the permanent of an $n \times n$ probability matrix P is 1 (see Propositions 1 and 2 in Section 3.1), when P contains exactly one 1 in each of its rows and columns. In this case, the system is considered to provide no anonymity as the attacker has determined all input-output message pairings with full certainty. The minimum value of per(P) is well known to be $n!/n^n$, when all entries in P are $1/n$ (see, for example, Egorychev [5]). This corresponds to the system providing full anonymity.

Definition 2 (Probabilistic Attacks Metric). *For any probabilistic attack resulting in an $n \times n$ probability matrix P, Edman et al. [3] define the system's degree of anonymity after that attack as:*

$$D(P) = \begin{cases} 0 & \text{if } n = 1, \\ \dfrac{log(per(P))}{log(n!/n^n)} & \text{otherwise.} \end{cases}$$

The permanent of the matrix of Fig. 3(b) works out to $1/9 \approx 0.11111$, while the minimum value of the permanent of a 4×4 probability matrix is $4!/4^4 = 0.09375$. By the above metric, the system's degree of anonymity after this attack is $log(1/9) \, / \, log(4!/4^4) \approx 0.9282$.

A Note on Our Naming Convention and Figures. As the rest of this paper deals with two different types of matrices, namely *biadjacency* matrices that have 0 and 1 entries and *probability* matrices with real values in the closed interval $[0, 1]$ as their entries, we adopt a consistent naming convention while discussing them. The name A is always used for discussing any biadjacency matrix, and P for any probability matrix. When the type of a matrix under consideration is not important, we use the name M.

In figures, biadjacency matrices are displayed in the plain format, as in Fig. 2(c), and probability matrices with shaded row and column titles, as in Fig. 3(b).

Finally, the infeasibility attacks metric d of Edman et al. [3], given in Definition 1, is defined for biadjacency matrices, while their probabilistic attacks metric D, given in Definition 2, is for probability matrices.

3 Shortcomings of Metric for Probabilistic Attacks

It is instructive to recapitulate the ranges of the permanent of matrices considered so far. These ranges are shown in Fig. 4. There are some similarities

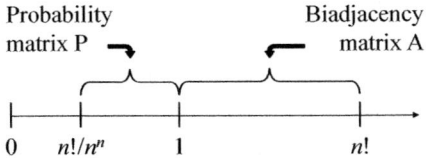

Fig. 4. Ranges of permanent: For an $n \times n$ biadjacency matrix A, per(A) is an integer from the set $\{1, 2, \ldots, n!\}$, and for an $n \times n$ probability matrix P, per(P) is a real value in the range $[n!/n^n, 1]$

between the metric expressions proposed by Edman et al. [3] for infeasibility attacks given by Definition 1 and probabilistic attacks given by Definition 2. First, in both cases, the argument of the logarithm in the denominator is the permanent of the matrix that corresponds to full anonymity. Second, the farther away from 1 the permanent of the underlying matrix (A for an infeasibility attack, and P for a probabilistic attack), the larger the system's degree of anonymity.

Despite these similarities, while the metric for infeasibility attacks in Definition 1 is sound, we show that the metric for probabilistic attacks in Definition 2 is not a good one. In this section, we demonstrate some shortcomings of this metric and, in the next section, we propose a better metric for probabilistic attacks.

3.1   Inadequacy of Matrix Permanent

The first shortcoming of the metric in Definition 2 for probabilistic attacks is that it is a function of just the permanent of the probability matrix. While the value of the permanent is necessary to take into account, we will show that it is not sufficient.

An Intuitive Understanding of Permanent. We begin by gaining a better understanding of the permanent of a matrix. Recall that S and T are the sets of n input and output messages of the system. Given any $n \times n$ biadjacency or probability matrix M, we define a *thread* of M to be any subset of its cells that contains exactly one cell from each row of M. Each thread therefore has exactly n cells. Additionally, a thread of M is a *diagonal* if no two of its cells lie in the same column of M. Let $T(M)$ and $X(M)$ denote, respectively, the sets of all threads and diagonals of M. Note that, a cell in the matrix M corresponds to an edge of the system's complete bipartite graph between S and T, a thread corresponds to a subgraph of that graph obtained by removing all but one edge connected to each $s \in S$ (i.e. a function from S to T), and a diagonal corresponds to a perfect matching between S and T. Clearly, M has n^n threads, of which $n!$ are diagonals.

Let the *weight* of any thread t of M, denoted $W(t)$, be the product of values in all cells of t. The following proposition follows immediately from the definitions so far.

Proposition 1. *For any biadjacency or probability matrix M,*

$$\sum_{x \in \mathcal{X}(M)} \mathcal{W}(x) = per(M).$$

In other words, $per(M)$ is the composite sum of weights of all diagonals of M. We first make the following important observation:

> *The values in M induce not just its permanent, but also a weight distribution on all its threads, including diagonals.*

Next, we improve our intuitive understanding of the permanent of a probability matrix by taking a closer look at the *information content* in it. The following proposition is also straightforward.

Proposition 2. *For any probability matrix P,*

$$\sum_{t \in \mathcal{T}(P)} \mathcal{W}(t) = 1.$$

Proof. Let P be $n \times n$. By definitions and algebraic rearrangement we have,

$$\sum_{t \in \mathcal{T}(P)} \mathcal{W}(t) = \sum_{j_1=1}^{n} \sum_{j_2=1}^{n} \cdots \sum_{j_n=1}^{n} p_{1j_1} p_{2j_2} \cdots p_{nj_n} = \prod_{i=1}^{n} (p_{i1} + p_{i2} + \cdots + p_{in}) = 1.$$

The last equality follows from the fact that the sum of each row of P is 1.   □

Consider the set T^S of all n^n functions $f : S \to T$. By assigning a probability to each edge in the set $S \times T$, the matrix P ends up inducing a probability on each function in T^S. The probability that P associates with any function $f \in T^S$ is $\prod \{p_{ij} \mid f(s_i) = t_j\}$, i.e. the weight of the thread in P corresponding to f. By Proposition 2, these weights add up to 1, i.e. we have a probability distribution on the entire set T^S. If a function f is now picked randomly from the set T^S according to the probability distribution defined by P, then by Proposition 1, $per(P)$ is the probability that f is a bijection, i.e. a perfect matching between S and T. The weights of the individual diagonals of P are the probabilities associated by P to their corresponding perfect matchings of being the true communication pattern of the system.[1]

A Better Indicator of Anonymity. Since the system's goal is to blend the true message communication pattern among others, the system's degree of anonymity should not be determined by simply answering the question:

> *What is the composite permanent of P?*

---

[1] As all column sums of P are also 1, P induces a similar probability distribution on the set S^T of all n^n functions $f : T \to S$. However, the bijections in S^T correspond to the bijections in T^S, and get identical probabilities in both distributions. This distribution therefore casts no further light on the meaning of $per(P)$.

The quintessential question is, rather:

How evenly is the permanent of P distributed as its diagonal weights?

By Proposition 1, it is possible for two matrices, say P_1 and P_2, to have identical permanents, but a significantly different diagonal weight distribution. If the weights of all diagonals of P_1 are closer to each other in comparison with those of P_2, then the system underlying P_1 should be considered as providing better anonymity, because the attack has better succeeded in exposing some of the perfect matchings of P_2 as being the likely ones.

The example in Fig. 5 illustrates this phenomenon on 3×3 matrices. The

P_1	t_1	t_2	t_3
s_1	.53	.25	.22
s_2	.20	.28	.52
s_3	.27	.47	.26

.0386 .1489   .0130 .0024   .0207 .0000

.1295 .0024   .0351 .0973   .0166 .0024

P_2	t_1	t_2	t_3
s_1	.53	.46	.01
s_2	.01	.53	.46
s_3	.46	.01	.53

Fig. 5. Two probability matrices with nearly identical permanent, 0.2535, but significantly different diagonal weight distributions (for each perfect matching, weights according to P_1 and P_2 shown of its corresponding diagonal)

diagonal weight distributions of these two matrices, in non-decreasing order, are:

$$P_1: \langle 0.0130, 0.0166, 0.0207, 0.0351, 0.0386, 0.1295 \rangle,$$
$$P_2: \langle 0.0000, 0.0024, 0.0024, 0.0024, 0.0973, 0.1489 \rangle.$$

Clearly, the weights of the diagonals of P_1 are more evenly distributed than those of P_2. Yet, $D(P_1) \approx D(P_2)$, because $\mathrm{per}(P_1) \approx \mathrm{per}(P_2)$. Later, in Section 4, we propose another metric that, by taking the diagonal weight distribution into account, ends up assigning almost twice as high degree of anonymity to the system underlying P_1 than to that of P_2.

Region of Acute Inadequacy of Permanent. Let the *diameter* of an $n \times n$ probability matrix P be the largest difference between weights of any two of its diagonals, i.e.

$$\max\{\mathcal{W}(x_1) - \mathcal{W}(x_2) \mid x_1, x_2 \in \mathcal{X}(P)\}.$$

Just as the permanent of P, its diameter is another rough indicator of the degree of anonymity of the underlying system. In general, the smaller the diameter, the higher the anonymity.

For any possible permanent value $p \in [n!/n^n, 1]$, let $\mathfrak{M}(p)$ be the set of all $n \times n$ probability matrices with permanent p. As illustrated in Fig. 6 for $n = 3$, for any value of p that is close to 1 or extremely close to $n!/n^n$, the diameters of all matrices in $\mathfrak{M}(p)$ are roughly the same. Using just p to determine the system's anonymity level for such matrices, although inaccurate, is somewhat acceptable. However, for any other value of p, i.e. in the middle range, matrices in $\mathfrak{M}(p)$ vary

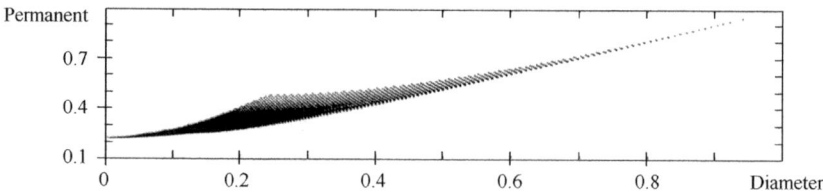

Fig. 6. Diameter spread of possible permanent values of 3×3 probability matrices

significantly in their diameters. It is in this region, where it is critical to consider the entire diagonal weight distribution of a probability matrix to determine the system's anonymity level, rather than just its permanent.

We end this discussion with the observation that the permanent of matrices in the example of Fig. 5 is approximately 0.2535. From Fig. 6 we can tell that the diameters of these two matrices are in fact not as far apart from each other as can be for some other two matrices with permanent, say around 0.4. Thus, even more convincing examples can be constructed to demonstrate the inadequacy of permanents as sole indicators of the anonymity level.

3.2   Incorrect Generalization of Infeasibility Attacks Metric

Another shortcoming of the metric in Definition 2 for probabilistic attacks is that it is not a generalization of the metric in Definition 1 for infeasibility attacks, despite the fact that probabilistic attacks are, in a sense, a generalization of infeasibility ones. We state this more precisely by giving an information-preserving embedding of infeasibility attacks into the wider class of probabilistic ones.

Diagonal Weight Profile. Let $\langle X_1, X_2, \ldots, X_{n!} \rangle$ be the sequence of diagonals of any $n \times n$ matrix M, ordered by the lexicographic ordering on their underlying index sets. In other words, if $\{(1, i_1), (2, i_2), \ldots, (n, i_n)\}$ is the set of indices of cells in a diagonal X_i, and $\{(1, j_1), (2, j_2), \ldots, (n, j_n)\}$ is the set of indices of cells in a diagonal X_j, then $i < j$ iff for some c, $i_c < j_c$ and for all $k < c$, $i_k = j_k$.

We define the *diagonal weight profile* (or just *profile*) of M to be the normalized sequence of weights of diagonals in the above sequence, given by:

$$\text{profile}(M) = \frac{1}{\text{per}(M)} \langle \mathcal{W}(X_1), \mathcal{W}(X_2), \ldots, \mathcal{W}(X_{n!}) \rangle.$$

As this paper only deals with matrices that have strictly positive permanents, the above sequence is well defined. A fixed ordering of diagonal weights in profiles, such as the lexicographic one given above, together with normalization, enable us to compare weights of corresponding diagonals across matrices.

From Proposition 1, it is seen that $\text{profile}(M)$ is a probability distribution on the diagonals of M, i.e. perfect matchings of its underlying bipartite graph. From the point of view of a *system-wide* anonymity metric, this is the most vital piece of information contained in M.

A Profile-Preserving Embedding. Let A be an $n \times n$ biadjacency matrix resulting from an infeasibility attack. Exactly $\text{per}(A)$ values in $\text{profile}(A)$ are $1/\text{per}(A)$, and the remaining values are 0. The metric $d(A)$ of Definition 1 is based on the premise that each of the $\text{per}(A)$ feasible perfect matchings corresponding to the nonzero values in $\text{profile}(A)$ are equally likely, and the remaining are not possible. We now proceed to construct a unique probability matrix C_A with the same profile as A. We will then show that while it is desirable and expected that $D(C_A) = d(A)$, in general it is not so.

We begin by observing that the reduced bipartite graph underlying A may contain edges that do not appear in any perfect matching as, for example, the edge $\langle s_3, t_2 \rangle$ in Fig. 2(b) and (c). Such nonzero entries in A are harmless since, by not being on any diagonal with nonzero weight, their presence affects neither $\text{per}(A)$ nor $\text{profile}(A)$, thus also not $d(A)$. Let $\hat{A} = [\hat{a}_{ij}]$ be the matrix identical to A, except that $\hat{A}$ contains a 0 entry for all such edges.

Now, let $\mathfrak{P}(A)$ be the set of all possible (doubly-stochastic) probability matrices conforming to the graph underlying A, i.e.

$$\mathfrak{P}(A) = \{ n \times n \text{ probability matrix } P = [p_{ij}] \mid$$
$$p_{ij} = 0 \text{ if } \hat{a}_{ij} = 0, \text{ for all } i, j\}.$$

In other words, $\mathfrak{P}(A)$ contains all possible probability distributions on the edges declared feasible by A. It is well known that $\mathfrak{P}(A)$ is nonempty iff $\text{per}(A) > 0$ (see, for example, Theorem 2.2.3 in Bapat and Raghavan [6]). Observe that any $P \in \mathfrak{P}(A)$ has no less information than A as it contains some probability distribution *in addition to* the feasibility information in A, i.e. an attack resulting in P is at least as strong as one resulting in A. It is therefore expected and desirable that $D(P) \leq d(A)$, but that does not always hold as the example matrix in Fig. 7 illustrates. This matrix, P, is chosen arbitrarily from $\mathfrak{P}(A)$, for the biadjacency matrix A in Fig. 2(c). While $d(A) \approx 0.436$, as computed at the end of Section 2.1, we have that $D(P) \approx 0.491$, a larger value. This phenomenon does not conform to the intuition behind anonymity metrics.

Let an $n \times n$ matrix $S = [s_{ij}]$ be called a *scaling* of an $n \times n$ matrix $M = [m_{ij}]$ if for some multiplier vectors $R = \langle r_1, r_2, \ldots, r_n \rangle$ and $C = \langle c_1, c_2, \ldots, c_n \rangle$ with strictly positive values, $s_{ij} = r_i m_{ij} c_j$, for all i, j. It is easily verified that the weight of any diagonal of S is the weight of the corresponding diagonal of M,

P	t_1	t_2	t_3	t_4
s_1	½	½	0	0
s_2	½	½	0	0
s_3	0	0	¼	¾
s_4	0	0	¾	¼

Fig. 7. An example $P \in \mathfrak{P}(A)$, for biadjacency matrix A of Fig. 2(c)

multiplied by the scaling factor $\lambda = \prod_{i=1}^{n} r_i c_i$. Thus, $\text{per}(S) = \lambda \cdot \text{per}(M)$ as well. This leads to the following proposition.

Proposition 3. *If S is a scaling of M, then $\text{profile}(S) = \text{profile}(M)$.*

We let $\mathfrak{S}(M)$ denote the set of all scalings of M.

Theorem 1. *For any $n \times n$ biadjacency matrix A resulting from an infeasibility attack, $\mathfrak{P}(A) \cap \mathfrak{S}(\hat{A})$ is a singleton set.*

Proof. When $\text{per}(A) > 0$, that the intersection is nonempty was established by Brualdi, Parter and Schneider [7]. Uniqueness, when nonempty, follows from the fact that distinct doubly-stochastic matrices cannot have identical profiles, given as Corollary 2.6.6 in Bapat and Raghavan [6]. □

The sole member of $\mathfrak{P}(A) \cap \mathfrak{S}(\hat{A})$ is the unique *canonical* probability matrix for A, denoted $\mathcal{C}_A$. It is the only doubly-stochastic matrix whose profile is identical to that of A. Fig. 8 shows an example matrix A, along with its $\mathcal{C}_A$. The matrix $\mathcal{C}_A$

A	t_1	t_2	t_3
s_1	0	1	1
s_2	1	0	1
s_3	1	1	1

$\mathcal{C}_A$	t_1	t_2	t_3
s_1	0	$(\sqrt{5}-1)/2$	$(3-\sqrt{5})/2$
s_2	$(\sqrt{5}-1)/2$	0	$(3-\sqrt{5})/2$
s_3	$(3-\sqrt{5})/2$	$(3-\sqrt{5})/2$	$\sqrt{5}-2$

Fig. 8. A biadjacency matrix A and its canonical probability matrix $\mathcal{C}_A$

can be viewed as the result of a probabilistic attack that has arrived at the same conclusion as the infeasibility attack resulting in A, in that the sets of perfect matchings called feasible by these attacks coincide and all those feasible perfect matchings are deemed equally likely by both attacks. As these two attacks are equally strong (in fact, identical), it is desirable that $D(\mathcal{C}_A) = d(A)$.

For the matrices shown in Fig. 8, $\text{per}(A) = 3$ and $\text{per}(\mathcal{C}_A) = 3(5\sqrt{5} - 11)/2$. However, $\text{profile}(A) = \text{profile}(\mathcal{C}_A) = \langle 0, 0, \frac{1}{3}, \frac{1}{3}, \frac{1}{3}, 0 \rangle$. And while $d(A) \approx 0.6131$, we have that $D(\mathcal{C}_A) \approx 0.8693 \neq d(A)$. Again, an undesirable behavior of the D metric. In Section 4, we present a new metric Δ that has the property $\Delta(\mathcal{C}_A) = d(A)$, for all biadjacency matrices A.

Construction of Canonical Probability Matrix. As for the construction of $\mathcal{C}_A$ from a given A, recall that $\mathcal{C}_A$ is a scaling of $\hat{A}$ with some row-multiplier vector R and column-multiplier vector C. For the example of Fig. 8, $A = \hat{A}$, and let $R = \langle r_1, r_2, r_3 \rangle$ and $C = \langle c_1, c_2, c_3 \rangle$. As the sums of the rows and columns of $\mathcal{C}_A$ should be 1, we get the following 6 equations:

$$r_1(c_2 + c_3) = 1 \qquad r_2(c_1 + c_3) = 1 \qquad r_3(c_1 + c_2 + c_3) = 1$$
$$c_1(r_2 + r_3) = 1 \qquad c_2(r_1 + r_3) = 1 \qquad c_3(r_1 + r_2 + r_3) = 1$$

We seek solutions to the above system of equations in which all r_i's and c_i's are positive. One solution for this particular scaling is:

$$R = \left\langle \frac{3 - \sqrt{5}}{2}, \frac{3 - \sqrt{5}}{2}, \sqrt{5} - 2 \right\rangle, \quad C = \left\langle \frac{1 + \sqrt{5}}{2}, \frac{1 + \sqrt{5}}{2}, 1 \right\rangle.$$

Although there are multiple such solutions, Sinkhorn [8] showed that all solutions are unique up to a scalar factor, i.e. if (R_1, C_1) and (R_2, C_2) are solutions to the above, then for some $\alpha > 0$, $R_2 = R_1 \alpha$ and $C_2 = C_1/\alpha$. However, due to the uniqueness of C_A all solutions lead to the same resulting matrix.

Sinkhorn and Knopp [9] gave another interesting characterization of C_A as the limit of an infinite sequence of matrices. Let f, g and h be functions from and to $n \times n$ real matrices, defined as follows:

$$f(M)_{ij} = M_{ij} \,/\, \textstyle\sum_{k=1}^{n} M_{ik} \quad (f \text{ normalizes each row of } M)$$
$$g(M)_{ij} = M_{ij} \,/\, \textstyle\sum_{k=1}^{n} M_{kj} \quad (g \text{ normalizes each column of } M)$$
$$h(M) = g(f(M))$$

Then, $C_A = \lim_{k \to \infty} h^k(A)$. In other words, a procedure that alternately normalizes all rows followed by all columns of A, ad infinitum, would converge to C_A. The accumulated row and column multipliers along the way also converge to the correct R and C values. However, as A contains just 0-1 values, multipliers accumulated after any finite number of iterations are only rational. As the example in Fig. 8 shows, the final solution can be irrational, the limit of an infinite sequence of rational approximations. So in general, this procedure requires an infinite number of iterations. A number of efficient algorithms have therefore been considered, as in Kalantari and Khachiyan [10] and Linial, Samorodnitsky and Wigderson [11], for producing in a finite number of steps, approximate solutions that are within acceptable error bounds.

4   A More Accurate Metric for Probabilistic Attacks

We now present a new metric for probabilistic attacks that overcomes the shortcomings mentioned in the previous section of the metric D of Edman et al. [3]. By being sensitive to the distribution of the permanent of a given probability matrix over its diagonals, the new metric results in a more accurate measurement of the underlying system's degree of anonymity. Furthermore, this metric has the welcome trait of correctly treating probabilistic attacks as generalizations of infeasibility attacks. This feature is exploited to make just this one metric suffice for both kinds of attacks.

The fundamental premise upon which our metric is constructed is that the permanent of a matrix can be broken down into a probability distribution over its diagonals, i.e. the perfect matchings of the system's complete bipartite graph. The profile of the matrix is essentially that distribution.

Ever since the works of Serjantov and Danezis [1] and Diaz et al. [2], Shannon entropy of a probability distribution is a well accepted measure of the system's degree of anonymity. We employ the same technique over the profile of the matrix as a measure of the attacker's uncertainty of which perfect matching is the system's true communication pattern.

Definition 3 (Unified Metric). *Let M be a given $n \times n$ biadjacency or probability matrix resulting from an attack, with profile$(M) = \langle w_1, w_2, \ldots, w_{n!} \rangle$. We define the underlying system's* degree of anonymity *after this attack as:*

$$\Delta(M) = \begin{cases} 0 & \text{if } n = 1, \\ \dfrac{-\sum_{i=1}^{n!} w_i \cdot log(w_i)}{log(n!)} & \text{otherwise.} \end{cases}$$

In the above summation, a subexpression $0 \cdot log(0)$ is interpreted as 0.

Observe that the above metric Δ is for biadjacency *as well as* probability matrices, whereas the metrics of Edman et al. [3] for these two kinds of matrices were separate. Their metric d, given in Definition 1, was for biadjacency matrices, while their metric D, given in Definition 2, was for probability matrices. We first establish that for biadjacency matrices, our Δ coincides with d.

Theorem 2. *For any biadjacency matrix A, $d(A) = \Delta(A) = \Delta(\mathcal{C}_A)$.*

Proof. The second equality follows from the fact that A and $\mathcal{C}_A$ have identical profiles. To show the first equality, we recall from Section 3.2 that exactly per(A) values in profile(A) are $1/\text{per}(A)$, and the remaining values are 0. The numerator of the expression in Definition 3 thus becomes:

$$-\text{per}(A) \left[\frac{1}{\text{per}(A)} \cdot log \left(\frac{1}{\text{per}(A)} \right) \right] = log(\text{per}(A)),$$

which is the numerator of the expression in Definition 1 of Section 2.1.   □

To understand the properties of our new metric better, we revisit some of our earlier examples. For the probability matrices P_1 and P_2 of Fig. 5 with equal permanent value of about 0.2535, we had that $D(P_1) \approx D(P_2) \approx 0.9124$. However, $\Delta(P_1) \approx 0.8030$, about twice as high as $\Delta(P_2) \approx 0.4544$. Our new metric Δ recognizes that the profile of P_2 is significantly more uneven than that of P_1, thus assigning the system underlying P_2 a far lower degree of anonymity.

For the biadjacency matrix of Fig. 2(c), we have $\Delta(A) = d(A) \approx 0.436$. The probability matrix P of Fig. 7 was arbitrarily chosen from the set $\mathfrak{P}(A)$. Of the 24 values in profile(P), $\langle \frac{1}{20}, \frac{9}{20}, \frac{1}{20}, \frac{9}{20} \rangle$ is the subsequence of nonzero values. While we saw that $D(P) \approx 0.491 > d(A)$, we have that $\Delta(P) \approx 0.3204 < d(A)$. This behavior conforms with our intuition that P has more information than A. The following theorem shows that this phenomenon is guaranteed by Δ.

Theorem 3. *For any biadjacency matrix A and $P \in \mathfrak{P}(A)$, such that $P \neq \mathcal{C}_A$, $\Delta(P) < \Delta(A)$.*

Proof. Let per$(A) = t$. Then, profile(A) has t nonzero values, and each of those values is $1/t$. Let $p_1, p_2, \ldots, p_t$ be the corresponding values in profile(P). As these are the only diagonals of P that may have nonzero weights, their sum is 1. We need to show that:

$$-\sum_{i=1}^{t} p_i \cdot \log(p_i) < -\sum_{i=1}^{t} (1/t) \cdot \log(1/t).$$

Although this property of Shannon entropy is well known in information theory (see, for example, Kapur [12] for a proof based on Jensen's inequality), here we give a short proof.

It is easily seen that, for all $\beta > 0$, we have $2\beta \leq 2^{\beta}$, with equality iff $\beta = 1$. Taking logarithms to the base 2 gives $1 + \log(\beta) \leq \beta$. As we interpret $0 \cdot \log(0) = 0$, we can substitute $\beta = (1/t)/p_i$, and simplify, to get that for all i, $p_i - p_i \cdot \log(p_i) \leq (1/t) - p_i \cdot \log(1/t)$, with equality iff $p_i = 1/t$. Summation over all i gives:

$$-\sum_{i=1}^{t} p_i \cdot \log(p_i) \leq \log(t) = -\sum_{i=1}^{t} (1/t) \cdot \log(1/t).$$

As $P \neq C_A$ and distinct doubly-stochastic matrices cannot have the same profile, we have that for some i, $p_i \neq (1/t)$, leading to a strict inequality.   □

We end this section with an example that demonstrates how different our new metric Δ can be from the old metric D of Edman et al. [3]. Fig. 9 shows two matrices, P_1 and P_2 for which, according to the D metric, P_1 seems to result in less anonymity than P_2, as $D(P_1) \approx 0.5658 < 0.7564 \approx D(P_2)$. However,

P_1	t_1	t_2	t_3
s_1	.04	.04	.92
s_2	.48	.49	.03
s_3	.48	.47	.05

P_2	t_1	t_2	t_3
s_1	.65	.01	.34
s_2	.01	.34	.65
s_3	.34	.65	.01

Fig. 9. Two probability matrices for which $D(P_1) < D(P_2)$, but $\Delta(P_1) > \Delta(P_2)$

$\Delta(P_1) \approx 0.4132 > 0.2750 \approx \Delta(P_2)$, i.e. according to our new metric, P_1 results in higher anonymity than P_2.

5   Conclusions and Future Work

Edman, Sivrikaya and Yener [3] introduced a method for arriving at a system-wide measure of the level of anonymity provided by a system. Their approach is based upon a complete bipartite graph that models all possible input and output message associations of the system. By rendering infeasible some edges of this graph, an *infeasibility* attack results in a reduced graph, thereby lowering anonymity. They proposed adopting the permanent of the biadjacency matrix of this reduced graph to determine the amount of anonymity remaining in the system in the aftermath of the attack.

Edman et al. [3] then suggest adopting a similar technique for a wider class of *probabilistic* attacks that, instead of removing infeasible edges from the system's complete bipartite graph, assign probabilities to all edges.

In this paper, we argue that while the metric given in [3] for the narrower class of infeasibility attacks is sound, their metric for probabilistic attacks has shortcomings. We show why using just the permanent of the underlying matrix for probabilistic attacks is inaccurate, as it at best gives only a rough measure of the system's anonymity level. We also show that this technique fails to correctly treat probabilistic attacks as generalizations of infeasibility ones.

We then present a new metric that overcomes these shortcomings. By recognizing that the permanent of a matrix can be broken down into a probability distribution on the perfect matchings of the underlying bipartite graph, our new metric provides an accurate measure of anonymity. It also has the desirable property of being a unified metric for both classes of attacks.

The basic metric of [3] for infeasibility attacks has since been extended for modified scenarios. Gierlichs et al. [13] enhanced it for situations where system users send or receive multiple messages. The equivalence relation on perfect matchings, induced by such multiplicity, causes a reduction in anonymity. Bagai and Tang [14] analyzed the effect of employing data caching within the mix network. Their modified metric captures an increase in anonymity due to such caching. We leave such extensions to the new metric proposed in this paper as future work.

Acknowledgements. We would like to thank Andrew Bradley of Stanford University for helpful discussions on matrix scaling that led to the example of Fig. 8. The research described in this paper has been partially supported by the United States Navy Engineering Logistics Office contract no. N41756-08-C-3077.

References

1. Serjantov, A., Danezis, G.: Towards an information theoretic metric for anonymity. In: Proceedings of the 2nd Privacy Enhancing Technologies Workshop, San Francisco, USA, pp. 41–53 (2002)
2. Diaz, C., Seys, S., Claessens, J., Preneel, B.: Towards measuring Anonymity. In: Proceedings of the 2nd Privacy Enhancing Technologies Workshop, San Francisco, USA, pp. 54–68 (2002)
3. Edman, M., Sivrikaya, F., Yener, B.: A combinatorial approach to measuring anonymity. In: IEEE International Conference on Intelligence and Security Informatics, New Brunswick, USA, pp. 356–363 (2007)
4. Asratian, A., Denley, T., Häggkvist, R.: Bipartite graphs and their applications. Cambridge University Press, Cambridge (1998)
5. Egorychev, G.: The solution of van der Waerden's problem for permanents. Advances in Mathematics 42(3), 299–305 (1981)
6. Bapat, R., Raghavan, T.: Nonnegative matrices and applications. Cambridge University Press, Cambridge (1997)

7. Brualdi, R., Parter, S., Schneider, H.: The diagonal equivalence of a nonnegative matrix to a stochastic matrix. J. Mathematical Analysis and Applications 16(1), 31–50 (1966)
8. Sinkhorn, R.: A relationship between arbitrary positive matrices and doubly stochastic matrices. Annals of Mathematical Statistics 35, 876–879 (1964)
9. Sinkhorn, R., Knopp, P.: Concerning nonnegative matrices and doubly stochastic matrices. Pacific Journal of Mathematics 21(2), 343–348 (1967)
10. Kalantari, B., Khachiyan, L.: On the complexity of nonnegative matrix scaling. Linear Algebra and its Applications 240, 87–103 (1996)
11. Linial, N., Samorodnitsky, A., Wigderson, A.: A deterministic strongly polynomial algorithm for matrix scaling and approximate permanents. Combinatorica 20(4), 545–568 (2000)
12. Kapur, J.: Maximum entropy models in science and engineering, 2nd edn. New Age International Publishers (2009)
13. Gierlichs, B., Troncoso, C., Diaz, C., Preneel, B., Verbauwhede, I.: Revisiting a combinatorial approach toward measuring anonymity. In: Proceedings of the ACM Workshop on Privacy in the Electronic Society, Alexandria, USA, pp. 111–116 (2008)
14. Bagai, R., Tang, B.: Data caching for enhancing anonymity. In: Proceedings of the 25th IEEE International Conference on Advanced Information Networking and Applications, Singapore, pp. 135–142 (2011)

DefenestraTor: Throwing Out Windows in Tor

Mashael AlSabah[1], Kevin Bauer[1,*], Ian Goldberg[1], Dirk Grunwald[2],
Damon McCoy[3], Stefan Savage[3], and Geoffrey M. Voelker[3]

[1] University of Waterloo
{malsabah,k4bauer,iang}@cs.uwaterloo.ca
[2] University of Colorado
grunwald@colorado.edu
[3] University of California, San Diego
{dlmccoy,savage,voelker}@cs.ucsd.edu

Abstract. Tor is one of the most widely used privacy enhancing technologies for achieving online anonymity and resisting censorship. While
conventional wisdom dictates that the level of anonymity offered by Tor
increases as its user base grows, the most significant obstacle to Tor
adoption continues to be its slow performance. We seek to enhance Tor's
performance by offering techniques to control congestion and improve
flow control, thereby reducing unnecessary delays.

To reduce congestion, we first evaluate small fixed-size circuit windows
and a dynamic circuit window that adaptively re-sizes in response to
perceived congestion. While these solutions improve web page response
times and require modification only to exit routers, they generally offer
poor flow control and slower downloads relative to Tor's current design.
To improve flow control while reducing congestion, we implement *N23*,
an ATM-style per-link algorithm that allows Tor routers to explicitly
cap their queue lengths and signal congestion via back-pressure. Our
results show that N23 offers better congestion and flow control, resulting
in improved web page response times and faster page loads compared to
Tor's current design and other window-based approaches. We also argue
that our proposals do not enable any new attacks on Tor users' privacy.

1 Introduction

Tor [10] is a distributed circuit-switching overlay network consisting of over
two-thousand volunteer-run *Tor routers* operating around the world. Tor clients
achieve anonymity by source-routing their traffic through three Tor routers using
onion routing [14].

Context. Conventional wisdom dictates that the level of anonymity provided by
Tor increases as its user base grows [8]. Another important, but often overlooked,
benefit of a larger user base is that it reduces suspicion placed on users simply
because they use Tor. Today, there are an estimated 150 to 250 thousand daily
Tor users [20]. However, this estimate has not increased significantly since 2008.

---

* Work was done at University of Colorado and University of California, San Diego.

S. Fischer-Hübner and N. Hopper (Eds.): PETS 2011, LNCS 6794, pp. 134–154, 2011.

One of the most significant road blocks to Tor adoption is its excessively high and variable delays, which inhibit interactive applications such as web browsing. Many prior studies have diagnosed a variety of causes of this high latency (see Dingledine and Murdoch [11] for a concise summary). Most of these studies have noted that the queuing delays often dominate the network latencies of routing packets through the three routers. These high queuing delays are, in part, caused by bandwidth bottlenecks that exist along a client's chosen circuit. As high-bandwidth routers forward traffic to lower-bandwidth downstream routers, the high-bandwidth router may be able to read data faster than it can write it. Because Tor currently has no explicit signaling mechanism to notify senders of this congestion, packets must be queued along the circuit, introducing potentially long and unnecessary delays for clients. While recent proposals seek to re-engineer Tor's transport design, in part, to improve its ability to handle congestion [18,29,36], these proposals face significant deployment challenges.

Improving Congestion and Flow Control. To reduce the delays introduced by uncontrolled congestion in Tor, we design, implement, and evaluate two classes of congestion and flow control. First, we leverage Tor's existing end-to-end window-based flow control framework and evaluate the performance benefits of using small fixed-size circuit windows, reducing the amount of data in flight that may contribute to congestion. We also design and implement a dynamic window resizing algorithm that uses increases in end-to-end circuit round-trip time as an implicit signal of incipient congestion. Similar solutions are being considered for adoption in Tor to help relieve congestion [6], and we offer a critical analysis to help inform the discussion. Window-based solutions are appealing, since they require modifications only to exit routers.

Second, we offer a fresh approach to congestion and flow control inspired by standard techniques from Asynchronous Transfer Mode (ATM) networks. We implement a per-link credit-based flow control algorithm called N23 [19] that allows Tor routers to explicitly bound their queues and signal congestion via back-pressure, reducing unnecessary delays and memory consumption. While N23 offers these benefits over the window-based approaches, its road to deployment may be slower, as it may require all routers along a circuit to upgrade.

Evaluation. We conduct a holistic experimental performance evaluation of the proposed algorithms using the ModelNet network emulation platform [35] with realistic traffic models. We show that the window-based approaches offer up to 65% faster web page response times relative to Tor's current design. However, they offer poor flow control, causing bandwidth under-utilization and ultimately resulting in poor download time. In contrast, our N23 experiments show that delay-sensitive web clients experience up to 65% faster web page responses and a 32% decrease in web page load times compared to Tor's current design.

2   Tor Background

The Tor network is a decentralized circuit-switching overlay consisting of volunteer-run Tor routers hosted around the world. Tor offers anonymity to clients by

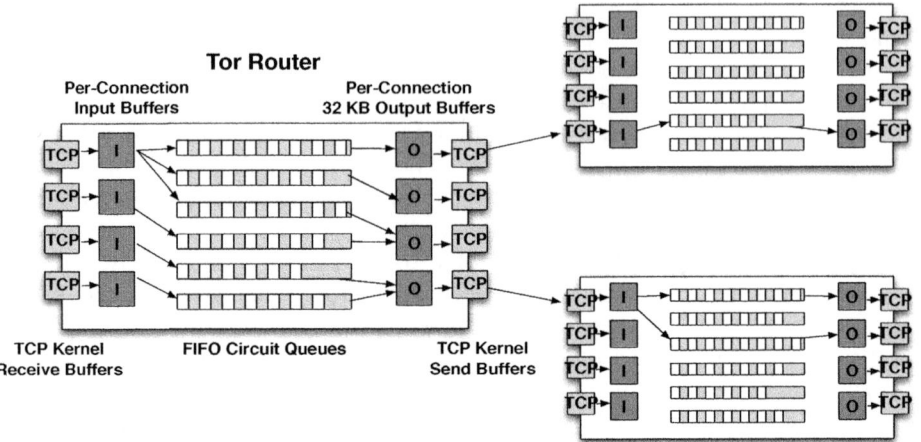

Fig. 1. A Tor router's queuing architecture

employing a layered encryption scheme [14] with three Tor routers. All data is sent in fixed-sized 512-byte units called cells. In general, the client selects routers to use on a circuit taking into account their bandwidth capacities, in order to balance the traffic load over the available router bandwidth. The first router on a circuit (called an "entry guard") is chosen carefully to reduce the threat of profiling and the predecessor attack [38]. Upon receiving a cell, the router removes its layer of encryption and forwards the cell to the next router on the circuit. Once the final (exit) router in the circuit removes its layer of encryption, the client's traffic is forwarded to the destination. A prior study found that the majority of Tor traffic by connection is interactive HTTP [21], and most of this traffic volume flows from the destination to the client. More details about Tor can be found in its design document [10] and its evolving protocol specification [9].

3   Tor's Approach to Congestion and Flow Control

Since the Tor network consists of volunteer-run routers from across the world, these routers have varying and often limited amounts of bandwidth available to relay Tor traffic. Consequently, as clients choose their circuits, some routers have large amounts of bandwidth to offer, while others may be bandwidth bottlenecks. In order for Tor to offer the highest degree of performance possible, it is necessary to have effective mechanisms in place to ensure steady flow control, while also detecting and controlling congestion. In this section, we discuss the many features that directly or indirectly impact congestion and flow control in Tor.

3.1   Congestion and Flow Control Mechanisms

Pairwise TCP. All packets sent between Tor routers are guaranteed to be delivered reliably and in-order by using TCP transport. As a result of using TCP, communications between routers can be protected with TLS link encryption. However, several circuits may be multiplexed over the same TCP connections, which could result in an unfair application of TCP's congestion control [29].

Tiered Output Buffers. Each Tor router's internal queuing architecture is illustrated in Figure 1. When a Tor router receives a cell on one of its TCP connections, the cell is first copied from the connection's receive kernel buffer into an application-layer input buffer to be decrypted. Next, the cell is pushed onto a FIFO *circuit queue* for the cell's respective circuit. For each outgoing TCP connection, a FIFO *output buffer* is maintained. The output buffer has a fixed size of 32 KiB, while the circuit queue has no explicit bound, but the circuit window size restricts how many cells may be in flight (described below). Since multiple circuits are often multiplexed over the same TCP connection, when there is space available in the outgoing connection's respective output buffer, the router must choose which circuits' cells to copy onto the output buffer. Initially, cells were chosen by round-robin selection across circuits. Recently, circuit prioritization has been proposed to give burstier circuits that likely correspond to interactive traffic priority over long-lived, bulk circuits [34].

Circuit and Stream Windows. Tor uses two layers of end-to-end window-based flow control between the exit router and the client to ensure steady flow control. First, a *circuit window* restricts how many cells may be in flight per circuit. By default, Tor uses a fixed 500 KiB (1000 cell) circuit window. For every 50 KiB (100 cells) received, an acknowledgment cell called a SENDME is sent, informing the sender that they may forward another 100 cells to the receiver[1].

Within each circuit window is a *stream window* of 250 KiB (500 cells) to provide flow control (or fairness) within a circuit. The receiver replies with a stream-level SENDME for every 25 KiB (50 cells) received. On receiving a stream-level SENDME, the sender may forward another 50 cells.

Both the stream-level and circuit-level windows are relatively large and static. To illustrate how this can degrade performance, consider the following scenario. Suppose a client downloads files through a circuit consisting of 10 MiB/s entry and exit routers and a 128 KiB/s middle router. Since the exit router can read data from the destination server faster than it can write it to its outgoing connection with the middle router, and the reli-

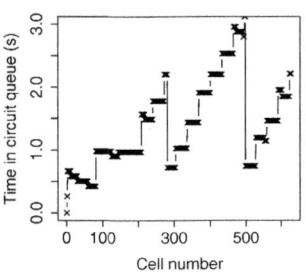

Fig. 2. The exit router's circuit queue delays for a 300 KiB download

able TCP semantics preclude routers from dropping cells to signal congestion, the exit router must buffer up to one full circuit window (500 KiB) worth of cells. Furthermore, as shown in Figure 2, these cells often sit idly for several seconds while the buffer is slowly emptied as SENDME cells are received. Since cells may

---

[1] Due to a bug, clients running Tor 0.0.0–0.2.1.19 erroneously reply with circuit-level SENDME cells after receiving 101 cells (rather than 100 cells).

travel down a circuit in large groups of up to 500 KiB followed by periods of silence while the exit router waits for SENDME replies, Tor's window-based flow control does not always keep a steady flow of cells in flight.

Token Bucket Rate Limiting. In order to allow routers to set limits on the amount of bandwidth they wish to devote to transiting Tor traffic, Tor offers token bucket rate limiting. Briefly, a router starts with a fixed amount of tokens, and decrements their token count as cells are sent or received. When the router's token count reaches zero, the router must wait to send or receive until the tokens are refilled. To reduce Tor's CPU utilization, tokens are refilled only once per second. However, it has been previously observed that refilling the tokens so infrequently contributes in part to Tor's overall delays [5].

3.2   Alternate Proposals to Reduce Congestion

There have been several recent proposals aimed specifically at reducing Tor's congestion. First, Tor has incorporated adaptive circuit-building timeouts that measure the time it takes to build a circuit, and eliminate circuits that take an excessively long time to construct [4]. The intuition is that circuits that build slowly are highly congested, and would in turn offer the user poor performance. While this approach likely improves the users' quality of service in some cases, it does not help to relieve congestion that may occur at one or more of the routers on a circuit *after* the circuit has been constructed.

In addition, user-level rate limiting has been proposed to throttle over-active or bulk downloading users. Here, the idea is to reduce the overall bandwidth consumption by bulk downloaders by using per-connection token bucket rate limiting at the entry guard. Early experiments indicate faster downloads for small file downloaders (the majority of Tor users), while harming bulk downloaders [7].

Finally, incentive schemes [17,24] have been proposed to reward users for operating fast Tor routers by offering them prioritized service. These proposals seek to reduce congestion and improve performance by increasing the bandwidth available for relaying Tor users' traffic.

4   Improving Tor's Congestion and Flow Control

Our primary goal is to improve Tor's performance, specifically by better understanding and improving Tor's congestion and flow control. We consider two broad classes of solutions. First, we wish to understand how much improvement is possible simply by adjusting Tor's existing end-to-end window-based flow control mechanisms to reduce the amount of data in flight, and thereby mitigate congestion. We also evaluate an end-to-end congestion control technique that enables exit Tor routers to infer incipient congestion by regarding increases in end-to-end round-trip time as a congestion signal. Second, we consider a fresh approach to congestion and flow control in Tor, eliminating Tor's end-to-end window-based flow control entirely, and replacing it with ATM-style, per-link flow control that caps routers' queue lengths and applies back-pressure to upstream routers to signal congestion.

4.1   Improving Tor's Existing End-to-End Flow Control

We first consider whether adjusting Tor's current window-based flow control can offer significant performance improvements. Keeping Tor's window-based mechanisms is appealing, as solutions based on Tor's existing flow control framework may be deployed immediately, requiring modifications only to the exit routers, not clients or non-exit routers.

Small Fixed-size Circuit Windows. The smallest circuit window size possible without requiring both senders and receivers to upgrade is 50 KiB (100 cells, or one circuit-level SENDME interval). We evaluate how fixed 50 KiB circuit windows impact clients' performance[2].

Dynamic Circuit Windows. It has been shown that protocols that use a small, fixed end-to-end window may achieve suboptimal throughput [28]. To avoid a potential loss in throughput that could result from an under-sized window, we next consider an algorithm that initially starts with a small, fixed circuit-window and dynamically increases the window size in response to positive end-to-end latency feedback. Inspired by latency-informed congestion control techniques for IP networks [3,37], we propose an algorithm that uses increases in perceived end-to-end circuit round-trip time (RTT) as a signal of incipient congestion.

The algorithm works as follows. Initially, each circuit's window size starts at 100 cells. First, the sender calculates the circuit's end-to-end RTT using the circuit-level SENDME cells, maintaining the minimum RTT (rtt_{min}) and maximum RTT (rtt_{max}) observed for each circuit. We note that rtt_{min} is an approximation of the base RTT, where there is little or no congestion on the circuit. Next, since RTT feedback is available for every 100 cells[3], the circuit window size is adjusted quickly using an additive increase, multiplicative decrease (AIMD) window scaling mechanism based on whether the current RTT measurement (rtt) is less than the threshold T, defined in Equation 1. This threshold defines the circuit's tolerance to perceived congestion.

$$T = (1 - \alpha) \times rtt_{min} + \alpha \times rtt_{max} \qquad (1)$$

Choosing a small α value ensures that the threshold is close to the base RTT, and any increases beyond the threshold implies the presence of congestion along the circuit[4]. For each RTT measurement (*e.g.*, each received circuit-level SENDME), the circuit window size (in cells) is adjusted according to Equation 2.

$$new\_window(rtt) = \begin{cases} old\_window + 100 & \text{if } rtt \leq T \\ \lfloor old\_window/2 \rfloor & \text{otherwise} \end{cases} \qquad (2)$$

---

[2] Due to the aforementioned bug, in practice, the window size should be 101 cells.

[3] Similar to the 50 KiB windows, SENDME cells may be available after 101 cells.

[4] For our experiments, we use $\alpha = 0.25$.

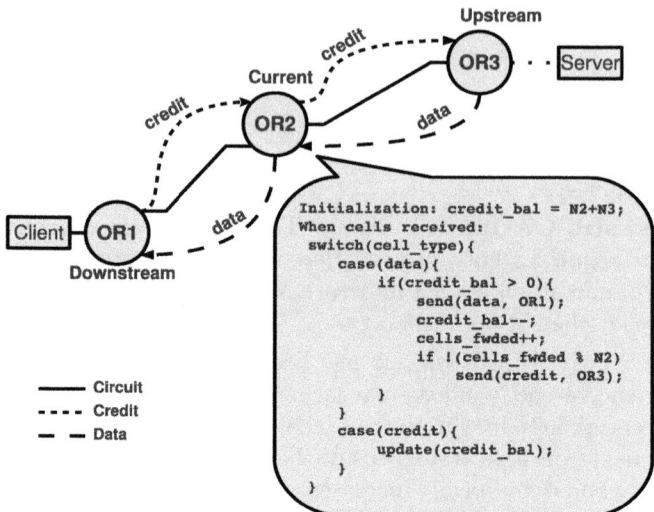

Fig. 3. N23 credit-based flow control in Tor

Finally, we explicitly cap the minimum and maximum circuit window sizes at 100 and 1000 cells, respectively[5]. Note that for long-lived circuits, rtt_{min} may become increasingly small and rtt_{max} may grow very large. In practice, these values should decay over time, for example, using an exponentially weighted moving average of each respective parameter.

4.2   ATM-Style Congestion and Flow Control for Tor

Because Tor's flow control works at the circuit's edges—the client and the exit router—we seek to improve performance by implementing per-link flow control to ensure a steady flow of cells while reducing congestion at the intermediate routers. Implementing per-link flow control in Tor resembles the problem of link-by-link flow control (LLFC) in ATM networks. While the goals of Tor and ATM are certainly different, there are many similarities. Both networks are connection-oriented, in the sense that before applications can send or receive data, virtual circuits are constructed across multiple routers or switches, and both have fixed-sized cells. Furthermore, it has been shown that ATM's credit-based flow control approaches, such as the N23 scheme, eliminate cell loss due to buffer overflows [16], a feature that makes such approaches similar to Tor, where no packets may be dropped to signal congestion.

N23 Flow Control for Tor. Figure 3 depicts the N23 scheme that we integrated into Tor, and it works as follows. First, when a circuit is built, each router along the circuit is assigned an initial *credit balance* of $N2 + N3$ cells,

---

[5] Note that a selfish Tor client could attempt to increase their circuit window by preemptively acknowledging data segments before they are actually received. Prior work in mitigating similar behavior in selfish TCP receivers may be applied here [30,32].

where $N2$ and $N3$ are system parameters. $N2$ cells is the available steady state buffering per circuit, $N3$ cells is the allowed excess buffering, and the circuit's queue length is strictly upper bounded by $N2 + N3$ cells. In general, $N2$ is fixed at the system's configuration time, but $N3$ may change over a circuit's lifetime.

When a router forwards a cell, it decrements its credit balance by one for that cell's circuit. Each router stops forwarding cells if its credit balance reaches zero. Thus, routers' circuit queues are upper bounded by $N2 + N3$ cells, and congestion is indicated to upstream routers through this back-pressure. Next, for every $N2$ cells forwarded, the downstream router sends a *flow control cell* to the upstream router that contains credit information reflecting its available circuit queue space. On receiving a flow control cell, the upstream router updates the circuit's credit balance and may forward cells only if the credit balance is greater than zero.

Adaptive Buffer Sizes and Congestion Control. The algorithm as described assumes a static $N3$. We also developed an adaptive algorithm that reduces the $N3$ value when there is downstream congestion, which is detected by monitoring the delay that cells experience in the connection's output buffer. When the congestion subsides, $N3$ can increase again. The value of $N3$ is updated periodically and is bounded by a minimum and a maximum value (100 and 500 cells, respectively).

Advantages. The N23 algorithm has two important advantages over Tor's current flow control. First, the size of the circuit queue is explicitly capped, and guaranteed to be no more than $N2 + N3$ cells. This also ensures steady flow control, as routers typically have cells available to forward. Tor's current flow control algorithm allows the circuit queue of a circuit's intermediate routers to grow up to one circuit window in size, which not only wastes memory, but also results in unnecessary delays due to congestion. In contrast, for typical parameter values ($N3 = 500$ and $N2 = 10$), N23 ensures a strict circuit queue bound of 510 cells, while these queues currently can grow up to 1000 cells in length.

The second advantage is that adaptive N3 reacts to congestion within a single link RTT. When congestion occurs at a router, the preceding router in the circuit will run out of credit and must stop forwarding until it gets a flow control cell.

5 Experiments and Results

To empirically demonstrate the efficacy of our proposed improvements, we offer a whole-network evaluation of our congestion and flow control algorithms using the ModelNet network emulation platform [35]. Briefly, ModelNet enables the experimenter to specify realistic network topologies annotated with bandwidth, delay and other link properties, and run real code on the emulated network[6].

Our evaluation focuses on performance metrics that are particularly important to the end-user's quality of service. First, we measure *time-to-first-byte*, which is how long the user must wait from the time they issue a request for

---

[6] More details about our experimental environment can be found in Bauer *et al.* [2].

Fig. 4. A simple topology with a middle router bandwidth bottleneck

data until they receive the first byte (or until a web client starts to see content load on their current web page). The time-to-first-byte is two end-to-end circuit RTTs: one RTT to connect to the destination web server, and a second RTT to issue a request for data (*e.g.*, HTTP GET) and receive the first byte of data in response[7]. Second, we measure *overall download time* (including time-to-first-byte), which is how long the user must wait for their web page to load. For all experiments, we use the latest development branch of the Tor source code (version 0.2.3.0-alpha-dev)[8].

5.1   Small-Scale Analysis

Setup. We emulate the topology depicted in Figure 4 on ModelNet where two Tor clients compete for service on the same set of routers with a bandwidth bottleneck at the middle router[9]. One client downloads 300 KiB, which roughly corresponds to the size of an average web page [27]. The second client, a bulk downloader, fetches 5 MiB. Both clients pause for a random amount of time between one and three seconds, and repeat their downloads. Each experiment concludes after the web client completes 200 downloads. Both clients use the wget web browser and the destination runs the lighthttpd web server.

End-to-end Window-based Solutions. Figure 5(a) shows that the time-to-first-byte for a typical web client using stock Tor is 4.5 seconds at the median, which is unacceptably high for delay-sensitive, interactive web users who must incur this delay for each web request. In addition, stock Tor's circuit queues fluctuate in length, growing up to 250 cells long, and remaining long for many seconds, indicating queuing delays, as shown in Figure 6(a). Reducing the circuit window size to 50 KiB (*e.g.*, one circuit SENDME interval) offers a median time-to-first-byte of less than 1.5 seconds, and dynamic windows offer a median time-to-first-byte of two seconds. In Figure 5(b), we see that the web client's download time is influenced by the high time-to-first-byte, and is roughly 40% faster with 50 KiB and dynamic windows relative to stock Tor. Also, the circuit queues are smaller with the 50 KiB and dynamic windows (see Figures 6(b) and 6(c)).

---

[7] Note that there is a proposal being considered to eliminate one of these RTTs [13].

[8] In our evaluation, we refer to unmodified Tor version 0.2.3.0-alpha-dev as *stock Tor*, 50 KiB (100 cell) fixed windows as *50 KiB window*, the dynamic window scaling algorithm as *dynamic window*, and the N23 algorithm as *N23*.

[9] Note that a 128 KiB/s router corresponds to the 65th percentile of routers ranked by observed bandwidth, as reported by the directory authorities. Thus, it is likely to be chosen fairly often by clients. Also, prior work [26] found the median round-trip time between live Tor routers to be about 80 ms.

(a) Web client's time-to-first byte (b) Web client's download time

(c) Bulk client's time-to-first-byte (d) Bulk client's download time

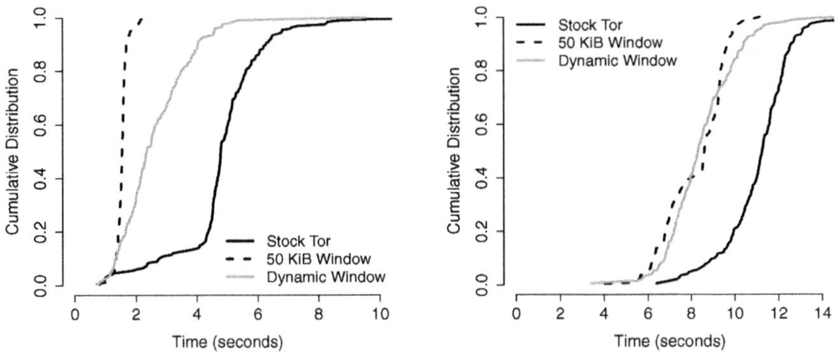

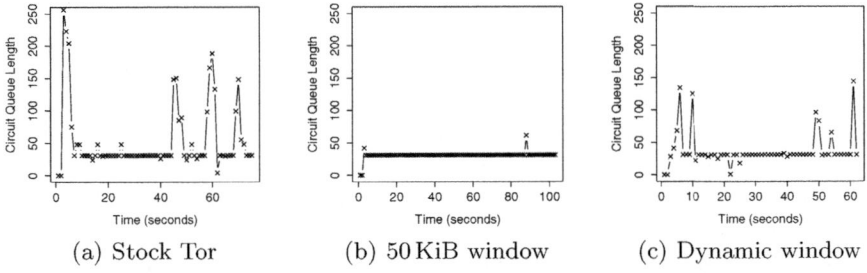

Fig. 5. Performance comparisons for window approaches in a bottleneck topology

(a) Stock Tor (b) 50 KiB window (c) Dynamic window

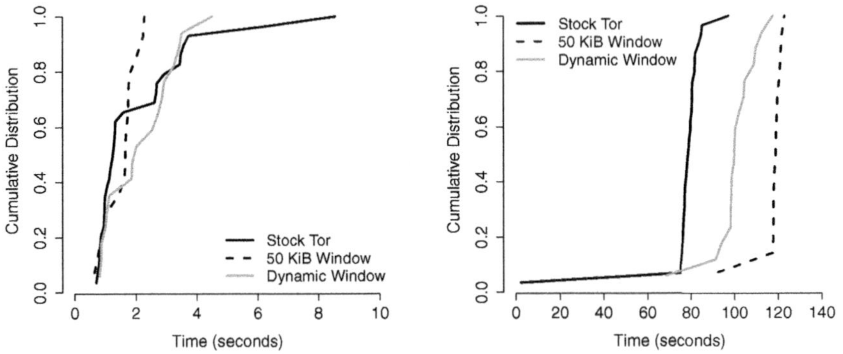

Fig. 6. Bulk client's circuit queues at the exit router over the course of a download

The bulk client experiences significantly less time-to-first-byte delays (in Figure 5(c)) than the web client using stock Tor. This highlights an inherent unfairness during congestion: web clients' traffic is queued behind the bulk traffic

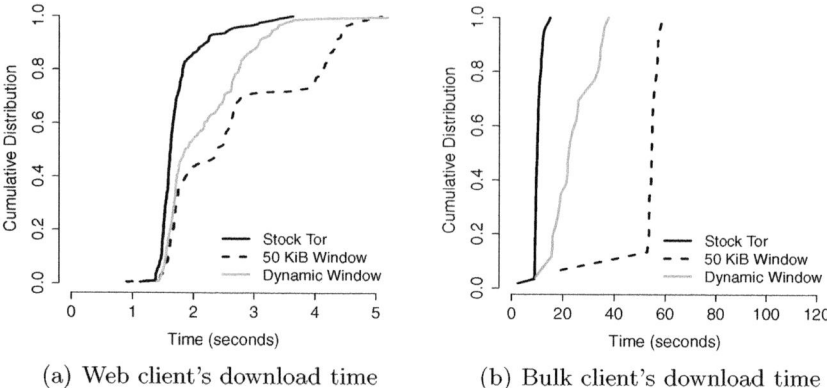

(a) Web client's download time   (b) Bulk client's download time

Fig. 7. Download time comparisons for windows in a non-bottleneck network

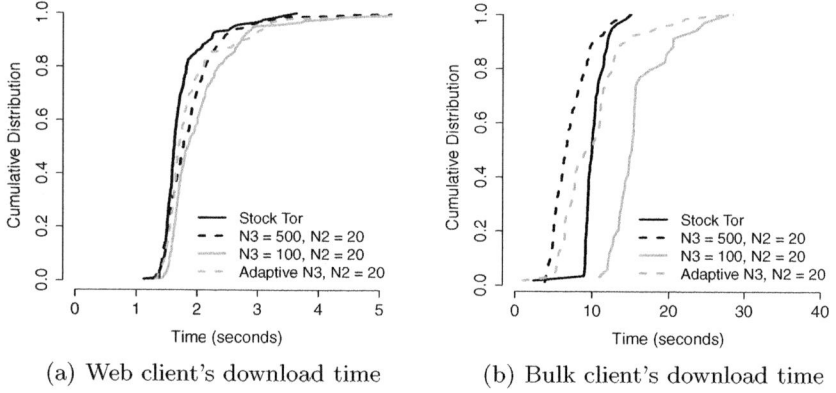

(a) Web client's download time   (b) Bulk client's download time

Fig. 8. Download time comparisons for Tor and N23 in a non-bottleneck network

and, consequently, delay-sensitive clients must wait longer than delay-insensitive bulk downloaders to receive their first byte of data. Using a small or dynamic window reduces this unfairness, since the bound on the number of unacknowledged cells allowed to be in flight is lower.

However, Figure 5(d) indicates that the bulk client's download takes significantly longer to complete with 50 KiB windows relative to stock Tor. Thus, 50 KiB windows enhance performance for web clients at the cost of slower downloads for bulk clients. The bulk clients experience slower downloads because they keep less data in flight and, consequently, must incur additional round-trip time delays to complete the download. Dynamic windows offer a middle-ground solution, as they ameliorate this limitation by offering an improvement in download time for web clients while penalizing bulk clients less than small windows, but bulk clients are still penalized relative to stock Tor's performance.

We next consider the same topology shown in Figure 4, except we replace the bottleneck middle router with a 10 MiB/s router. In such a topology, congestion is minimal, as evidenced by a median time-to-first-byte of 0.75 s for both the web and bulk clients (regardless of the window size). However, because the 50 KiB and dynamic windows generally keep less data in flight, these solutions offer slower downloads relative to stock Tor, as shown in Figures 7(a) and 7(b). We also found that manipulating Tor's circuit windows in combination with circuit-level prioritization offers even more improvement for the web client, while not further harming the bulk client's performance. These results are in Appendix A.

Despite the improvements in time-to-first-byte in the presence of bandwidth bottlenecks, we find that smaller circuit windows may under-utilize the available bandwidth[10] and the dynamic window scaling algorithm is unable to adjust the window size fast enough, as it receives congestion feedback infrequently (only every 100 cells). Also, even in the non-bottleneck topology, the 50 KiB window web client's time-to-first-byte is higher than the optimal delay from two circuit RTTs, which is 0.64 s. Lastly, 50 KiB windows offer worse flow control than Tor's current design, since only 50 KiB can be in flight, and the exit router must wait for a full circuit RTT until more data can be read and sent down the circuit.

Based on these drawbacks, we conclude that in order to achieve an improvement in both time-to-first-byte and download speed, it is necessary to re-design Tor's fundamental congestion and flow control mechanisms. We next offer an evaluation of per-link congestion and flow control for Tor.

Per-link Congestion and Flow Control. We first implemented N23 with fixed values of N2 and N3 (*static N23*) and then with N3 values that react to network feedback (*adaptive N3*). We disabled Tor's window-based flow control, so that exit routers ignored SENDMEs they received from clients. We discuss the results of adaptive N3 with our large-scale experiments. In this section, we present the results of N23 for both the bottleneck and non-bottleneck topologies.

For the non-bottleneck topology, we see in Figure 8(b) that N23 provides a substantial improvement in download time for the 5 MiB downloads compared to stock Tor only for higher values of N3 — 500 cells, comparable to stock Tor's stream window size. The graph shows that there is a 25% decrease in delay for 50% of the bulk downloads when N23 is used. Since the maximum throughput is bounded by W/RTT, where W is the link's TCP window size and RTT is the link's round-trip time, and since N23's per-link RTT is significantly smaller than a stock Tor's complete circuit RTT, throughput is increased when N23 is used. This improvement suggests that in non-bottleneck scenarios, bulk traffic data cells are

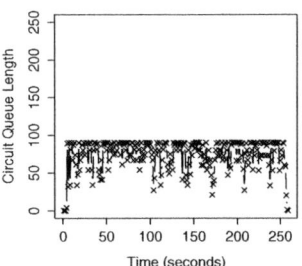

Fig. 9. Circuit queue length with bottleneck: N3 = 70, N2 = 20

---

[10] We note that bandwidth under-utilization may only be a problem if there is not sufficient demand from Tor clients to fully consume the network's bandwidth.

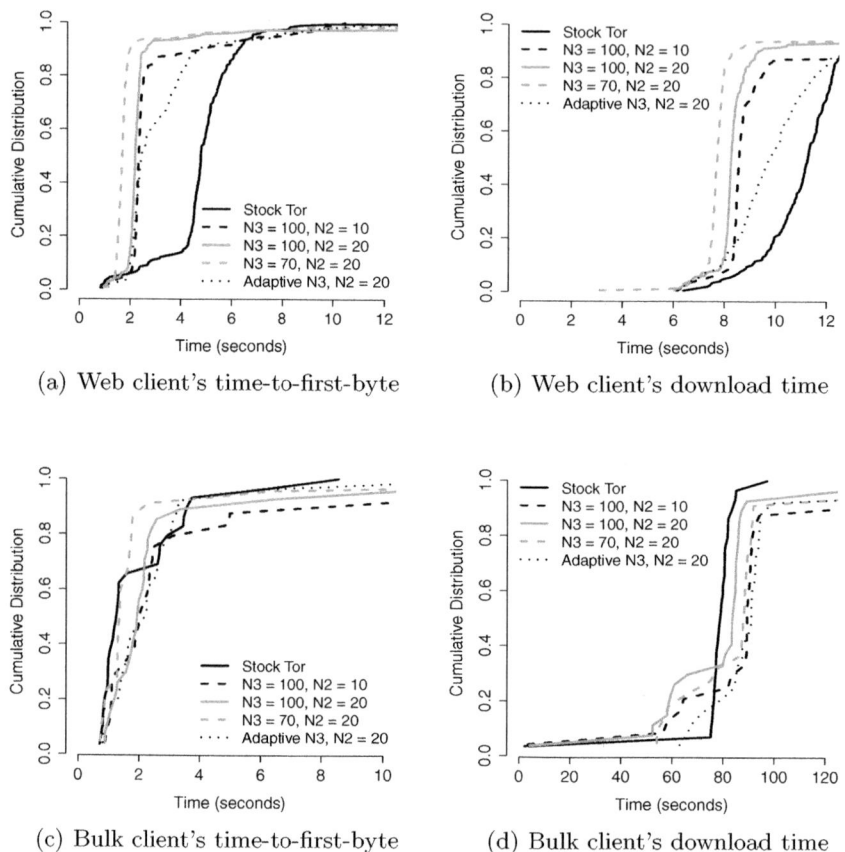

(a) Web client's time-to-first-byte

(b) Web client's download time

(c) Bulk client's time-to-first-byte

(d) Bulk client's download time

Fig. 10. Performance comparisons for Tor and N23 in a bottleneck topology

unnecessarily slowed down by Tor's flow control at the circuit's edges. For web traffic, Tor's current flow control and N23 have similar performance for fixed and adaptive N3, as shown in Figure 8(a). Also, the median time-to-first-byte is the same for the web and bulk clients at 0.75 s.

For bottleneck scenarios, Figures 10(a) and 10(b) show that smaller values of N3 improve both the download time and time-to-first-byte for the bursty web traffic. For example, the web browsing client experiences a 20% decrease in download time for 80% of the requests when N23 is used. Also, the web client's time-to-first-byte is only two seconds for 90% of the requests, whereas for the stock Tor client, 80% of web requests take more than four seconds to receive the first byte. Figure 9 shows that the circuit queue length is upper bounded by $N2 + N3 = 90$ cells.

To understand how N23 performs with different $N2$ values, we repeated the bottleneck experiments while varying that parameter. Although a higher value for $N2$ has the undesirable effect of enlarging the circuit buffer, it can be seen in Figures 10(a) and 10(b) that when $N3$ is fixed at 100 cells, increasing $N2$ to 20 cells slightly improves both download time and time-to-first-byte. It can be observed from Figure 10(a) that time-to-first-byte is significantly improved by keeping a smaller $N3 = 70$ and a larger $N2 = 20$. Decreasing $N3$ to 70 cells makes up for the increase in the $N2$ zone of the buffer, which means we gain the benefits of less flow control overhead, and the benefits of a small buffer of $N2 + N3 = 90$ cells. While performance is improved for the web clients, the bulk client's time-to-first-byte is not affected greatly, as seen in Figure 10(c), but its downloads generally take longer to complete, as we see in Figure 10(d). In addition, adaptive N3 offers improved time-to-first-byte and download times for the web client, while slowing downloads for the bulk client. By N23 restricting the amount of data in flight, the bandwidth consumed by bulk clients is reduced, improving time-to-first-byte and download time for delay-sensitive web clients.

We also evaluate N23 in combination with circuit-level prioritization in a bottleneck topology. We observe that circuit-level prioritization with N23 offers no performance benefit over N23 alone. The full results are in Appendix B.

Finally, the bandwidth cost associated with the N23 scheme is relatively low. For instance, with $N2 = 10$, a flow control cell must be sent by each router on the circuit for every 10 data cells forwarded, which requires a 10% bandwidth overhead per router. For $N2 = 20$, a flow control cell is sent for every 20 data cells, which is only a 5% overhead per router. While this cost is higher than Tor's window-based flow control (*e.g.*, one stream-level SENDME for every 50 data cells and one circuit-level SENDME for every 100 data cells, resulting in a 3% overhead per circuit), the cost of N23 is nonetheless modest.

5.2   Larger-Scale Analysis

Setup. We next evaluate the window-based solutions and N23 with adaptive N3 in a more realistic network topology[11]. We deploy 20 Tor routers on a ModelNet topology whose bandwidths are assigned by sampling from the live Tor network. Each link's round-trip time is set to 80 ms. Next, to generate a traffic workload, we run 200 Tor clients. Of these, ten clients are bulk downloaders who fetch files between 1–5 MiB, pausing for up to two seconds between fetches. The remaining 190 clients are web clients, who download files between 100–500 KiB (typical web page sizes), pausing for up to 30 seconds between fetches. This proportion of bulk-to-non-bulk clients approximates the proportion observed on the live Tor network [21]. To isolate the improvements due to our proposals, circuit-level prioritization is disabled for this experiment.

Results. For web clients, Figure 11(a) shows that both the 50 KiB fixed and dynamic windows still offer improved time-to-first-byte. However, both algorithms perform worse than stock Tor in terms of overall download time, as shown in Figure 11(b). Note that this observation holds for both web clients and bulk downloaders. Because smaller windows provide less throughput than larger windows when there is no bottleneck, non-bottlenecked circuits are under-utilized.

---

[11] In this experiment, we only consider N23 with adaptive N3 because in practice, N23 should discover the right buffer size for the given network conditions.

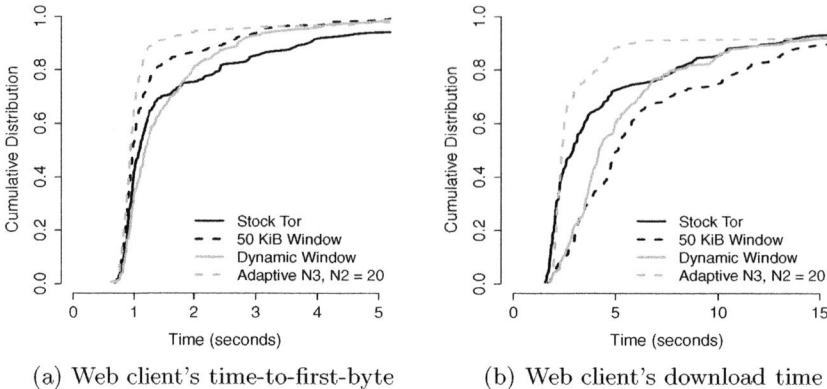

(a) Web client's time-to-first-byte   (b) Web client's download time

Fig. 11. Performance results for large-scale experiments

N23 with the adaptive N3 algorithm, in contrast, has the ability to react to congestion quickly by reducing routers' queue lengths, causing back pressure to build up. Consequently, our results indicate that N23 offers an improvement in both time-to-first-byte *and* overall download time for web clients, while bulk clients experience roughly the same performance as stock Tor.

These experiments again highlight the potential negative impact of 50 KiB and small dynamic windows, since even in a larger network with a realistic traffic load, smaller windows offer worse performance for typical delay-sensitive web requests relative to Tor's current window size. Thus, to achieve maximal improvements, we suggest that Tor adopt N23 congestion and flow control.

6 Discussion

Having empirically evaluated our proposed congestion and flow control approaches, we next discuss a variety of open issues.

6.1 Limitations of Experiments and Results

The results presented in Section 5 generally show an improvement in time-to-first-byte and download time with N23 flow control relative to end-to-end windows. However, these results were obtained in a testbed environment with a single, artificial traffic load; thus, an analysis of expected performance as the traffic load varies, on the live Tor network with real traffic loads, and with exhaustive N23 parameter configurations is future work.

6.2 Incremental Deployment

In order for our proposed congestion and flow control mechanisms to be practical and easily deployable on the live Tor network, it is important that any modifications to Tor's router infrastructure be incrementally deployable. Any solutions based on Tor's existing window-based flow control require upgrades only to the exit routers; thus they can be slowly deployed as router operators upgrade. N23 may also be deployed incrementally, however, clients may not see substantial performance benefits until a large fraction of the routers have upgraded.

6.3   Anonymity Implications

A key question to answer is whether improving Tor's performance and reducing congestion enables any attack that was not previously possible. It is well known that Tor is vulnerable to congestion attacks wherein an attacker constructs circuits through a number of different routers, floods them with traffic, and observes if there is an increase in latency on a target circuit, which would indicate a shared router on both paths [22]. More recent work has suggested a solution that would mitigate bandwidth amplification variants of this attack, but not the shared router inference part of the attack [12]. We believe that by reducing congestion (and specifically, by bounding queue lengths), our proposed techniques may increase the difficulty of mounting congestion attacks.

However, if only a fraction of the routers upgrade to our proposals and if clients only choose routers that support the new flow control, then an adversary may be able to narrow down the set of potential routers that a client is using. Thus, it is important to deploy any new flow control technique after a large fraction of the network has upgraded. Such a deployment can be controlled by setting a flag in the authoritative directory servers' consensus document, indicating that it is safe for clients to use the new flow control.

Another well-studied class of attack is end-to-end traffic correlation. Such attacks endeavor to link a client with its destination when the entry and exit points are compromised, and these attacks have been shown to be highly accurate [1,23,25,31,33]. Reducing latency might improve this attack; however, Tor is already highly vulnerable, so there is little possibility for additional risk.

Finally, previous work has shown that network latency can be used as a side channel to infer a possible set of client locations [15]. By decreasing the variance in latency, we might expose more accurate RTT measurements, thus improving the effectiveness of this attack. However, reducing congestion does not enable a new attack, but rather may potentially increase the effectiveness of a known attack. To put this attack in perspective, Tor's design has already made many performance/anonymity trade-offs, and thus, we believe that our performance improvements outweigh any potential decrease in anonymity brought about by reducing the variance in latency.

7   Conclusion

We seek to improve Tor's performance by reducing unnecessary delays due to poor flow control and excessive queuing at intermediate routers. To this end, we have proposed two broad classes of congestion and flow control. First, we tune Tor's existing circuit windows to effectively reduce the amount of data in flight. However, our experiments indicate that while window-based solutions do reduce queuing delays, they tend to suffer from poor flow control, under-utilizing the available bandwidth, and consequently, smaller windows provide slower downloads than unmodified Tor.

To solve this problem, we offer a fresh approach to congestion and flow control in Tor by designing, implementing, and experimentally evaluating a per-link congestion and flow control algorithm from ATM networks. Our experiments indicate that this approach offers the promise of faster web page response times and faster overall web page downloads.

Acknowledgments. We thank the anonymous reviewers and our shepherd, Roger Dingledine, for their helpful comments and suggestions. We also thank Ken Yocum for his invaluable assistance with ModelNet. This work was supported in part by NSERC, MITACS, The Tor Project, Qatar University, National Science Foundation grants NSF-0433668, DGE-0841423, a CRA/NSF Computing Innovation Fellowship, the Office of Naval Research MURI grant N000140911081, and by generous research, operational and/or in-kind support from the UCSD Center for Networked Systems (CNS).

References

1. Bauer, K., McCoy, D., Grunwald, D., Kohno, T., Sicker, D.: Low-resource routing attacks against Tor. In: Proceedings of the Workshop on Privacy in the Electronic Society (WPES 2007), Washington, DC, USA (October 2007)
2. Bauer, K., Sherr, M., McCoy, D., Grunwald, D.: ExperimenTor: A testbed for safe and realistic Tor experimentation. Technical Report CACR 2011-12 (May 2011), http://www.cacr.math.uwaterloo.ca/techreports/2011/cacr2011-12.pdf
3. Brakmo, L.S., O'Malley, S.W., Peterson, L.L.: TCP Vegas: New techniques for congestion detection and avoidance. In: Proceedings of the Conference on Communications Architectures, Protocols and Applications, SIGCOMM 1994, pp. 24–35. ACM, New York (1994)
4. Chen, F., Perry, M.: Improving Tor path selection (July 2008), https://gitweb.torproject.org/torspec.git/blob_plain/HEAD:/proposals/151-path-selection-improvements.txt
5. Dhungel, P., Steiner, M., Rimac, I., Hilt, V., Ross, K.W.: Waiting for anonymity: Understanding delays in the Tor overlay. In: Peer-to-Peer Computin. IEEE, Los Alamitos (2010)
6. Dingledine, R.: Prop 168: Reduce default circuit window (August 2009), https://gitweb.torproject.org/torspec.git/blob_plain/HEAD:/proposals/168-reduce-circwindow.txt
7. Dingledine, R.: Research problem: adaptive throttling of Tor clients by entry guards (September 2010), https://blog.torproject.org/blog/research-problem-adaptive-hrottling-tor-clients-entry-guards

8. Dingledine, R., Mathewson, N.: Anonymity loves company: Usability and the network effect. In: Workshop on the Economics of Information Security (June 2006)
9. Dingledine, R., Mathewson, N.: Tor Protocol Specificiation (2010), https://gitweb.torproject.org/tor.git/blob_plain/HEAD:/doc/spec/tor-spec.txt
10. Dingledine, R., Mathewson, N., Syverson, P.: Tor: The second-generation onion router. In: Proceedings of the 13th USENIX Security Symposium (August 2004)
11. Dingledine, R., Murdoch, S.: Performance improvements on Tor or, why Tor is slow and what we're going to do about it (March 2009), http://www.torproject.org/press/presskit/2009-03-11-performance.pdf
12. Evans, N., Dingledine, R., Grothoff, C.: A practical congestion attack on Tor using long paths. In: Proceedings of the 18th USENIX Security Symposium (2009)
13. Goldberg, I.: Prop 174: Optimistic data for Tor: Server side, https://trac.torproject.org/projects/tor/ticket/1795
14. Goldschlag, D.M., Reed, M.G., Syverson, P.F.: Hiding routing information. In: Proceedings of Information Hiding: First International Workshop (May 1996)
15. Hopper, N., Vasserman, E.Y., Chan-Tin, E.: How much anonymity does network latency leak? In: Proceedings of ACM CCS (October 2007)
16. Jain, R.: Congestion control and traffic management in ATM networks: Recent advances and a survey. Computer Networks and ISDN Systems (1995)
17. Jansen, R., Hopper, N., Kim, Y.: Recruiting new Tor relays with BRAIDS. In: Proceedings of the ACM CCS (2010)
18. Kiraly, C., Bianchi, G., Cigno, R.L.: Solving performance issues in anonymiziation overlays with a L3 approach. University of Trento Information Engineering and Computer Science Department Technical Report DISI-08-041 (September 2008)
19. Kung, H.T., Blackwell, T., Chapman, A.: Credit-based flow control for ATM networks: credit update protocol, adaptive credit allocation and statistical multiplexing. SIGCOMM Comput. Commun. Rev. 24, 101–114 (1994)
20. Loesing, K.: Measuring the Tor network: Evaluation of client requests to the directories. Tor Project Technical Report (June 2009)
21. McCoy, D., Bauer, K., Grunwald, D., Kohno, T., Sicker, D.: Shining light in dark places: Understanding the Tor network. In: Proceedings of the 8th Privacy Enhancing Technologies Symposium (July 2008)
22. Murdoch, S.J., Danezis, G.: Low-cost traffic analysis of Tor. In: Proceedings of the 2005 IEEE Symposium on Security and Privacy. IEEE CS, Los Alamitos (2005)
23. Murdoch, S.J., Zieliński, P.: Sampled traffic analysis by Internet-exchange-level adversaries. In: Privacy Enhancing Technologies Workshop (June 2007)
24. Ngan, T.W.J., Dingledine, R., Wallach, D.S.: Building Incentives into Tor. In: Proceedings of Financial Cryptography (January 2010)
25. Øverlier, L., Syverson, P.: Locating hidden servers. In: Proceedings of the 2006 IEEE Symposium on Security and Privacy. IEEE CS, Los Alamitos (2006)
26. Pries, R., Yu, W., Graham, S., Fu, X.: On performance bottleneck of anonymous communication networks. In: Parallel and Distributed Processing (2008)
27. Ramachandran, S.: Web metrics: Size and number of resources, https://code.google.com/speed/articles/web-metrics.html
28. Rapier, C., Bennett, B.: High speed bulk data transfer using the SSH protocol. In: 15th Mardi Gras Conference on Distributed Applications. ACM, New York (2008)
29. Reardon, J., Goldberg, I.: Improving Tor using a TCP-over-DTLS tunnel. In: Proceedings of the 18th USENIX Security Symposium (August 2009)

30. Savage, S., Cardwell, N., Wetherall, D., Anderson, T.: TCP congestion control with a misbehaving receiver. SIGCOMM Comput. Commun. Rev. 29, 71–78 (1999)
31. Serjantov, A., Sewell, P.: Passive attack analysis for connection-based anonymity systems. In: Snekkenes, E., Gollmann, D. (eds.) ESORICS 2003. LNCS, vol. 2808, pp. 116–131. Springer, Heidelberg (2003)
32. Sherwood, R., Bhattacharjee, B., Braud, R.: Misbehaving TCP receivers can cause Internet-wide congestion collapse. In: Proceedings of the 12th ACM Conference on Computer and Communications Security (2005)
33. Shmatikov, V., Wang, M.H.: Timing analysis in low-latency mix networks: Attacks and defenses. In: Gollmann, D., Meier, J., Sabelfeld, A. (eds.) ESORICS 2006. LNCS, vol. 4189, pp. 18–33. Springer, Heidelberg (2006)
34. Tang, C., Goldberg, I.: An improved algorithm for Tor circuit scheduling. In: Proceedings of the 2010 ACM Conference on Computer and Communications Security. ACM, New York (2010)
35. Vahdat, A., Yocum, K., Walsh, K., Mahadevan, P., Kostić, D., Chase, J., Becker, D.: Scalability and accuracy in a large-scale network emulator. SIGOPS Oper. Syst. Rev. 36, 271–284 (2002)
36. Viecco, C.: UDP-OR: A fair onion transport. HotPETS (July 2008)
37. Wang, Z., Crowcroft, J.: Eliminating periodic packet losses in the 4.3-Tahoe BSD TCP congestion control algorithm. SIGCOMM Comput. Commun. Rev. 22, 9–16 (1992)
38. Wright, M.K., Adler, M., Levine, B.N., Shields, C.: The predecessor attack: An analysis of a threat to anonymous communications systems. ACM Trans. Inf. Syst. Secur. 7(4), 489–522 (2004)

A   End-to-End Windows with Circuit Prioritization

Circuit-level prioritization has been proposed [34] to enable routers to process bursty circuits ahead of bulk circuits. In this appendix, we evaluate small and dynamic circuit windows in combination with circuit-level prioritization[12]. For the web client using stock Tor, the time-to-first-byte is reduced from 4.5 seconds (see Figure 5(a)) to 3 seconds, and the time-to-first-byte for 50 KiB and dynamic windows are roughly the same. However, as shown in Figure 12(a), roughly 25% of requests experience no significant improvement when using small or dynamic circuit windows. For these same requests, stock Tor's large window allows more data in flight without acknowledgment and, as shown in Figure 12(b), induces faster downloads (compared to Figure 5(b)). However, for the remaining 75%, small and dynamic windows offer faster downloads. The bulk client's time-to-first-byte and overall download times are not significantly altered by the circuit prioritization, as shown in Figures 12(c) and 12(d), relative to non-prioritized circuit scheduling (see Figures 5(c) and 5(d)). These observations are consistent with the claims made by Tang and Goldberg [34].

---

[12] For all prioritization experiments, we set `CircuitPriorityHalflifeMsec` to 30 seconds, the current value used on the live Tor network.

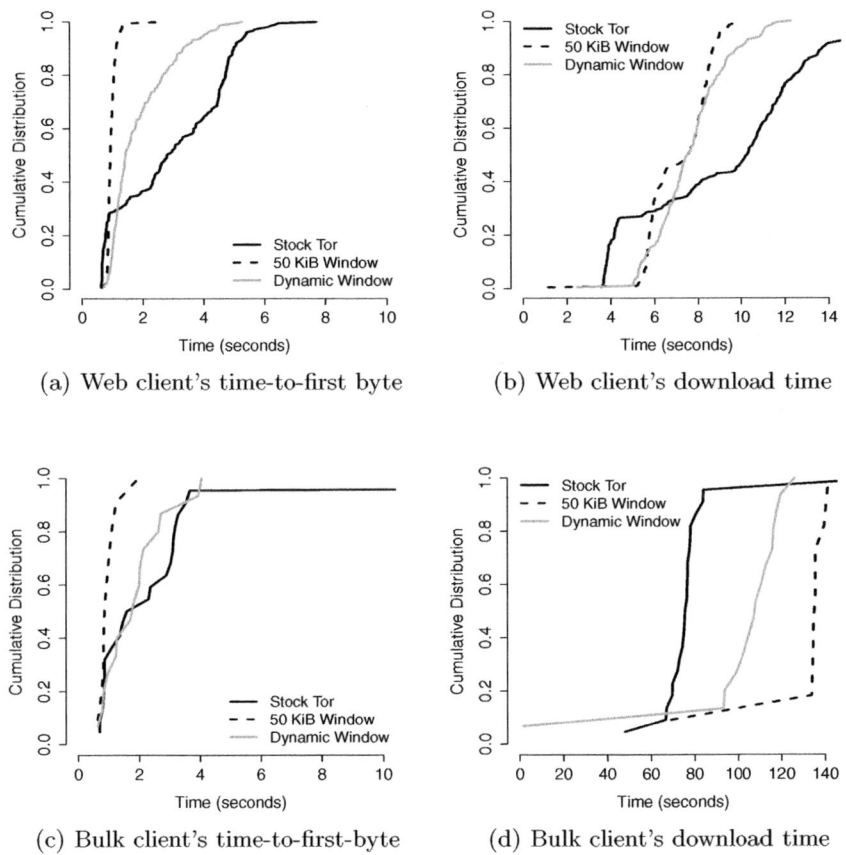

(a) Web client's time-to-first byte

(b) Web client's download time

(c) Bulk client's time-to-first-byte

(d) Bulk client's download time

Fig. 12. Performance for window-based flow control with circuit prioritization

B   N23 with Circuit Prioritization

The circuit-level prioritization algorithm enhances the bursty clients' experience because it remembers how many cells each circuit has recently sent, and gives more priority to the circuits that have sent less. For stock Tor, this algorithm is useful since circuit queues can grow to 1000 cells, which means bulk-traffic circuits can grow large queues and are able to send continuously. However, with N23, circuit queue sizes are significantly smaller and are equal for both bulk and bursty clients. This allows both applications to have a fairer share of the bandwidth. Therefore, for N23, circuit-level prioritization does not provide any performance benefits. Figures 13(a)–13(d) depict the results of the performance of N23 in combination with circuit-level prioritization. Both time-to-first-byte and download times are unaffected by enabling prioritization.

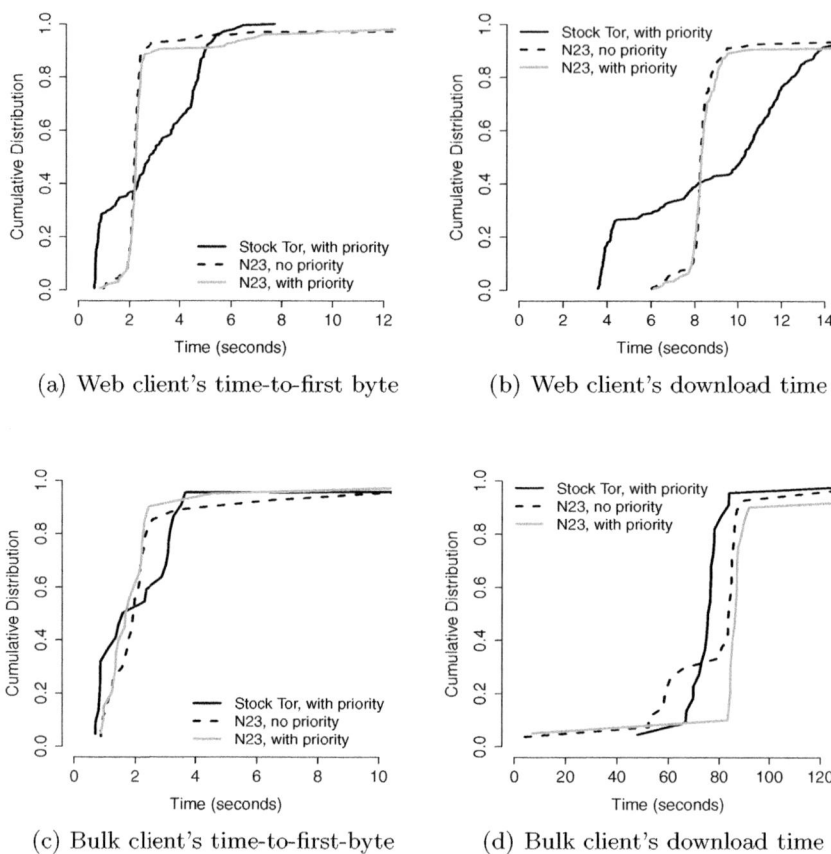

(a) Web client's time-to-first byte

(b) Web client's download time

(c) Bulk client's time-to-first-byte

(d) Bulk client's download time

Fig. 13. Performance for N23 ($N3 = 100$, $N2 = 20$) with circuit prioritization

Privacy-Implications of Performance-Based Peer Selection by Onion-Routers: A Real-World Case Study Using I2P

Michael Herrmann and Christian Grothoff

Technische Universität München, Munich, Germany
{herrmann,grothoff}@net.in.tum.de

Abstract. I2P is one of the most widely used anonymizing Peer-to-Peer networks on the Internet today. Like Tor, it uses onion routing to build tunnels between peers as the basis for providing anonymous communication channels. Unlike Tor, I2P integrates a range of anonymously hosted services directly with the platform. This paper presents a new attack on the I2P Peer-to-Peer network, with the goal of determining the identity of peers that are anonymously hosting HTTP services (Eepsite) in the network.

Key design choices made by I2P developers, in particular performance-based peer selection, enable a sophisticated adversary with modest resources to break key security assumptions. Our attack first obtains an estimate of the victim's view of the network. Then, the adversary selectively targets a small number of peers used by the victim with a denial-of-service attack while giving the victim the opportunity to replace those peers with other peers that are controlled by the adversary. Finally, the adversary performs some simple measurements to determine the identity of the peer hosting the service.

This paper provides the necessary background on I2P, gives details on the attack — including experimental data from measurements against the actual I2P network — and discusses possible solutions.

1 Introduction

Onion routing [13] is an established technique to provide sender- or receiver-anonymity for low-latency network applications. Both Tor [2] and I2P [15] provide anonymity to their users via an open network of onion routers run by volunteers. However, there are significant differences in the details of how these networks implement the basic technique. For many of the differences, the existing related work does not provide a clear answer as to which approach is better.

In this paper, we report on our exploitations of some of the *design choices* in I2P to deanonymize I2P services, specifically I2P Eepsites.[1] An Eepsite is a website hosted anonymously within the I2P network and accessed via HTTP tunneled through the I2P network, which also acts as an anonymizing SOCKS

---

[1] Our basic technique could be applied to other kinds of I2P services as well.

S. Fischer-Hübner and N. Hopper (Eds.): PETS 2011, LNCS 6794, pp. 155–174, 2011.

proxy. Our attack requires a modest amount of resources; the only special requirement, to run I2P peers in several different /16 peers, can also be met by any Internet user, for example by using cloud based services. While this requirement may put us outside of the I2P attacker model, our other requirements — participation in the I2P network and a modest amount of bandwidth — are easily within common attacker models for anonymizing P2P networks, including I2P and Tor. We have implemented and tested the attack on the extant I2P network in early 2011, making our attacker a credible real-world adversary.

Our attack is primarily based on exploiting I2P's performance-based selection of peers for tunnel construction, I2P's usage of unidirectional tunnels and the fact that Eepsites are located at a static location in the network. Using a combination of peers that participate as monitors in the network and other peers that selectively reduce the performance of certain other peers, our attack deduces with high degree of certainty the identity of the peer hosting the targeted Eepsite. In contrast to previous deanonymization attacks (such as [9,3]), our attack does not rely on congestion-induced changes to latency. In fact, the denial-of-service component of the attack focuses on peers that are not known to participate in the Eepsite's active tunnels at the time.

We have evaluated our technique not merely in simulation or a testbed but against the real I2P network. This paper presents experimental results obtained in early 2011 using I2P version 0.8.3, modified for our attack.

The main contributions of this paper are as follows:

- An independent characterization of the I2P protocol
- A novel attack on anonymity based on the heuristic performance-based peer selection for uni-directional tunnels
- Experimental evaluation of the attack
- Recommendations for improving the I2P design to thwart the attack

The rest of the paper is structured as follows. Section 2 provides a detailed overview of the I2P network. Section 3 describes our attack and Section 4 presents the experimental results. Finally, Section 5 discusses possible solutions and relates our attack to previous work on deanonymization for similar systems.

2   Background: I2P

I2P is a multi-application framework for anonymous P2P networking written in Java. On top of the native Internet protocol, I2P specifies the use of two different peer-to-peer transport protocols. The first is called *NIO-based TCP* (NTCP), where NIO refers to the Java New I/O library. The second is called *Secure Semireliable UDP* (SSU), providing UDP-based message transfer.

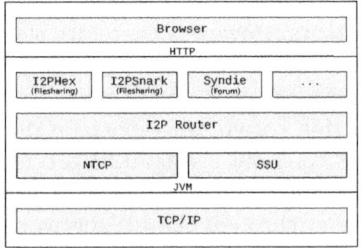

I2P Architecture

The core of the I2P framework is the I2P router, which implements key components of the I2P protocol. Tasks of the I2P router include: maintaining peer statistics, performing encryption/decryption and building tunnels. I2P applications rely on the anonymizing tunnels provided by the I2P router for privacy protection; consequently, the I2P router is central to the security of all I2P applications and the analysis presented in this paper.

Many Internet applications can be implemented on top of the I2P router. An application provided by a particular I2P peer is referred to as a service. For example, I2P includes services to host HTTP servers, to provide IRC-based communication and to perform POP/SMTP-based email transfer. Most I2P services are controlled and used via a web browser interface.

2.1 Peer and Service Discovery

Like most other P2P networks, I2P has to deal with the problem of finding peers and subsequently the services offered by those peers. Every peer in the I2P network is uniquely identified by a data structure called *routerInfo*. This data structure holds all the key information about the peer, including public keys of the peer, a 256 bit hash-identifier and information about how the peer can be contacted. I2P addresses the bootstrapping problem, the problem of initially discovering some other peer in the network, by using a non-anonymous HTTP download of a list of routerInfos for available I2P peers from a fixed location.

I2P's DHT: the netDB. After bootstrapping, I2P uses a super-peer DHT to build a network database, called the *netDB*, with information about all the peers and services available in the network. The super-peers that maintain this database are called *floodfill* peers; each floodfill peer is responsible for the information closest to its ID. Proximity is determined using Kademlia's XOR distance metric [8]. If a peer has sufficient bandwidth and its configuration allows it, a peer can promote itself to floodfill status and will do so as soon as the number of active floodfill peers in the network drops below a certain threshold.

Storing Data in the netDB. Information about how to contact a service provided by an I2P peer is kept in a so-called *leaseSet*. LeaseSets are stored in the same netDB that also contains routerInfos; nevertheless, leaseSets and routerInfos are independent entities that only share the same storage facility. A leaseSet primarily specifies a set of entry points (called *leases*) to the service. An entry point is the identification of an inbound tunnel at a peer currently serving as an inbound gateway to the service.

The lookup and storage of leaseSets and routerInfos is achieved by sending the respective requests to a floodfill server. Figure 1 illustrates the storage process for a leaseSet. After a floodfill peer receives a request, it replicates the information at seven additional closest floodfill peers and sends a confirmation to the initiator.

Retrieving Data from the netDB. Retrieving routerInfos and leaseSets is also performed via tunnels. The request is transmitted to the — with respect to the destination address — two closest floodfill peers known to the requester.

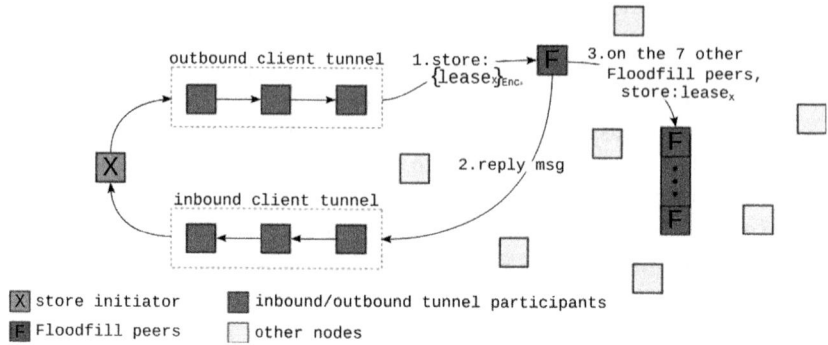

Fig. 1. I2P uses tunnels to store a lease in the floodfill database to hide the identity of the (HTTP) server

If a floodfill peer does not have the requested information, a list of other close floodfill peers is sent back. The replies are transmitted to the initiator using an inbound tunnel. If both floodfill peers do not have the requested information, the requesting peer queries two other floodfill peers until all known floodfill peers have been contacted.

2.2   I2P Tunnels

I2P uses *tunnels* to hide the IP address of a participant in an online interaction. I2P tunnels closely resemble onion routing as implemented in Tor with circuits [2]: the initiator selects the route through the network, no artificial delays are introduced when forwarding, and link- and layered-encryption are used to protect the data against observers.

I2P Tunnels are Unidirectional. Tunnels in I2P only transfer payload data in one direction. In order to achieve bi-directional communication, I2P uses *inbound* and *outbound* tunnels. Inbound tunnels are used to transmit data to the peer that constructed the tunnel and outbound tunnels are used to transfer data from the peer that constructed the tunnel. Note that only the peer that constructed the tunnel knows all of the peers in the tunnel.

For outbound tunnels, multiple layers of encryption are added by the creator of a message; each one is then removed by the corresponding peer as the message traverses the outbound tunnel.

For inbound tunnels, adding all layers of encryption at the first peer is not possible; this would require the first inbound node to know the secret tunnel keys for all of the participants of the tunnel. Instead, every node in an inbound tunnel *adds* an additional layer of encryption. Finally, the creator of the tunnel, who knows the tunnel keys used by each peer from the tunnel construction phase, removes all layers of encryption to obtain the original message.

Tunnel Diversity. Every I2P peer creates multiple tunnels; the specific number of tunnels and the tunnel length depend on the peer configuration. The length of the tunnel is considered to be a trade-off between speed and anonymity and I2P gives the end-user control over this setting. The user specifies two non-negative numbers, x and y. For each tunnel, I2P selects a random number $r \in [-y, y]$ and constructs a tunnel of length $\max(x + r, 0)$.

In addition to the distinction between inbound and outbound tunnels based on the tunnel's transfer direction, I2P further distinguishes between *exploratory* and *client* tunnels. Exploratory tunnels are for routerInfo queries to the netDB and for tunnel management. They are not used for privacy-sensitive operations. Client tunnels are used for all typical application level network messages, for example to provide tunnels for Eepsites and for leaseSet operations on the netDB.

Tunnel Construction. In order to select peers for tunnel construction, I2P first categorizes all known peers into tiers. Depending on the type of tunnel that is being created, the peer selection algorithm then attempts to select peers exclusively from a particular tier. In addition to selecting peers from particular tiers, I2P also avoids the selection of multiple peers from the same /16 (IPv4) network for the same tunnel.

After selecting peers for the tunnel, the initiator sends tunnel construction requests (via that partially built tunnel) to the selected peers. A peer receiving a tunnel construction request is free to either accept to participate in the tunnel or reject the request, indicating a reason for the refusal. Naturally, tunnels can still fail if peers that accepted a tunnel construction request are later unable to sustain the tunnel. The behavior of a peer faced with tunnel construction requests (including the reason given for rejection) as well as tunnel failures are important for the performance evaluation of peers, which is used for assigning peers to tiers.

Tier-based Peer Selection. An I2P peer chooses other peers randomly from a particular tier depending on the type of the tunnel. A tier consists of peers that share certain performance characteristics. I2P places certain well-performing peers into two special tiers:

Fast tier. Peers with high throughput
High-capacity tier. Peers that will accept a tunnel request with high probability.

The fast tier is considered the most valuable tier and is used for constructing client tunnels. In the theoretical case where the fast tier does not have a sufficient number of peers, I2P falls back to using peers from the high-capacity tier for peer selection in the construction of client tunnels. In practice, we were unable to observe this behavior since the fast tier was always sufficiently populated during our evaluation.

The high-capacity tier is the default choice for exploratory tunnels. Peers must also be in the high-capacity tier to be eligible for the fast tier. All other peers are only used as fallback options if the fast and high-capacity tiers lack available peers. In practice, this is unlikely to happen.

Peers are placed into tiers based on certain performance metrics. A peer is put in a particular tier if its corresponding performance value exceeds a threshold calculated by I2P for that tier.[2] The size of the fast and high-capacity tiers is bounded. For the fast tier the number of peers is between 8 and 30 and for the high-capacity tier between 10 and 75. If the number of peers in those tiers drops below the threshold, the best-performing peers from lower tiers are promoted. If the number of peers in a tier exceeds the upper limit, the lowest rated peers are demoted.

The I2P router keeps track of various performance statistics in order to sort peers into the correct tiers. Performance metrics are gathered more often for peers in the fast and high-capacity tiers, since performance metrics are always gathered if a peer is used for a tunnel. Furthermore, performance scores are cumulative; this generally results in higher performance values for peers in the fast and high-capacity tiers and reduces fluctuation.

Metrics for Tier Assignment. I2P is careful about only including performance metrics that are hard to manipulate, relying only on measurements entirely controlled by the peer for throughput and tunnel maintenance properties. In particular, information about tunnels created by other peers is not taken into consideration.

The *capacity value* of a peer is based on the number of times the peer accepts a tunnel request, the number of tunnel rejections and the number of tunnel failures that happen after a peer accepted to participate in a tunnel.

The goal of the capacity calculation is to estimate how a peer is likely to behave in the future in terms of its participation in tunnels. The calculation is primarily based on the accept, reject and failure actions of that peer. Furthermore, if the peer rejected events in the last 5 minutes, the reason given for the rejection is also considered. A detailed description of the capacity calculation algorithm can be found in [4]; the main point for this paper is that peers accepting tunnel requests score high, peers rejecting tunnel requests score low and peers participating in tunnels that then failed score very low in terms of their capacity value.

A peer's *speed value* is the mean of its three highest, one second throughput measurements in any tunnel established by the measuring peer over the course of the last day. Throughput is measured whenever data is sent through a peer via a tunnel created by the measuring peer. Naturally, throughput is bounded by the throughput capacity of the measuring peer as well as, for each individual measurement, the slowest peer in the tunnel. While it would be nice to be able to influence speed values of other peers, the fact that I2P uses the observed maximum over an entire day makes this unattractive: attacking a peer to reduce its speed for a whole day is expensive.

---

[2] The complex threshold calculation is described in detail in [4].

2.3 Eepsites

The I2P software comes with the *Jetty* web server[3]. Using Jetty, every I2P user can offer HTTP web pages to the I2P network using a domain under the .i2p TLD. Given such a domain name, I2P creates inbound and outbound client tunnels for the service and (periodically) publishes a leaseSet in the netDB.

Accessing an Eepsite involves several steps (illustrated in Fig. 2):

1. Eepsite host (server) creates inbound and outbound tunnels for sender-anonymity and publishes gateway information as a leaseSet in the netDB (as described in Section 2.1). Fresh tunnels and corresponding leaseSet updates are created at least every 10 minutes.
2. The peer running the HTTP client (client) uses a tunnel to access the netDB and retrieves the leaseSet information.
3. The client uses inbound and outbound tunnels (for receiver-anonymity) to contact the gateways from the leaseSet.
4. A handshake is performed via the tunnels for end-to-end encryption between server and client, using the public key in the leaseSet.
5. The HTTP request is transmitted through the outbound tunnel of the client and the inbound tunnel of the server.
6. The HTTP response is transmitted through the outbound tunnel of the server and the inbound tunnel of the client.

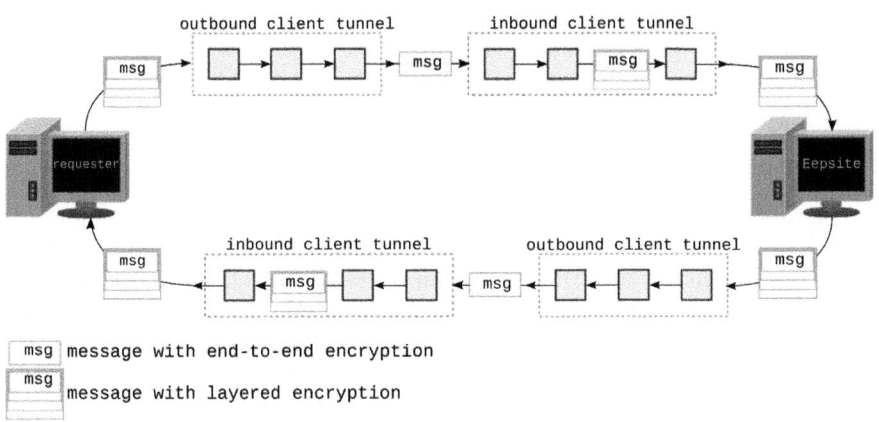

Fig. 2. Accessing an I2P Eepsite

Steps 5 and 6 can then be repeated; I2P reuses the resulting channel for subsequent HTTP requests to improve performance. This is somewhat relevant to the attack presented in this paper since it allows an attacker to repeatedly query the HTTP server without the need to perform the costly tunnel setup operations each time.

---

[3] http://jetty.codehaus.org/jetty/

Table 1. Key technical differences between Tor and I2P

Tor	I2P
3-hop tunnels	user-configurable, randomized number of hops
bi-directional tunnels	uni-directional tunnels
guards, bandwidth-based peer selection	performance-based peer selection
7 directory servers with complete data	super-peer DHT (floodfill peers)
link- and layered-encryption, but not (necessarily) end-to-end-encryption	end-to-end-, link- and layered-encryption
many exit nodes, few hidden services	one exit node, many integrated services
hidden services are external TCP servers	build-in servers for many services
implemented in C	implemented in Java
transport over TCP only	transport over TCP or UDP

2.4 Threat Model

The I2P project does not specify a formal threat model, it instead provides a list of possible well-known attack vectors (such as intersection / partitioning, tagging, DoS, harvesting, sybil and analysis attacks) and the authors discuss how the design relates to these attack vectors.[4]

Based on the scenarios described, I2P's attacker model closely resembles that of Tor: malicious peers are allowed to participate in the network, collect data and actively perform requests. However, the attacker is assumed to be unable to monitor the entire network traffic, should not control a vast number of peers (80% is used as an example) and should not be able to break cryptographic primitives.

2.5 Summary: I2P vs. Tor

The key philosophical difference between the well-known Tor network and I2P is that I2P tries to move existing Internet services into the I2P network and provide service implementations within the framework whereas Tor enables anonymous access to external Internet services implemented and operated separately. While Tor has hidden services and I2P has exit nodes, the canonical usage of Tor is accessing external services and the canonical usage of I2P is accessing integrated services.

I2P and Tor also differ in a number of technical details, some of which are key to the attack presented in the following section. Table 1 summarizes the main technical differences between the two projects.

3 Our Attack

Our attack assumes an adversary that actively participates in the network. Malicious nodes are distributed over different /16 subnets. The adversary should be

---

[4] http://www.i2p2.de/how_threatmodel.html

distributed in order to work around I2P's restriction of one node per subnet per tunnel and to provide reasonably well-performing malicious peers as neighbors regardless of the location of the victim on the Internet. Each of the participating peers is expected to have resources comparable to typical normal peers in the I2P network. The peers participate in the I2P network according to the network protocol. Our adversary does not have the capability to monitor the traffic of any other node. Our attack influences the performance of I2P peers likely to be chosen by the host of an Eepsite — the victim — for creating its client tunnels.

The goal of the attacker is to identify the peer "anonymously" hosting a given Eepsite with high probability. Furthermore, it is assumed that the Eepsite is available to the entire I2P network for the duration of the attack and hence resists intersection and partitioning attacks.

For our attack, the adversary uses three types of peers (illustrated in Fig. 3). The first type, a *monitor* peer, simply participates in the I2P network as "normal" peer, but reports certain statistics about tunnel operations back to the adversary. The most expensive operation (in terms of time and/or bandwidth) is getting the victim to select these monitor peers as its direct neighbors during tunnel construction. While there is always a (small) chance that the victim will select the adversary's monitor peers, the adversary uses a second type of peer, an *attack* peer (which performs a limited type of DoS attack) to influence the victim's tiers to the adversary's benefit. Note that, in contrast to [11], the goal of the attack is to change the fast tier, not to impact the availability or reachability of the Eepsite. Finally, the adversary also uses one peer to act as a "normal" visitor to the Eepsite, querying the I2P NetDB for leaseSets and issuing HTTP requests to the Eepsite. The leaseSets are used to determine which peers should be attacked (by the attack peers), and the HTTP requests are used to create a pattern which is detected by the monitor peers.

3.1   Distributed Monitoring

The main goal for the adversary is to control the nodes closest to the victim in the inbound and outbound tunnels of the Eepsite. I2P never picks two nodes from the same /16 network for the same tunnel twice. This makes it highly beneficial to use a distributed attacker that deploys monitor nodes across many /16 networks.

The attacker needs to only control the guard node and not multiple nodes per tunnel. Still, it is necessary to distribute the attacker across many /16 networks because for inbound tunnels, the guard node is the last node being chosen. So if the attacker's monitor nodes were all from the same /16 network, none of the attacker's monitor nodes must have been picked previously to participate in the tunnel before the guard node is selected in order to allow I2P to pick an attacker's monitor node as the guard node. If tunnels are of length n and the adversary controls a out of s (where $s = 30$ for the current version of I2P) monitor peers from the same /16 network in the victim's fast tier, the probability of being chosen as guard node would be only $\left(\frac{a}{s}\right)^n$ if all monitor peers are from the same /16 network. Even for small values of n, the attacker's /16 network

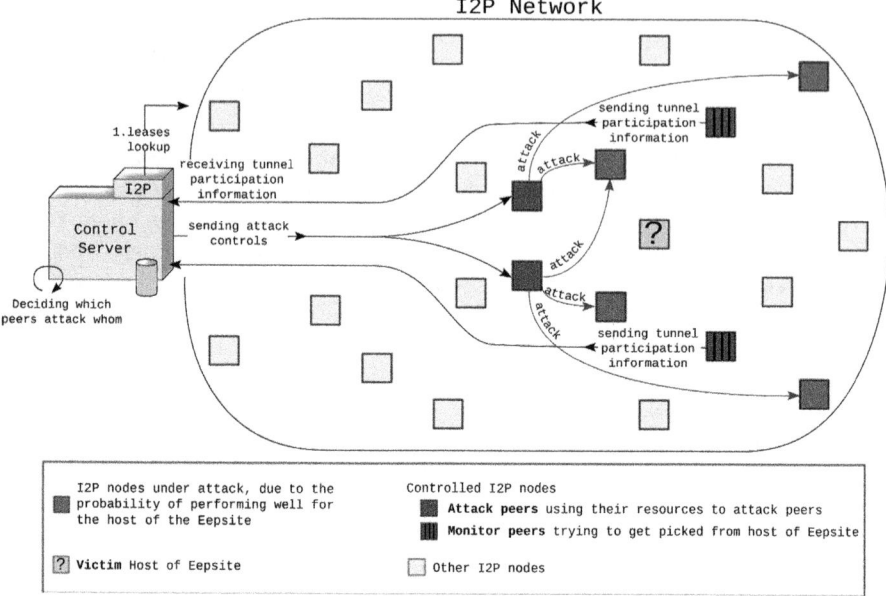

Fig. 3. Our attack on I2P uses several participating peers in different roles. Monitor peers gather statistical evidence, attack peers accelerate getting the monitor peers into the right position and the control server orchestrates activities.

would be blocked from being selected as the guard node most of the time. Since our attacker distributes his monitor nodes over many /16 networks, the chance of successfully becoming a guard node for the incoming tunnel is $\frac{a}{s}$, independent of the path length n.

3.2   Taking over the Victim's Fast Tier

The main challenge for the adversary is to force the victim to use the adversary's monitoring peers in its fast tier. Naturally, this requires the adversary to run several well-behaved and fast (monitor) peers. Clearly, depending on the size of the I2P network, just having a few monitor peers participate in the network would make it unlikely that the victim chooses these peers. Our attack takes advantage of the peer selection algorithm of I2P, which tries to select only well-performing peers for the tunnels. Thus, the adversary can increase its chances of entering the victim's fast tier by actively hampering the performance of the peers that are currently in the fast tier. While our goal is to enter the victim's fast tier, I2P's use of the highest observed speed over the last 24h makes it impractical to remove peers from the fast tier directly. Furthermore, the adversary may not be able to simply perform faster than the fastest s peers in the network — not to mention the victim may normally take a long time to even evaluate nodes controlled by the adversary. Thus, our attack makes use of the fact that I2P only allows high-capacity peers to remain in the fast tier; as a result, our attack influences the peer selection algorithm by causing peers to reject tunnels, which in turn makes it likely that they will be removed from the high-capacity tier (and thereby also the fast tier). This increases the chance that the victim will then select the adversary's monitoring peers as replacements.

Before the adversary can get peers from the victim's fast tier to reject tunnel requests, the current nodes in the victim's fast tier must be identified. Our attack uses nodes that were recently specified in the leaseSet of the Eepsite as good targets. After all, nodes that are in the leaseSet must be in the fast tier of the victim at that time, and are thus likely to remain in the fast tier for a while. We found that this method worked better than trying to predict the fast tier from performance measurements done by adversarial nodes.

Given a (small) set of peers that are likely in the fast tier, the adversary performs a denial-of-service (DoS) attack against these peers. Possible venues we considered were attacks against the CPU (by forcing the victims to perform many public key operations) and bandwidth exhaustion. In the end, overloading the peers with a large number of idle tunnels turned out to be the most cost-effective strategy for the current I2P release. This attack either exhausts the amount of bandwidth the peer is configured to use, or, if that limit is rather high, creates more than the 2500 tunnels that an I2P peer can participate in at any time. It should be noted that the specifics of the DoS attack are not terribly relevant to the big picture of the attack, and alternative strategies would likely work as well.

3.3   Confirmation via Traffic Analysis

The final step of the attack is to observe the victim's participation in a pair of tunnels carrying the adversary's signal with monitor peers adjacent to the victim in both directions.

There are many established traffic analysis techniques to confirm that two endpoints are participating in the same low-latency tunnel [6,7]. Existing theoretical models typically assume that a single message moves through the tunnel largely unmodified with only small chances of message loss. For I2P, the situation is a bit different; HTTP requests are explicitly converted into an HTTP responses, and, moreover, individual HTTP requests result in two distinct peaks in the packet frequency plots (see Fig. 5 (a)). Thus, we deployed a simple, application-specific method for detecting this particular traffic pattern instead of using more complex, generic methods that do not incorporate this domain knowledge.

A periodic HTTP request at a fixed frequency t is issued by the adversary's control server to create a statistical pattern that is then used to identify the correct tunnels at the monitor peers (Fig. 4). For our experiments we use $t = 15s$. For each tunnel, each monitoring peer counts the number of packets received in buckets representing time intervals of packet arrival times modulo t. If the total number of packets is smaller than those transmitted by the adversary to the Eepsite, the circuit is ignored. If the number of packets is close to or exceeds the expected number, the monitoring peers compute how many standard deviations the largest bucket size is from the average bucket size. If the resulting

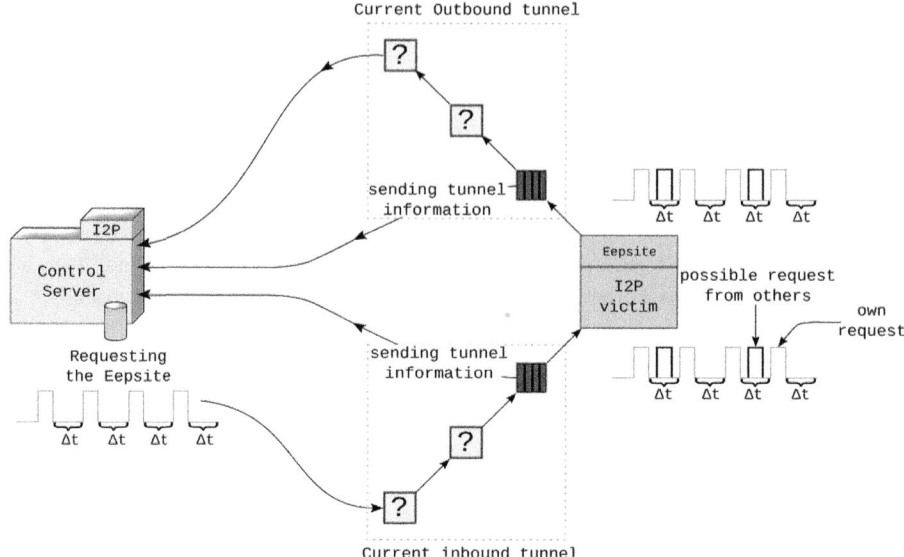

Fig. 4. A periodic signal is induced by the control server and detected by the monitor nodes. They report likely Eepsite hosts to the control server which aggregates the information.

factor is large, the packets were not equally distributed. Then, to exclude false-positives from short, non-periodic bursts, the monitoring peers perform the same calculation, this time for a time interval modulo q where $gcd(t, q) = 1$ and $|t - q|$ is small (we use $q = 16s$). If the signal had a frequency of t, the resulting factor should be very small; however, if a burst caused a false-positive, the resulting factor should be about as big as for the calculation modulo t. If the distribution is normalized modulo q, the tunnel is reported to the adversary as detected. If two monitoring peers report a peer between them at the same time, that peer is flagged as likely to be the Eepsite host. The sensitivity used for the standard deviation factor threshold determines how often the same peer needs to be flagged before the adversary can be certain.

4   Experimental Results

In this section, we present results from our experiments based on extending the extant I2P network with 70 "malicious" nodes (corresponding to less than 3.6% of the nodes in the network) on PlanetLab [12]. Monitor and attacker peers were configured to use at most 64 kb/s upstream and downstream bandwidth. We set up the control peer on a machine we controlled to minimize jitter. Furthermore, one of our peers was set up to host an Eepsite to serve as a victim for testing. This host was configured to use the standard I2P bandwidth settings (96 kb/s downstream and 40 kB/s upstream).

Table 2. Accuracy of the prediction for peers in the fast and high-capacity tiers using the n most recently observed peers from the lease set. The given percentage refers to the fraction of the peers from the n most recent leases that are actually in the respective tier. The fast tier typically consists of $s = 30$ peers, the high-capacity tier typically has 75 peers. At the time of the measurement, the I2P network contained at least 1921 peers in total.

# leases (most recent)	% nodes from lease set in fast tier	% nodes from lease set in high-capacity tier
5	60%	60%
10	40%	50%
15	40%	47%
20	45%	55%
25	36%	52%
30	30%	50%

All tests were performed by having all of our peers join the live I2P network and participate normally (except, of course, for attack-specific behavior). For our tests, we used 40 attack peers and 30 monitor peers. The 40 attack peers consistently utilized their 64 kb/s bandwidth; utilization of the 30 monitor peers differed widely depending on how they were used by normal I2P traffic. The I2P network contained *at least* 1921 peers at the time of our experiments.

We should note that the main impact of our experiments on the public I2P network was that a small fraction (about 1–2%) of the network was slowed down for a few hours. No personally identifiable information was collected. Despite our expectation that the impact of the experiment on the network would be small, an I2P developer did notice "strange" behavior (a significant increase in tunnels and traffic) when his node was (by chance) chosen as one of the targets for the attack. Those members of the I2P community we interacted with generally approved of us doing these kinds of (limited) experiments on I2P. Naturally, given an open community of anonymous participants, asking for everyone's approval is not possible.

4.1 Tier Evolution

First, we wanted to see how well the adversary would be able to predict the victim's fast tier from the public leaseSets for the Eepsite. This determines how much of the attack actually has a chance to have an effect on the victim's peer selection algorithm. Table 2 shows what fraction of the last n peers observed in the leaseSet were actually in the fast tier of the victim at the time. We configured the victim to use only one inbound and one outbound tunnel (I2P's default is two tunnels for each direction). This configuration captures the worst case scenario from the point of view of the adversary; with more tunnels, more leases could be learned and the adversary would get a better picture of the victim's fast tier.

Table 3. Direct impact of the tunnel acceptance rate of a peer under attack from various number of attackers with a configured bandwith limit of 64 kb/s. Note that an increasing number of attackers not only causes the peer under attack to reject tunnels, but additionally causes requests for tunnels to be lost and hence not be answered at all.

	normal	under attack, number of attackers				
	normal	2	3	5	7	10
Tunnels accepted	82%	63%	52%	16%	9%	1%
Tunnels rejected	18%	36%	41%	40%	36%	28%
Tunnels lost	0%	1%	7%	44%	55%	71%

Table 4. Impact of the DoS attack on the network using 40 peers with a configured bandwidth limit of 64 kb/s. This table shows the increase in the churn for the high-capacity and fast tiers of the victim that the attacker tries to deanonymize. Each value represents the churn of nodes per 45 seconds tier evaluation cycle of the victim. Note that the attack uses our (limited-precision) leaseSet-based prediction heuristic (Section 3.2) to determine which peers to attack. If the attacker could be certain about which peers are in the respective tiers, the increase in churn would be significantly higher. Monitor peers provided by the attacker are not subjected to the attack.

	normal	under attack
High-capacity tier churn	0.89 peers/cycle	3.41 peers/cycle
Fast tier churn	0.76 peers/cycle	1.71 peers/cycle

4.2   Attack Effectiveness

Next, we determined the impact of the DoS attack, first on the attacked peers (to confirm that the attack works as expected), and then on peer fluctuation in the fast and high capacity tier. Table 3 shows the impact of our attack on a single peer. It compares the tunnel request acceptance rate of an ordinary peer with the acceptance rate when that peer is attacked by several attackers. Table 4 shows the typical churn rate for peers in the high-capacity and fast tiers of the victim in two states: under normal operation, and under attack. The data corresponds to the adversary attacking the last 30 peers observed as leases (with the expected inaccuracies as listed in Table 2). The data shows that the DoS attack is effective at obstructing tunnel operations and that the victim reacts to these obstructions by replacing peers in its high-capacity and fast tiers more often.

4.3   Deanonymization

Finally, we measured how effective our statistical analysis is at determining the victim once the monitor peers are in place. First, we will provide some examples for what the statistical patterns observed by the monitor peers (Section 3.3) look like. Figure 5a shows a representative pattern for the case where the adversary observes the correct circuit with the signal and performs the statistical analysis

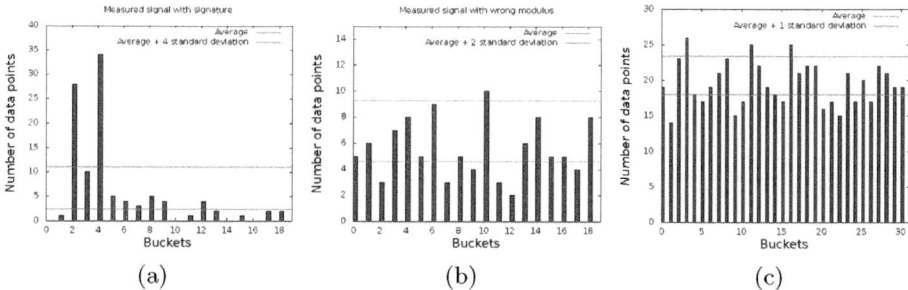

     (a)   (b)   (c)

Fig. 5. Subfigure (a) shows a packet frequency plot for a circuit containing the signal (with timestamps calculated modulo the correct modulus t). Subfigure (b) shows the same packet frequency plot, but with timestamps calculated modulo a different modulus q. Finally, Subfigure (c) shows a packet frequency plot for a typical circuit not created by the adversary. In all plots, average and standard deviation are calculated over the distribution excluding the two largest values (since we expect two peaks).

using the correct modulus (here $t = 15$). Internals of the I2P implementation typically create two distinct (and close) peaks if the signal is present. Since we expect to see these two peaks, we remove them from the distribution when calculating the average and standard deviations.

Figure 5b shows the same data using a different modulus (here $q = 16$), resulting in the peaks being destroyed. This would not be the case if the signal was not due to requests at the adversaries frequency of t. Sometimes, a circuit may experience spikes in load at a single point in time. Such spikes would show up as false-positive signals   mod t, but also as spikes   mod q. Our analysis eliminates these false-positives by only considering signals valid that show up mod t but are extinguished   mod q.

Finally, Figure 5c shows a typical pattern for a circuit that does not contain the signal. It should be noted that during our experiments, most circuits never reached the required minimum number of messages (approximately the number of messages transmitted by the adversary via the tunnel) and were hence filtered long before this statistical analysis is even performed. As a consequence, the adversary also does not have to worry about small sample sizes for calculating averages and standard deviations.

Figure 6 shows the ROC curves with the ratios for true-positives and false-positives for different standard deviation thresholds (in the range of 0 to 10 standard deviations). Tunnels with too few packets to carry the adversary's signal are not considered; for instance, for the 1-hop experiment, 47,503 out of 62,366 tunnels (76%) did not carry a sufficient number of packets. If such tunnels were included, the false-positive rate of the analysis would be lower.

The data from Figure 6 was obtained over the course of four hours with the victim manipulated to give the attacker control over the entire fast tier (to control this variable in the experiment). In practice, during a long-term measurement the adversary would not know at what times his monitor peers

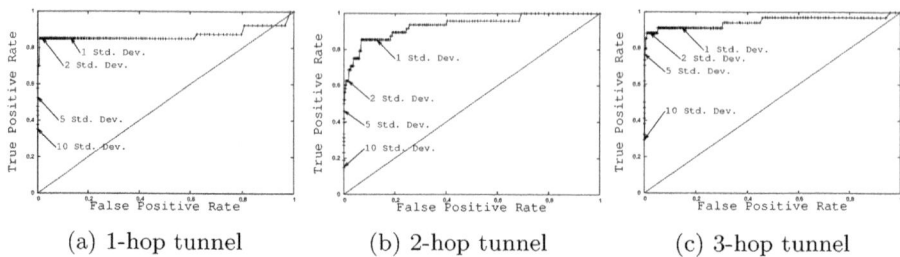

| (a) 1-hop tunnel | (b) 2-hop tunnel | (c) 3-hop tunnel |

Fig. 6. Final result of the statistical analysis. For each tunnel length, the monitor peers collected 4h worth of data. During this time, the victim created 40, 48 and 34 tunnels for 1-hop (Fig. 6a), 2-hop (Fig. 6b) and 3-hop (Fig .6c) tunnels respectively. The true-positive rates represent the fraction of those tunnels flagged by the statistical analysis for the given threshold. The monitor peers also observed a varying number of other tunnels (with a sufficient number of packets) unrelated to the victim (14,823 for 1-hop (Fig. 6a), 11,861 for 2-hop (Fig. 6b) and 5,898 for 3-hop (Fig. 6c)). The false-positive rates represent the fraction of those tunnels flagged by the statistical analysis for the given threshold. We marked the 1, 2, 5 and 10 standard deviation thresholds in the charts.

are in the correct position, making false-positive measurements more frequent. If the adversary is weak, he might rarely be in the correct position and hence would need to apply an aggressively high threshold to avoid false-positives. For example, if the adversary is only able to observe the signal 10% of the time, the ratio between the target and the top FP peer must be significantly larger than 10:1 to avoid identifying the wrong peer as the host.

Using a threshold of just one standard deviation would be a bit low, given that the adversary must expect many more non-victim tunnels over the duration of an experiment. During our experiment, the ratio was 40:14,823 for the 4h measurement with 1-hop tunnels. In reality, the adversary should expect even higher ratios because the adversary is likely to control a smaller fraction of the fast tier of the victim. Figure 6 shows that the signal is strong enough to be detected even when using a wide range of thresholds that are so high that there are virtually no false-positives. There are also no significant differences in the quality of the results between 1, 2 and 3-hop tunnels. Additional experimental results are included in [4].

5   Discussion

This work confirms the well-known result [1] that attacks on availability or reliability of an anonymizing service can be used to compromise anonymity. What we have shown specifically is that anonymizing networks that have a strong bias towards well-performing peers for tunnel construction are particularly vulnerable to this type of attack. Once the tunnel is compromised, other researchers have shown that latency measurements could be used to determine the likely identity of the victim [5].

5.1   Simplifying the Attack

The presented attack uses both monitor peers and attack peers. In theory, the attack could work without the attack peers, after all, the attack peers only speed-up the churn rate in the fast and high-capacity tiers of the victim. However, without attack peers, it is quite possible that the victim may rarely, if ever, choose the adversary's monitor peers: they might be too slow or not even ever measured by the victim.

In our attack, the attack peers more than doubles the churn in the fast tier, so we can expect that they cut down the time for the attack by about a factor of two. Using twice as many monitor peers would have been about as expensive; thus using a small number attackers to double the effect of the monitor peers represents a reasonable trade-off (as long as doubling the monitor peer effect is about as expensive as doubling the number of monitors). Using even more attackers would allow us to attack more peers; however, given that our knowledge about the fast tier of the victim is limited, the ratio between attack bandwidth and attack effect quickly gets worse. Using significantly fewer attacker peers also does not work — at 64 kb/s, a handfull of attackers might not cause a significant increase in the number of rejected tunnel requests.

5.2   Uni-directional vs. Bi-directional Tunnels

Because of the uni-directional nature of the I2P tunnels the attacker has to wait a longer time to observe the victim in the correct position for deanonymization; monitoring peers have to be in the correct position for both the inbound and the outbound tunnel. Thus, with a being the number of monitor peers in the fast tier of the victim, the probability for deanonymization in a fast tier of size s is $\left(\frac{a}{s}\right)^2$. For bi-directional tunnels the attacker would only need one peer in the correct position, resulting in a probability of $\frac{a}{s}$. This shows that the attacker has to wait t times longer to be in a position to confirm the victim in the uni-directional case when compared to the bi-directional case.

However, the chance of being correct about the deanonymization is different for both cases as well. To really compare the two styles, we need to consider the probability of deanonymizing the wrong peer (false-positive). For the uni-directional case, it is possible to accuse the wrong peer if the same ordinary tunnel participant happens to be adjacent to the victim for both the inbound and the outbound tunnel. For this to happen, the peer running the Eepsite has to first choose an ordinary, non-malicious peer for the first hop of the inbound tunnel. This happens with probability $\frac{a-s}{s}$. The same peer then also needs to be in the outbound tunnel, which happens with probability $\frac{1}{s}$. Additionally, the victim has to choose a monitor peer for the second hop of the inbound and the outbound tunnel, which happens with probability $\left(\frac{a}{s-1}\right)^2$. Combining all these probabilities, the probability for false-positives with uni-directional tunnels is:

$$\frac{s-a}{s}\frac{1}{s}\left(\frac{a}{s-1}\right)^2 = \frac{s-a}{s^2}\left(\frac{a}{s-1}\right)^2 \approx a^2\frac{s-a}{s^4} \tag{1}$$

With bi-directional tunnels, the probability for a false-positive is higher, because any other peer between a monitor peer and the victim can be falsely accused. The overall probability for a bi-directional 2-hop tunnel is:

$$\frac{s-a}{s}\frac{a}{s-1} \approx a\frac{s-a}{s^2} \tag{2}$$

We now relate the probabilities for getting a false-positive for uni-directional and bi-directional tunnels. Dividing (1) and (2) we get $\frac{a}{s^2}$, which shows that the accuracy for the uni-directional case is up to s^2 times higher when compared to the bi-directional case.

This result indicates that uni-directional tunnels help an attacker due to the much higher certainty an attacker gets once the monitor peers are in the correct position. Considering this, using uni-directional seems to be a bad design decision; it makes the statistical evaluation for the adversary easier for the attack presented in this paper. However, it should be said that the false-positive rate of bi-directional paths is not tremendously high and might still be manageable for an attacker.

5.3   Suggestions for Improvements to I2P

While making the I2P network more robust towards DoS attacks is always a good goal, we do not believe that this would address the main problem: the ability of the adversary to influence peer selection. While I2P's heuristics seem to make it hard for an adversary to directly influence the metrics used for peer selection, influencing performance itself is likely always possible. Hence, a better solution would be to limit churn in the fast and high-capacity tiers. Furthermore, when the Tor network was subjected to a similar attack [10], guard nodes were introduced into the design of Tor; this would also help in the case of I2P.

Another problem is the fact that Eepsites allow repeated measurements, giving the attacker the opportunity to possibly collect data for many months. This problem is not unique to I2P, but also applies in exactly the same way to Tor's hidden services. The I2P developers are currently working on integrating a version of the secure distributed Tahoe filesystem [14], which may address this issue.

I2P could try to detect the specific attack, for example by watching for periodic requests. However, such a defense would likely not be effective because an adversary could use signals that are much harder to detect, for example using [6].

Most importantly, I2P should avoid leaking information about its fast tier by selecting random peers for the leases. This would make it harder for an adversary to determine which peers should be attacked with the DoS attack while maintaining performance advantages for the rest of the tunnel.

6   Conclusion

Biasing peer selection towards well-performing peers has previously been seen as a mostly theoretical issue. This work shows that combined with a limited, selective DoS attack on a few peers it enables an adversary to compromise the anonymity of long-running services. This work also shows that peers reacting quickly to changes in observed network performance can be detrimental to anonymity.

Acknowledgments

This work was funded by the Deutsche Forschungsgemeinschaft (DFG) under ENP GR 3688/1-1. We thank Katie Haus for her help with the figures and Nathan Evans, Matthew Wright and the anonymous reviewers for their feedback on the paper.

References

1. Borisov, N., Danezis, G., Mittal, P., Tabriz, P.: Denial of service or denial of security? How attacks on reliability can compromise anonymity. In: CCS 2007: Proceedings of the 14th ACM Conference on Computer and Communications Security, pp. 92–102. ACM Press, New York (2007)
2. Dingledine, R., Mathewson, N., Syverson, P.: Tor: The second-generation onion router. In: Proceedings of the 13th USENIX Security Symposium (August 2004)
3. Evans, N.S., Dingledine, R., Grothoff, C.: A practical congestion attack on tor using long paths. In: 18th USENIX Security Symposium, pp. 33–50. USENIX (2009)
4. Herrmann, M.: Privacy-Implications of Performance-Based Peer Selection by Onion-Routers: A Real-World Case Study using I2P. Master's thesis, Technische Universität München (2011)
5. Hopper, N., Vasserman, E.Y., Chan-Tin, E.: How much anonymity does network latency leak? ACM Transactions on Information and System Security 13(2) (2010)
6. Houmansadr, A., Borisov, N.: Swirl: A scalable watermark to detect correlated network flows. In: NDSS 2011 (2011)
7. Levine, B., Reiter, M., Wang, C., Wright, M.: Timing attacks in low-latency mix systems. In: Juels, A. (ed.) FC 2004. LNCS, vol. 3110, pp. 251–265. Springer, Heidelberg (2004)
8. Maymounkov, P., Mazières, D.: Kademlia: A peer-to-peer information system based on the xor metric, pp. 53–65 (2002)
9. Murdoch, S.J., Danezis, G.: Low-cost traffic analysis of Tor. In: SP 2005: Proceedings of the 2005 IEEE Symposium on Security and Privacy, May 2005, pp. 183–195. IEEE Computer Society Press, Washington, DC, USA (2005)
10. Øverlier, L., Syverson, P.: Locating hidden servers. In: SP 2006: Proceedings of the 2006 IEEE Symposium on Security and Privacy, pp. 100–114. IEEE Computer Society Press, Washington (2006)
11. Øverlier, L., Syverson, P.: Valet services: Improving hidden servers with a personal touch. In: Danezis, G., Golle, P. (eds.) PET 2006. LNCS, vol. 4258, pp. 223–244. Springer, Heidelberg (2006)

12. Peterson, L.: PlanetLab: Version 3.0. Tech. Rep. PDN–04–023, PlanetLab Consortium (October 2004)
13. Syverson, P., Goldschlag, D., Reed, M.: Anonymous Connections and Onion Routing. In: IEEE Symposium on Security and Privacy, Oakland, California, vol. 7, pp. 44–54 (1997)
14. Wilcox-O'Hearn, Z., Warner, B.: Tahao – the least-authority filesystem. In: Proceedings of the 4th ACM international workshop on Storage security and survivability. ACM Press, New York (2008)
15. zzz, Schimmer, L.: Peer profiling and selection in the i2p anonymous network. In: PET-CON 2009.1., TU Dresden, Germany (March 2009)

Privacy-Friendly Aggregation for the Smart-Grid

Klaus Kursawe[1], George Danezis[2], and Markulf Kohlweiss[2]

[1] Radboud Universiteit Nijmegen
kursawe@cs.ru.nl
[2] Microsoft Research, Cambridge, U.K.
{gdane,markulf}@microsoft.com

Abstract. The widespread deployment of smart meters for the modernisation of the electricity distribution network, but also for gas and water consumption, has been associated with privacy concerns due to the potentially large number of measurements that reflect the consumers behaviour. In this paper, we present protocols that can be used to privately compute aggregate meter measurements over defined sets of meters, allowing for fraud and leakage detection as well as network management and further statistical processing of meter measurements, without revealing any additional information about the individual meter readings. Thus, most of the benefits of the Smart Grid can be achieved without revealing individual data. The feasibility of the protocols has been demonstrated with an implementation on current smart meters.

1 Introduction

Smart-grid deployments are actively promoted by many governments, including the United States as well as the European Union. Yet, current smart metering technologies rely on centralizing personal consumption information, leading to privacy concerns. We address the problem of security aggregating meter readings without the provider learning any information besides the aggregate, or to compare an aggregate with a known value to detect fraud or leakage (the latter is more relevant for water and gas metering).

Aggregates of consumption across different populations are used for fraud detection, forecasting, tuning production to demand, settling the cost of production across electricity suppliers, and getting a clear picture on the supply of consumer generated energy, e.g., through solar panels. Aggregation protocols will also be used to detect leakages in other utilities, e.g., water (which is a big issue in desert countries) and gas (where a leakage poses a safety problem).

Privacy in Smart Metering. The area of smart metering for electricity, but also other commodities such as gas and water is currently experiencing a huge push; for example, the European commission has formulated the goal to provide 80% of all households with smart electricity meters by the year 2020 [1], and the US government has dedicated a significant part of the stimulus package towards a smart grid implementation. Simultaneously, privacy issues are mounting – in

S. Fischer-Hübner and N. Hopper (Eds.): PETS 2011, LNCS 6794, pp. 175–191, 2011.

2009, the Dutch Senate stopped a law aimed to make the usage of smart meters compulsory based on privacy and human rights issues [2]. On the US side, NIST has identified privacy as one of the main concerns in a smart grid implementation, and both NIST and the European Comission propose using the "privacy by design" approach [3,4] to alleviate them. While it is not clear yet how much data can be derived from actual meter readings, the high frequency suggested (i.e., about 15 minute reading intervals), together with the difficulty to temporarily hide one's behaviour (as one can do, for example, by turning off a mobile phone), gives rise to serious privacy concerns. For water and gas leakage detection privacy preserving protocols are even more desirable since measurements need to be frequent to detect potentially dangerous leaks as soon as possible. Our protocols allow for a business positive view on privacy. As the aggregator does not learn anything about the individual contributions, the granularity of the input to the protocol can be much finer than otherwise possible. For example, one vision for the smart grid is to remotely tune down flexible applicances such as fridges and air-conditioners during times of energy shortage. Due to privacy protecting aggregation, it is possible that the meter reports the consumption of such devices (and willingness to tune down) separately without an additional privacy risk, which allows the energy supplier to predict better how much energy consumption could be reduced that way.

An important aspect in privacy preserving metering protocols is to take into account the rather limited resources on such meters, both in terms of bandwidth and in terms of computation. We therefore push as much workload as possible to the back-end, leaving the minimal work possible on the meter itself. In terms of communication, the messages sent out by the meters should increase only minimally. Furthermore, meters should ideally act independently, without requiring any interaction with other meters wherever possible and minimal interaction when not.

For statistical analysis, our protocols support the division of meters into independent sets over which the aggregation is to be done. This allows for different use-cases that require only statistical accuracy to be combined without any additional effort on the meters. We have validated the practicality of our protocols in a real setting with an implementation on a production meter in collaboration with the meter manufacturer, and by defining the usecases together with several energy suppliers.

Related work. Privacy preserving metering aggregation and comparison has been introduced by Garcia and Jacobs [5]. Their protocol requires $O(n^2)$ bytes of interaction between the individual meters as well as relatively expensive cryptography on the meters. Fu. et all [6], highlight the privacy related threats of smart metering and propose an architecture for secure measurements, that rely on trusted components outside of the meter. Rial and Danezis [7] propose a protocol using commitments and zero knowledge proofs to privately derive and prove the correctness of bills, but not for aggregation across meters.

2   Basic Protocols

The protocols we propose follow the principle of [8] by relying on masking the meter consumptions $c_{i,j}$ output by meter j for a reading i, in such a way that an adversary cannot recover individual readings. Yet, the sum of the masking values across meters sums to a known value (for simplicity we set it to be zero here; however, in a practical setting, a non-zero value does allow for aggregating over several different sets of meters and easier group management). As a result summing the masked readings uncovers their sum or a one-way function of their sum. To prevent linking masked values, the masks are recomputed for every measurement either by a symmetric protocol with communication between the meters, or by an asymmetric one that does not require such. We refer to the combination of a meter and a user as a metered home, or home in short. We consider two types of protocols:

In the first, which we refer to as *aggregation protocols*, metered homes use masking values $x_{i,j}$ to output blinded values $x_{i,j} + c_{i,j}$. After the masking values have canceled each other out, the result of the protocol is $\sum c_{i,j}$.

In the second type of protocols, homes output $g_i^{x_j + c_{i,j}}$ and the result of the protocol is $g_i^{\sum c_{i,j}}$. We call the latter protocols *comparison protocols*, because they require that the aggregator already knows the (approximate) sum of the values she is aggregating (through a feeder meter), and needs to determine whether her sum is sufficiently close to the aggregate obtained from home meters. However, as shown in Section 4.6, the comparrison protocol can easily be turned into a full aggregation protocol with low overhead.

Comparison protocols offer advantages for cryptographic protocol design, as protocol values can be exponents in cryptographic groups for which the computation of discrete logarithms are in general hard. One advantage that can be garnered from this is that in contrast to aggregation protocols, no fresh $x_{i,j}$ are needed. For random x_j and g_i, $g_i^{x_j}$ are indistinguishable from $g_i^{x_{i,j}}$, where the $x_{i,j}$ are chosen freshly for each g_i, under the Decisional Diffie-Hellman assumption.

The basic comparison protocol. Let $\mathbb{G}$ be a suitable Diffie-Hellman group, and $H : \{0,1\}^* \to \mathbb{G}$ a hash function mapping arbitrary strings onto elements of $\mathbb{G}$.[1] Let x_j be a pre-shared secret for home j such that $\sum_j x_j = 0$. We assume that each measurement round has a unique identifier i that is shared by all homes and the aggregator, e.g., a serial number or the time and date of the measurement.

For each reading $c_{i,j}$, the home computes a common group element $g_i = H(i)$. It then computes $g_{i,j} = g_i^{c_{i,j} + x_j}$. The value $g_{i,j}$ is then send to the aggregator. The aggregator collects all values of $g_{i,j}$, and computes $g_a = \prod_j g_{i,j}$.

By construction, we have $\prod_i g_{i,j} = \prod_i g_i^{c_{i,j}} \cdot \prod_i g_i^{x_i} = g^{\sum_i c_{i,j}}$, i.e., g_a is g_i to the power of the aggregated measurements. As the aggregator has it's own

---

[1] For our security analysis we will make use of the random oracle model to guarantee the randomness of the g_i values [9].

measurement c_a of the total consumption of the connected meters, it now needs to verify if g_a roughly equals g^{c_a}. This can be done by brute forcing values of $g^{c_a}, g^{c_a-1}, g^{c_a+1}, \ldots$ until either a match is found or a sufficiently large interval has been tested to raise an alarm.

In the bare protocol, the consumer can easily modify outgoing messages by multiplying with or dividing by g_i. This can easily be prevented by either usign authenticated messages, or by deriving g_i using a keyed hash-function. In the later case, the consumer can still maniulate the outut, but no longer in a controled way, which will triggen an alarm with high probability.

3   Concrete Protocols

As we have seen, the general framework of our protocols requires a number of meters or users to have a secret value x_j per meter or $x_{i,j}$ per meter per round, such that they all add up to zero. Then the aggregation protocols can be used by each party publishing $x_{i,j} + c_{i,j}$, or the comparison protocol by publishing $g_i^{x_j+c_{i,j}}$. Concrete protocols provide different ways for a number of meters or users to derive the necessary $x_{i,j}$ or $g_i^{x_j}$.

We propose four such protocols each with different advantages: (1) a protocol that offers unconditional security based on secret sharing; (2,3) two protocols based on Diffie-Hellman key exchange that allow blinding to be verifiably done outside the meter; (4) finally a protocol based on computations on the meter, but with negligible communication overhead.

3.1   Interactive Protocol

Our first protocol uses simple additive secret sharing. For each round i of measurements, a subset of the homes is (deterministically) chosen as *leaders*[2]; all parties compute completely random secret shares, encrypt them, and send them to the leaders. The leaders then computes their final shares in a way that all shares together sum to zero. Shares at each home are added together with the meter reading to mask it; an aggregator can sum up all shares such that they cancel out and reveal the sum of all consumption across the homes.

More formally, we assume an aggregation set of n homes and one aggregator (substation). We call p the privacy parameter; this is the number of leaders in a run of the protocol. At system setup, each home has its own private encryption key K_j, as well as the public encryption keys $PK_1, \ldots, PK_n$ for all other homes in the same aggregation set.

- To generate masking values, each home j first computes p random values $s_{j,1}, \ldots, s_{j,p}$. It then computes the leader identities $\ell_1, \ldots, \ell_p$ of the p leaders, and encrypts $s_{j,k}$ with PK_{ℓ_k}, $1 \leq k \leq p$. The set of p encrypted shares is

---

[2] Alternatively, leaders could be trusted third parties that do not contribute any consumption values themselves.

sent to the aggregator that sends each leader its corresponding encrypted shares.
- Each leader ℓ_k collects $n - 1$ shares $s_{j,k}$, $1 \le j \le n$, $j \ne \ell_k$, and computes its own share $s_{\ell_k,k}$ such that all shares together sum to the value 0 (modulo 2^{32}).
- Finally, all parties add all their shares $s_{j,1}, ..., s_{j,p}$ to get the main share s_j.

For the basic aggregation protocol, $x_{i,j} = s_j$. To update the masking values, the above steps are repeated with a different set of leaders for each reading i; the results for each meter is added to it's current share. To send a reading $c_{i,j}$, a meter computes $b_{i,j} = c_{i,j} + s_{i,j}$ mod 2^{32}. The aggregator collects all this data, and computes $\sum_i b_{i,j} = \sum_i c_{i,j}$.

The interactive protocol can also be used in combination with the basic comparison protocol by setting $x_j = s_j$, removing the need for updating shares.

3.2 Diffie-Hellman Key-Exchange Based Protocol

Our second scheme is based on the standard Diffie-Hellman key exchange protocol, combined with a modified variant of the Dining Cryptographer's anonymity protocol [10,11]. We assume that each meter j has a secret key X_j, and a corresponding public key Pub_j.

- For each round i, let $g_i = H(i)$ be a generator of a Diffie-Hellman group $\mathbb{G}$. The generator g_i is the same as for the basic comparison protocol.
- In the first phase of the protocol, each home computes a round specific public key $\text{Pub}_{i,j} = g_i^{X_j}$, certifies it, and distributes it to all other members of the aggregation set.
- Homes receive and verify public keys $\text{Pub}_{i,1}, \ldots, \text{Pub}_{i,n}$.
- Each home can now compute the following value:

$$g_i^{x_j} = \prod_{k \ne j} \text{Pub}_{i,k}^{(-1)^{k<j} X_j} ,$$

where $k < j$ is an indicator variable taking value 1, if the name/index of meter k is lexicographically smaller than the name of meter j, and zero otherwise. As required the sum of all x_j is equal to 0:

$$\sum_j x_j = \sum_j \sum_{k \ne j} (-1)^{k<j} p_k \cdot p_j = 0 .$$

- Therefore each meter can compute $g_{i,j}$ as required by the comparison protocol as: $g_{i,j} = g_i^{c_{i,j}} \cdot g_i^{x_j} = g_i^{c_{i,j}+x_j}$.

Note that x_j cannot be known or recovered by any of the meters. This precludes the use of this protocol as an aggregation protocol, but is not an impediment to using it as a comparison protocol.

3.3   Diffie-Hellman and Bilinear-Map Based Protocol

The DH-based scheme can be extended to only require a fixed public key per
meter. The construction is similarly to the modified Dining-Cryptographers pro-
tocols in [12]. Let $\mathbb{G}_1$, $\mathbb{G}_2$, and $\mathbb{G}_T$ be groups in which the Decisional Bilinear Diffie-
Hellman assumption [13] holds with a bi-linear map function $e(\mathbb{G}_1, \mathbb{G}_2) \rightarrow \mathbb{G}_T$.
Each meter only has to produce once a fixed public key $\text{Pub}_j = \hat{g}_0^{X_j}$ where $\hat{g}_0$ is
a generator of $\mathbb{G}_1$. Let $H(\{0,1\}^*) \rightarrow \mathbb{G}_2$ be a hash function mapping arbitrary
strings onto elements of $\mathbb{G}_2$.

- In round i, compute $\hat{g}_i = H(i)$ and $g_i = e(\hat{g}_0, \hat{g}_i)$. Homes can now compute
  $g_i^{x_j}$ as:

$$g_i^{x_j} = \left(\prod_{k \neq j} e(\text{Pub}_k, \hat{g}_i)^{(-1)^{k<j}} \right)^{X_j} ,$$

  where $k < j$ is an indicator variable taking value 1 or 0 depending on the
  result of the comparison. As required the sum of all x_j is 0:

$$\sum_j x_j = \sum_j \sum_{k \neq j} (-1)^{k<j} p_k \cdot p_j = 0 .$$

- Therefore each meter can compute $g_{i,j}$ as required by the comparison protocol as: $g_{i,j} = g_i^{c_{i,j}} \cdot g_i^{x_j} = g_i^{c_{i,j}+x_j}$.

Note that as in the pure Diffie-Hellman protocol x_j cannot be known or recovered
by any of the meters. This is not an impediment to using it as a comparison
protocol. As noted by [12], the map e can be instantiated with the Weil pairing
over a suitable elliptic curve.

3.4   Low-Overhead Protocol

As for the Bilinear map based scheme, we assume that all meters have a fixed
public key $\text{Pub}_j = g^{X_j}$ where g is a fixed globally known generator of a group
in which the Computational Diffie-Hellman assumption holds.

- Each meter is initialised with the public keys of all other meters, and computes a set of shared keys, as: $K_{j,k} = H(\text{Pub}_k^{X_j})$ Once the set of shared
  keys have been computed the original public keys of the other meters can be
  discarded.
- For each round i of masking value generation each meter j outputs:

$$x_{i,j} = \sum_{k \neq j} (-1)^{k<j} H(K_{j,k} \| i) .$$

For the basic aggregation protocol, only 32 bits of $x_{i,j}$ are needed, and $b_{i,j} = c_{i,j} + x_{i,j} \bmod 2^{32}$. The values $b_{i,j}$ are short 4 byte unsigned integers, and the aggregator can compute the sum simply by adding all the outputs together $\sum_j c_{i,j} = \sum_j b_{i,j} \mod 2^{32}$.

The low-overhead protocol can also be used in combination with the basic comparison protocol by setting $x_j = x_{i',j}$ for a fixed i'. This removes the need for creating additional masking values. To allow for cryptographic verification of correct computation of $g_{i,j} = g_i^{c_{i,j}+x_j}$, the meter can output a commitment $g^{x_j} h^{open_{x_j}}$ together with a signature σ_{x_j} on this commitment under the meter's secret key.

4 Comparison between Concrete Protocols

We proposed four concrete protocol variants to achieve private aggregation or comparison. In this section we compare them with regards to *cryptographic verifiability, cost & performance, availability, forward secrecy, group management, interoperability with other protocols* and finally their applicability to *further applications*.

4.1 Cryptographic Verifiability

The metering setting presented so far includes meters and an aggregator jointly computing the sum of consumption or comparing it to a known value. In practice meters are resource constraint devices in terms of memory, bandwidth, latency and storage, and to a lesser extent computation. Furthermore the architecture of smart-meters separates the certified metrological core, from other functions such as any user interface or communications logic, further constraining resources available for privacy protocols. For these reasons it might be beneficial to perform the bulk of any computations necessary for the aggregation protocol outside the meter or at least outside the certified metrological unit. Yet, despite off-loading those computations on untrusted hardware, under the control of the customer, we would like to ensure the correctness of the protocols – namely that the sum extracted through the aggregation protocol is indeed the sum of all readings from the meters.

Existing privacy-reserving billing protocols [7] have proposed a simple modification to meters that enables further privacy preserving computations: meters output commitments to their readings (such as Petersen commitments [14] of the form $C_{c_{i,j}} = g^{c_{i,j}} h^{open_{i,j}}$) and a signature over them. The customer associated with meter can open those commitments but can also use them as input to certify further computations. Let us evaluate how our proposed protocols are amenable to such certification.

In the context of verification we consider a meter, a customer, and an aggregator. The meter outputs signed commitments to its readings, as well as the raw readings to the customer. The customer performs the necessary steps of the aggregation or comparison protocol, but also outputs a universally verifiable cryptographic proof that protocol messages are correct. The aggregator receives the inputs of all customers, and can use the certified readings as well as the proof of all messages to ensure no customer has deviated from the valid protocol.

We use several existing results to prove statements about discrete logarithms, such as, proofs of knowledge of a discrete logarithm [15] and proofs of knowledge of the equality of elements in different representations [16]. These results are often given in the form of Σ-protocols but with the help of hash functions they can be turned into non-interactive zero-knowledge arguments in the random oracle model [17]. When referring to the proofs above, we follow the notation introduced by Camenisch and Stadler [18].

The *interactive protocol* can be verified by using a simple version of a verifiable secret sharing scheme [14] to certify that all protocol messages are well formed. For every round of aggregation i each customer outputs a commitment $C_{x_{i,j}}$ to a random value $x_{i,j}$, as well as commitments $C_{s_{j,k}}$ to the shares $s_{j,k}$. Then it provides a proof in zero-knowledge that the sum of the shares is equal to the committed random value, and that the output value $c_{i,j} + x_{i,j}$ is indeed the sum of the random value and the genuine meter reading. Each leader further proves that their random share $s_{i,k}$ added to all the shares they received sums to the value zero. The proofs only involve statements about revelation of commitments and sums of commitments and are extremely efficient if a commitment scheme with an additive homomorphism is used, such as Petersen commitments.

The *DH based protocol* is also amenable to cryptographic verification. The customer can produce the value $g_{i,j}$ along with a certificate to prove it is correctly formed given their public key $\mathrm{Pub}_j = g^{X_j}$ and the commitment to the meter reading $C_{c_{i,j}}$. First, the customer needs to create a new public key using the generator g_i associated with the reading time i, and prove that it has the same secret key X_j. This public key $\mathrm{Pub}_{i,j}$ is published for all to retrieve.

Then using the public keys $\mathrm{Pub}_{i,k}$ of all other customers k, it needs to prove that the value $g_{i,j}$ is well formed given its own secret key. This involves a standard zero-knowledge proof that:

$$\mathrm{NIZK}(X_j, c_{i,j}, \mathrm{open}_{i,j})\{\mathrm{Pub}_j = g^{X_j} \wedge \mathrm{Pub}_{i,j} = g_i^{X_j} \wedge C_{c_{i,j}} = g^{c_{i,j}} h^{\mathrm{open}_{i,j}}$$

$$\wedge\ g_{i,j} = g_i^{c_{i,j}} \cdot \left(\prod_{k \neq j} \mathrm{Pub}_{i,k}^{(-1)^{i<j}} \right)^{X_j} \}\ .$$

The *bilinear map based protocol* can also be verified cryptographically. Each meter has to prove that the value $g_{i,j}$ is formed correctly. This can be done efficiently with a proof that:

$$\mathrm{NIZK}(X_j, c_{i,j}, \mathrm{open}_{i,j})\{\mathrm{Pub}_j = \hat{g}_0^{X_j} \wedge C_{c_{i,j}} = g^{c_{i,j}} h^{\mathrm{open}_{i,j}}$$

$$\wedge\ g_{i,j} = g_i^{c_{i,j}} \left(\prod_{k \neq j} e(\mathrm{Pub}_k, \hat{g}_i)^{(-1)^{k<j}} \right)^{X_j} \}\ .$$

This is similar to the proofs in [12], except that we do not have to worry about collisions in the Dining Cryptographers protocol. In fact, our protocol presupposes that every home contributes some value $g_i^{c_{i,j}}$ as a contribution to the sum $\sum_i c_{i,j}$.

Finally the *low-overhead protocol* is based on symmetric key primitives that do not exhibit the mathematical relations necessary for efficient zero-knowledge proofs. While it could in theory be cryptographically verified though decomposing it into a circuit, this would not be a practical protocol. Therefore this protocol has to be run within the trusted meter hardware.

When using the low-overhead protocol together with the basic comparison protocol some amount of cryptographic verifiability is possible. Cryptographic verifiability can, however, be guaranteed only for the correct construction of $g_{i,j}$ from the values committed in signed commitments C_{x_j} and $C_{c_{i,j}}$. This can be done efficiently with a proof that:

$$\text{NIZK}(x_j, \text{open}_{x_j}, c_{i,j}, \text{open}_{i,j})\{C_{c_{x_j}} = g^{x_j} h^{\text{open}_{x_j}}$$
$$\wedge\, C_{c_{i,j}} = g^{c_{i,j}} h^{\text{open}_{i,j}} \wedge g_{i,j} = g_i^{x_j + c_{i,j}}\}\,.$$

This might be useful for aggregating values that are not known to the meter (such a demographics, e.g. the number of people sharing a home). In such cases the meter can provide a signed commitment that is augmented by another certified item outside the meter.

4.2   Computation and Communication Overheads

Whether the proposed protocols are executed by meters or by customers our protocols always impose some overhead over a privacy invasive solution.

The DH based protocol in its most secure form is the most expensive protocol, requiring $O(N^2)$ total messages to be exchanged as all participants need to have access to a new set of DH public keys $\text{Pub}_{i,j}$ for the aggregation of each meter reading. A related version of the protocol could allow participants to only share keys with p other participants reducing the communication cost to $O(N \cdot p)$. The protocol requires $O(N)$ modular multiplications but only $O(1)$ exponentiations per participant.

The interactive protocol only requires $O(N \cdot p)$ messages to be sent from the normal participants to the leaders, and a further $O(p)$ messages from the leaders. The setup cost requires public key distribution which could cost from $O(N^2)$ messages to $O(N \cdot p)$ if leader are fixed. Computations are very fast as they only involve addition over large integers, but secrecy of shares forces each participant

Table 1. Performance comparison

	Initialization	Communication	Computation
Interactive (agg)	$O(N^2) \cdot |PK|$	$O(N \cdot p) \cdot \mathbb{Z}_q$	$O(p) \cdot \text{Enc}$
Interactive (comp)	$O(N^2) \cdot |PK|$ $+O(N \cdot p) \cdot \mathbb{Z}_q$	$O(N) \cdot \mathbb{G}$	$O(1) \cdot E$
DH	$O(N^2) \cdot \mathbb{G}$	$O(N^2) \cdot \mathbb{G}$	$O(N) \cdot M + O(1) \cdot E$
Pairing	$O(N^2) \cdot \mathbb{G}$	$O(N) \cdot \mathbb{G}$	$O(N) \cdot P + O(1) \cdot E$
Low-overhead (agg)	$O(N^2) \cdot \mathbb{G}$	$O(N) \cdot \mathbb{Z}_{2^{32}}$	$O(N) \cdot H$
GC [5]	$O(N^2) \cdot |PK|$	$O(N^2) \cdot \mathbb{Z}_{n^2}$	$O(N) \cdot \text{Enc} + O(1) \cdot \text{Dec}$

to perform $O(p)$ public key encryptions and each leader $O(N)$ decryptions. Its cryptographic proof can use homomorphisms involving multiplications and $O(1)$ exponentiations for each customer.

The pairing based scheme is the most economical in terms of communication overhead. The key distribution setup requires $O(N^2)$ messages for all homes to be made aware of the long term public keys of all other meters. After that for each reading only $O(N)$ messages are required from the meters to the aggregator. Each participant needs to perform $O(N)$ pairing operations and $O(1)$ exponentiations.

The low-overhead protocol has to be run within the meter but is extremely compact and computationally efficient. Key distribution requires a one-off exchange of public keys which costs overall $O(N^2)$ messages and $O(N)$ exponentiations per participant. Subsequently, only $O(N)$ hash function applications are required, and only $O(N)$ small integer values are transmitted to the aggregator. This is the same communication cost as today's meters – giving the final protocol its name. We provide an experimental evaluation of this protocol in Section 5.

4.3 Availability, Privacy and Forward Secrecy

Considerations of whether to run the protocols in the meter or over customer hardware need to take into account the need for availability, or the principle "utility robustness" as it is known in the energy industry. The principle means that all parts necessary for the correct functioning of the energy supply system, including fraud detection, should be under the control of the energy industry. The key fear is that the energy supplier may not have the authority to replace a component when it fails, or is disabled. Therefore when the aggregation and comparision protocols are used for critical monitoring it is advisable to run them in the meters. When they are only used for non-critical tasks (such as tuning seasonal profiles of consumption) they can be off-loaded on customer machines and performed when the user is on-line.

Privacy is a key property of our protocols and it is maintained as long as all participants are honest-but-curious and do not collude. In case of passive collusion different protocols provide different guarantees. The DH based protocol, the bilinear maps based protocol, and the low-overhead protocol ensure that the anonymity set within which meter readings are aggregated includes all the non colluding meter readings. The interactive protocol has a similar property for any number of colluding nodes that does not include all leaders. If all leaders collude all privacy is lost.

Active attackers, that can break their meters, can disrupt the protocol so that the reported aggregate is different than the actual sum of consumptions. This is, however, at the heart of the fraud detection mechanism: the total may be different and thus has to be compared with the aggregator meter. Colluding attackers can also shift their reported consumption to appear as if some are consuming more or less subject to the sum being equal. While this attack does not change the total energy consumed it might still be beneficial for customers with variable tariffs. In case cryptographically verifiable protocols are used active adversaries should not be able to interfere with the integrity of the protocol messages unless they have compromised the physical meters, or have physically bypassed the meter – which is common.

Forward secrecy [19,13,20] is desirable to minimize the impact of a potentially leaked private key. The interactive and DH based protocols can be modified to provide some forward secrecy. The interactive protocol participants can use ephemeral keys to encrypt shares sent to the leaders, that are forgotten after a certain epoch. Similarly fresh DH keys can be used for each round of aggregation using the DH protocol, by signing them with the long term keys instead of proving they are the same. The overhead to modify the protocols in this manner is not high, since they already require $O(N^2)$ messages per round. On the other hand it is difficult to modify either the Bilinear map based protocol or the low-overhead protocol to provide forward secrecy while keeping their messages volumes at a similar level. Re-keying these protocols will require a fresh setup and $O(N^2)$ messages.

4.4   Key Establishment and Group Management

All proposed protocols require participants to be aware of the keys of meters, and other participants, including signature keys and encryption keys. In all cases we assume that meters contain a signature key to authenticate genuine messages. A private decryption key is used by some protocols to either communicate with leaders or build secure channels. These can be shared with the customers.

In case cryptographic certification is used to off-load computations a further secure channel is required between customers and meters to ensure only authorised customers can open the certified commitments to readings. In that case meters do not need to be aware of the keys of other parties, keeping them cheap.

Setup phases when keys are exchanged take from $O(l \cdot N)$ messages for the interactive protocol to $O(N^2)$ messages for the other protocols. For the bilinear maps based protocol and the low-overhead protocol this is a one-off cost, after which only $O(N)$ messages need to be exchanged.

In some cases keys will have to be rotated, either to ensure forward secrecy (as for example when the owner of a house changes) or to introduce or retire meters to groups. Adding, changing, or removing the key of a meter from a group only requires $O(N)$ messages, to notify all participants of the new certified key.

The security of the proposed schemes depends on the compositions of the meter groups. As we have already discussed a single honest participant within a group that is totally controlled by the adversary cannot expect any privacy. For this work we assume that the energy industry is in charge of specifying meter groups, and meters or participants can audit the group composition to detect whether they are tricked into participating in compromised groups. For this purpose a tamper evident log of group participants can be kept by the meters or the certified aggregates can be kept by users to prove any deviation from the genuine groups. Pragmatically energy providers are likely to be curious but unlikely to engage in behaviour that can be shown to deviate from their obligations, be it contractual or regulatory.

Individual customer may wish to opt-out of smart metering all together. Supporting regions with such customers is not a problem for the aggregation protocols but a challenge for our comparison protocols. Consider a single meter within a region not participating in computing the privacy friendly aggregate that is also metered by the aggregate meter: the difference between two sum of participating readings and the aggregate meter will end up being the consumption of the meter that has opted out. This is perverse as it results in a privacy sensitive user being even more vulnerable by opting out than by participating in the protocol.

4.5   Support for Settlement, Profiling and Forecasting

The primary aim of the aggregation protocol is to detect whether the sum of meter readings corresponds, or at least is close to, the reading of an aggregate meter. This allows electricity distributors to detect whether any fraud might be taking place, in the case the sum of reported readings are substantially below what is reported by the aggregate meter. In this settling meter groups must correspond to the physical distribution network since there should be a correspondence between the computed aggregate and the metered aggregate.

Other processes in the energy industry rely on aggregate of readings, which do not have such a straight forward correspondence. We will concentrate on two particular processes, namely *settlement* and *profiling*, and discuss how our aggregation protocols could be used to solve them in a privacy friendly manner. For the purposes of the discussion we assume it is practical to extract the aggregate as from the protocols, and not merely to match it to a known consumption.

First we give an overview of *settlement* and *profiling* in the energy industry – both processes that are buried deep in the infrastructure:

Settlement. The UK energy market works by separating the supply of energy from its generation. A number of suppliers draft contracts with generators to produce a certain amount of electricity within a sequence of half-hourly time periods. Yet, the actual load of the network is monitored by the UK grid, that may also issue orders to increase or reduce generation in the short term to meet the actual demand. The settlement process determines whether the contracts of suppliers with generators covered the actual demand of their customers, or whether specific suppliers need to pay more for any extra generation, or under consumption. To determine whether the production of electricity for each supplier matched their demand an estimate of the total amount of electricity consumed by customers of each supplier has to be produced. We therefore discuss how our protocols could be used to supply such estimates.

Profiling. Both suppliers and national grids need data on which to base electricity models and forecasts. Short term forecasts are related to very short term demand and whether. Longer term forecasts depend on other factors including the effects new devices have on consumption, socio-economical profiles of users, different patterns of consumption per region or sector of the economy. When raw data is available an analysts can use them to train their models.

In the absence of raw data volunteers are recruited or payed to construct profiles. We show that our protocols can be used to extract load profiles for different populations despite aggregation.

Trivial solutions. Both issues of settlement and profiling boil down to computing aggregates over different sets of meters. For settlement it would suffice to compute aggregates of meters associated with each distinct supplier to estimate the total energy consumption of their user base over time. This would be a far superior estimate than those produced by current methods (based on aggregate consumption and average profiles). A trivial solution for profiling would require meters to be groups according to the profile criteria: different temperatures, regions, socio-economic class, etc.

The trivial solution could work but might not be practical. For settlement, there is no uncertainty about the association of meter and supplier. Yet, changing the meter group requires expensive re-keying in all our protocols. Depending on how dynamic the energy market is this may happen multiple times every year. For profiling the task of grouping meters according to pre-determined categories is even harder. For example analysts may be interested in observing the effect temperature has on the energy consumption of a household over the winter holidays. Yet, it is not easy to predict the exact temperatures to group meters accordingly. Similarly, it is difficult to group meters by family size or composition of family, as demographics are subject to frequent change. In the case of socio-economic profiling, the data may simply not be available at an individual level to assign meters into groups – and further privacy concerns may arise if this is attempted.

Finally the trivial solution require meters groups to be tuned to extracting particular aggregates, or require them to output readings associated with multiple groups. Depending on the scheme used this increases computation and communication costs, while degrading the quality of privacy protection.

Inference on random population meter groups. Meters may be assigned to arbitrary groups, within which readings are aggregated, and yet and regression analysis can be applied to extract statistics from arbitrary meter populations. This approach decouples the assignment of meters into groups from any consideration of what statistics are to be extracted at a later time, alleviating the shortcomings of the trivial solution.

Consider a number N of meter groups $\mathcal{G}_i$ which run our protocols to calculate at each time period an aggregate of their consumption $S(\mathcal{G}_i)$. We denote as $\boldsymbol{S}$ the column ($N \times 1$) matrix with elements $S(\mathcal{G}_i)$. An arbitrary partition of meters and a function $\mathcal{P}$ that is applied to each group $\mathcal{G}_i$ returns the number of meters $\mathcal{P}(\mathcal{G}_i)$ in the group within that partition. The domain of $\mathcal{P}(\mathcal{G}_i)$ is as expected $[0, |\mathcal{G}_i|]$.

The mean consumption of the meters within the partition $\mathcal{P}$ can be estimated from the aggregate readings $S(\mathcal{G}_i)$. We construct $\mathcal{M}$ a $N \times 2$ matrix with elements $\mathcal{P}(\mathcal{G}_i)$ and $|\mathcal{G}_i| - \mathcal{P}(\mathcal{G}_i)$, and compute:

$$\mathcal{R} = (\mathcal{M}^T \mathcal{M})^{-1}(\mathcal{M}^T \boldsymbol{S})$$

The 2×1 matrix $\mathcal{R}$ is the least squares estimator of the mean of the consumption of the population in $\mathcal{P}$ (in position 1×1) and the population of meters not in $\mathcal{P}$ (in position 2×1). This is a standard linear regression, and it can be extended to estimating mean consumptions of multiple partitions of meters simultaneously. Efficient techniques based on LU decompositions avoid the need for a matrix inversion in case multiple population partitions are required.

4.6   Converting an Comparison Protocol Back into an Aggregation Protocol

The scheme as we described allows an aggregator to verify if an aggregate it already knows corresponds to the sum private measurement values it received. In many settings, however, an aggregator cannot measure the aggregated value - for example, a utility may be interested in the aggregate of the power output of all houses with photovoltaic energy generation, which are not connected to the same substation. Note that in this case the masking values do not cancel out – however, the aggregator can simply be provided with the sum of the masking values and thus effectively get the same effect.

While the comparison protocol supports fraud detection it requires reading from an aggregate meter. In some settings, such as gathering statistics, one may need to extract the sum of meter readings instead of comparing it to a known value.

A typical smart meter reading is a four byte value. If we assume up to 250 devices in one group, that would give us a 40 bit value for the aggregated reading. However, in most cases, the aggregator has a fairly good idea on the rough total consumption, as energy usage is fairly predictable - this would easily reduce the set of possible values into an area a normal computer can brute-force in a reasonable short time (Note that the brute force will only reveal the aggregate, while the individual contributions are still secure).

If the either the number of measurements of the measurement domain gets too big, the meters can easily split the measurement in a high- and low part and report both parts independently. The aggregator can then brute force both parts individually, reducing the computational effort on the backend to a level it can handle in a practical setting. The only setting in which this approach does not work is if the aggregation is performed over a large number of devices, e.g., a million meters. In this case, however, the entire protocol can be run independently on different subgroups of the devices without any loss of privacy.

5   Prototype Implementations

We implemented the *low-overhead* variant of the proposed scheme (described in Section 3.4) in the Python language. The code core with the cryptographic operations spans 89 lines of code. It uses the standard library hash function SHA-256, and a separate pure-python implementation of Curve25519 [21] for Diffie-Hellman key generation and derivation yielding 32 byte public keys. Readings and their cipher texts are represented using 4 bytes.

We tested our protocols in the setting of 100 meters reporting their aggregate consumption. Key generation took 0.013 s / meter and lead to 4790 bytes of total storage required for the 100 public keys and their associated meta-data. Key derivation, i.e. the computation of the secrets shared with other meters, took 1.371 s / meter. The 100 EC point multiplications using Curve25519 per meter dominate the cost of this operation. Each subsequent computations of the blinding factors required for obscuring readings took less than 0.001 s / meter. All reported figures are averages over 100 experiments.

The pure python implementation of Curve25529 is orders of magnitude slower than a native or optimised implementation, and dominates the cost of deriving shared keys. Such key derivation only happens when meter groups are formed, and can be amortised over an arbitrary period of time when groups are stable. The recurring cost of calculating blinding factors for readings take a negligible time as they only require the application of comparatively fast hash functions.

To validate the practicallity of the proc ocol on the meter side and investigate the practical behaviour of our code in a realistic setting, we also collaborated with a meter manufacturer to implement the low overhead variant on a set of real devices. To this end, Elster Group SE prototyped the protocol on their smart meters. The computation for each measurement in the integrated version was below one second. Thus, given a normal measurement frequency is 15 minutes, the protocols can easily work within the real smart grid infrastructure, and have enough reseves for overhead due to advancd usage (e.g., aggregating over several independent inputs, or additional mechanism to increase the reliability).

Implementation of regression techniques. The stability of meter groups can be maintained while extracting statistics about arbitrary partitions of the meters using the proposed regression based techniques. We partitioned a population of 1 million meters into 1000 groups of 1000 meters each reporting collectively their aggregated consumption. We then partitioned meters into two populations consuming electricity according to a population with different means μ_a and μ_b. We ensured that at least 50 meters from both populations are present in each meter group, and inferred the means μ_a and μ_b using our regression analysis.

The regression algorithm for inferring μ_a and μ_b took less than 0.001 seconds to run, and was implemented in 30 lines of pure python with standard numerical libraries. As expected it returns the values of the means with negligible error. (See [22] for a detailed treatment of error analysis in regression.) This demonstrates that computing statistics from aggregate measurements using regression analysis is computationally feasible even at a national scale.

6   Conclusion

A naive way of implementing privacy-friendly aggregation and comparison protocols would involve a trusted party collecting all raw readings to aggregate them. This is indeed the approach currently discussed for the UK smart-metering deployment and others. We argue this is not necessary and present a family of protocols to achieve the same functionality without the need to ever disclose raw meter readings. Different protocols have different advantages we discuss, in terms of their properties, their cost, their deployment model, and how they interrelate with other smart-metering privacy technologies. Similar approaches could be extended to aggregates for other utilities as well as a general set of techniques to gather real time statistics without revealing private data.

Acknowledgements. We would like to thank Michael John for insightful comments on the reality of smart metering as well as his contribution towards making the implementing the protocols on real smart meters happen, and Lejla Batina and Jaap-Henk Hoepman, for helpful discussions and for taking the patience to read and comment on early versions of this papers.

The work described in this paper has been supported (in part) by the European Commission through the ICT programme under contract ICT-2007-216676 ECRYPT II.

References

1. European Parliament: DIRECTIVE 2009/72/EC (2009)
2. Cuijpers, C., Koops, B.J.: Het wetsvoorstel slimme meters: een privacytoets op basis van art. 8 evrm. Technical report, Tilburg University, October, Report (in Dutch) (2008)
3. The Smart Grid Interoperability Panel Cyber Security Working Group: Smart Grid Cybersecurity Strategy and Requirements. US National Institute for Standards and Technology, NIST (2010),
   http://csrc.nist.gov/publications/nistir/ir7628/nistir-7628_vol2.pdf
4. European Commission: Smart grids: from innovation to deployment (April 2011)
5. Garcia, F.D., Jacobs, B.: Privacy-friendly energy-metering via homomorphic encryption. In: 6th Workshop on Security and Trust Management, STM (2010)
6. Molina-Markham, A., Shenoy, P., Fu, K., Cecchet, E., Irwin, D.: Private memoirs of a smart meter. In: 2nd ACM Workshop on Embedded Sensing Systems for Energy-Efficiency in Buildings (BuildSys 2010), Zurich, Switzerland (November 2010)
7. Rial, A., Danezis, G.: Privacy-preserving smart metering. Technical Report MSRTR- 2010-150, Microsoft Research (November 2010)
8. Kursawe, K.: Some Ideas on Privacy Preserving Meter Aggregation. Technical Report ICIS–R11002, Radboud University Nijmegen (February 2011)
9. Bellare, M., Rogaway, P.: Random oracles are practical: A paradigm for designing efficient protocols. In: ACM Conference on Computer and Communications Security, pp. 62–73 (1993)
10. Chaum, D.: The dining cryptographers problem: Unconditional sender and recipient untraceability. J. Cryptology 1(1), 65–75 (1988)
11. Hao, F., Zieliński, P.: A 2-Round Anonymous Veto Protocol. In: Christianson, B., Crispo, B., Malcolm, J.A., Roe, M. (eds.) Security Protocols. LNCS, vol. 5087, pp. 202–211. Springer, Heidelberg (2009)
12. Golle, P., Juels, A.: Dining Cryptographers Revisited. In: Cachin, C., Camenisch, J.L. (eds.) EUROCRYPT 2004. LNCS, vol. 3027, pp. 456–473. Springer, Heidelberg (2004)
13. Canetti, R., Halevi, S., Katz, J.: A forward-secure public-key encryption scheme. In: Biham, E. (ed.) EUROCRYPT 2003. LNCS, vol. 2656, pp. 255–271. Springer, Heidelberg (2003)

14. Pedersen, T.P.: Non-interactive and Information-Theoretic Secure Verifiable Secret Sharing. In: Feigenbaum, J. (ed.) CRYPTO 1991. LNCS, vol. 576, pp. 129–140. Springer, Heidelberg (1992)
15. Schnorr, C.: Efficient signature generation for smart cards. Journal of Cryptology 4(3), 239–252 (1991)
16. Chaum, D., Pedersen, T.P.: Wallet Databases with Observers. In: Brickell, E.F. (ed.) CRYPTO 1992. LNCS, vol. 740, pp. 89–105. Springer, Heidelberg (1993)
17. Fiat, A., Shamir, A.: How to Prove Yourself: Practical Solutions to Identification and Signature Problems. In: Odlyzko, A.M. (ed.) CRYPTO 1986. LNCS, vol. 263, pp. 186–194. Springer, Heidelberg (1987)
18. Camenisch, J., Stadler, M.: Proof systems for general statements about discrete logarithms. Technical Report TR 260, Institute for Theoretical Computer Science, ETH Zürich (March 1997)
19. Diffie, W., van Oorschot, P.C., Wiener, M.J.: Authentication and authenticated key exchanges. Des. Codes Cryptography 2(2), 107–125 (1992)
20. Borisov, N., Goldberg, I., Brewer, E.A.: Off-the-record communication, or, why not to use pgp. In: Atluri, V., Syverson, P.F., di Vimercati, S.D.C. (eds.) WPES, pp. 77–84. ACM, New York (2004)
21. Bernstein, D.J.: Curve25519: New Diffie-Hellman Speed Records. In: Yung, M., Dodis, Y., Kiayias, A., Malkin, T. (eds.) PKC 2006. LNCS, vol. 3958, pp. 207–228. Springer, Heidelberg (2006)
22. Gelman, A., Hill, J.: Data Analysis Using Regression and Multilevel/Hierarchical Models, 1st edn. Cambridge University Press, Cambridge (2006)

Plug-In Privacy for Smart Metering Billing

Marek Jawurek, Martin Johns, and Florian Kerschbaum

SAP Research
firstname.lastname@sap.com

Abstract. Traditional electricity meters are replaced by Smart Meters in customers' households. Smart Meters collect fine-grained utility consumption profiles from customers, which in turn enables the introduction of dynamic, time-of-use tariffs. However, the fine-grained usage data that is compiled in this process also allows to infer the inhabitant's personal schedules and habits. We propose a privacy-preserving protocol that enables billing with time-of-use tariffs without disclosing the actual consumption profile to the supplier. Our approach relies on a zero-knowledge proof based on Pedersen Commitments performed by a plug-in privacy component that is put into the communication link between Smart Meter and supplier's back-end system. We require no changes to the Smart Meter hardware and only small changes to the software of Smart Meter and back-end system. In this paper we describe the functional and privacy requirements, the specification and security proof of our solution and give a performance evaluation of a prototypical implementation.

1 Introduction

1.1 Motivation

Smart Metering has been mandated by EU directive 2009/72/EC and promoted by the US Energy Independence and Security Act of 2007 and Smart Meter roll-outs have begun all over the world [1]. Smart Meters record a fine-grained consumption profile of a certain service (electricity, heat or water) and report it to the supplier of the service who bills the customer accordingly. Traditionally only a single, compiled value for a whole reporting period has been reported to the supplier (e.g., the total consumed electrical energy of the last year). In contrast, Smart Meters transmit a detailed set of many data points which document consumption for short time intervals (e.g. every 15 minutes). This enables the suppliers to introduce more dynamic pricing schemes and to collect precise data about their customer base's usage patterns.

Besides the technical motivation, also legal reasons come into play in respect to the current push towards Smart Metering: For instance, in Germany starting October 2010 suppliers must offer either time or load dependent tariffs (see §40 [20]). These tariffs necessarily require Smart Meters with fine-grained consumption recording.

S. Fischer-Hübner and N. Hopper (Eds.): PETS 2011, LNCS 6794, pp. 192–210, 2011.

However, such detailed data has privacy implications: A listening third party, the supplier or even an employee of the supplier could learn the consumption behavior of a customer and might use this information maliciously for other purposes than intended (e.g, to learn behavioral patterns, such as sleep/wake cycles or vacation time, of a given customer based on his energy usage). Recently, customers have become aware of the potential privacy implications of such consumption profiles. In the Netherlands Smart Meter roll-outs have been stopped because of the public outcry about the invasion of customer privacy [15].

Grid operators and suppliers now face a dilemma: On the one hand, they need to implement Smart Metering for legal and technical reasons. But, on the other hand, they face on-going problems in respect to public acceptance of the technology due to the outlined privacy problems.

1.2   Our Solution

We provide a solution to this conflict by introducing a new consumption profile reporting protocol for time-of-use tariffs. We introduce a plug-in privacy component into the standardized Smart Meter / Meter Data Management (MDM) reporting communication link. This component hides the actual consumption profile from the MDM and therefore also from the supplier. We require only small changes compared to current Smart Meter reporting. The plug-in privacy component intercepts Smart Meter readings, then uses tariff information provided externally (over the Internet or by the MDM) to calculate the billing amount and sends only the resulting billing amount to the MDM. A Zero-Knowledge Proof ensures the correctness of the calculation.

The advantages of our approach are the following:

1. The Smart Meter's hardware complexity remains the same, because all calculations are conducted by the stand-alone plug-in component. Such a plug-in component can be realized by off-the-shelf computing hardware like a router or Wifi access point or even by software running on a standard personal computer.

2. The supplier does not have to trust the plug-in privacy component. The privacy component's output suffices to check whether it calculated the final billing amount honestly and correctly, i.e. based on the correct tariff and on the correct readings provided by the Smart Meter. Therefore the privacy component does not require hardware-protected components and can be quite simple and cheap. The correct operation of the privacy component can be verified only by its output.

3. Plaintext, fine-grained consumption profiles never even leave the household, if a privacy component is used. This prevents any abuse of this data, either by intercepting it in transit, by leakage in the MDM systems or by the MDM's operator himself. It also spares the MDM expensive security measures for the protection of the massive amount of privacy related data – the consumption profiles of his customers.

1.3   Paper Outline

The remainder of this paper is structured as follows: Section 2 motivates the problem, gives a short introduction into Smart Metering and its privacy problems and defines our problem statement. In Section 3 we describe the underlying cryptographic method of our solution before we explain the setup of our solution, the specification of the protocol and its security analysis in Section   4. We evaluate a prototypical implementation in Section 5. Furthermore we show how our protocol might fit into existing Smart Meter communication protocols and how it fulfills the stakeholder requirements. Finally, we give an overview of related work in Section 6, provide an outlook on future work in Section 7 and conclude with a summary in Section 8.

2   Smart Metering's Implications for Privacy

2.1   Naming Conventions

Before we explore the Smart Meter billing process and deduct its privacy implications, we briefly specify the terms used in the rest of this paper:

Customer: The term "customer" represents the household, family or person that receives the service from a supplier.

Supplier: The term "supplier" stands as placeholder for all companies that cooperate in order to provide the service to customers and also want to subsequently invoice the customers for this service.

Consumption profile: The term "consumption profile" stands for the consumption data collected by Smart Meters for service in a certain interval over a certain period of time. This is applicable to many utilities (electricity, water, heat, gas, etc.).

Back-end system: Usually, the Smart Meter is directly connected to a MDM which just collects consumption data. Tariffs, are then applied in the supplier's billing systems where the data is subsequently transported to. In this paper, "back-end system" (BS) stands for the collection of all IT-systems that collect consumption profiles and use them to calculate the invoice for the customer based on tariffs.

Tariff: The term "tariff" stands for the price schema, i.e., the price of service consumption at a specific interval. In the following we restrict ourselves to a time-of-use pricing scheme, but our protocol could also handle load-dependent billing with little modification.

2.2   Smart Metering Billing

Smart Metering refers to the collection of consumption profiles at customer's households with the help of so called Smart Meters (SM). Smart Meters measure electricity consumption in households and communicate their readings at regular intervals to the back-end system. Alternatively, the back-end system can also

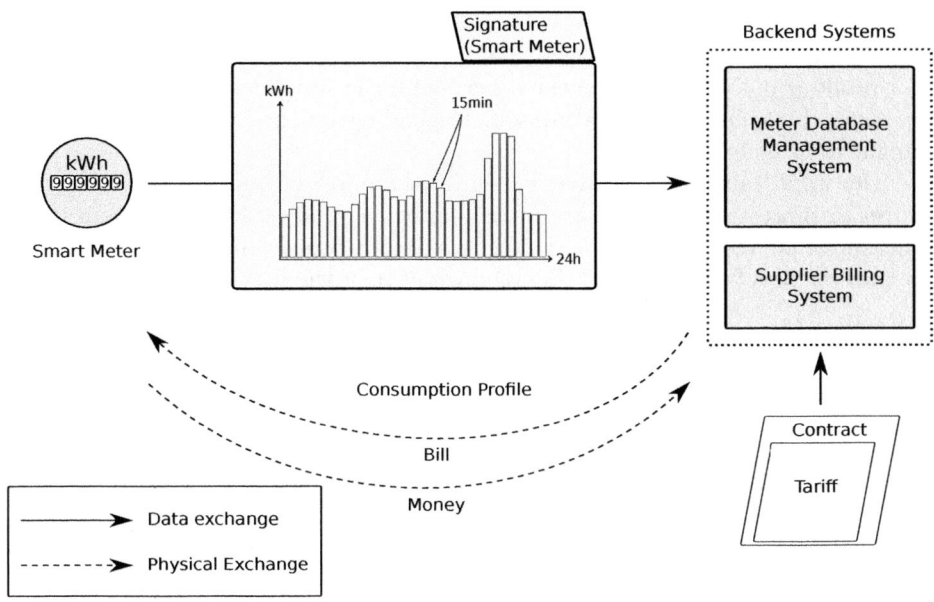

Fig. 1. Traditional setup of Smart Meter and back-end system

query the Smart Meter for its data (pull). A Trusted Platform Module (TPM) in the Smart Meter holds key material and creates signatures over the data to ensure authenticity and integrity until it arrives at the back-end system. There the consumption profile and the tariff data from the respective customer's contract are used to calculate the price the customer has to pay for the time period covered by the profile. Figure 1 displays the usual Smart Meter setup.

2.3 Privacy Concerns

Smart Metering has encountered massive privacy concerns from media [16], data privacy experts [8] and consumers [15]. The fact that whole consumption profiles of households are transmitted to and stored by suppliers is troubling w.r.t. customer privacy. Data confidentiality can be easily protected in transit between SM and BS. However, their storage at the suppliers' IT-systems still endangers customer privacy. Depending on resolution and the availability of different services' profiles (e.g. water, heat, electricity) one can read the profile and "see" more or less clearly what happens in the household: For instance, when family members wake up (light switched on), whether they shower in the morning (water, heat, and electricity for water heater), whether they drink hot beverages with their breakfast and when or if they leave for work or school. Furthermore, the frequency of washing and drying clothes, cooking or the amount of time the TV is turned on can be inferred. For further research on what electricity consumption profiles tell about the inhabitants see [4], [13], [14], [24] or [29].

These inferences make consumption profiles very privacy-sensitive data and these profiles might even have value in the advertising market, for instance. On one hand, disgruntled employees or external attackers might attempt to steal it for profit or out of malice. On the other hand, the supplier could seek subsidiary revenues by selling this data himself. Depending on the local jurisdiction, this might even be legal.

The important point is, that currently there are no reliable, technical measures in place to prevent abuse of consumption profiles. Merely organizational measures, policies or laws sanction the abuse of privacy related data but require a trace or proof of abuse and do not prevent it in the first place.

2.4 Problem Statement

The problem we tackle in this paper is to enable suppliers to do billing using Smart Metering data without actually receiving privacy related data.

Supplier's requirements. The supplier's requirement regarding consumption profiles is the ability to reliably use the data in the consumption profile to calculate the customer's bill for received electricity. The consumption profile V is a vector of n values v_i that represent the amount of utility used in the interval i of one day. The time-of-use tariff T is a vector of n t_i where interval i is priced with t_i. t_i and v_i are integers. Then the formula for calculating the time-of-use price for consumption of one day is

$$P(V, T) = \sum_{i=0}^{n} t_i * v_i$$

It is crucial for the supplier that the consumption profiles are accurate and trustworthy. Clearly, a customer might be inclined to report lower consumption than actually consumed, because it lowers his bill. Therefore the Smart Meters are equipped with the TPM in order to ensure that the reported consumption profiles are trustworthy and reliable.

Customers' requirements. In addition to the requirements of traditional metering (accuracy of the bill), a customer of Smart Metering is concerned about his privacy. The less information is leaked by the customer, the better for him. We strive for ideal privacy, i.e. the view of the consumption profile by the supplier is indistinguishable from a uniformly chosen consumption profile with the same price, i.e. supplier obtains no additional information to the price. Furthermore, complicated tariffs will necessitate a way for customers to verify their bill in a trustworthy manner. Being able to do so, without relying on the suppliers billing systems, is a secondary requirements that customers will have with Smart Metering.

Infrastructure constraints. A major constraint for the infrastructure investments in Smart Metering is cost. Suppliers have to replace conventional meters in every household with a new Smart Meter. This is a significant amount of money for a complete roll-out even for a utilities' provider. Therefore every technology built into a Smart Meter faces scrutiny w.r.t. to costs.

This also includes the security measures like TPMs and secure storage. The development and verification of a secure TPM is very expensive and therefore it is common practice to keep its functionality minimal. One naive approach to privacy-preserving billing of consumption profiles would be to calculate the price in the TPM itself. But this would require that tariff information is retrieved and verified by the TPM. In turn, this would require adding an input communication channel and module to the TPM and would consequently increase the costs for building and verifying the TPM considerably.

Legal constraints. Depending on the jurisdiction, metering can be subject to legal requirements. In Germany, for instance, metrology laws [21] govern require a certain degree accuracy of the meter and measurements and the tamperproofness of the meter. Privacy laws [22] require the confidentiality of readings to protect consumers' privacy. We translate this into the technical requirements of Smart Meter integrity and integrity and confidentiality of consumption profiles on the wire and in computer systems.

3   Pedersen Commitments

The core of our proposed solution (which we present in Sec. 4) relies on Pedersen Commitments [26]. In this section we briefly introduce the basics of this cryptographic method. For further information on the scheme please refer to [26].

A commitment is a cryptographic tool with two functions:

- *Commit(x, r)* $\longrightarrow$ *c* takes as input a value x and a random number r. As output it produces the commitment c.
- *Open(c, x, r)* $\longrightarrow$ $\top/\bot$ takes as input a commitment c, a value x and a random number r. It outputs $\top$, if c is indeed a commitment to x and $\bot$, if not.

Commitments have two security properties:

- *Secret*: Given c it is hard to compute x.
- *Binding*: Given c, x and r it is hard to compute an $x' \neq x$ and r', such that $Open(c, x', r') = \top$, i.e. c is a commitment for x' as well.

They are used in the following way: Alice chooses a value x. She computes a commitment c and sends it to Bob. Now, Alice and Bob may, for example, engage in some computation that depends on Alice's input x, but where Alice may no longer change her mind. Alice opens her commitment and shows that everything was indeed computed according to the value x she choose at the beginning.

A typical example is fair coin flip. Alice chooses a random s and sends the commitment c of s to Bob. Bob chooses a random number t and sends it to Alice. Alice now opens her commitment. The fair coin flip is $x = s \oplus t$ (where $\oplus$ denotes "exclusive-or"). If the commitment was not secret, Bob could choose x. If the commitment was not binding, Alice could choose x.

Pedersen commitments operate over a group $\mathbb{G}$. This group $\mathbb{G}$ can be the same elliptic curves as used of EC-DSA in the secure hardware of the Smart Meter, but in our implementation we use the group $\mathbb{Z}_p^*$. Let g and h be two generators of $\mathbb{G}$. Pedersen commitments are computed as follows:

- *Commit(x, r)*:
$$c = g^x h^r$$

- *Open(c, x, r)*:
$$c \stackrel{?}{=} g^x h^r \cong c \stackrel{?}{=} Commit(x, r)$$

The proofs of their security properties can be found in [26].

Pedersen commitments have another very useful property we exploit in this paper. They are homomorphic, i.e. a multiplication of two commitments results in a commitment to the sum of their committed values.

$$Commit(x, r)Commit(y, s) = Commit(x + y, r + s)$$

A commitment can also be multiplied by a plain factor y

$$Commit(x, r)^y = Commit(xy, ry)$$

Note that both operations change the commitment c, such that the binding security property is not violated. Instead one needs to open with the new input values of the commitment.

4   The Private Billing Protocol

In this section we describe our privacy-preserving Smart Meter billing protocol. First we give a very abstract description in Section 4.1, then we provide the full specification in Section 4.2 and provide a security analysis in Section 4.3.

4.1   Components and Specification

The main idea of our approach is that the plaintext consumption profiles never leave the household, but only after they have been processed by a pseudo-random one-way function. Therefore, ideal privacy is preserved. We propose to introduce a privacy component (PC) into the communication link of the Smart Meter and the supplier's back-end system. Its objective is to intercept reports of consumption profiles and to let only processed information pass-through. The PC is invisible to the SM and only the supplier will notice it: The PC directly interacts

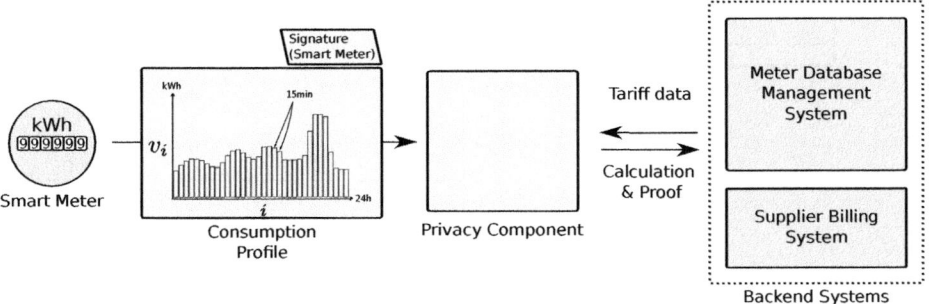

Fig. 2. Setup of proposed solution with intermediate privacy component

with the supplier's systems and consumption profiles will look different if a PC
is used. This setup is illustrated in Figure 2.

The major difference to a standard Smart Metering setup is that the price
function $P(V, T)$ is not calculated at the supplier's system. It is calculated in the
PC which is supposed to be located in the household. For this, the PC intercepts
the consumption profile and signed commitments sent to it by the Smart Meter
and removes the plaintext consumption profile. Then the PC obtains the tariff
information from the supplier and calculates the bill with the original consumption profile. It then presents the invoice, the signed commitments and a Zero
Knowledge Proof to the supplier who verifies the bill's validity using the homomorphic property of the used commitment scheme: The supplier determines the
correctness of the bill by appropriate operations on the received signed commitments and the tariff. If the commitments can be verified on the presented bill,
then the presented bill is trustworthy and correct. The homomorphic commitment scheme we use on the Smart Meter side is Pedersen Commitment [26] and
is shortly outlined in Section 3.

4.2 Protocol Specification

Initiation. Initially, the SM and BS need to employ some signature scheme
which allows the SM to secure the integrity of data sent to the BS. This is
usually already the case with Smart Meters. They are either part of a PKI or
both, the SM and the BS, have access to a symmetric key for a symmetric signing
scheme. We denote such signing key with $\text{Sign}_{\text{priv}}$.

Secondly, the TPM in the Smart Meter must be able to use the Pedersen
Commitment scheme (see Section 3) with public generators g and h. How keys
(or the public parameters, such as the generators) are distributed to Smart
Meters is beyond the scope of this paper, but it is already common practice in
on-going Smart Meter deployments.

Consumption profile reporting and invoice calculation. Figure 3 illustrates the communication that takes place between the different actors and the
following enumeration of steps describes the protocol in detail:

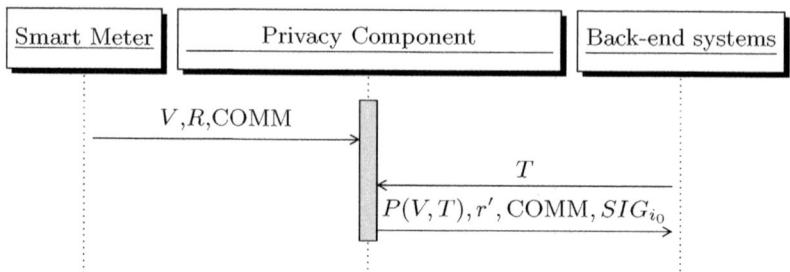

Fig. 3. Communication sequence

1. The SM prepares a consumption profile to be reported to BS. The profile basically consists of a vector of consumption values $V = \{v_{i_0}, v_{i_1}, ..., v_{i_n}\}$. v_{i_k} represents the energy consumption of the household in the interval i_k. i_k stands for the interval number, incremented since a fictive first interval, analogous to the definition of the UNIX time stamp.
2. For values in V the SM now creates commitments. The commitment of v_{i_k} is $Comm_{i_k} = Commit(v_{i_k}, r_{i_k})$. Where $Commit(a, r)$ stands for the Pedersen Commitment of a and a random value r with the generators g and h known to the TPM and the BS.
3. Now, the SM would like to send the data to the BS. Before that can happen, it protects the data from being manipulated on the way. It creates a signature SIG_{i_0} (with its signing key $Sign_{priv}$) over (i_0, COMM) and sends it together with the vector V, the vector $\text{COMM} = \{Comm_{i_0}, Comm_{i_1}, ..., Comm_{i_n}\}$ and the vector $R = \{r_{i_0}, r_{i_1}, ..., r_{i_n}\}$ towards the supplier's back-end system.
4. The PC intercepts all the traffic between the SM and the BS.
5. The PC obtains the tariff vector $T = \{t_{i_0}, t_{i_1}, ...t_{i_n}\}$ from BS and performs the following two calculations:
    (a) $P(V, T) = \sum_{k=i_0}^{i_n} v_k * t_k$ This is the actual price the customer has to pay for the reporting period represented by V.
    (b) In addition it also calculates r' from the vector R it intercepted in step 4: $r\prime = \sum_{k=i_0}^{i_n} r_k * t_k$
6. The PC now sends $P(V, T)$, r', COMM, SIG_{i_0} to BS and has finished its work.

Verification. These are the steps performed by the BS subsequently to the reporting in order to verify that the $P(V, T)$ was correctly calculated:

7. First of all, the BS verifies that the signature SIG_{i_0} over i_0 and the commitments is intact which means that the commitments it received has been signed by the TPM and stands for the next vector $V = \{v_{i_0}, v_{i_1}, ..., v_{i_n}\}$ starting from i_0.

8. BS now computes $\text{COMM}_{\text{Tariff}}$ with the $Comm_i$ it received in step 6 and the tariff vector T that it made available to PC in step 5:

$$\text{COMM}_{\text{Tariff}} = \prod_{k=i_0}^{i_n} Comm_k^{t_k}$$

9. Whether the $P(V,T)$ sent by the PC has been calculated truthfully with the correct v_i and t_i can now be verified by opening the aggregated commitment $\text{COMM}_{\text{Tariff}}$. For that, the BS uses $P(V,T)$ and the aggregate random value r' that it received in step 6.

$$Open(\text{COMM}_{\text{Tariff}}, P(V,T), r')$$

$$= \text{COMM}_{\text{Tariff}} \stackrel{?}{=} Commit(P(V,T), r')$$

4.3   Analysis

Theorem 1. *Our private billing protocol is complete, sound and honest-verifier zero-knowledge.*

Proof. For completeness, i.e. if the PC truthfully computes the tariff, then the BS accepts, we observe the following equation:

$$Commit(P(V,T), r')$$

$$= Commit(\sum_{k=i_0}^{i_n} t_k v_k, \sum_{k=i_0}^{i_n} t_k r_k)$$

$$= \prod_{k=i_0}^{i_n} Commit(t_k v_k, t_k r_k)$$

$$= \prod_{k=i_0}^{i_n} Commit(v_k, r_k)^{t_k}$$

$$= \prod_{k=i_0}^{i_n} Comm_k^{t_k}$$

$$= \text{COMM}_{\text{Tariff}}$$

It follows that $\text{COMM}_{\text{Tariff}}$ is a Pedersen commitment for $P(V,T)$ with the random number r'.

For soundness we prove that if the PC does not truthfully compute the tariff, then the BS must reject. That is given v_i, the PC cannot forge a view $Comm_i$, $P(V,T)$ and r' of the protocol that is accepted by the BS.

We will prove by contradiction. First, observe that we assume that the PC cannot forge the $Comm_i$ commitments, since they are signed by the TPM. Second, as follows from completeness, the subsequently computed $COMM_{Tariff}$ is a Pedersen commitment to $P(V, T)$ and r'. If, the PC could present $P'(V, T) \neq P(V, T)$ and r'', such that $COMM_{Tariff} = Commit(P'(V, T), r'')$ is opened correctly, then this would be a contradiction to the binding property of Pedersen commitments as established in [26].

For honest-verifier zero-knowledge, we present a simulator of the view of the BS given only its input and output. The values $Comm_i$ and r' from the view of the protocol are uniformly and independently distributed in $\mathbb{Z}_p^*$. The tariff $P(V, T)$ is public output of the protocol (and input to the verification operation).

The signature $Sig_{i_0}(Comm_1, \ldots, Comm_n)$ of the TPM cannot be trivially simulated, since the BS only holds the public key. Nevertheless, since it is only a signature of randomly distributed values, we could simulate it by inverting the signature verification operation on a random signature. This rather strange simulation is an artifact of our unconventional setup of proving having the PC compute on input from another party – the TPM. In a strict sense, the signature is not part of the Zero Knowledge Proof, since it is computed by the TPM and not the PC.

5   Implementation and Evaluation

In this section, we give details on our prototypical implementation, show how our component can be integrated in real world Smart Meter deployments, and discuss how our solution fulfills the functional and security requirements which were identified in Section 2.4.

5.1   Implementation of the Core Algorithm

We implemented an exemplary system to identify load on the respective hardware systems during the execution of our protocol. For this purpose, we modeled the SM, the PC and the BS in Java as much as necessary to execute our protocol. In our implementation the SM creates a consumption profile from 96 fake readings and enriches the profile with commitments over the individual readings. It generates Pedersen Commitments in $\mathbb{Z}_p^*$ where p has bit length 1024, with respective bit lengths of 32 for the readings and the tariff, 160 bits for r and the generators $g = 2$, $h = 3$. We use the BigInteger class and its methods for representing and handling commitments and randoms. However, we used our own implementation of modular exponentiation with precomputed powers of g/h which is faster than the built-in method of the BigInteger class (see time differences in Table 1).

For the evaluation of performance we chose a Java Benchmarking framework explained in [7]. It provides us with a method to calculate means and standard deviations in a statistically sound manner, dealing with different Java specialties like dynamic optimization, resource reclamation and caching.

Table 2 displays the means and standard deviations of the respective calculations in the protocol. Execution times were measured on a Intel(R) Core(TM) i5

Table 1. Creation of commitments in SM (96 commitments) with built-in BigInteger.modPow vs own implementation

Method	Mean	Standard deviation
BigInteger.modPow	174.373 ms	3.400 ms
Our implementation	126.396 ms	6.175 ms

Table 2. Execution time means and standard deviations for the different computations in the protocol

Computation	Component	Mean	Standard deviation
Creation of commitments (step 2)	SM	126.396 ms	6.175 ms
Aggregation of randoms (step 5b)	PC	24.359 us	183.239 us
Aggregation of commitments (step 8)	BS	7.443 ms	1.736 ms
Opening of aggregated commitment (step 9)	BS	1.442 ms	984.345 us

CPU M540 at 2.53GHz on a OpenJDK Runtime Environment (IcedTea6 1.8.1) on a Ubuntu 10.10 system.

From the numbers in Table 2 one can see that most time is spent in the SM and the BS. The most expensive calculation is performed by the Smart Meter and its hardware, respectively the TPM performing the actual calculations. It is usually several scales inferior to our test system but we believe that the SM is able to perform its part of the protocol in a timely manner [5]. After all, irrespective of other constraints, it has one day before it needs to perform the next protocol run.

On the supplier's system side one has to take into account that the supplier's systems will need to participate in several thousand instances of this protocol per day, one for every associated household. If we assume that the supplier buffers the received verification data of concurrent protocol instances it can spread verification (where all of its time is spent) over the course of a whole day. Then, one such system (with our hardware) should be able to handle approx. one million protocol instances per day. This could be further increased by only verifying a random choice of reported prices. This shows, that a supplier should be able to implement our protocol for millions of users with negligible resources.

Our protocol necessitates higher data volumes to be transported between the SM, the PC and the BS than in a naive reporting protocol. In the most basic reporting protocol (with our assumptions that readings are 32bits wide) the SM has to sent 96 values (per day) to the BS. In addition to that, our protocol requires commitments (of 1024bits) and randoms (of 160bits) to be sent from the SM to the PC for every reading. The PC then forwards only 96 commitments, one aggregated random and one price. Table 3 displays the data volumes of our protocol. In total, our protocol requires 27284bytes to be transported over communication links, 26900bytes upstream (SM over PC to BS) and 384bytes downstream from BS to PC per reporting period (day). Although, our protocol poses a significant overhead with approx. factor 70 over the naive reporting

Table 3. Data volumes of our protocol vs a naive reporting protocol without privacy

Description	Source	Destination	Volume in bytes
Reporting of 96 readings (naive reporting without privacy)	SM	BS	$96 * 4 = 384$
Reporting of 96 readings, commitments and randoms	SM	PC	$96 * (128 + 20 + 4) = 14592$
Transport of tariff information for 96 time slots per day	BS	PC	$96 * 4 = 384$
Forwarding of 96 commitments and aggregated random	PC	BS	$96 * 128 + 20 = 12308$
Total amount of data volume in privacy-preserving reporting	*	*	$14592 + 384 + 12308 = 27284$

protocol those volumes can still be handled even by slow GPRS connections. In this analysis we disregarded additional readings, meta-data and signatures that would have to be transported in the naive protocol as well as in our protocol.

5.2 Integration in Real World Scenario

The technology used by the Smart Meter to communicate to the Back-end system dictates how a Privacy Component could be introduced into this setup. Wireless communication links like ZigBee or Wifi would require that the SM is explicitly configured to report to the PC instead of the BS. Wireless communication links like GPRS would implicate higher costs, as the SM would need to communicate with the PC and the PC would need to establish an additional connection to the BS. Wired communication links, on the other hand, allow our scheme to be introduced more easily. The PC would then interrupt the physical link and act as physical gateway between the SM and the BS.

Regarding the integration of our approach into current Smart Meter reporting protocols, we have identified two relevant application layer protocol specifications (from [9]) for SM to BS reporting: The universal DLMS/COSEM standard suite (IEC 62056 / EN 13757-1) [2] and the simple Smart Metering Language (SML) [10] specification. Landis+Gyr, recently nominated [31] leader in Smart Metering, supports DLMS with its Landis+Gyr ZMD100 AP/AS residential meters and SML with its E750 Industrial and Commercial Smart Meters.

The Smart Meter Language (SML) describes an application and presentation layer and Smart Meters operate either in a push (SM initiates) or pull (SM reacts) scenario. All data is encoded in either an SML request or SML response message. Encryption of SML messages on the application or presentation layer is not part of the SML specification.

DLMS/COSEM is an application layer protocol. DLMS specifies how one can talk about energy metering objects. Energy Metering objects are described by the COSEM specification.The standard does not dictate specific transport protocols. The Smart Meter operates as server and communication follows the pull-strategy from the view of the BS system. Read and write access is realized by transmitting respective COSEM objects in APDUs (Application Protocol Data Units). The server's application context determines whether APDUs are encrypted.

How the privacy component can be embedded in environments employing SML or DLMS/COSEM depends on a multitude of factors: The actual protocols used on the network/transport layers, the used push/pull strategy as well whether encryption is used. Those factors determine whether the PC acts as transparent or visible proxy, how it intercepts messages and whether it needs key material to decipher messages.

For SML we see a simple straightforward solution how to implement the privacy component on the application layer: In SML actual consumption profiles are sent as tables with one row for each recorded value. The columns can describe one entry further with entries like time of recording, error conditions and so on. The whole table but also individual columns of the table can be signed which allows us to fit our protocol into SML messages easily: For every query (pull-scenario) of consumption values the SM answers with a table with the columns: $i,v_i,Comm_i,r_i$. The SM signs all columns independently but the PC intercepts the SML response, deletes the columns v_i and r_i from the table and inserts $P(V,T),r'$ and COMM into the message. Sig_{i_0} is represented by the i's and $Comm_i$'s columns' intact signatures. This only requires, that the part of the Smart Meter responsible for creating signatures also create commitments. The BS system will notice that columns v_i and r_i are missing and will therefore switch into a mode where it communicates with a privacy component and performs the verification part of our protocol. If a privacy component was not employed the whole table is transferred intact and the BS system performs its normal operation and stores the plaintext values in its database.

For DMLS/COSEM the approach works analogously but with COSEM objects and properties instead of SML tables. However, in DLMS/COSEM encryption could make it impossible for the PC to understand the intercepted APDUs. In such a case, the Smart Meter either needs to be reconfigured not to use encryption or to use the public key of the PC instead of the supplier's public key. This will allow the PC to read and manipulate the APDU and possibly re-encrypt it for the supplier with the supplier's public key.

5.3   Fulfillment of Stakeholder's Requirements

In Section 2.4 we listed requirements of the different stakeholders for Smart Metering. We will show in this Section how our approach fulfills these requirements.

- In Section 2.4 we mentioned that the supplier's requirement is the trustworthiness of reported consumption values. Our protocol fulfills this by providing a trustworthy price instead of individual consumption values. We have given a soundness proof of our Zero Knowledge proof for the correct calculation of the price.

– In Section 2.4 we also stated that the customer wants privacy-aware billing. Our approach achieves a privacy-aware billing with ideal privacy as the consumption profile never leaves the household unprocessed, but only the price. We have proven the zero knowledge property of our Zero Knowledge Proof, i.e. the supplier will learn nothing, but the price. And while our approach was primarily developed for the fulfillment of the privacy-property it can also provide means to the customer to make billing reproducible. The PC can store intercepted consumption profiles and display them, together with the calculated prices, to the customer. This way, the customer can have real-time information about his energy consumption and current costs and also verify the invoice eventually sent out by the supplier.

– The infrastructure requirement listed in Section 2.4 is a low-cost Smart Metering solution. Our approach achieves this by only minimal changes to the software of Smart Meters and supplier's back-end system. The privacy component itself is simple and untrustworthy. It can therefore be implemented in inexpensive hardware or even in software.

– Finally, in Section 2.4 we mention several requirements regarding the tamperproofness, accuracy and confidentiality of the Smart Meter. As our approach does not interfere with the Smart Meter's normal operation accuracy and tamperproofness of the Smart Meter are not changed. We conform to any regulation we are aware of.

In addition, the supplier might benefit from the use of a privacy component as well, as less privacy-related data has to be stored in his systems for legal retention periods. The supplier needs to store all data that he receives from the PC for being able to reproduce invoice calculation for a certain retention time but that data is not privacy-related. The commitment values do not disclose useful information and the only privacy-related data item is the final price. This reduces the supplier's need for special security measures of his systems against internal or external attackers.

Based on the discussion above, it is safe to conclude that our approach fulfills all identified requirements (see Section 2.4) for a privacy-respecting billing of Smart Metering consumption profiles. Furthermore, as shown in Sections 5.1 and 5.2, an implementation of our algorithm is suitable to be deployed on a large scale and fits well with existing standards and infrastructures.

6   Related Work

General references concerning security aspects of Smart Metering: Abstract predictions about security and privacy challenges potentially coming with the evolution of the current grid to the Smart Grid are described in [17] while [11],[25] and [8] give more information on the topics of security, privacy and trust in Smart Grids/Smart Metering and Advanced Metering Infrastructures (AMI).

In [8] Ontario's (Canada) Information and Privacy Commissioner provides an overview of what the Smart Grid is, how it will affect electricity consumers and how their privacy might be at risk by the Smart Grid and Smart Metering. Furthermore she promotes the idea of building privacy into the Smart Grid from the start.

In [23] the authors first perform an informal threat analysis of Smart Metering and provide a sketch for an attested Smart Meter architecture. Using virtualization, mandatory network access control and trusted computing techniques this architecture enables multiple applications to use the Smart Meter hardware and to work in a privacy-preserving and integer manner. The article names applications for billing the customer very closely to the data origin (in the household) and applications that provide the consumer with a consumer portal. They achieve privacy-preserving Smart Metering billing by remote attestation of the billing software in the TPM of the Smart Meter. For that, in contrast to our solution, they require quite powerful hardware capable of virtualization and they have a higher attack surface due to a more complicated Smart Meter design.

Privacy aspects of smart meter-based billing: In [12] a privacy-preserving detection algorithm for leakages in electricity distribution has been proposed. By aggregation across several Smart Meters the developed algorithm protects individual meter readings while allowing grid operators to detect illegitimate/unknown load. Their approach does not allow individual billing, yet this is the main application of our paper.

Furthermore, in [6] a model for measuring privacy in Smart Metering is developed and subsequently two different solutions to privacy are presented: A Trusted Third Party-based approach, where individual consumption profiles are aggregated at the third party and only sums are communicated to the supplier. The other approach attempts to mask consumption profiles by adding randomness to the actual profile with an expectation of the random distribution of zero. In contrast to our solution, both of their approaches cannot handle billing of time-of-use tariffs but only provide either sums or not-accurate profiles. Furthermore, our approach does not require a trusted third party and provides exact results for every computation (as required by some legislations).

Finally, in [27] also a twofold approach is presented: The first solution employs a sophisticated Trusted Platform Module (TPM) in the Smart Meter to obtain signed tariff data from the supplier and calculate a trustworthy bill. The second solution makes use of the electrical grid infrastructure as a third party to anonymize up-to-date consumption values sent out constantly by Smart Meters. Our approach can be distinguished as it only addresses billing but only requires a very simple TPM that creates commitments.

Concurrent work [28] also covers the aspect of billing in Smart Metering. It focuses on realizing different tariff types where we provide practical information on how our scheme can be combined with existing Smart Metering reporting protocols.

Similar applications of homomorphic commitments: The articles [3] and [18] describe how privacy-preserving electronic toll pricing can be implemented using commitments to protect the time and location of cars. On-board-units continuously collect their location, time and the price of the consumed service (the driven route). They send commitments to the traffic authority. Eventually, using random spot checking, the traffic authority challenges on-board-units to open their commitments for places and times where their cars have been recorded by cameras. In contrast to our scheme, they use commitments to mostly protect auxiliary information used for computing the price, i.e. the time and place. Our work uses commitments to hide the private information from which the price is directly computed on the commitments, i.e. the energy volume per time slot. Consequently, we never need to open any input data commitment.

Pedersen commitments: Due to their homomorphic properties Pedersen commitments are an effective means to verify the correctness of statistics computation. In [30] it has been applied in the outsourced database setting. Statistics and dot product computation can be useful for in many application areas. An example from the database community again is privacy-preserving data mining [32]. An example from the business software community is collaborative benchmarking [19].

Our work is the first in providing a very high degree of privacy for customers by not disclosing consumption profiles in time-of-use smart meter billing scenarios.

7   Future Work

Dynamic, time-dependent billing is only one application of fine-grained consumption data. In addition, a profile of a household's energy consumption can be utilized by the supplier to create predictions of this household's energy demand in the future. Our proposed solution does not cover this usage of consumption profiles. Realizing a privacy friendly method for calculating such predictions is subject to future research. However, one must realize that privacy and the ability to create predictions potentially conflict with each other and this conflict should be investigated further also in the field of Smart Metering.

8   Conclusion

In this paper we have proposed a protocol for privacy-preserving reporting of consumption profiles in a Smart Metering scenario by the use of a plug-in component. We have identified and analyzed the requirements of different stakeholders. Based on this analysis, we devised a billing scheme which allows privacy-related consumption profiles to remain within the household while preserving provable correctness of the billable amounts. The privacy sensitive data therefore is not susceptible to interception in transit or leakage in the supplier's back-end system.

We have provided the specification for the utilized components, for the introduction into a traditional Smart Metering setup, and for the communication and calculation during the three protocol stages (initialization, reporting, verification). After proving the soundness, completeness and zero-knowledge property of the verification, we investigated the execution times of our prototypical implementation and showed that it is a viable solution for Smart Metering hardware. Finally, we discussed how our protocol could be executed using existing Smart Metering reporting specifications and showed that our approach fulfills the previously identified stakeholder's requirements.

Our protocol is one step towards the idea of building privacy into the Smart Grid [8]. By preserving customer privacy we mitigate trust issues that privacy experts, the media and the public have raised about the privacy implications of Smart Metering.

References

1. Smart metering projects map (2010),
   http://maps.google.com/maps/ms?ie=UTF8&oe=UTF8&msa=0&msid=115519311058367534348.0000011362ac6d7d21187
2. D. U. Association. DLMS/COSEM: Device language message specification/companion specification for energy metering (2010), http://www.dlms.com/organization/index.html
3. Balasch, J., Rial, A., Troncoso, C., Geuens, C., Preneel, B., Verbauwhede, I.: Pretp: Privacy-preserving electronic toll pricing. In: 19th Usenix Security Symposium, Association, pp. 63–78, USENIX (2010)
4. Bauer, G., Stockinger, K., Lukowicz, P.: Recognizing the use-mode of kitchen appliances from their current consumption. In: Barnaghi, P., Moessner, K., Presser, M., Meissner, S. (eds.) EuroSSC 2009. LNCS, vol. 5741, pp. 163–176. Springer, Heidelberg (2009)
5. Bichsel, P., Camenisch, J., Groß, T., Shoup, V.: Anonymous credentials on a standard Java card. In: ACM Conference on Computer and Communications Security, pp. 600–610 (2009)
6. Bohli, J.-M., Ugus, O., Sorge, C.: A privacy model for smart metering. In: Proceedings of the First IEEE International Workshop on Smart Grid Communications (in conjunction with IEEE ICC 2010) (2010)
7. Boyer, B.: Companion material for robust java benchmarking article series (2010)
8. Cavoukian, A., Polonetskyand, J., Wolf, C.: Smart Privacy for the Smart Grid: embedding privacy into the design of electricity conservation. Identity in the Information Society 3(2), 275–294 (2010)
9. Craemer, K.D., Geert, D.: Analysis of state-of-the-art Smart Metering communication standards. In: Young Researcher Symposium edition 2010, Leuven, Belgium (2010)
10. Wisy, M.: Emsycon GmbH: Smart Meter language specification (SML) (January 2008)
11. Lenzini, M.O.G., Teeuw, W.: Trust, security, and privacy for the advanced metering infrastructure. Technical report (July 2009)
12. Garcia, F., Jacobs, B.: Privacy-friendly energy-metering via homomorphic encryption. In: Proceedings of the 6th International Workshop on Security and Trust Management (2010)
13. Hart, G.: Nonintrusive appliance load monitoring. Proceedings of the IEEE 80(12), 1870–1891 (1992)

14. Hart, G.W.: Residential energy monitoring and computerized surveillance via utility power flows. In: IEEE Technology and Society Magazine (June 1989)
15. Heck, W.: Smart energy meter will not be compulsory. NRC Handelsblad (April 2009),
    http://www.nrc.nl/international/article2207260.ece/
    Smart_energy_meter_will_not_be_compulsory
16. Jamieson, A.: Smart Meters could be spy in the home. Telegraph (UK) (October 2009), http://www.telegraph.co.uk/finance/newsbysector/energy/6292809/Smart-meters-could-be-spy-in-the-home.html
17. Jawurek, M., Johns, M.: Security challenges of a changing energy landscape. In ISSE 2010, Securing Electronic Business Processes, pages 249–259, Vieweg+Teubner (2010)
18. Jonge, W., Jacobs, B.: Privacy-Friendly Electronic Traffic Pricing via Commits, pp. 143–161. Springer-Verlag, Heidelberg (2009)
19. Kerschbaum, F.: Practical privacy-preserving benchmarking. In: Proceedings of the 23rd IFIP International Information Security Conference, vol. 278, pp. 17–31. Springer, Heidelberg (2003)
20. German Legislation: Energiewirtschaftsgesetz (2005)
21. German Legislation: Gesetz über das Meß und Eichwesen (Eichgesetz) (2008)
22. German Legislation: Bundesdatenschutzgesetz (2009)
23. Lemay, M., Gross, G., Gunter, C.A., Garg, S.: Unified architecture for large-scale attested metering. In: in Hawaii International Conference on System Sciences, Big Island. ACM Press, New York (2007)
24. Lisovich, M.A., Mulligan, D.K., Wicker, S.B.: Inferring personal information from demand-response systems. IEEE Security and Privacy 8(1), 11–20 (2010)
25. McDaniel, P., McLaughlin, S.: Security and privacy challenges in the Smart Grid. IEEE Security and Privacy 7, 75–77 (2009)
26. Pedersen, T.P.: Non-interactive and information-theoretic secure verifiable secret sharing. In: Feigenbaum, J. (ed.) CRYPTO 1991. LNCS, vol. 576, pp. 129–140. Springer, Heidelberg (1992)
27. Petrlic, R.: A privacy-preserving concept for Smart Grids. In: Sicherheit in vernetzten Systemen: 18. DFN Workshop. Books on Demand GmbH, pp. B1–B14 (2010)
28. Rial, A., Danezis,G.: Privacy-preserving smart metering. Technical report, Microsoft Research (November 2010)
29. Sultanem, F.: Using appliance signatures for monitoring residential loads at meter panel level. IEEE Transactions on Power Delivery 6(4), 1380–1385 (1991)
30. Thompson, B., Haber, S., Horne, W.G., Sander, T., Yao, D.: Privacy-preserving computation and verification of aggregate queries on outsourced databases. In: Privacy Enhancing Technologies, pp. 185–201 (2009)
31. Torchia, M.: Idc marketscape: North American AMI Communication Network 2011 vendor assessment (2011)
32. Vaidya, J., Zhu, Y.M., Clifton, C.W.: Privacy Preserving Data Mining (Advances in Information Security). Springer, New York (2005)

Scramble! Your Social Network Data

Filipe Beato[1], Markulf Kohlweiss[1,2], and Karel Wouters[1]

[1] Katholieke Universiteit Leuven
Dept. Electrical Engineering - ESAT/SCD/IBBT-COSIC
Kasteelpark Arenberg 10, Leuven-Heverlee (Belgium)
[2] Microsoft Research, Cambridge, UK

Abstract. Social network sites (SNS) allow users to share information with friends, family, and other contacts. However, current SNS sites such as Facebook or Twitter assume that users trust SNS providers with the access control of their data. In this paper we propose Scramble, the implementation of a SNS-independent Firefox extension that allows users to enforce access control over their data. Scramble lets users define access control lists (ACL) of authorised users for each piece of data, based on their preferences. The definition of ACL is facilitated through the possibility of dynamically defining contact groups. In turn, the confidentiality and integrity of one data item is enforced using cryptographic techniques. When accessing a SNS that contains data encrypted using Scramble, the plugin transparently decrypts and checks integrity of the encrypted content.

1 Introduction

Social Network Sites (SNS) such as Facebook, MySpace, LinkedIn, and Twitter are becoming increasingly popular. Millions of users access these sites as part of their daily routine. These sites provide technological features that allow users to share content and build communities around shared interests. Users can assess, analyse, and modify privacy preferences made available by the service providers, but they cannot control the enforcement of these preferences.

SNS users often post a large amount of privacy sensitive information on SNS, such as their date of birth, their daily activities, or political views. As already mentioned, users have to rely on privacy preferences enforced by the SNS providers to protect this data. However, these policies and privacy preferences are often extremely coarse and difficult to locate [19], which lead to potential misconfigurations [7]. Nevertheless, the SNS provider still has access to all users' data and can share it with external parties, like targeted advertisement companies. Therefore, the user does not have full control over his data. In addition, SNS may offer application programming interfaces that may expose and share the users' information with other services. Finally, policies may be changed intentionally by providers, to help them strike a balance between the interests of advertisers, application providers, and usability.

All of this may leads to serious privacy concerns. The need for a mechanism that returns control over both access-control policy configuration and

S. Fischer-Hübner and N. Hopper (Eds.): PETS 2011, LNCS 6794, pp. 211–225, 2011.

enforcement for user-generated content to the users themselves has been identified in previous works [1,2,12,14,15,18]. Clearly, this is highly desirable for SNS, but is also relevant for other Web 2.0 services.

In this paper, we present Scramble, a client side application implemented as a Firefox extension to help users keep their data confidential. Scramble allows users to encrypt their posted content in the SNS. Therefore, Scramble guarantees confidentiality of users' data towards the SNS-provider. To support audience segregation [11,20], scramble contains an easy-to-use user interface for defining the set of users the user's content should be shared with.

Our implementation of Scramble is SNS independent and is suitable for immediate deployment as open source software. We make use of the OpenPGP[1] standard to enforce confidentiality and integrity. Several SNS providers have a length limitation for posted content, e.g., Twitter[2], and do not allow publication of encrypted text defined on their Terms of Service, like Facebook. For those reasons, we provide an implementation of an external tiny link server. The server stores the encrypted data and produces a short link that works as an index to the posted encrypted content. The scramble prototype is part of research performed within the EU-PrimeLife[3] project.

The remainder of this paper is organised as follows: In Section 2 we review related work and compare it with our proposal. We introduce our goals and assumptions in Section 3. In Section 4 we present a detailed description of the Scramble design, and in Section 5 we describe our implementation. Section 6 gives a security, performance and usability analysis of our implementation. Finally, in Section 7 we discuss future work and conclude by summarising our results.

2   Related Work

We discuss existing approaches for enforcing access control rules in SNS: Social network providers, such as Facebook and MySpace, implement access control mechanisms for user-generated data. These mechanisms, however, offer no protection against the SNS providers themselves, since they through their control of the servers running the service have access to all of a user's information. To avoid access by the SNS, Lockr [3] hides pictures posted in the SNS by replacing it by a link, and storing the picture at a third party server in unencrypted format. This approach relies on a third-party that might not be trustworthy – instead of trusting the SNS provider one now has to trust the third party server. In [8] the authors apply the concept of virtual private networks to social networks. Whilst, this solution is SNS independent and allows users to replace the original attribute data with some pseudo information. The real information is then sent and stored in friends machines. Thus, besides creating a bargain on

---

[1] OpenPGP represents the IETF RFC 4880 - http://www.openpgp.org/

[2] Twitter allows a maximum of 140 characters per post.

[3] This project aims at providing significant improvements to protect privacy in emerging digital world. http://www.primelife.eu

friends machines instead of delegating to the server, it does not allow users to selective enforce access control over their posted data.

There are several proposals that use encryption to protect a user's information that target Facebook. flyByNight [16] is a Facebook application that protects user data by storing it in encrypted form in Facebook. This application is Facebook dependent and relies on Facebook servers for its key management. The decryption algorithm is implemented in JavaScript and is retrieved from the Facebook application. Thus, while browser independent, it is not secure against active attacks by the provider – Facebook. In contrast, Scramble is a client side application that has no SNS dependencies.

NOYB (*None Of Your Business*) [13] is a system that targets Facebook and uses encryption to protect private information. The personal details of users, such as name and gender, are divided into multiple pieces of data, called atoms. These atoms are separated and shuffled with atoms of other users, acting as a random substitution cipher. The encryption method used by NOYB just replaces the privacy details of user A with those of random users B and C. Only the user himself and his friends can reverse the process and reconstruct the profile. However, this can only be applied to the personal details on the user's profile, and does not allow encryption of free text entries as frequently found in social networks.

FaceCloak [17] is a Firefox extension that uses a symmetric key to encrypt user's information in Facebook. The encrypted data is stored in the FaceCloak server, and replaced in Facebook by random text fetched from wikipedia. The symmetric keys are shared with the set of users authorised to read the content. The random text acts as an index to the encrypted data on the server.

One of the problems with the FaceCloak and NOYB model is, that using random meaningful text retrieved from Wikipedia or other users may lead to social conflicts, if other users take them to be genuine user content.One could argue that the goal of natural-text as either cipher-text or index by NOYP and FaceCloak respectively is an important anti-censorship mechanism against a SNS that sees threads to it's advertising revenues. Should the need arise, Scramble could make use of similar techniques. However, we believe that other solutions to this dilemma, such as client-side privacy friendly advertising mechanisms may be more desirable.

Moreover, FaceCloak has a complicated and inefficient key distribution system. For each piece of content, the user accessing the content has to use an offline channel to retrieve the key. Scramble uses a simpler and more reliable approach for key distribution. The encryption of the content is done using public keys, and thus a user with access rights just needs to use his own secret key for decryption. As a usability compromise we restrict the use of PGP's web-of-trust mechanism to power-users and adopt leap-of-faith authentication as the default key-distribution paradigm.

The schemes defined above have proposed mechanism to protect users' sensitive information in Facebook. However, they are Facebook dependent, while Scramble is SNS independent.

Diaspora[4] presented a new privacy friendly, open source social network. The project offers users the possibility to share privately information using OpenPGP mechanisms, like Scramble. It uses its own distributed network for storing the encrypted data. However, while it offers a new service to protect the privacy of its users, it does not support the existing and highly popular centralised social networks services.

3   Goals and Assumptions

We represent a social network as a graph $\mathcal{G} = (\mathcal{V}, \mathcal{E})$, whose vertices represent users and whose edges represent the undirected connections between users. Each u establishes a set of relationships $\mathcal{R}_u \in \mathcal{V}$ that contains all users to which u has a connection. Formally, $(u, v) \in \mathcal{E}$ if and only if $v \in \mathcal{R}_u$.

We now describe our thread model and our assumptions, as well as the goals of our system.

Threat model. Our threat model considers the SNS providers as potentially adversarial. SNS providers have access to all of the user's private information. SNS providers can leak information to external parties and have the power to tamper or replace user generated content on the SNS. Therefore, users may be vulnerable to data leakage, impersonations and false judgements.

We consider curious users seeking sensitive information to be a weaker adversary than the provider. Such users benefit from the SNS as a channel to listen and obtain sensitive content from other SNS users and may use it for their own profit. Providers commonly enforce default privacy settings to protect against such threat, but these settings are often permissive [2] and subject to frequent change. Thus, users lack control about which other SNS users can access their content.

We rely on the integrity of users' personal environment, such as their browser and computer. We assume that no external party has access to or can compromise a user's environment. We assume that each user u has a public and secret key pair (pk_u, sk_u), where pk_u is known by all $\mathcal{R}_u$ and sk_u is only known by u. We assume that users u and v exchange their public keys when a friendship relation is established using an authenticated offline channel.[5]

Goals. Users need to be able to control their own data, and specify who can access it, preferably without relying on third party servers, such as the SNS providers. Any user u can create new content d for the SNS, e.g., as a wall post or some other message. Thus, the desired goals for Scramble are the following:

Privacy Preservation: A user u should be able to define the subset $\mathcal{S}_d$ of recipients from $\mathcal{R}_u$ that are authorised to read d. Only users in $\mathcal{S}_d$ are able to read d.

---

[4] Diaspora: https://joindiaspora.com/

[5] For the sake of reducing the entrance barrier for ordinary users, we will, sometimes willingly break the last assumption and allow users to start communicating using unauthenticated keys. Users are, however, advised to check the authenticity of keys using key fingerprints, and to get suspicious if keys change without premonition.

Both S_d and the content of d should be kept hidden from the provider. The confidentiality of d should be protected by cryptographic techniques. However, once d is distributed among the users in S_d, there is no way to prevent a *malicious* user in S_d from storing or re-distribute the content of d. In this case, the receiving user is said to break the social contract associated with the establishment of the friendship relation.

Publisher Integrity: Scramble should guarantee d's integrity when posting d in the SNS using cryptographic techniques. This prevents attackers from tampering with the content of d and impersonating u.

Deployability: Scramble is meant to be deployed in the real world. Thus, it must be stable, compatible with different environments, and SNS independent.

Usability: Scramble should present a user interface that is easy to use. In order to overcome usability issues, such as those presented in [21], the operations should be simple and the cryptographic techniques transparent. Operations like the generation, import and export of keys should be effortless or hidden. If a user v is not authorised to read d, then Scramble should hide d from v.

4   Scramble

In this section we describe and motivate the design details and functionalities of Scramble. We first discuss design decisions specific to key management, access control policies, and the employed cryptographic mechanisms. Then, we describe the process flow of Scramble from a user perspective.

4.1   Key Management, Access Control Policies, and Cryptography

Key Management. In Scramble, each user u holds a OpenPGP key pair, composed of public key pair pk_u and a secret key pair sk_u. The public and private key pairs consist of the public respectively private keys of an ElGamal encryption and a DSA signature scheme. The keys can be either generated (default behavior) or imported (power-user behavior) by the user upon Scramble initialisation. If the user Alice[6] wants to share d with the set S_d, she must possess the associated public keys pk of all users in S_d. All pk of S_d are stored in Alice's machine, and are managed by Scramble.

Key management is a hard problem due to the possibility of key tampering and the fact that it is counterintuitive to ordinary users. A malicious user v or the SNS provider can replace the pk_u of the user u to impersonating u. Thus, it is important that users can correctly distribute their public keys, as they are used for encryption when posting content. If users, however, are not able to exchange any keys and resort to unencrypted alternatives, they are even worse off.

Users have to be able to exchange their pk when a friendship connection is established. They can make their public key available using the provider or a

---

[6] For the sake of concreteness, we sometimes use Alice and Bob for the user u that posts a new d and the intended reader v respectively.

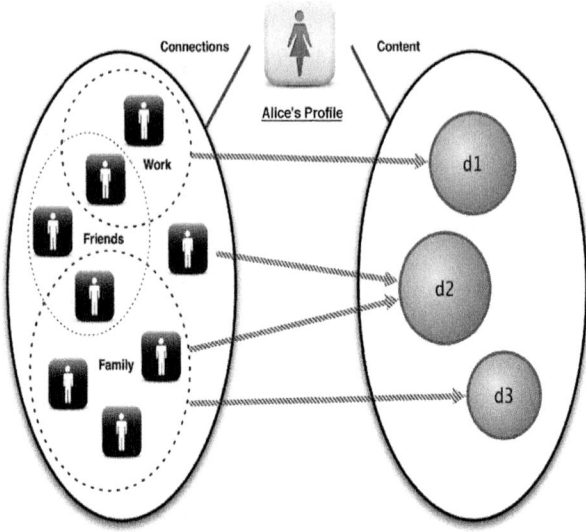

Fig. 1. Access control mapping example

key server and should verify fingerprints using an offline channel to verify the authenticity of a public key. As Scramble makes use of the OpenPGP standard we can make use of any public PGP server. We opted to verify the authenticity of keys manually as the current OpenPGP web of trust has proved to be too complicated for ordinary users [21]. Users have to either take the leap-of-faith or check the fingerprints. For future versions it should be easy to introduce a web-of-trust mechanism, if this is desired by power-users.

Alternatively, our key management model could be extended by making public keys available over an SNS-based mechanism such as the one proposed by [5], where users cross certify their digital certificates using SNS relationship connections. The cross certification is achieved by users signing other users' digital certificates, which are composed by the public key together with some Personal Identifiable Information (PII).

For key revocation or key update users are required to distribute a new public key. However, this only affects new content.

Access Control Policies. We consider that $\mathcal{R}_u$ is represented in Scramble by the public keys of the users in $\mathcal{R}_u$. Moreover, a user u can define groups $G_i \subset \mathcal{R}_u$ in order to separate $\mathcal{R}_u$ into categories.

Whenever u publishes a new document d in the SNS he can define with whom to share. For that, u selects a subset $\mathcal{S}_d$ from his $\mathcal{R}_u$ that is to be authorised to read d. $\mathcal{S}_d$ can be composed of single users $v_i \in \mathcal{R}_u$, of a set of pre-defined groups G_i or of a mix of both. The set $\mathcal{S}_d$ can be different for each d posted. For any $\mathcal{S}_d$ update d is required to be re-posted.

Figure 1 represents an example of our approach for defining access rights. Alice has relationships $\mathcal{R}_{Alice}$ and posts contents $\{d_i\}$. $\mathcal{R}_{Alice}$ is represented by three groups *Work, Friends, Family* and a single relationship *Bob*. This helps Alice to define her $\mathcal{S}_d$ in an easier way. When Alice posts new content d she may, e.g., defines $\mathcal{S}_d = \{Bob \cup Work\}$. In this way, Alice keeps d private to a limited audience defined by $\mathcal{S}_d$. Moreover, the audience defined by $\mathcal{S}_d$ is only known to her.

Cryptographic primitives. For the confidentiality and integrity of d we had the choice between traditional hybrid-encryption techniques, like OpenPGP [22], or broadcast encryption such as [4,6]. In both cases, the users' public keys in $\mathcal{S}_d$ would be used to create the access list that would be attached to the final posted content. The confidentiality of d is then achieved using an encryption algorithm, while integrity of d is assured by signing d before encryption.

$$d' \leftarrow \text{Encrypt}_{\mathcal{S}_d}(\text{Sign}(d, sk_u))$$

We chose OpenPGP as it is a well deployed standard with support for multiple recipients encryption using hybrid encryption. Moreover, most broadcast encryption schemes such as [6] do not provide key privacy, with the exception of [4]. The latter, however, also uses a hybrid-encryption approach internally and does not offer performance advantages. We discuss weaknesses of OpenPGP that we are aware of in Section 6, but we believe that it is more reasonable to fix OpenPGP, than to abandon it as a design choice.

Thus, d is encrypted with a one time random-generated secret key k using a symmetric algorithm. Then, $|\mathcal{S}_d|$ encryptions of k are generated using the public key of each subject in $|\mathcal{S}_d|$. The integrity of d is assured by signing d before encryption. Hence, d is published as follows.

> *Let* $\mathcal{S}_d = \{Alice, Bob, Charlie\}$ *be set by* u
>
> $\sigma_d \leftarrow \text{Sign}(d, sk_u)$
>
> $\text{C} \leftarrow \text{SymEnc}_k(\sigma_d || d)$
>
> $d' \leftarrow \{\text{PKEnc}_{pk_{Alice}}(k) || \text{PKEnc}_{pk_{Bob}}(k) || \text{PKEnc}_{pk_{Charlie}}(k) || \text{C}\}$

The public key encrypted values of k are appended to the symmetric encryption and represent an anonymous version of $\mathcal{S}_d$ that specifies which other users are allowed to see d. This will indeed increase the storage overhead on the server side, but it will save the user from managing a large number of different keys for every new d on his machine. In addition, this allows the user to keep his defined access sets anonymised, and enforce different access control rights for each document d. It is important to note, that OpenPGP uses a separate ElGamal encryption key and DSA signing key to perform the previous operations.

In order to keep the set of recipients hidden, we use the *hidden-recipient* option. This option conceals the key IDs of recipients in the encrypted content. In this way, only the users in $\mathcal{S}_d$ are able to retrieve the value of d. Other users, and the SNS provider stay oblivious of the raw value of d, learning only d'. However, the length of the output is directly affected by the size of $\mathcal{S}_d$.

4.2   User Interaction Flow

The Scramble system consists of two modules. The first and main element, Scramble, is a Firefox extension that contains the cryptographic primitives to enforce the access rights, and the key and group management. The second and optional element is a TinyLink server. This server just receives content posts and returns a link to the location of the content. We assume that users can choose their external server or set their own server with our provided implementation.

We describe the two elements using the flow of operations needed to to publish and retrieve data on a SNS. The process flow is preceded by an initialisation phase.

Initialisation. In this phase, Alice generates her key pair (pk_u, sk_u), uploads it to the key server, obtains keys for her contacts $\mathcal{R}_u$, and creates her groups G_i. In order to import her relationship contacts, Alice could, in future version, extract the contacts from the SNS provider directly using the mechanism described in [9]. For now, imports need to be done manually based on the email address of users.

Posting content. Alice is a user that wishes to post a new d in the SNS (Figure 2). Therefore Alice (1) selects $\mathcal{S}_d = \{Bob, Charlie, ..., Dave\}$ using Scramble. Then, Scramble signs d and encrypts d with the keys of the authorised users in $\mathcal{S}_u$. If the SNS limits the length of the posted d, then (2) Scramble posts d', the encryption of d, in the TinyLink server that returns a tiny link to the stored location. (3) Scramble posts the encrypted value d' or the tiny link to d' in the SNS. The value of d' is transmitted from Scramble in encrypted format, keeping a possible attacker oblivious.

Retrieving content. The decryption of encrypted content from the SNS is transparent to the user (Figure 3). First, (1) Scramble reads the encrypted value of d from the SNS. If the content is a tiny link, then (2) Scramble uses the tiny link retrieves d', the encrypted value of d from the TinyLink server. Subsequently, (3) Scramble tries to decrypt and if successful, verifies if d' was not tampered with and that it was in fact Alice who signed d. Since d came from Alice and Bob is in $\mathcal{S}_d$, Bob is authorised to read d. Thus, Scramble presents the value of d to Bob. Otherwise, the decryption fails, and the retrieved value d' is not shown.

5   Implementation

Our implementation represents the design functionalities in software. We have implemented Scramble as an open source application[7] under the EPL licence [10]. In this section we outline our implementation by describing the details of the application modules along with the functional aspects.

The main module of the implementation is the Firefox extension, that manages and enforces the access control lists. Our implementation is composed by the following two modules.

---

[7] Scramble version can be found in the project website `http://tinyurl.com/ScrambleIt`.

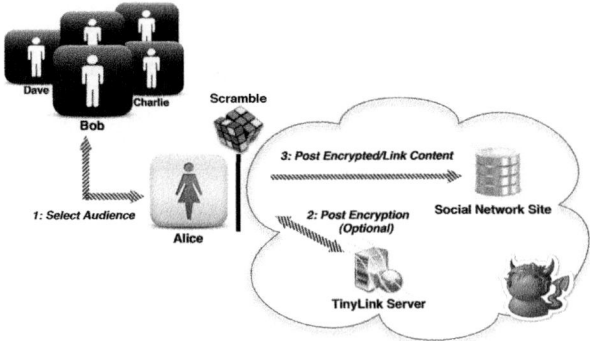

Fig. 2. Posting new Content Process

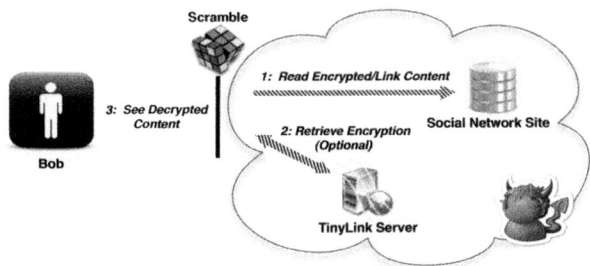

Fig. 3. Reading Content Process

Firefox extension. Scramble is a client-side application implemented as a Firefox extension, that allows cross-platform client-side encryption and key management. Due to the fact that a Firefox extension is developed mainly in JavaScript, we have used a Java XPCOM[8] component to improve performance of the cryptographic module. The Java XPCOM component contains an implementation of the OpenPGP standard. The component executes either a BouncyCastle[9] (BC) OpenPGP implementation or the GnuPG[10] binary module that implements the OpenPGP standard. By means of having the two different implementations, the user can choose to have an embedded OpenPGP implementation with a dedicated key ring with BC, or to execute the general GnuPG module with a key ring that can be shared with other programs.

Key management. The key management is handled by Scramble. The OpenPGP key pair can be generated or imported by the user Alice during installation, however, it can be changed afterwards. Alice can then upload her key to the public key server in order to allow her friends to download it. The group management

---

[8] http://www.mozilla.org/projects/xpcom/
[9] http://www.bouncycastle.org/
[10] http://www.gnupg.org/

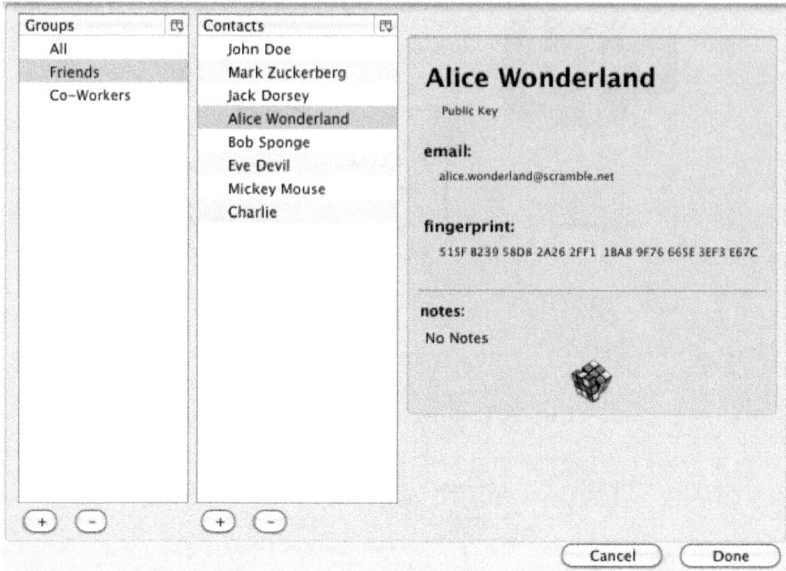

Fig. 4. Access Control Definition User Interface

and their definition is defined by Alice, by operating on a simple user-interface (Figure 4). The OpenPGP pk of all users $v \in \mathcal{R}_u$ are stored in Alice's machine, and act as their identification. In order to import those keys, Alice uses the key server mechanism to import it by referring to them using her friends email addresses. The fingerprint of an imported key pk_v of Bob can then used by Alice to verify the authenticity of his key. The full or a part of the fingerprint should be communicated using a secure offline channel. Thus, $\mathcal{R}_u$ in Scramble represents a subset of the relationship graph on the SNS.

Publish data operation. To perform the operation where Alice wants to post a new d into the SNS in encrypted format, Alice is required to write d into a field in the SNS and select it. Scramble then allows Alice to define the $\mathcal{S}_d$ for d from her circle of trust $\mathcal{R}_u$. The values of the pk of each users in $\mathcal{S}_d$ are loaded and used in the encryption algorithm. Scramble retrieves the selected text from the DOM[11] tree of the SNS website's displayed HTML page and posts the value of d in encrypted format or the tiny link to d', the encrypted value of d. This is only readable by users in $\mathcal{S}_d$.

Retrieve data operation. For the decryption operation, Scramble parses the DOM tree of the website and searches for Scramble tags representing encrypted blocks of text. If the user belongs to the set and thus has access, Scramble automatically and transparently decrypts the content presenting the unencrypted data d to the

---

[11] http://www.w3.org/DOM/

user. Otherwise, the data is hidden or is indicated by a pre-defined message, like "Non-authorised content". This is done by only replacing the encrypted text independently from the DOM's tree style.

In order to perform the operations to store and retrieve data from the tiny link server, Scramble executes `XMLHttpRequest Post` and `Get` calls in JavaScript.

Users that are not using Scramble will see the encrypted data (Figure 5). This can be either the full encrypted block d' or a link to the block.

Tiny Link Server. The Tiny Link Server was developed to target the limitation of content size imposed by SNS providers. The PHP[12] server stores encrypted data and returns a tiny link (short URL) which represents the index of d', the encryption of d. This server can be controlled by the users directly or outsourced into a cloud server, that may or may not require extra authentication. We provide the users with the source code and details for their own implementation.

6   Security Analysis, Performance and Usability

In this section we proceed with a security analysis of our implementation. Then, we present our performance and usability results.

Security analysis. We analyze the resilience of the current implementation of scramble against a number of potential attacks.

Recipients Set Anonymity Scramble keeps the content document d confidential using OpenPGP encryption. In order to anonymise the recipients set for outsiders, Scramble uses the OpenPGP option *hidden-recipients* to conceal the key IDs. However, this does not offer anonymity of the set of recipients towards a malicious user in the set, as shown in [4]. We note that Scramble does not provide protection against traffic analysis, meaning that the provider could infer who has access to the content by analysing download and upload operations. Protection against this kind of attacks is left as a subject of future work.

Active Attacks. In an active attack, a malicious service provider attempts to tamper with the content item, by compromising content integrity and confidentiality. In Scramble the user posts the item d in encrypted format on the server to ensure the confidentiality of d. A malicious server can also have the objective of fooling or impersonating users by changing or replacing d. In order to prevent such attacks, the user posts d together with a signature on d in encrypted format.

Performance. To be usable, Scramble must minimise its implementation overhead. The use of an XPCOM component allows to execute either a BC Java OpenPGP implementation or the binary command line GnuPG module. Both of which provide very efficient encryption, decryption and signing operations.

In order to analyse the performance of our implementation, we focus on the cryptographic algorithms that represent the most expensive operations and the

---

[12] http://php.net/

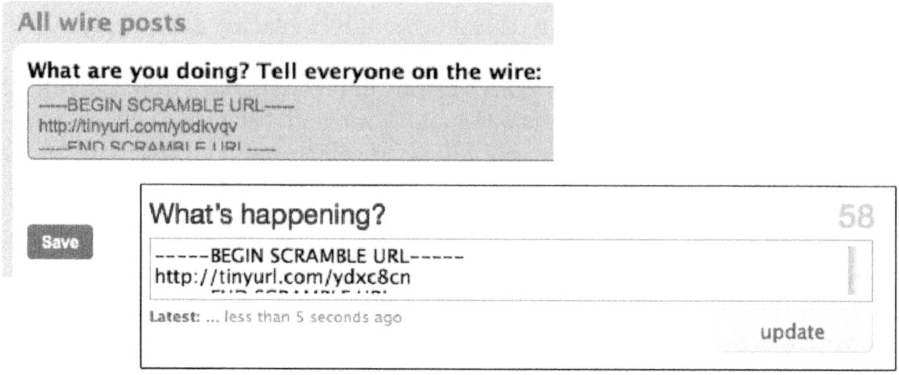

Fig. 5. Scramble in *(Private)* Twitter

response of the tiny link server, which include the network latency and server process. Therefore, Scramble depends directly on the amount of recipients $r = |\mathcal{S}_d|$ per encrypted block d. The encryption and decryption costs are represented in Figure 6, where the size of the contact set for encryption and decryption operations goes from 0 to 720 contacts[13]. The public key operations are the most costly operations compared to the use of a symmetric encryption algorithm. The performance complexity details are described as follow.

Publish operation. is affected by the efficiency of the encryption and signing algorithm E and t_s. The efficiency of E is directly affected by r. Thus, the overall performance is $t_s + O(r)$.

Retrieval operation. is affected by the number of encrypted items per page n, by the efficiency of decryption and verification algorithm D and t_s. Whilst a user in $\mathcal{S}$ is required to perform an average $r/2$ decryptions, a user that does not have access rights is required to perform r. Thus, the overall performance for retrieving information is $n(t_s + O(r))$.

Usability. We have performed some user tests with local Belgian students, where Scramble was well received in terms of user experience and functionality. Scramble was also submitted to a usability expert evaluation conducted by KAU[14] in the scope of the EU-PrimeLife project. However, a more advanced user experience test targeting a larger audiences is left for future work.

7   Future Work and Conclusions

In this section we start to enumerate some discussion points on the current implementation and future directions. Then, we conclude by presenting our results.

---

[13] Tests performed on a 2GHz AMD Athlon(tm) XP 2400+, with 1Gb RAM.

[14] Karlstad University - http://www.kau.se/

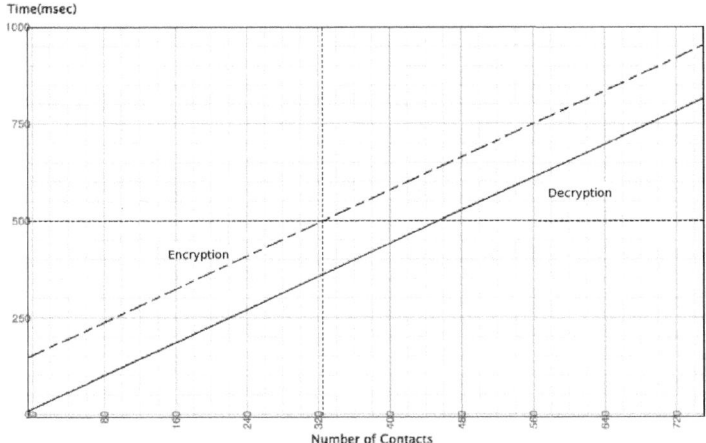

Fig. 6. Performance of Scramble operations per contact set

Future work. At the moment, it is the user himself who is responsible for defining $G \subset \mathcal{R}_u$. In the future, we intend to extend Scramble to be able to infer the privacy policies information from social network specific tags during an initialisation state. These tags are added to the content or can be derived from the context, as shown in [9].

In order to attract a large set of users and extend to other systems, we are currently developing a Scramble version as a Google Chrome application. In addition, a mobile device extension of Scramble would be attractive.

Conclusions. We designed and implemented Scramble, a Firefox extension that allows users to define and enforce selective access control preferences for data published on social network sites. Scramble is SNS independent and can be used in diverse SNS, like Twitter, Facebook, Clique[15] and MySpace. Through the integration into a Firefox extension, the encrypted content is automatically decrypted by the browser for authorised users. The extension also allows the definition of groups to define audience segregation, and the encryption of content under the keys of all group members.

Using a public key encryption scheme we are able to protect the integrity and confidentiality of user created data, especially towards the SNS provider, by means of encryption. At the moment, the implementation just allows content encryption as wall posts, private messages and news status. However, it is also possible to extend to other content types, such as pictures, by following the same directions.

Due to the fact that it has been designed to be general and SNS independent, it can also be used with other Web 2.0 services, such as blogs, forums and wikis. Potentially, it allows users to store data in encrypted format in any cloud service.

---

[15] http://clique.primelife.eu/

Acknowledgements

This work have been supported in part by the Concerted Research Action (GOA) Ambiorics 2005/11 of the Flemish Government, by the IAP Programme P6/26 BCRYPT of the Belgian State (Belgian Science Policy), and in part by the European Commission through the ICT program under the following contract: ICT-216483 PRIMELIFE. The authors would like to thank Ronald Leenes and Jan Camenisch for the useful discussions, and Venelin Gornishki and Elmar Tischhauser for helping during the development, test and dissemination phases of the tool.

References

1. (Under)mining Privacy in Social Networks, Google Inc. (2008)
2. Acquisti, A., Gross, R.: Imagined Communities: Awareness, Information Sharing, and Privacy on the Facebook (2006)
3. Tootoonchian, G.S.A., Hatahet, A.Z.: Fine grained access control in online social networks. Technical report (2007)
4. Barth, A., Boneh, D., Waters, B.: Privacy in encrypted content distribution using private broadcast encryption. In: Di Crescenzo, G., Rubin, A. (eds.) FC 2006. LNCS, vol. 4107, pp. 52–64. Springer, Heidelberg (2006)
5. Bichsel, P., Müller, S., Preiss, F.-S., Sommer, D., Verdicchio, M.: Patrik Bichsel, Samuel Müller, Franz-Stefan Preiss, Dieter Sommer, and Mario Verdicchio. Security and trust through electronic social network-based interactions. In: IEEE International Conference on Computational Science and Engineering, vol. 4, pp. 1002–1007 (2009)
6. Boneh, D., Gentry, C., Waters, B.: Collusion resistant broadcast encryption with short ciphertexts and private keys. In: Shoup, V. (ed.) CRYPTO 2005. LNCS, vol. 3621, pp. 258–275. Springer, Heidelberg (2005)
7. Bonneau, J., Preibusch, S.: The privacy jungle: On the market for data protection in social networks. In: The Eighth Workshop on the Economics of Information Security, WEIS 2009 (2009)
8. Conti, M., Hasani, A., Crispo, B.: Virtual private social networks. In: Proceedings of the First ACM Conference on Data and Application Security and Privacy, ACM CODASPY 2011 (page to appear) (2011)
9. Danezis, G.: Inferring privacy policies for social networking services. In: AISec 2009: Proceedings of the 2nd ACM workshop on Security and artificial intelligence, pp. 5–10. ACM, New York (2009)
10. Eclipse Foundation: Eclipse public license (epl) frequently asked questions (2007) (accessed December 2007)
11. Goffman, E.: The Presentation of Self in Everyday Life. Doubleday, Garden City, New York (1959)
12. Gross, R., Acquisti, A.: Information revelation and privacy in online social networks (the Facebook case). In: Proceedings of the 2005 ACM Workshop on Privacy in the Electronic Society, pp. 71–80 (2005)
13. Guha, S., Tang, K., Francis, P.: Noyb: privacy in online social networks. In: WOSN 2008: Proceedings of the first workshop on Online social networks, pp. 49–54. ACM, New York (2008)

14. Khajeh-Hosseini, A., Sommerville, I., Sriram, I.: Research challenges for enterprise cloud computing. In: CoRR, abs/1001.3257 (2010)
15. Krishnamurthy, B., Wills, C.E.: Characterizing privacy in online social networks. In: WOSN 2008: Proceedings of the First Workshop on Online Social Networks, pp. 37–42. ACM, New York (2008)
16. Lucas, M.M., Borisov, N.: Flybynight: mitigating the privacy risks of social networking. In: Proceedings of the 7th ACM Workshop on Privacy in the Electronic Society (WPES), pp. 1–8. ACM Press, New York (2008)
17. Luo, W., Xie, Q., Hengartner, U.: FaceCloak: An architecture for user privacy on social networking sites. In: 2009 International Conference on Computational Science and Engineering (CSE), vol. 3, pp. 26–33. IEEE, Los Alamitos (2009)
18. Sun, S.-T., Beznosov, K.: Open problems in web 2.0 user content sharing (June 2009)
19. New York Times. Facebook privacy: A bewilldering tangle of options, http://www.nytimes.com/interactive/2010/05/12/business/facebook-privacy.html
20. van den Berg, B., Leenes, R.: Audience segregation in social network sites. In: SocialCom/PASSAT, pp. 1111–1116 (2010)
21. Whitten, A., Tygar, J.D.: Why johnny can't encrypt: a usability evaluation of pgp 5.0. In: Proceedings of the 8th conference on USENIX Security Symposium, vol. 8, pp. 14–14. USENIX Association, Berkeley (1999)
22. Zimmermann, P.R.: The official PGP users guide. MIT Press, Cambridge (1995)

A Constraint Satisfaction Cryptanalysis of Bloom Filters in Private Record Linkage

Mehmet Kuzu[1], Murat Kantarcioglu[1], Elizabeth Durham[2], and Bradley Malin[2]

[1] Dept. of Computer Science, University of Texas at Dallas
Richardson, TX, 75080 USA
{mxk093120,muratk}@utdallas.edu
[2] Dept. of Biomedical Informatics, Vanderbilt University
Nashville, TN, 37232 USA
{ea.durham,b.malin}@vanderbilt.edu

Abstract. For over fifty years, "record linkage" procedures have been refined to integrate data in the face of typographical and semantic errors. These procedures are traditionally performed over personal identifiers (e.g., names), but in modern decentralized environments, privacy concerns have led to regulations that require the obfuscation of such attributes. Various techniques have been proposed to resolve the tension, including secure multi-party computation protocols, however, such protocols are computationally intensive and do not scale for real world linkage scenarios. More recently, procedures based on Bloom filter encoding (BFE) have gained traction in various applications, such as healthcare, where they yield highly accurate record linkage results in a reasonable amount of time. Though promising, no formal security analysis has been designed or applied to this emerging model, which is of concern considering the sensitivity of the corresponding data. In this paper, we introduce a novel attack, based on constraint satisfaction, to provide a rigorous analysis for BFE and guidelines regarding how to mitigate risk against the attack. In addition, we conduct an empirical analysis with data derived from public voter records to illustrate the feasibility of the attack. Our investigations show that the parameters of the BFE protocol can be configured to make it relatively resilient to the proposed attack without significant reduction in record linkage performance.

1 Introduction

There are many societal needs, as well as legal requirements, for organizations to share data about their constituents in support of a wide range of endeavors, ranging from homeland security to biomedical research. At the same time, increasing decentralization of our world has led to the storage of an individual's personal information across independent organizations. To ensure accurate analytics, it is critical to apply "record linkage" techniques to integrate information that corresponds to the same individual. Record linkage is a relatively mature field and a sizable number of algorithms have been refined to support the task [1]. Yet, record linkage has traditionally been applied to explicit identifiers, such

S. Fischer-Hübner and N. Hopper (Eds.): PETS 2011, LNCS 6794, pp. 226–245, 2011.

as names and Social Security Numbers, and there are concerns that sharing such information beyond an organization's boundaries can endanger an individual's privacy. To mitigate risk, various private record linkage (PRL) protocols have been developed to enable data integration without revealing the identity of the corresponding individuals (e.g., [2–6]).

Most data sources contain records with typographical (e.g., "ei" vs. "ie") or semantic errors (e.g., maiden vs. married name) [7, 8], so it is critical that PRL protocols enable similarity tests between records. It has been demonstrated that such tests can be accomplished through the use of sophisticated cryptographic methods based on secure multi-party computation (SMC) [9, 10]. Unfortunately, protocols based on SMC are not practical for large dataset integration because they incur substantial computational costs and require continuous interaction between the organizations involved in the protocol [11]. More recently, a PRL protocol based on Bloom filter encoding (BFE) was proposed to measure the similarity of records in a more efficient manner, which is particularly notable because it has gained traction in the medical environment [12]. Although the accuracy and performance of the BFE approach are promising for real world applications [4], a detailed cryptanalysis has not been performed. Given the sensitivity of the data which BFEs are being proposed to protect (e.g., medical information), we believe a formal analysis is necessary and timely. In this paper, we construct a novel attack for BFEs, based on a combination of constraint satisfaction and intelligent heuristics. We use real personal identifiers, derived from publicly available resources, to empirically illustrate that the attack can compromise a significant amount of private data if the parameters of the BFE are selected as suggested in the literature. In summary, there are several notable contributions of this paper:

Frequency-Aware Constraint Satisfaction Model: We frame the attack against the BFE protocol as a constraint satisfaction problem (CSP). Though a cryptanalytic method based on constraint satisfaction was previously proposed for simple substitution ciphers [13], it does not directly apply to BFEs, which are significantly more complex due to the ingredients involved in the encoding process (see Section 2). The proposed cryptanalytic approach integrates frequency analysis into the construction of the CSP to reduce the complexity.

Statistically Reliable Constraints: The CSP attack on the BFE protocol leverages constraints that are approximately correct (i.e., accurate with a very high probability). While the constraints in a CSP should be accurate, an over-specified system can lead to high computational costs when solving the problem. By utilizing statistically reliable constraints, we enable a complex CSP to be solved efficiently by pruning the search space of the CSP solver.

Empirical Vulnerability Assessment: We show that the BFE protocol is vulnerable to attack, provided that the adversary has a certain amount of reasonable background information. At the same time, we explore the relationship between the encoding parameters (e.g., filter length) and vulnerability through extensive experiments. Our investigations show that BFE can be made relatively resilient to the proposed attack by tuning the BFE parameters appropriately.

The remainder of the paper is organized as follows. Section 2 provides background information and describes the adversarial model. Section 3 presents the proposed attack. We then report our experimental analysis in Section 4. We review related work in Section 5 and conclude in Section 6.

2   Background

We begin with an overview of the BFE techniques and our threat model. A legend for the notation used throughout the paper is provided in Table 1.

Table 1. Symbol Definitions

Symbol	Description	Symbol	Description
A, B	datasets of Alice and Bob	A^T, B^T	encoded versions of A, B
G	global dataset	D, D^T	$(A \cup B), (A^T \cup B^T)$
g	string encoding function	f	n-gram encoding function
bf	belief function	X_i	variable of CSP
v_i	value assigned to X_i	q_i, Q_{X_i}	single n-gram, n-gram set of X_i
m	filter length	k	number of hash functions in f

2.1   Bloom Filter Encoding

A Bloom filter [14] is a bit array of length m that is affiliated with k hash functions. Each function maps a given element to one bit location with a uniform probability. For the purposes of this work, we define an element as a string, $S \in \Sigma^*$, over an alphabet Σ.

In the BFE model described in [12], S is represented as the set of substrings of length n, or n-grams such that $Q_S = \{q_1, \ldots, q_z\}$. Each n-gram is subject to each hash function and the corresponding bit indices are set to 1. The encoding of a string is then obtained by combining the n-gram encodings with the bitwise OR ($\vee$) operation. Formally, let $f : \Sigma^n \mapsto \{0,1\}^m$ be the n-gram encoding function obtained by combining k hash functions and $g : \Sigma^* \mapsto \{0,1\}^m$ be the string encoding function that converts any string into its BFE:

$$g(S) = \bigvee_{i=1}^{z} f(q_i) \tag{1}$$

Example 2.1 *:* In Figure 1, the bigrams of "amy" are encoded with two hash functions. Notice "_a" and "y_" are mapped to the same index by one of the hash functions.

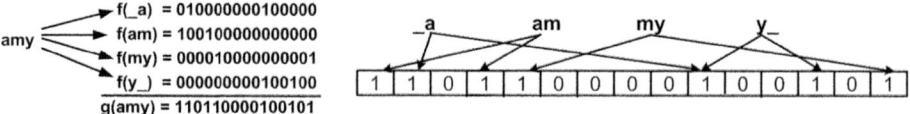

Fig. 1. Sample BFE: $Q_{amy} = \{\_a, am, my, y\_\}$

2.2   Threat Model

In this paper, the linkage of data sources A and B, owned by Alice and Bob, respectively, is facilitated through a third party, Charlie. The utilization of the third party is a common practice in real world privacy preserving data sharing environments for healthcare (e.g., [15]). First, the data owners agree on the filter length, the keyed hash functions, and the secret keys. Next, the owners convert their strings into the BFEs. Then, the owners transfer the BFE lists $(A^T \cup B^T)$ (Henceforth, we will use D and D^T to refer $(A \cup B)$ and $(A^T \cup B^T)$, respectively.) to Charlie who compares the BFEs using a set-based similarity measure to find matching pairs of records.

In this setting, we assume Charlie is the adversary and does not collude with Alice or Bob. Charlie attempts to expose the original records based on their BFEs without access to the secret keys. However, we assume that Charlie has access to the following practical background knowledge:

Assumption 1: Charlie knows the global dataset G from which A and B are drawn, such that $D \subseteq G$. This is reasonable because record linkage is typically performed with personal identifiers (e.g., names and addresses), which in many countries, can be found in public resources.

Assumption 2: Charlie knows the number of hash functions (k) that are part of the Bloom encoding function. This is reasonable because Charlie can infer the number of hash functions from the number of bits set in the Bloom filters. Due to hash collisions, Charlie can only estimate this number, but it can be restricted to a small range, such that the proposed attack can be applied for all values in the range.

3   Overview of the Attack

Here, we provide an overview of the attack Charlie can execute on the BFE system. Without loss of generality, let D be represented in relational form $D(Attr_1, \ldots, Attr_y)$ with string-valued attributes that correspond to personal identifiers (e.g., surnames). For each record $t_i \in D$, the Bloom encoding process results in an encoding $t_i^T = (g(t_i.Attr_1), \ldots, g(t_i.Attr_y))$. An attribute encoding $t_i^T.Attr_j$ is said to be compromised, if Charlie learns $g^{-1}(t_i^T.Attr_j) = t_i.Attr_j$. The components of the attack are presented in subsections 3.2 to 3.4 and we refer the reader to Appendix C for a visualization of the attack flow.

3.1   Motivating Example

Consider the scenario in Figure 2. Alice and Bob generate BFEs, which are transferred to Charlie, who initiates the attack by calculating the frequency distribution of the items in D^T. Next, Charlie performs a statistical analysis on G to form frequency intervals of the items in an arbitrary dataset of size equal to D^T. The possible encodings that could be associated with a particular string is reduced significantly via frequency analysis as illustrated in the following example.

Example 3.1.1 (Frequency Utilization): In Figure 2, Charlie estimates the frequency interval of "adrianna" as [0.25, 0.4] by performing a statistical analysis on G. Charlie then observes that the frequencies {0.375, 0.25} of BFEs {0111101101, 0111001010} are the only ones in the interval of "adrianna". As a result, possible encodings for "adrianna" is reduced to these BFEs.   □

In addition to frequency analysis, Charlie can use BFEs and the properties of the encoding for the attack as illustrated in the following example.

Example 3.1.2 (Encoding Utilization): In Figure 2, "david" contains 6 bigrams {_d, da, av, vi, id, d_} with a possible encoding set {0111101101, 0111001010}. Notice, the encoding of "david" cannot contain more than six 1's according to the construction of the BFE. The only encoding that satisfies this condition is {0111001010}. Once "david" is mapped to {0111001010}, "adrianna" can only be mapped to {0111101101} since encoding function is one-to-one with very high probability (see Section 3.3). It should be noted that each mapping of a name to an encoding reveals additional knowledge about the behavior of the encoding function. For instance, once "sam" is mapped to {0100000011}, it is known that the encoding function can only set the second, ninth, and tenth bit locations when applied on the set of bigrams {_s, sa, am, m_}. And, this type of knowledge revision can be used to reveal further assignments. Notice that after the mappings of "david", "adrianna" and "sam", the possible encodings for "adam" contains {0101000111, 1000110110}. But "adam" consists of the bigrams {_a, ad, da, am, m_} which have been included in previous mappings. Thus, to be compatible with previous mappings, the first bit location of the encoding for "adam" cannot be set to 1. The only encoding that satisfies this constraint is {0101000111}, so "adam" is correctly assigned to it.   □

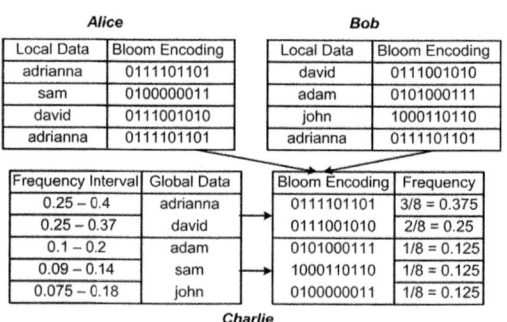

Fig. 2. Records are embedded into a 10 bit Bloom filter with 1 hash function

3.2   Bloom Encoding Analysis

Some constraints can be derived from the properties of f, the n-gram encoding function. The derived constraints should be satisfied by the mapping between the original strings and the corresponding BFEs. Therefore, the problem of discovering the mappings can be modeled as a CSP. Generally, a CSP is defined by a set of variables $\{X_1, X_2, \ldots, X_p\}$, and a set of constraints $\{C_1, C_2, \ldots, C_r\}$ [16]. Each variable X_i has a nonempty domain of possible values. Each constraint C_i is related to some variables and allows only some combination of assignments between the variables and values in their domains. A state of the problem is defined by an assignment of some, or all, variables to values, such that $\{X_1 = v_1, \ldots, X_p = v_p\}$ and it is said to be *consistent* if all the constraints are satisfied by the assignments of the given state.

The variables of the CSP for BFE cryptanalysis are obtained from the global dataset. The domain of the variables are BFEs and the constraints are derived from the properties of f. We assemble a CSP for each attribute of the dataset independently because each attribute may be encoded with different encoding parameters (e.g., filter length). More formally, the components of the CSP in this context can be stated as follows:

Variable: Let record $t_i \in G$. Then $t_i.Attr_j$ is a candidate variable for attribute $Attr_j$. Consider the example in Figure 2, values for the forename attribute in G such as "david" and "sam" are candidate variables. The domain of the CSP variables consists of the values obtained from the encoded dataset. Since $D \subseteq G$, only some of the candidates have corresponding encoding in D^T. CSP variables are selected from the candidates according to the frequency of the item sets such that selected candidate has an encoding in D^T with very high probability. The selection procedure is described in Section 3.3.

Domain: Let record $t_i^T \in D^T$. Then $t_i^T.Attr_j$ is a candidate value for attribute $Attr_j$. In Figure 2, the encoded values for the forename attribute, such as "0100000011" and "0111101101" are candidate values for the domain of forename variables. The domains of variables are determined in two steps. In the first step, certain values are eliminated based on the number of bit locations set to 1. With respect to BFEs, each hash function that is applied to encode n-grams sets one bit location in the filter. Therefore, any value in the domain of variable X_i can contain at most $k \cdot z_i$ 1's if X_i contains z_i distinct n-grams. Values with more than $k \cdot z_i$ 1's can be eliminated from the domain of X_i. In the second step, frequency analysis is performed to refine the domains. This procedure is described in Section 3.3.

Constraints: The deterministic behavior of f and the number of hash functions are utilized for defining constraints. When f is applied on a particular n-gram, only particular bit locations are set to 1. When a BFE contains 0's in certain bit locations, Charlie can conclude f does not set those locations for the n-grams that are part of the corresponding string. This assertion is captured in the Theorem 1. Since, in our threat model we assume that k is known by the attacker, the maximum number of bit locations that can be set by f when applied on any n-gram is known to be k. In addition, the minimum number of bit locations that will be set by f can be determined probabilistically as asserted by Theorem 2.

Theorem 1. *Let variable X_i contain n-grams $Q_{X_i} = \{q_1, ..., q_z\}$, and let state $CS = \{X_1 = v_1, ..., X_p = v_p\}$ be a consistent state. If the value of bit location $\bar{l}$ is 0 in v_i, then $f(q_x)[\bar{l}] = 0$ for any $q_x \in Q_{X_i}$.*

Theorem 2. *Let $num1s : \{0,1\}^m \mapsto N$ be a function that returns the number of bit locations with value 1 for the given encoding and w be an integer in range [1,k]. For any n-gram q_i, $num1s(f(q_i)) \geq w$ with probability p such that:*

$$p = \frac{\sum_{i=w}^{k} \binom{m}{i}\binom{k-1}{k-i}}{\binom{m+k-1}{k}} \tag{2}$$

Proof. We refer the reader to Appendix A for the proof of both theorems.

Another important information resource for defining constraints is available assignments in a CSP state which accommodates some knowledge about f. This knowledge is accumulated through a belief function:

Definition 3.2.1 (Belief Function): Belief function $bf : \Sigma^n \mapsto \{0,1\}^m$ is a function, that takes n-grams as input and yields a BFE as output, which simulates f on each n-gram. In its initial state, for any n-gram q_i, it is believed that $f(q_i)$ may set any bit location. The belief function reflects this knowledge by satisfying the equation $bf(q_i)[\bar{l}] = 1$ for $1 \leq \bar{l} \leq m$.

Once a new assignment $\{X_i = v_i\}$ is added to the current state of the CSP, the belief function is modified to satisfy Theorem 1. Basically, the new belief about the encoding of any q_i that is part of variable X_i is obtained by applying the bitwise AND ($\wedge$) operation to current belief $bf(q_i)$ and v_i. Let variable X_i contain n-grams $Q_{X_i} = \{q_1, ...q_z\}$. Then for each $q_i \in Q_{X_i}$:

$$bf(q_i)_{updated} = bf(q_i)_{current} \wedge v_i \tag{3}$$

Equation 3 extracts the knowledge from the assignment, such that if v_i contains 0 in $\bar{l}$, then $f(q_i)[\bar{l}] = 0$ for an updated state of the CSP.

Example 3.2.1 (Belief Update): An illustration of the belief update process is presented in Figure 3. Initially, $bf(jo) = 11111$. Now, suppose $\{joe = 10001\}$ is added to the current state of the CSP. According to Theorem 1, f does not set the second, third, or fourth bit locations when applied on the bigrams of $\{joe\}$, so we can update $bf(jo)$ to be 10001. After the assignment $\{john = 10110\}$, we learn that the second and fifth bit locations cannot be set to 1 if f is applied on the bigrams of $\{john\}$. Therefore, $bf(jo) = 10000$.

Belief Validity Constraint (BVC): The belief validity constraint is based on Equation 1 and belief function. Let $CS = \{X_1 = v_1, ..., X_p = v_p\}$ be a consistent state. Then all assignments $\{X_i = v_i\}$ should be compatible with the current belief function. Compatible means Equation 1 should be satisfiable with the current belief function and the known assignments. Let X_i contain the n-gram set $Q_{X_i} = \{q_1, ..., q_z\}$. Then,

jo → 11111	jo → 10001	jo → 10000
oh → 11111	oh → 11111	oh → 10110
hn → 11111	hn → 11111	hn → 10110
oe → 11111	oe → 10001	oe → 10001
kn → 11111	kn → 11111	kn → 11111
(a) initial belief	(b) joe = 10001	(c) john = 10110

Fig. 3. Belief Update

$$v_i = \bigvee_{i=1}^{z} bf(q_i) \quad \forall \{X_i = v_i\} \in CS \tag{4}$$

Example 3.2.2 (BVC Check): Imagine a belief state such that $bf(\_j) = bf(jo) = 10001$ and $bf(oe) = bf(e\_) = 01001$ and suppose $\{joe = 11001\} \in CS$. Now, consider the potential assignment $\{john = 00111\}$. If this assignment is performed, then $bf(\_j) = bf(jo) = 00001$. Yet, to satisfy the BVC, $(bf(\_j) \vee bf(jo) \vee bf(oe) \vee bf(e\_) = 11001)$ should hold true, which is not the case. As a result, the assignment $\{john = 00111\}$ is not permitted in this state. □

Min-Location Constraint (MLC): The minimum location constraint is based on Theorem 2 and belief function. Let w be the threshold for the minimum number of bit locations set by f, then we can enforce the following constraint:

$$num1s(bf(q_i)) \geq w \tag{5}$$

If w could be set to a large value, the search space of the CSP solver could be reduced significantly, and the CSP could be solved in a more timely manner. However, according to Theorem 2, w should be set to 1 to satisfy $num1s(bf(q_i)) \geq w$ with probability $p = 1$. By reducing p slightly, w could be increased significantly. At the same time, a reduction in p could lead to an unsatisfiable CSP, since $num1s(bf(q_i)) \geq w$ may not hold with probability $1 - p$. As a result, there is a tradeoff between solving a complex CSP in a timely manner and accepting the risk of converting a satisfiable CSP into an unsatisfiable one. In this setting, the risk is controlled by p (i.e., if p is large the risk is small). Once p is fixed, the threshold w can be calculated via Equation 2.

Example 3.2.3 (MLC Check): Consider the state prior to the potential assignment $\{joe = 11000\}$, such that $bf(jo) = 10111$. After the assignment, $bf(jo) = 10000$ and $num1s(bf(jo)) = 1$. If the threshold w is 2, then $num1s(bf(jo)) \geq w$ no longer holds true after the assignment. Therefore, the assignment $\{joe = 11000\}$ is not permitted in this state. □

3.3   Frequency Analysis

In section 3.2, the problem of discovering the mappings between original strings and their BFEs is modeled as a CSP with candidate variables and domains.

To select the variables and their domains from candidates, the frequency distribution of the elements in sets G and D^T can be used. CSPs are generally hard problems to solve, however they can be solved in a timely manner by minimizing the domains of the variables and using heuristics based on domain restrictions. Such restrictions can be achieved by leveraging frequency analysis. In particular, we introduce a fair assumption to form the basis of frequency analysis.

Assumption 3.3.1 (g is a 1-1 function): It can be assumed that there is a one-to-one mapping between each distinct string and each distinct BFE. Let S_1 and S_2 be two strings, then

$$g(S_1) = g(S_2), \quad \text{if } S_1 = S_2$$
$$g(S_1) \neq g(S_2), \quad \text{otherwise} \tag{6}$$

It is guaranteed that $g(S_1) = g(S_2)$ when $S_1 = S_2$ by the construction of the encoding. It is highly unlikely that $g(S_1) = g(S_2)$ if $S_1 \neq S_2$. In this context, two strings are defined to be distinct if they have at least one distinct n-gram. Suppose $q_x \in Q_{S_1}$ and $q_x \notin Q_{S_2}$, then $g(S_1) = g(S_2)$ if and only if the Bloom filter check on $g(S_2)$ indicates membership of q_x in S_2. The probability of such false positives (p_f) depends on k, m, and the size of $Q_{S_2}(s)$ such that $p_f = (1 - e^{-ks/m})^k$ (see [17]). Notice that p_f becomes negligible with large k and m. In fact, k and m should be large in a PRL protocol; otherwise record matching quality would degrade significantly. We can derive additional information if we know that g is a 1-to-1 function, such as frequency conservation:

Corollary 3.3.1 (Frequency Conservation): Let fr_i be the frequency of X_i in set D. Then the frequency of $g(X_i)$ in set D^T is also fr_i. Given Equation (6), any string with value X_i will be mapped to the same encoding $g(X_i)$. Strings with values other than X_i will not be mapped to the $g(X_i)$. Therefore, the frequencies are preserved during transformation.

Definition 3.3.1 (Relative Frequency (fr)): Let $freq : \Sigma^* \times Z \mapsto N$ be a function that returns the number of occurrences of x in Z. Then the relative frequency of x is defined as:

$$fr_Z(x) = \begin{cases} \frac{freq(x,Z)}{|Z|} & \text{if } x \in Z \\ 0 & \text{otherwise} \end{cases} \tag{7}$$

If we know that Z is a random sample of size $|Z|$ from G, we can bound the relative frequency of any item in Z using statistics learned from G. This implies we can draw multiple samples of size $|Z|$ from G using Monte Carlo techniques [18] and, for each sample set U from G, we can compute $fr_U(x)$ to determine the frequency intervals in which the true value of $fr_Z(x)$ belongs with high confidence. Using these samples, for any X_i, we can compute α_{X_i} and β_{X_i} such that $\alpha_{X_i} \leq fr_Z(X_i) \leq \beta_{X_i}$ with high confidence. In our problem setting, D is a random sample of size $|D|$ and D^T is the encoded dataset such that $X_i \in D \rightarrow g(X_i) \in D^T$. Now, suppose $\alpha_{X_i} \leq fr_D(X_i) \leq \beta_{X_i}$ for each $X_i \in D$ with 99% confidence, then $\alpha_{X_i} \leq fr_{D^T}(g(X_i)) \leq \beta_{X_i}$ for each $g(X_i) \in D^T$ with 99% confidence by the frequency conservation principle.

In the attack model, Charlie can calculate the relative frequency of items in D^T, but can also learn α_{X_i} and β_{X_i} for any $X_i \in G$. CSP construction could then be finalized using this set of knowledge. Variables of the CSP and their domains could be selected from the candidates (see Section 3.2) as follows:

Variable Selection: Let X_i be a candidate variable. Then X_i could be selected as a CSP variable if and only if $\alpha_{X_i} > 0$. This means that $X_i \in G$ is expected to have the corresponding encoding $g(X_i) \in D^T$ if $\alpha_{X_i} > 0$.

Domain Selection: Let v_i be a candidate value for the domain of X_i, then v_i could be selected for the domain of X_i if and only if $\alpha_{X_i} \leq fr_{D^T}(v_i) \leq \beta_{X_i}$.

Example 3.3.1 (Variable & Domain Selection): Imagine the dataset D^T consists of 20,000 records. Charlie draws a sample dataset of size 20,000 from G multiple times. Given these samples, Charlie obtains an approximate sampling distribution of $fr_Z(X_i)$ for each $X_i \in G$ for the forename attribute. Now imagine $\alpha_{john} = 0.08$ and $\beta_{john} = 0.1$. Since $\alpha_{john} > 0$, 'john' could be selected as a variable. When Charlie receives D^T, he calculates $fr_{D^T}(v_i)$ for each $v_i \in D^T$ for the forename attribute. Suppose $fr_{D^T}(11001) = 0.09$ and $fr_{D^T}(01000) = 0.04$. Then '11001' is in the domain of the variable {john} while '01000' is not because $\alpha_{john} \leq fr_{D^T}(v_i) \leq \beta_{john}$ is satisfied for $v_i = 11001$, but not for $v_i = 01000$.

Clearly, the frequency analysis should also consider possible erroneous records in D because they may affect the relative frequency of items in the dataset. A simple approach to deal with errors is to update the frequency intervals of the variables by considering the possible error rate that can affect the records. Error rates could be determined by domain experts or could be extracted from the historical data [7]. Once the error rates are determined, frequency intervals could be updated accordingly. Let the amount of reduction and increment in the relative frequency of an item be at most err_r and err_i respectively, then $\alpha_{X_{i_{updated}}} = (1 - err_r) \times \alpha_{X_i}$ and $\beta_{X_{i_{updated}}} = (1 + err_i) \times \beta_{X_i}$. The effect of the erroneous records on the attack is examined in Section 4.

Notice that if the frequency of all the elements in the global dataset is similar, frequency analysis is not useful to Charlie. In such a case, domain of the variables cannot be reduced. Even worse, the variables cannot be determined since α_{X_i} will be 0 for most of the candidates. However in real life, the frequencies of items tend not to be similar. The distribution of a wide variety of natural and man made phenomena such as frequencies of family names follow power-law distribution [19]. In our problem, such frequent elements in G will have a corresponding encoding in the transformed dataset with high probability. In fact, the proposed variable selection method only allows the selection of such frequent items.

3.4   CSP Solver

Initially, the adversary models the mapping of BFEs to strings as a CSP according to the procedures described in sections 3.2 and 3.3. Once the problem is modeled, a CSP solver is applied to associate BFEs with corresponding strings.

Standard algorithms such as backtracking search [16] could be applied to solve the CSP. The performance of this search can be improved via additional heuristics. One of the most successful heuristics is dom/deg [20], which selects the variable with the smallest *domain* involved in the greatest number of constraints (i.e., maximum *degree*). For the BFEs, constraints are defined over the n-grams of the variables through the belief function. If a variable contains frequently used n-grams, then it is said to be involved in most of the constraints. In this setting, the degree of a variable is the sum of the frequencies of its n-grams.

Definition 3.4.1 (dom/deg): Let $ngramFreq : \Sigma^n \mapsto N$ be a function that returns the number of occurrences of a particular n-gram in all variables of the CSP. Let X_i be a variable in the CSP with domain size $dsize_{X_i}$ such that X_i contains the n-grams $\{q_1, ..., q_z\}$. Then the dom/deg of X_i is defined as:

$$dom/deg_{X_i} = \frac{dsize_{X_i}}{\sum_{i=1}^{z} ngramFreq(q_i)}$$

In any state of the CSP, the variable with the smallest dom/deg is selected as the next variable to assign. The CSP solver applies backtracking search directed by dom/deg to assign variables according to defined constraints. We provide the summary of our CSP solver in Algorithms 1 and 2 in Appendix B.

4   Experimental Results

In this section, we present the experimental evaluation of the proposed attack. To perform our evaluation, we selected a publicly available dataset of real personal identifiers, derived from the North Carolina voter registration list (NCVR), which contains 6,190,504 records [21]. NCVR was used as dataset G from which a random sample of 20,000 records was selected to form dataset D. We investigated the success of the attack with the forename attribute, but note that the attack could be repeated for each attribute. The resulting dataset contained approximately 3,500 unique forenames. To evaluate the effect of typographical and semantic name errors, we also generated a perturbed version of D by implementing a data corrupter based on the errors typically observed in practice [7]. The corrupter introduced errors based on optical character recognition, phonemes, and typography at rates typical of real datasets.

We use precision (i.e., ratio of correctly assigned names to all assigned names) and recall (i.e., ratio of matched names to all available names) as metrics for the attack's success.

4.1   Attack on BFEs Based on Parameters in the Literature

In this part, we evaluate the success of the proposed attack and the effects of the CSP parameters on the computational complexity with a fixed BFE setting. The encoding of D was obtained using the parameters: k (number of hash functions): 15, m (filter length): 500 and n (encoding unit): 2 that are reported in [12]. The effect of varying encoding parameters is then examined in subsection 4.2.

To select CSP variables and domains, frequency intervals were constructed via a Monte Carlo sampling of 10,000 datasets with 20,000 records each from G. The 400 most frequent names in G were selected as the CSP variables according to this analysis ($\alpha_{X_i} > 0$ holds for only 400 names). For the experiments with perturbed data, the frequency intervals were updated according to the data corrupter's error rates, such that $error_r = 0.5$ and $error_i = 0$ (see Section 3.3).

Number of variables (s_v): The effect of s_v is depicted in Figure 4(a) and 4(b). In Figure 4(a) we observe that the recall and precision of the assignments increases with s_v. This is because the constraints of the CSP become stronger with an increasing number of assignments (i.e., belief function updates). Once the constraints are sufficiently strong, only the correct assignment satisfies the constraints. We note that recall has an upper bound of approximately 0.11 (400/3500) due to the outcome of the frequency analysis. In fact, recall of the proposed attack reaches this upper bound along with precision 1.

In Figure 4(b), it can be seen that the complexity of the CSP increases significantly with s_v. This is because, variables with larger domains are added to the CSP as s_v grows, which makes the search space larger. For the perturbed data analysis, the attack becomes more time consuming to execute because the frequency intervals are broadened to compensate for error, which leads to variables with larger domains. For instance, although the assignment of 400 variables is fulfilled in 94 sec. in unperturbed case, it takes 870 sec. for the perturbed dataset.

Min-Location Threshold (w) : Figure 4(c) illustrates that the CSP's complexity depends on the threshold w associated with the Min-Location constraint (MLC). Specifically, MLC becomes more restrictive as w increases. Therefore, the search space of the CSP solver shrinks, which permits the problem to be solved more quickly. However, w can only be increased up to a certain point, after which the CSP becomes unsatisfiable. In this setting, w was initially set to 10 with 0.99 probability (based on Equation 2), and the CSP solver correctly assigned all the variables up to this threshold. The CSP solver could not propose a solution for higher w because, during the pruning of the search space, some of the true mappings were eliminated due to the wrong w constraint.

In summary, the results reported in Figure 4 indicate that proposed attack can compromise 11% of the records with precision close to one in a reasonable amount of time even under the corrupted data scenario.

4.2   Tuning BFE Parameters to Mitigate Attack

The previous experiments show that BFEs are vulnerable when the parameters are set according to recommendations in the literature. However, given that the values of the parameters can be tuned, we set out to determine if the security of BFEs can be strengthened without sacrificing record linkage accuracy. To investigate, we performed a systematic analysis with the number of variables in the CSP fixed to 50. This is a smaller set than the 400 used in the previous experiments, but Figure 4(b) shows that the assignment time grows exponentially with the number of variables, and certain experiments required several days to

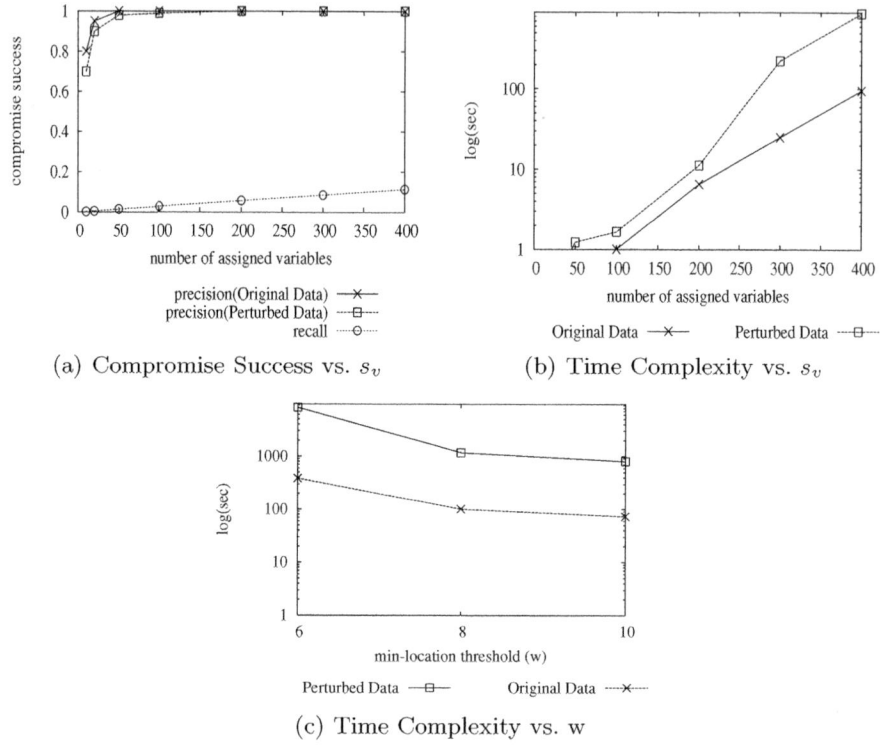

(a) Compromise Success vs. s_v (b) Time Complexity vs. s_v

(c) Time Complexity vs. w

Fig. 4. CSP Evaluation

complete. As a result, for the following experiments, the recall of the attack is fixed to 1.43%. Since the main use of BFEs is to tolerate errors in records during PRL, all experiments were conducted over perturbed data .

Encoding unit: We note that BFEs gain resistance to the attack as n increases. Specifically, the complexity of the CSP rapidly increases and the precision of the assignments drops off as shown in Figure 5(a) and 5(b). For instance, while 50 assignments were achieved in several seconds for $n = 2$, it required almost 2 days for $n = 4$. Additionally, this was accompanied by a 12% reduction in precision. This is an expected finding because as n grows the constraints become less restrictive. Both BVC and MLC constraints depend on the belief function, such that the more accurate the belief function is, the more restrictive the constraints are. If n becomes larger, the quality of the belief function degrades significantly. This is because records share fewer n-grams as n increases, which leads to less accurate reasoning about the n-gram encoding function.

To characterize the effect of increasing n on record linkage accuracy, we attempted to match the records in the perturbed version of the dataset (P) with the ones in the unperturbed version (O). Once encoding of the datasets was formed (P^T and O^T), each item in P^T was associated with exactly one item in O^T according to similarity between encodings. Similarity was measured with

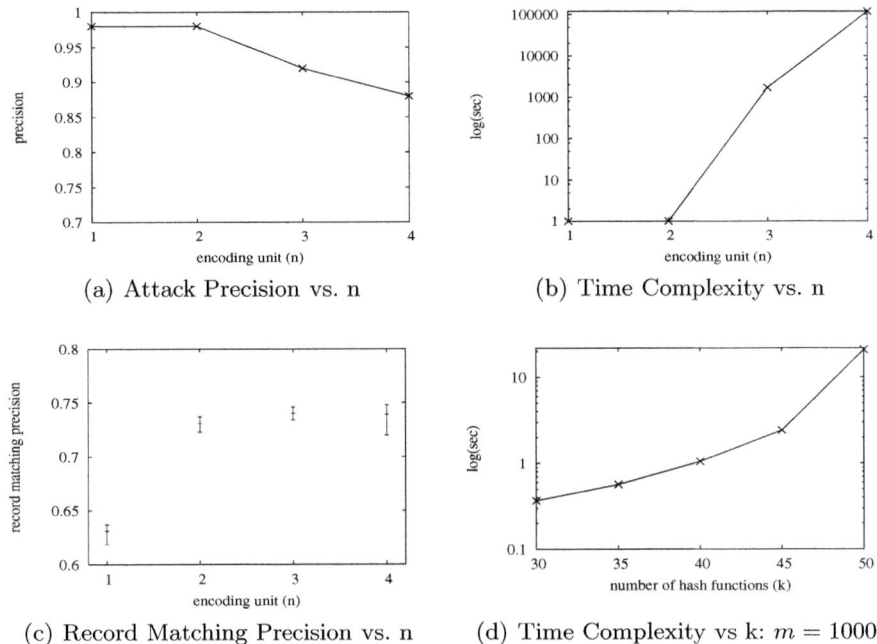

(a) Attack Precision vs. n   (b) Time Complexity vs. n

(c) Record Matching Precision vs. n   (d) Time Complexity vs k: $m = 1000$

Fig. 5. $k = 25$, $m = 1000$ for a, b and c

Dice-coefficient [12] which is a set based similarity measure. The experiments, summarized in Figure 5-c, show that as n increases the record matching precision (i.e., ratio of correct associations to all associations) is only slightly affected. These results suggest that large n (e.g., $n = 4$) may provide sufficient record matching accuracy, while significantly reducing the recall rate of the attack and increasing its computational cost.

Bloom filter length(m) and Number of hash functions(k): According to our empirical observations, the security of the encoding does not depend on m or k independently, but rather on their ratio. As the m/k decreases, the number of bit locations set by individual n-gram encodings decreases. Therefore, the strength of the constraints that are dependent on the distinction between individual n-gram encodings via belief function diminishes. The complexity of the CSP increases with less restrictive constraints as shown in Figure 5(d). On the other hand, record matching quality degrades if m/k becomes smaller (see [12]). This is because less distinction between n-gram encodings leads to more false positives in the record matching process.

In summary, BFEs become more resistant to the proposed attack with increasing n and decreasing m/k.

5   Related Work

Various protocols for private record linkage (PRL) have been developed [2–5]. PRL protocols tend to use two primary mechanisms for protecting sensitive information: secure multi-party computation (SMC) and data transformation. Although SMC protocols provide strong security guarantees, they are impractical for many real data integration tasks due to their reliance on inefficient cryptography. As an alternative to heavyweight SMC, there are approaches to selectively reveal information through transformation [22–25]. Such approaches perturb, as opposed to encrypt, private information to protect individual identity. Unlike SMC, transformation can leave data vulnerable to compromise due to the presence of partial information. In fact, several attack models have emerged against transformation techniques. Of note, the disclosure risk of pseudonymization [26] is examined in [22], and the approach is particularly applicable for situations in which the attacker has some background information (e.g, frequency distribution of anonymized items). Another popular approach for data transformation relies on distance preserving data perturbation (e.g., [25]). Disclosure risk of such approaches is examined in [27] and [28]. Their research demonstrated that an adversary can discover the original values with high confidence if mutual distances between data objects is known. While attacks and security investigations have been reported for various transformation methods, to the best of our knowledge ours is the first work to explicitly address BFEs.

In addition to attack scenarios against privacy preserving protocols, information theoretic measures have been proposed to evaluate the degree of the privacy provided by such protocols, especially in the context of anonymous routing ([29], [30], [31]). The quality of the privacy is measured according to the amount of information an attacker can gain after observing the message flow (see [29] and [30]) under various attack scenarios. The quality assessment is extended in [31] by considering the possible prior knowledge of the attackers. Available information theoretic metrics can be used as a basis to evaluate the degree of privacy provided by BFE with different BFE parameter settings. In fact, our work provides a particular attack scenario to enable such analysis for BFE.

6   Conclusions and Future Work

In this paper, we proposed an adversarial model against private record linkage protocols based on Bloom filter encoding (BFE). BFEs are part of an important emerging record linkage model for real world application domains, such as healthcare, because they enable approximate data matching with low computational resources. We modeled the problem of learning the original data from their encoded versions as a constraint satisfaction problem (CSP) using the properties of the encoding function and the frequency distribution of the identifiers in encoded and global unencoded datasets from which the encodings are derived. The unencoded records are assigned to the encoded versions iteratively, according to the constraints. We experimentally evaluated the attack with real data derived from a publicly available voter registration list. We illustrated that the attack can be highly successful if encoding is applied with the settings published in existing literature. However, we also demonstrated that the encodings can be made more resistant to the attack by adjusting encoding parameters with only a slight reduction in record matching quality.

In future work, we plan to extend the attack to determine if additional encodings, or portions of the encodings, can be compromised. In particular, the current CSP is designed to crack high frequency encodings, but items with lesser frequencies may be predictable using the knowledge learned about the encoding function.

Acknowledgments. This work was partially supported by Air Force Office of Scientific Research MURI Grant FA9550-08-1-0265, National Institutes of Health Grants 1R01LM009989, 2-T15LM07450-06, National Science Foundation (NSF) Career Grant CNS-0845803, and NSF Grants CCF-0424422, CNS-0964350, and CNS-1016343.

References

[1] Elmagarmid, A., Ipeirotis, P., Verykios, V.: Duplicate record detection: a survey. IEEE Transactions on Knowledge and Data Engineering 16, 1–16 (2007)

[2] Churches, T., Christen, P.: Blind data linkage using n-gram similarity comparisons. In: Dai, H., Srikant, R., Zhang, C. (eds.) PAKDD 2004. LNCS (LNAI), vol. 3056, pp. 121–126. Springer, Heidelberg (2004)

[3] Clifton, C., Kantarcioglu, M., Doan, A., Schadow, G., Vaidya, J., Elmagarmid, A., Suciu, D.: Privacy-preserving data integration and sharing. In: Proceedings of the 9th ACM SIGMOD Workshop on Data Mining and Knowledge Discovery, pp. 19–26 (2004)

[4] Durham, E., Xue, Y., Kantarcioglu, M., Malin, B.: Private medical record linkage with approximate matching. In: Proceedings of the 2010 American Medical Informatics Association Annual Symposium, pp. 182–186 (2010)

[5] Inan, A., Kantarcioglu, M., Bertino, E., Scannapieco, M.: A hybrid approach to private record linkage. In: Proceedings of the 24th IEEE International Conference on Data Engineering, pp. 496–505 (2008)

[6] Verykios, V., Karakasidis, A., Mitrogiannis, V.: Privacy preserving record linkage approaches. International Journal of Data Mining, Modelling and Management 1, 206–221 (2009)

[7] Christen, P., Pudjijono, A.: Accurate synthetic generation of realistic personal information. In: Proceedings of the 13th Pacific-Asia Conference on Knowledge Discovery and Data Mining, pp. 507–514 (2009)

[8] Hernandez, M., Stolfo, S.: Real-world data is dirty: data cleansing and the merge/purge problem. Data Mining and Knowledge Discovery 2, 9–37 (1998)

[9] Atallah, M., Kerschbaum, F., Du., W.: Secure and private sequence comparisons. In: Proceedings of the 2003 ACM Workshop on Privacy in the Electronic Society, pp. 39–44 (2003)

[10] Feigenbaum, J., Ishai, Y., Nissim, K., Strauss, M., Wright, R.: Secure multiparty computation of approximations. ACM Transactions on Algorithms 2, 435–472 (2006)

[11] Goldreich, O.: The Foundations of Cryptography, vol. 2. Cambridge University Press, Cambridge (2004)

[12] Schnell, R., Bachteler, T., Reiher, J.: Privacy-preserving record linkage using Bloom filters. BMC Medical Informatics and Decision Making 9, 41 (2009)

[13] Lucks, M.: A constraint satisfaction algorithm for the automated decryption of simple substitution ciphers. In: Menezes, A., Vanstone, S.A. (eds.) CRYPTO 1990. LNCS, vol. 537, pp. 132–144. Springer, Heidelberg (1991)

[14] Bloom, B.: Space/time trade-offs in hash coding with allowable errors. Communications of the ACM 13, 422–426 (1970)

[15] Quantin, C., Bouzelat, H., Allaert, F., Benhamiche, A., Faivre, J., Dusserre, L.: Automatic record hash coding and linkage for epidemiological follow-up data confidentiality. Methods of Information in Medicine 37, 271–277 (1998)

[16] Russell, S., Norvig, P.: Artificial Intelligence: A Modern Approach, 2nd edn. Prentice-Hall, Englewood Cliffs (2003)

[17] Mitzenmacher, M., Upfal, E.: Probability and computing: An introduction to randomized algorithms and probabilistic analysis. Cambridge University Press, Cambridge (2005)

[18] Mooney, C.: Monte Carlo Simulation. Sage Publications, Thousand Oaks (1997)

[19] Newman, M.: Power laws, pareto distributions and zipf's law. Contemporary Physics 46, 323–351 (2005)

[20] Bessire, C., Regin, J.: Mac and combined heuristics: Two reasons to forsake fc (and cbj?) on hard problems. In: Freuder, E.C. (ed.) CP 1996. LNCS, vol. 1118, pp. 61–75. Springer, Heidelberg (1996)

[21] North Carolina Voter Registiration Database (2011), ftp://www.app.sboe.state.nc.us/data

[22] Lakshmanan, L., Ng, R., Ramesh, G.: On disclosure risk analysis of anonymized itemsets in the presence of prior knowledge. ACM Transactions on Knowledge Discovery from Data 2, 13 (2008)

[23] Agrawal, R., Srikant, R.: Privacy preserving data mining. In: Proceedings of the 2000 ACM SIGMOD Conference on Management of Data, pp. 439–450 (2000)

[24] Kargupta, H., Datta, S., Wang, Q., Sivakumar, K.: Random data perturbation techniques and privacy preserving data mining. Knowledge and Information Systems 7, 387–414 (2005)

[25] Chen, K., Liu, L.: Privacy preserving data classification with rotation perturbation. In: Proceedings of the 2005 IEEE Interanational Conference on Data Mining, pp. 589–592 (2005)

[26] Pfitzmann, A.: Anonymity, unobservability, and pseudonymity - a proposal for terminology. In: Proceedings of the Privacy Enhancing Technologies Workshop, pp. 1–9 (2001)

[27] Liu, K., Giannella, C.M., Kargupta, H.: An attacker's view of distance preserving maps for privacy preserving data mining. In: Fürnkranz, J., Scheffer, T., Spiliopoulou, M. (eds.) PKDD 2006. LNCS (LNAI), vol. 4213, pp. 297–308. Springer, Heidelberg (2006)

[28] Turgay, E.O., Pedersen, T.B., Saygın, Y., Savaş, E., Levi, A.: Disclosure risks of distance preserving data transformations. In: Ludäscher, B., Mamoulis, N. (eds.) SSDBM 2008. LNCS, vol. 5069, pp. 79–94. Springer, Heidelberg (2008)

[29] Diaz, C., Seys, S., Claessens, J., Preneel, B.: Towards measuring anonymity. In: Dingledine, R., Syverson, P.F. (eds.) PET 2002. LNCS, vol. 2482, pp. 54–68. Springer, Heidelberg (2003)

[30] Serjantov, A., Danezis, G.: Towards an information theoretic metric for anonymity. In: Dingledine, R., Syverson, P.F. (eds.) PET 2002. LNCS, vol. 2482, pp. 41–53. Springer, Heidelberg (2003)

[31] Deng, Y., Pang, J., Wu, P.: Measuring anonymity with relative entropy. In: Dimitrakos, T., Martinelli, F., Ryan, P.Y.A., Schneider, S. (eds.) FAST 2006. LNCS, vol. 4691, pp. 65–79. Springer, Heidelberg (2007)

[32] Koshy, T.: Discrete Mathematics with Applications. Elsevier, Amsterdam (2003)

APPENDIX

A   Proof of Theorems

Proof of Theorem 1: Let us assume $v_i[\bar{l}] = 0$ and $f(q_x)$ set $\bar{l}$ in the Bloom filter to 1. According to the following equation, that is derived from Equation 1

$$v_i[\bar{l}] = \left(\bigvee_{q_i \in (Q_{X_i} - q_x)} f(q_i)[\bar{l}] \right) \bigvee f(q_x)[\bar{l}] \tag{8}$$

Notice, $(f(q_x)[\bar{l}] = 1) \rightarrow (v_i[\bar{l}] = 1)$ by the definition of bitwise OR and Equation 8. Since $f(q_x)[\bar{l}] = 1$, it follows that $v_i[l_x] = 1$, which contradicts the initial fact that $(v_i[\bar{l}] = 0) \equiv true$. Therefore, by contradiction, we conclude that $f(q_x)[\bar{l}] = 0$ provided that $(v_i[\bar{l}] = 0)$ is satisfied and $q_x \in QX_i$.

Proof of Theorem 2:   Each hash function $hash_i$ for $1 \le i \le k$, sets a random bit location in Bloom filter for each input q_j. Consider the set $L = \{1, 2..., m\}$, which contains the bit locations in the Bloom filter, and the multiset $MS = \{l_1, ..., l_k\}$, such that $l_i = hash_i(q_j)$ and $l_i \in L$. MS is a multiset since some hash functions may set same bit locations of filter. MS could be considered as a k-multicombination [32] from set L and the number of all such multisets is:

$$n_1 = \binom{m + k - 1}{k}$$

Let MS^w be a multiset of size k from L with exactly w distinct elements, MS_i^w be a set that contains w distinct elements selected from L, and MS_r^w be a multiset that contains $(k - w)$ elements such that $l_i \in MS_r^w \rightarrow l_i \in MS_i^w$. Then $MS^w = MS_i^w \cup MS_r^w$. In other words, multiset MS^w is constructed by selecting w distinct elements from set L and selecting the remaining $(k-w)$ elements from initially selected w elements. MS_i^w is also defined to be w-combination [32] from L and the number of all such sets is $C(\ell, w)$. MS_r^w is $(k - w)$ multicombination from MS_i^w and the number of all such sets is $C(k - 1, k - w)$. Then the number of multisets MS^w is $C(m, w)C(k - 1, k - w)$, since MS^w is the union of MS_i^w and MS_r^w. As a result, the number of multisets of size k from set L with at least w distinct elements is:

$$n_2 = \sum_{i=w}^{k} \binom{m}{i} \binom{k - 1}{k - i}$$

n_1 represents the number of all possible encodings of length m with k hash functions. n_2 represents the number of encodings of length m with k hash functions such that at least w of them set different locations in the Bloom filter. As a result, n_2/n_1 is the probability p such that at least w locations of Bloom filter are set by k hash functions. Since at least w distinct locations are set, there are at least w 1's exist in the corresponding encoding with probability p.

B   CSP Solver Algorithm

As described in Section 3.3, the frequency analysis is applied to select the CSP variables and their domains. However, we may want to assign only a portion of these variables to reduce the complexity. In Algorithm 1, s_v items with the smallest domains are retrieved. As described in Section 3.2, the belief function is proposed to simulate the n-gram transformation function. At the implementation level, the belief function could be represented by a hashtable. Each n-gram q_i is a key in this hashtable, and belief about the n-gram encodings are the values[1].

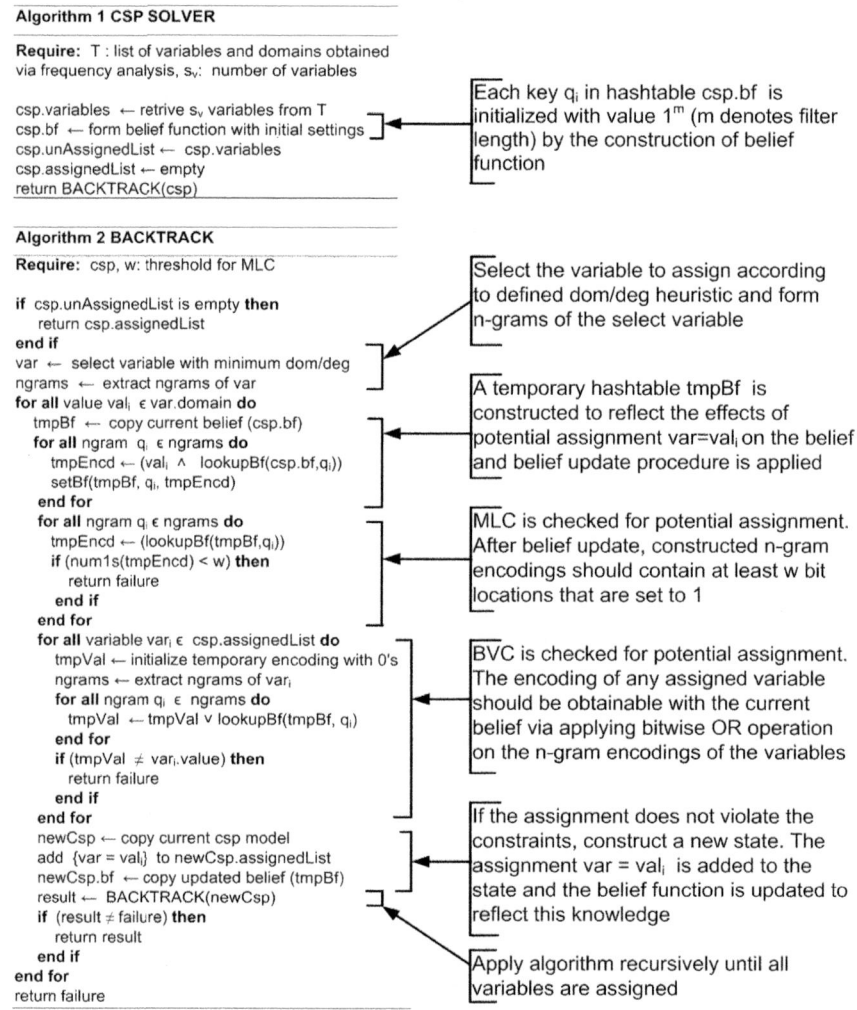

Fig. 6. CSP Solver

---

[1] setBf(H,K,V) sets the value of key K as V, lookupBf(H,K) returns the value for the key K in hashtable H.

C   Attack Flow

The attack flow that is executed on BFEs is depicted in Figure 7. In this setting, the adversary attempts to compromise BFEs received from Alice and Bob.

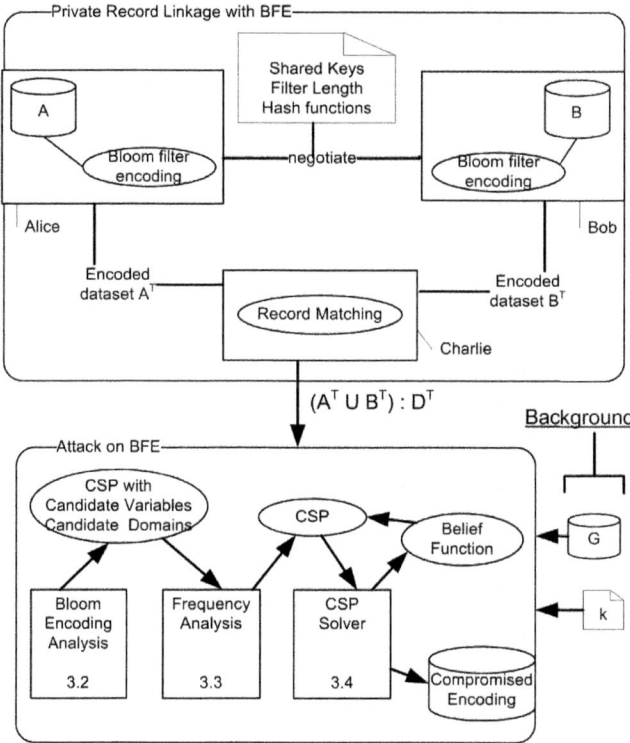

Fig. 7. A schematic of BFE data sharing and the attack issued by the third party

Efficient Proofs of Attributes in Pairing-Based Anonymous Credential System

Amang Sudarsono[1,*], Toru Nakanishi[2], and Nobuo Funabiki[2]

[1] Electronic Engineering Polytechnic Institute of Surabaya (EEPIS), Indonesia
[2] Department of Communication Network Engineering, Okayama University, Japan
nakanisi@cne.okayama-u.ac.jp

Abstract. An anonymous credential system allows the user to convince a verifier of the possession of a certificate issued by the issuing authority anonymously. One of the applications is the privacy-enhancing electronic ID (eID). A previously proposed anonymous credential system achieves constant complexity in the number of finite-set attributes of the user. However, the system is based on the RSA. In this paper, we show how to achieve the constant complexity in a pairing-based anonymous credential system excluding the RSA. The key idea of the construction is the use of a pairing-based accumulator. The accumulator outputs a constant-size value from a large set of input values. Using zero-knowledge proofs of pairing-based certificates and accumulators, we can prove AND and OR relations with constant complexity in the number of finite-set attributes.

1 Introduction

Electronic identification has been widely applied to access authorization to buildings, use of facilities, Web services, etc. Currently, electronic identity (eID) such as eID card is often used. The eID is issued by a trusted organization such as the government, company, or university, and is used for services provided by the organization. Trusted ID is very attractive for secondary use in commercial services. The eID includes attributes of the user such as the name, the address, the gender, the occupation, and the date of birth. In commercial cases, the attribute-based authentication can be desired. For example, a service provider can refuse the access from kids, by checking the age in the eID.

One of serious issues in the existing eID systems is user's privacy. In the systems, the eID may reveal the user's identity. The service provider can collect the use history of each user. Anonymous credential systems [13], [12], [10] are one of the solutions.

Anonymous credential systems allow an issuer to issue a certificate to a user. Each certificate is a proof of membership, qualification, or privilege, and contains user's attributes. The user can anonymously convince a verifier for the possession of the certificate, where the selected attributes can be disclosed without revealing any other information about the user's privacy. The user can prove complex

---

* This work was done while this author was with Okayama university.

S. Fischer-Hübner and N. Hopper (Eds.): PETS 2011, LNCS 6794, pp. 246–263, 2011.

relations of the attributes using AND and OR relations. AND relation is used when proving the possession of all of the multiple attributes. For example, the user can prove that he is a student, and has a valid student card, when entering the faculty building. OR relation represents the proof for possession of one of multiple attributes. For example, he can prove that he is either a staff or a teacher when using a copy machine in a laboratory. An implementation of eID on a standard java card is shown in [5].

In [13], Camenisch and Lysyanskaya firstly proposed an anonymous credential system based on RSA. Unfortunately, it suffers from a linear complexity in the number of user's attributes in proving AND and OR relations. Hence, this system is not suitable for small devices such as smart cards. In [10], Camenisch and Groß extended the scheme to solve the drawback. They classify attribute types into two categories: string attributes and finite-set attributes. The former can be represented as a string, such as name and ID number. The latter can be represented as an element from relatively small finite-set, such as gender and profession. There are much fewer string type of attributes, and thus the costs on finite-set attribute types impacts the total efficiency. In Camenisch-Groß system, by encoding a large number of finite-set attributes into prime numbers, one value for the finite-set attributes can be embedded into the certificate. Then, the AND and OR relations are proved with the constant complexity in the number of finite-set attributes using zero-knowledge proofs of integer relations on prime numbers.

In this paper, for a pairing-based anonymous credential system using BBS+ signatures [7], we show how to prove AND and OR relations with constant complexity. The key idea of the construction is the use of a pairing-based accumulator [12]. The accumulator outputs a constant-size value from a large set of input values. We consider that the input values are assigned to attributes. Then, we utilize an extended BBS+ signatures to certify a set of attributes as the accumulator. Using zero-knowledge proofs of BBS+ signatures and accumulators, we can prove AND and OR relations with constant complexity in the number of finite-set attributes. The drawback is that the size of public key is depending on the number of attribute values. It varies from 200 KBytes to 2 MBytes for the number of attribute values $1,000$ to $10,000$. In the current mobile environments, the data size is sufficiently practical, since the public key is not changed after it is distributed.

Remark 1. In the RSA-based anonymous credential system with efficient complexity [10], NOT relation is also equipped. Namely, the prover can prove that a specified attribute is not in his certificate. On the other hand, our system does not have the protocol to directly prove NOT relation. However, OR relation substitutes NOT relation. In an attribute type, we consider the set of attribute values except for the attribute value targeted by NOT relation. Then, proving that an attribute value in the set is in his certificate means that the target attribute value is not in the certificate. For example, for proving that the user is not student, we can prove that she has some of other profession attribute values.

2   Preliminaries

2.1   Bilinear Groups

Our scheme utilizes the following bilinear groups:

1. $\mathcal{G}$ and $\mathcal{T}$ are multiplicative cyclic groups of prime order p,
2. g is a randomly chosen generator of $\mathcal{G}$,
3. e is an efficiently computable bilinear map: $\mathcal{G} \times \mathcal{G} \to \mathcal{T}$, i.e., (1) for all $u, u', v, v' \in \mathcal{G}$, $e(uu', v) = e(u, v)e(u', v)$ and $e(u, vv') = e(u, v)e(u, v')$, and thus for all $u, v \in \mathcal{G}$ and $a, b \in Z$, $e(u^a, v^b) = e(u, v)^{ab}$, and (2) $e(g, g) \neq 1$.

2.2   Assumptions

The security of our scheme is based on the q-SDH assumption [7,8], the q-HSDH (Hidden SDH) assumption [9], and q-TDH (Triple DH) assumption [4] for the underlying signatures, and n-DHE assumption [12] for the accumulator, where q, n are non-negative integer.

Definition 1 (q-SDH assumption). *For all PPT algorithm $\mathcal{A}$, the probability*

$$\Pr[\mathcal{A}(u, u^a, \ldots, u^{a^q}) = (b, u^{1/(a+b)}) \wedge b \in Z_p]$$

is negligible, where $u \in_R \mathcal{G}$ and $a \in_R Z_p$.

Definition 2 (q-HSDH assumption). *For all PPT algorithm $\mathcal{A}$, the probability*

$$\Pr[\mathcal{A}(u, v, u^a, (u^{1/(a+b_1)}, u^{b_1}, v^{b_1}), \ldots, (u^{1/(a+b_q)}, u^{b_q}, v^{b_q})) = (u^{1/(a+b)}, u^b, v^b)$$
$$\wedge \forall i \in [1, q] : u^b \neq u^{b_i}]$$

is negligible, where $u, v \in_R \mathcal{G}$, $a \in_R Z_p$, and $b, b_i \in Z_p$.

Definition 3 (q-TDH assumption). *For all PPT algorithm $\mathcal{A}$, the probability*

$$\Pr[\mathcal{A}(u, u^a, u^b, (c_1, u^{1/(a+c_1)}), \ldots, (c_q, u^{1/(a+c_q)})) = (u^{ra}, u^{rb}, u^{rab})$$
$$\wedge \forall i \in [1, q] : c \neq c_i \wedge r \neq 0]$$

is negligible, where $u \in_R \mathcal{G}$, $a, b \in_R Z_p$, and $c_i, c \in Z_p$.

Definition 4 (n-DHE assumption). *For all PPT algorithm $\mathcal{A}$, the probability*

$$\Pr[\mathcal{A}(u, u^a, \ldots, u^{a^n}, u^{a^{n+2}}, \ldots, u^{a^{2n}}) = u^{a^{n+1}}]$$

is negligible, where $u \in_R \mathcal{G}$ and $a \in_R Z_p$.

2.3   Extended Accumulator with Efficient Updates

In [12], the accumulator with efficient updates is proposed. the accumulator is generated from a set of values, and we can verify that a single value is accumulated. Thus, for k values, we have to verify that each value is accumulated multiple times. This means that the complexity depends on the number of proved values, k. Here, we extend the accumulator to verify that k values are accumulated with the constant complexity.

Here, we consider that some values in $\{1, \ldots, n\}$ with size n are accumulated. Let V be a set of accumulated values that is a subset of $\{1, \ldots, n\}$. Let $U = \{i_1, \ldots, i_k\}$ be a subset of V with size k. The accumulator allows us to confirm that all elements of U belong to V, i.e., $U \subseteq V$, all at once.

AccSetup: This is the algorithm to output the public parameters. Select bilinear groups $\mathcal{G}, \mathcal{T}$ with a prime order p and a bilinear map e. Select $g \in_R \mathcal{G}$. Select $\gamma \in_R Z_p$ and compute and publish $p, \mathcal{G}, \mathcal{T}, e, g, g_1 = g^{\gamma^1}, \ldots, g_n = g^{\gamma^n}, g_{n+2} = g^{\gamma^{n+2}}, \ldots, g_{2n} = g^{\gamma^{2n}}$ and $z = e(g,g)^{\gamma^{n+1}}$ as the public parameters.

AccUpdate: This is the algorithm to compute the accumulator using the public parameters. The accumulator acc_V of V is computed as $acc_V = \prod_{i \in V} g_{n+1-i}$.

AccWitUpdate: This is the algorithm to compute the witness that values are included in an accumulator, using the public parameters. Given V and the accumulator acc_V, the witness of values $i_1, \ldots, i_k$ in U is computed as $W = \prod_{i \in U} \prod_{j \in V}^{j \neq i} g_{n+1-j+i}$.

AccVerify: This is the algorithm to verify that values in U are included in an accumulator, using the witness and the public parameters. Given acc_V, U, and W, accept if

$$\frac{e(\prod_{i \in U} g_i, acc_V)}{e(g, W)} = z^k.$$

Theorem 1. *Under the n-DHE assumption, any adversary cannot output (U, V, W) where $U \subseteq \{1, \ldots, n\}, V \subseteq \{1, \ldots, n\}$ on input $p, \mathcal{G}, \mathcal{T}, e, g, g_1, \ldots, g_n, g_{n+2}, \ldots, g_{2n}$ and z s.t. **AccVerify** accepts U, acc_V, W and $U \setminus V \neq \emptyset$.*

Proof. Assume an adversary which outputs (U, V, W) s.t. **AccVerify** accepts U, acc_V, W and $U \setminus V \neq \emptyset$. Let $U_1 = U \setminus V$ and $U_2 = U \cap V$. $U \setminus V \neq \emptyset$ (i.e., $U_1 \neq \emptyset$) implies $|U_2| \neq k$.

Since **AccVerify** accepts these,

$$\frac{e(\prod_{i \in U} g_i, acc_V)}{e(g, W)} = z^k = e(g, g_{n+1})^k,$$

where $g_{n+1} = g^{\gamma^{n+1}}$. From $acc_V = \prod_{i \in V} g_{n+1-i}$,

$$\frac{e(\prod_{i \in U} g_i, \prod_{i \in V} g_{n+1-i})}{e(g, W)} = e(g, g_{n+1})^k,$$

$$e(g, \prod_{\tilde{i} \in U} \prod_{i \in V} g_{n+1-i+\tilde{i}}) = e(g, W g_{n+1}{}^k).$$

Thus, we have

$$\prod_{\tilde{i} \in U} \prod_{i \in V} g_{n+1-i+\tilde{i}} = W g_{n+1}{}^k,$$

$$\prod_{\tilde{i} \in U_1} \prod_{i \in V} g_{n+1-i+\tilde{i}} \cdot \prod_{\tilde{i} \in U_2} \prod_{i \in V} g_{n+1-i+\tilde{i}} = W g_{n+1}{}^k,$$

$$(\prod_{\tilde{i} \in U_1} \prod_{i \in V} g_{n+1-i+\tilde{i}}) \cdot g_{n+1}{}^{|U_2|} \prod_{\tilde{i} \in U_2} \prod_{i \in V, i \neq \tilde{i}} g_{n+1-i+\tilde{i}} = W g_{n+1}{}^k,$$

$$\prod_{\tilde{i} \in U_1} \prod_{i \in V} g_{n+1-i+\tilde{i}} \cdot \prod_{\tilde{i} \in U_2} \prod_{i \in V, i \neq \tilde{i}} g_{n+1-i+\tilde{i}} = W g_{n+1}{}^{k-|U_2|}.$$

We obtain

$$g_{n+1} = (W^{-1} \cdot \prod_{\tilde{i} \in U_1} \prod_{i \in V} g_{n+1-i+\tilde{i}} \cdot \prod_{\tilde{i} \in U_2} \prod_{i \in V, i \neq \tilde{i}} g_{n+1-i+\tilde{i}})^{1/(k-|U_2|)},$$

where $k - |U_2| \neq 0$ due to $|U_2| \neq k$.

For any $\tilde{i} \in U_1$ and any $i \in V$, $g_{n+1-i+\tilde{i}} \neq g_{n+1}$, due to $U_1 \cap V = \phi$. Also, for any $\tilde{i} \in U_2$ and any $i \in V$ satisfying $i \neq \tilde{i}$, $g_{n+1-i+\tilde{i}} \neq g_{n+1}$. Therefore, we can compute g_{n+1} given $g_1, \ldots, g_n, g_{n+2}, \ldots, g_{2n}$, which contradicts n-DHE assumption.   □

2.4   Modified BBS+ Signatures

We utilize an extension from BB signature scheme [6], called BBS+ signatures. The extension is informally introduced in [7] and the concrete construction is shown in [15,1]. This scheme allows us to sign a set of messages. Our system requires that the accumulator is signed. In the BBS+ signature, the messages to be signed are set in exponents (elements of Z_p), whereas the accumulator is the product of g_i's from $\mathcal{G}$. Thus, we modify the BBS+ signature to be able to sign on g_i's, as follows.

mBBS+Setup: Select bilinear groups $\mathcal{G}, \mathcal{T}$ with a prime order p and a bilinear map e. Select $g, g_0, h_1, \ldots, h_L \in_R \mathcal{G}$. Select $\gamma \in_R Z_p$ and compute $g_1 = g^{\gamma^1}, \ldots, g_n = g^{\gamma^n}, g_{n+2} = g^{\gamma^{n+2}}, \ldots, g_{2n} = g^{\gamma^{2n}}$.

mBBS+KeyGen: Select $X \in_R Z_p$ and compute $Y = h^X$. The secret key is X and the public key is $(p, \mathcal{G}, \mathcal{T}, e, g, g_0, g_1, \ldots, g_n, g_{n+2}, \ldots, g_{2n}, h_1, \ldots, h_L, Y)$.

mBBS+Sign: Given messages $m_1, \ldots, m_n, m_{n+2}, \ldots, m_{2n} \in \{0, 1\}$, $M_1, \ldots, M_L \in Z_p$, select $w, r \in_R Z_p$ and compute

$$A = (\prod_{\substack{1 \leq j \leq 2n \\ j \neq n+1}} g_j{}^{m_j} \prod_{1 \leq j \leq L} h_j{}^{M_j} g_0^r g)^{1/(X+w)}.$$

The signature is (A, w, r).

mBBS+Verify: Given messages $m_1, \ldots, m_n, m_{n+2}, \ldots, m_{2n}, M_1, \ldots, M_L$ and the signature (A, w, r), check

$$e(A, Yg^w) = e(\prod_{\substack{1 \leq j \leq 2n \\ j \neq n+1}}^{j \neq n+1} g_j^{m_j} \prod_{1 \leq j \leq L} h_j^{M_j} g_0^r g, g).$$

The modified BBS+ signature is unforgeable against adaptively chosen message attack under the q-SDH assumption. It is shown in a similar way to [2], as follows.

BB signatures. Since the security is proved using the security of the underlying BB signatures [6], we briefly show the scheme.

BBSetup: Select bilinear groups $\mathcal{G}, \mathcal{T}$ with a prime order p and a bilinear map e. Select $g \in_R \mathcal{G}$.
BBKeyGen: Select $X \in_R Z_p$ and compute $Y = g^X$. The secret key is X and the public key is $(p, \mathcal{G}, \mathcal{T}, e, g, Y)$.
BBSign: Given message $m \in Z_p$, compute $B = g^{1/(X+m)}$. The signature is B.
BBVerify: Given message m and the signature B, check $e(B, Yg^m) = e(g, g)$.

BB signatures are existentially unforgeable against *weak* chosen message attack under the q-SDH assumption [6]. In this attack, the adversary must choose messages queried for the signing oracle, before the public key is given.

Theorem 2. *mBBS+ signature is unforgeable against adaptively chosen message attack under the q-SDH assumption.*

Proof. This proof is derived from [2].

Assume that $\mathcal{A}$ breaks the unforgeability of mBBS+ signatures, and we construct the following simulator $\mathcal{B}$ breaking BB signatures that are secure under the q-SDH assumption.

$\mathcal{B}$ chooses random messages $w_1, \ldots, w_{q-1}$ for BB signatures, and is given the corresponding BB signatures $B_i = g^{1/(X+w_i)}$ with the public key $(p, \mathcal{G}, \mathcal{T}, e, g, Y)$. Then, $\mathcal{B}$ selects $w^*, k^*, a^* \in_R Z_p$, and compute $g_0 = ((Yg^{w^*})^{k^*} g^{-1})^{1/a^*} = g^{((X+w^*)k^*-1)/a^*}$. Also, $\mathcal{B}$ selects $\gamma, \mu_1, \ldots, \mu_L \in_R Z_p$, and compute $g_1 = g_0^{\gamma^1}$, $\ldots, g_n = g_0^{\gamma^n}, g_{n+2} = g_0^{\gamma^{n+2}}, \ldots, g_{2n} = g_0^{\gamma^{2n}}$, and $h_1 = g_0^{\mu_1}, \ldots, h_L = g_0^{\mu_L}$. $\mathcal{B}$ sets the public key of mBBS+ signatures $(p, \mathcal{G}, \mathcal{T}, e, g, g_0, g_1, \ldots, g_n, g_{n+2}, \ldots, g_{2n}, h_1, \ldots, h_L, Y)$, and runs $\mathcal{A}$. Out of q signing queries from $\mathcal{A}$, $\mathcal{B}$ randomly selects a query, which called $*$ query. For messages $(m_{1,i}, \ldots, m_{n,i}, m_{n+2,i}, \ldots, m_{2n,i}, M_{1,i}, \ldots, M_{L,i})$ of the i-th query, define

$$t_i = \sum_{\substack{1 \leq j \leq 2n \\ j \neq n+1}}^{j \neq n+1} m_{j,i} \gamma^j + \sum_{1 \leq j \leq L} M_{j,i} \mu_j.$$

To the queries except $*$, $\mathcal{B}$ responds using the BB signature (B_i, w_i) as follows. $\mathcal{B}$ selects $r_i \in_R Z_p$, and compute $a_i = r_i + t_i$ and the following A_i.

$$
\begin{aligned}
A_i &= B_i^{(1 - \frac{a_i + (w_i - w^*)a_i k^*}{a^*})} g^{\frac{a_i}{a^*} k^*} \\
&= B_i^{(1 - \frac{a_i}{a^*})} g^{\frac{-(w_i - w^*)a_i k^* + a_i k^*(X + w_i)}{(X + w_i)a^*}} \\
&= B_i^{(1 - \frac{a_i}{a^*})} (g^{\frac{a_i}{a^*} k^*})^{\frac{-w_i + w^* + X + w_i}{X + w_i}} \\
&= B_i g^{\frac{-a_i + a_i k^*(X + w^*)}{a^*(X + w_i)}} \\
&= B_i g_0^{\frac{a_i}{(X + w_i)}} = (g g_0^{a_i})^{\frac{1}{X + w_i}}
\end{aligned}
$$

$\mathcal{B}$ returns (A_i, w_i, r_i).

To the $*$ query, $\mathcal{B}$ sets $r^* = a^* - t_i$, computes $A^* = g^{k^*} = (g g_0^{a^*})^{1/(X + w^*)}$ and returns (A^*, w^*, r^*).

Finally, $\mathcal{A}$ outputs the forged signature (A', w', r') on message $(m'_1, \ldots, m'_n, m'_{n+2}, \ldots, m'_{2n}, M'_1, \ldots, M'_L)$. There are three cases. Define

$$
a' = r' + \sum_{\substack{1 \le j \le 2n \\ j \ne n+1}} m'_j \gamma^j + \sum_{1 \le j \le L} M'_j \mu_j.
$$

– Case I [$w' \notin \{w_1, \ldots, w_q, w^*\}$]: $\mathcal{B}$ computes the following B'.

$$
\begin{aligned}
B' &= (A' g^{\frac{-k^*}{a^*} a'})^{\frac{a^*}{a^* - a' - k^* a'(w' - w^*)}} \\
&= ((g g^{\frac{(X + w^*)k^* a' - a'}{a^*}})^{\frac{1}{X + w'}} g^{\frac{-k^*}{a^*} a'})^{\frac{a^*}{a^* - a' - k^* a'(w' - w^*)}} \\
&= (g^{\frac{a^* + (X + w^*)k^* a' - a' - k^* a'(X + w')}{a^*(X + w')}})^{\frac{a^*}{a^* - a' - k^* a'(w' - w^*)}} \\
&= (g^{\frac{a^* - a' - k^* a'(w' - w^*)}{a^*(X + w')}})^{\frac{a^*}{a^* - a' - k^* a'(w' - w^*)}} = g^{\frac{1}{X + w'}}
\end{aligned}
$$

This means that a BB signature for a new message w' is forged, which contradicts q-SDH assumption.

– Case II [($w' = w_i$ and $A' = A_i$ for some i) or ($w' = w^*$ and $A' = A^*$)]: Consider $w' = w_i$ and $A' = A_i$ (The other case is similar). From $A'^{X + w'} = A_i^{X + w_i}$, $g g_0^{a'} = g g_0^{a_i}$ holds and we obtain $a' = a_i$. Thus, letting $\Delta r = r' - r_i$, $\Delta m_j = m'_j - m_{j,i}$, and $\Delta M_j = M'_j - M_{j,i}$,

$$
\Delta r + \sum_{\substack{1 \le j \le 2n \\ j \ne n+1}} \Delta m_j \gamma^j + \sum_{1 \le j \le L} \Delta M_j \mu_j = 0.
$$

Some Δm_j is not 0 or some ΔM_j is not 0. If $\Delta M_j \ne 0$, the above equation means that we can compute μ_j in case that $\mu_j = \log_{g_0} h_j$ is unknown. This contradict the DL assumption and then the q-SDH assumption. If $\Delta m_j \ne 0$, we can compute $\gamma^j \mod p$ and thus γ, given $g_0, g_0^\gamma, \ldots, g_0^{\gamma^n}, g_0^{\gamma^{n+2}}, \ldots, g_0^{\gamma^{2n}}$. This means that, given $g, g^\gamma, \ldots, g^{\gamma^{2n}}$, we can compute $(c, g^{1/(\gamma + c)})$ for any $c \in Z_p$, which contradicts the q-SDH assumption, where $q = 2n$.

- Case III [$w' \in \{w_1, \ldots, w_q, w^*\}$ and $A' \notin \{A_1, \ldots, A_q, A^*\}$]: With the probability $1/q$, $w' = w^*$. Then, from

$$A' = (gg_0^{a'})^{1/(X+w^*)} = g^{(a^* + a'(X+w^*)k^* - a')/(a^*(X+w^*))},$$

compute the following B'.

$$B' = (A'g^{\frac{-k^* a'}{a^*}})^{\frac{a^*}{a^* - a'}}$$
$$= (g^{\frac{a^* - a'}{a^*(X+w^*)}})^{\frac{a^*}{a^* - a'}}$$
$$= g^{\frac{1}{X+w^*}}$$

This means that a BB signature for a new message w^* is forged, which contradicts q-SDH assumption.   □

The security proof assumes that valid g_j's are signed, instead of any element from $\mathcal{G}$. Thus, for proving the knowledge of this signature, we have to ensure the correctness of g_j's by other technique, the following F-secure BB signatures.

2.5   F-secure BB Signatures

We also adopt another variant of BB signature scheme, called F-secure signature [4].

FBBSetup: Select bilinear groups $\mathcal{G}, \mathcal{T}$ with a prime order p and a bilinear map e. Select $g, \tilde{g} \in_R \mathcal{G}$.

FBBKeyGen: Select $\tilde{X}, \hat{X} \in_R Z_p$ and compute $\tilde{Y} = g^{\tilde{X}}, \hat{Y} = g^{\hat{X}}$. The secret key is $(\tilde{X}, \hat{X})$ and the public key is $(p, \mathcal{G}, \mathcal{T}, e, g, \tilde{g}, \tilde{Y}, \hat{Y})$.

FBBSign: Given message $M \in Z_p$, select $\mu \in_R Z_p - \{\frac{\tilde{X} - M}{\hat{X}}\}$ and compute $S = g^{1/(\tilde{X}+M+\hat{X}\mu)}, T = \hat{Y}^\mu, U = \tilde{g}^\mu$. The signature is (S, T, U).

FBBVerify: Given the signature (S, T, U) on message M, check $e(S, \tilde{Y}g^M T) = e(g, g)$ and $e(\tilde{g}, T) = e(U, \hat{Y})$.

Define bijection F as $F(M) = (g^M, \tilde{g}^M)$ for message M. The F-security means that no adversary cannot output $(F(M), \sigma)$ where σ is the signature on message M s.t. he has never previously obtained the signature after his adaptive chosen message attacks. The security is proved under the q-HSDH and q-TDH assumptions [4].

2.6   Proving Relations on Representations

We adopt zero-knowledge proofs of knowledge (PKs) on representations, which are the generalization of the Schnorr identification protocol [11]. Concretely we utilize a PK proving the knowledge of a representation of $C \in \mathcal{G}$ to the bases $g_1, g_2, \ldots, g_t \in \mathcal{G}$, i.e., $x_1, \ldots, x_t$ s.t. $C = g_1^{x_1} \cdots g_t^{x_t}$. This can be also constructed on group $\mathcal{T}$. The PK can be extended to proving multiple representations with equal parts.

Since we use only prime-order groups, we can extract the proved secret knowledge given two accepting protocol views whose commitments are the same and whose challenges are different.

3   Proposed System

3.1   Construction Idea

As in [10], we categorize finite-set attributes and string attributes. In the finite-set attributes, the values are binary or from a pre-defined finite set, for example, gender, degree, nationality, etc. On the other hand, name and identification number are the string attributes.

Our proposal is based on the pairing-based anonymous credential system using the BBS+ signatures, which is described in [12] for example. In the underlying system, the certificate is a BBS+ signature [7], where each attribute type is expressed as an exponent on a base assigned to the attribute type, such as $g_j^{M_j}$, and all parts of $g_j^{M_j}$ have to be signed. Namely, the certificate is (A, w, r) s.t.

$$A = (\prod_{1 \le j \le L'} h_j^{M_j} h_{L'+1}{}^x g_0^r g)^{1/(X+w)},$$

where x is a secret identity that only the user with the certificate knows. Then, proving the knowledge of the signature needs the cost depending on the number of attribute types.

To express the finite-set attributes (For the string type, we still use the exponent), we use a pairing-based accumulator in [12]. Let all attribute values in all finite-set attribute types be numbered. The j-th attribute value is assigned to an input value g_j's in the accumulator. The multiple inputs (i.e., attribute values) are accumulated into a single value. When V is the set of indexes of the attribute values for a user, they are accumulated to $acc_V = \prod_{j \in V} g_{n+1-j}$. We consider that the accumulated value is signed by an extended BBS+ signature,

$$A = (acc_V \cdot \prod_{1 \le j \le L} h_j^{M_j} h_{L+1}{}^x g_0^r g)^{1/(X+w)},$$

where the original representation $h_j^{M_j}$ is still used for the string type.

However, in the PK of the extended BBS+ signature, acc_V is committed for secrecy. That is, the validity of the committed value (i.e., it is the form of acc_V) is unknown to the verifier. The PK for representations only proves the form of $A = (R \cdot \prod_{1 \le j \le L} h_j^{M_j} h_{L+1}{}^x g_0^r g)^{1/(X+w)}$, for some $R \in \mathcal{G}$. However, the security proof of the modified BBS+ signatures assumes that the message is the product of g_j's, i.e., $\prod_{1 \le j \le 2n}^{j \ne n+1} g_j^{m_j}$. For example, we can show the following forge by manipulating the value of acc_V:

$$acc_V = \prod_{1 \le j \le 2n}^{j \ne n+1} g_j^{m_j} \cdot (\prod_{1 \le j \le L} h_j^{-M_j}) h_{L+1}^{-x} \cdot g_0^{-r} g^{-1} Y g^w, \quad A = g.$$

It is unknown whether this forge is meaningful or not. However, we cannot prove the security of our protocols, if the validity of acc_V is unknown and the modified BBS+ signature is forgeable. Thus, we add another signature on acc_V by signing the exponent $\sum_{j \in V} \gamma^{n+1-j}$. This approach is also used in [12] to ensure the g_j in the membership certificate. They use a weakly secure BB signature [6], based on interactive HSDH assumption [3] or HSDHE assumption [12]. We consider that it is a rather strong assumption. This is why we use the F-secure BB signature [4] derived from fully secure BB signature, based on the better assumptions (HSDH assumption and TDH assumption).

AND relation. For AND relation $(a_1 \wedge \cdots \wedge a_k)$, it is needed to prove that a specified set of attributes $(a_1, \ldots, a_k)$ are all embedded into the user's certificate. Using **AccVerify** in the extended accumulator, we can prove that multiple values are accumulated to the accumulator in the certificate with constant complexity. By the similar way to [12], we can obtain the PK of **AccVerify** with constant complexity.

OR relation. For OR relation $(a_1 \vee \cdots \vee a_k)$, it is needed to prove that one (denoted as $\tilde{a}$) of a specified set of attributes $(a_1, \ldots, a_k)$ is embedded into the user's certificate. Similarly to AND relation, using **AccVerify**, a signer can prove that a value $\tilde{a}$ is accumulated to the accumulator in the certificate. Furthermore, the verifier prepares another accumulator acc' from specified attributes $a_1, \ldots, a_k$. Then, the signer proves that the same value $\tilde{a}$ is accumulated to the additional accumulator acc'.

3.2   Proposed Construction

Setup. The inputs of this algorithm are ℓ, n, and L, where ℓ is the security parameter, n is the maximum number of finite-set attribute values, and L is the maximum number of string attribute types. The outputs are issuer's public key ipk and issuer's secret key isk.

1. Select bilinear groups $\mathcal{G}$, $\mathcal{T}$ with the same order p with length ℓ and the bilinear map e.
2. Select $g, g_0, \tilde{g}, \hat{g}, h_1, \ldots, h_{L+1} \in_R \mathcal{G}$. Select $X, \tilde{X}, \hat{X}, \tilde{X}', \hat{X}', \gamma \in_R Z_p^*$, compute $Y = g^X, \tilde{Y} = g^{\tilde{X}}, \hat{Y} = g^{\hat{X}}, \tilde{Y}' = g^{\tilde{X}'}$ and $\hat{Y}' = g^{\hat{X}'}$. Compute $g_1 = g^{\gamma^1}, \ldots, g_n = g^{\gamma^n}, g_{n+2} = g^{\gamma^{n+2}}, \ldots, g_{2n} = g^{\gamma^{2n}}$, and $z = (g, g)^{\gamma^{n+1}}$. Select hash function $H : \{0, 1\}^* \to Z_p$.
3. For every $g_j = g^{\gamma^j}$ with $1 \le j \le n$, select $\mu_j \in_R Z_p - \{\frac{\tilde{X}' - \gamma^j}{\hat{X}'}\}$ and compute the F-secure BB signature on g_j as follows:

$$\tilde{S}_j = g^{1/(\tilde{X}' + \gamma^j + \mu_j \hat{X}')}, \quad \tilde{T}_j = \hat{Y}^{\mu_j}, \quad \tilde{U}_j = \tilde{g}^{\mu_j}, \quad \tilde{F}_j = \tilde{g}^{\gamma^j}.$$

4. Output the issuer public key $ipk = (p, \mathcal{G}, \mathcal{T}, e, H, g, \tilde{g}, \hat{g}, g_0, g_1, \ldots, g_n, g_{n+2}, \ldots, g_{2n}, h_1, \ldots, h_{L+1}, z, (\tilde{S}_1, \tilde{T}_1, \tilde{U}_1, \tilde{F}_1), \ldots, (\tilde{S}_n, \tilde{T}_n, \tilde{U}_n, \tilde{F}_n), Y, \tilde{Y}, \hat{Y}, \tilde{Y}', \hat{Y}')$, and the issuer secret key $isk = (X, \tilde{X}, \hat{X}, \tilde{X}', \hat{X}', \gamma)$.

Issuing Certificate. This is an interactive protocol between the issuer **Issuer** and user **User**. The common inputs of this protocol consist of ipk, and (SA, FA) that are sets of string attribute values and finite-set attribute values of the user, respectively. Each string attribute value of the j-th attribute type in SA is represented by an element M_j from Z_p^* (If the user does not have any attribute value in the attribute type, we assign an attribute value implying not applicable). Each finite-set attribute value is represented by an index in $\{1, \ldots, n\}$. Thus, set SA consists of attribute values and set FA consists of indexes of attribute values (sets TSA and TFA shown later are similar). The input of **Issuer** is isk. The output of **User** is the certificate $cert$.

1. [**User**]. Select $x, r' \in_R Z_p^*$. Compute $A' = h_{L+1}{}^x g_0^{r'}$. Send A' to **Issuer**. In addition, prove the validity of A' using PK for representations, i.e., prove the knowledge of x, r' s.t. $A' = h_{L+1}{}^x g_0^{r'}$.
2. [**Issuer**]. Given the user's attributes (SA, FA), compute the accumulator of the finite-set attributes as $acc = \prod_{a \in FA} g_{n+1-a}$. Select $w, r'' \in_R Z_p^*$. Compute the modified BBS+ signature as follows:

$$A = (acc(\prod_{1 \le j \le L} h_j^{M_j})A'g_0^{r''}g)^{1/(X+w)} = (acc(\prod_{1 \le j \le L} h_j^{M_j})h_{L+1}^x g_0^{r'+r''}g)^{1/(X+w)}.$$

In addition, select $\mu \in_R Z_p - \{\frac{\tilde{X} - \sum_{a \in FA} \gamma^{n+1-a}}{X}\}$ and compute an F-secure BB signature ensuring acc as follows:

$$S = g^{1/(\tilde{X} + \sum_{a \in FA} \gamma^{n+1-a} + \mu \hat{X})}, \quad T = \hat{Y}^\mu, \quad U = \tilde{g}^\mu, \quad F = \tilde{g}^{\sum_{a \in FA} \gamma^{n+1-a}}.$$

   Return (A, S, T, U, F, w, r'') to **User**.
3. [**User**] Compute $r = r' + r''$, verify:

$$e(A, Yg^w) \stackrel{?}{=} e(acc(\prod_{1 \le j \le L} h_j^{M_j})h_{L+1}^x g_0^r g, g)$$

$$\wedge\ e(S, \tilde{Y} \cdot acc \cdot T) \stackrel{?}{=} e(g, g) \wedge\ e(\tilde{g}, T) \stackrel{?}{=} e(U, \hat{Y}) \wedge e(\tilde{g}, acc) \stackrel{?}{=} e(F, g).$$

   Output $cert = (A, S, T, U, F, x, w, r)$.

Attribute Proofs. This is an interactive protocol between the user and the verifier. The common inputs are ipk, and (TSA, TFA) are subsets of string attributes and finite-set attributes respectively, which are referenced in proofs, and user's secret inputs are $cert$ and (SA, FA).

Proving AND Relation. For TFA $= \{a_1, \ldots, a_k\}$ with $a_j \in \{1, \ldots, n\}$, the prover shows his possession of the certificate which includes all of the attributes, i.e., $a_1 \wedge a_2 \wedge \ldots \wedge a_k$.

1. The prover computes the witness that $a_1, \ldots, a_k$ are included in the accumulator of FA as: $W = \prod_{1 \le j \le k}(\prod_{a \in FA}^{a \ne a_j} g_{n+1-a+a_j})$. Set $D = \prod_{1 \le j \le k} g_{a_j}$.

2. The prover selects $\rho_A, \rho_S, \rho_T, \rho_U, \rho_F, \rho_a, \rho_W \in_R Z_p^*$, and compute commitments $C_A = A\hat{g}^{\rho_A}$, $C_S = S\hat{g}^{\rho_S}$, $C_T = T\hat{g}^{\rho_T}$, $C_U = U\hat{g}^{\rho_U}$, $C_F = F\hat{g}^{\rho_F}$, $C_a = acc \cdot \hat{g}^{\rho_a}$, and $C_W = W\hat{g}^{\rho_W}$.
3. The prover selects $\rho_w, \rho' \in_R Z_p^*$, sets $\alpha = w\rho_A$, $\zeta = \rho_S\rho_a$ and $\xi = \rho_S\rho_T$. The prover computes auxiliary commitments $C_w = g^w\hat{g}^{\rho_w}$ and $C_{\rho_S} = g^{\rho_S}\hat{g}^{\rho'}$. Then, the prover sets $\rho_\alpha = \rho_w\rho_A$, $\rho_\zeta = \rho'\rho_a$, and $\rho_\xi = \rho'\rho_T$.
4. The prover sends the commitments $(C_A, C_S, C_T, C_U, C_F, C_a, C_W, C_w, C_{\rho_S})$ to the verifier.
5. By using the proof of knowledge (PK) for representations, the prover proves the knowledge of $x, w, r, \rho_A, \rho_S, \rho_T, \rho_U, \rho_F, \rho_a, \rho_W, \rho_w, \rho', \alpha, \zeta, \xi, \rho_\alpha, \rho_\zeta, \rho_\xi$, and M_j for $M_j \notin$ TSA s.t.

$$C_w = g^w\hat{g}^{\rho_w}, 1 = C_w^{\rho_A}g^{-\alpha}\hat{g}^{-\rho_\alpha}, \tag{1}$$

$$e(C_A, Y)e(C_a(\prod_{1\le j\le L, M_j\in\text{TSA}} h_j^{M_j})g, g)^{-1} = (\prod_{1\le j\le L, M_j\notin\text{TSA}} e(h_j, g)^{M_j})$$

$$\cdot e(h_{L+1}, g)^x e(g_0, g)^r e(\hat{g}, Y)^{\rho_A} e(\hat{g}, g)^\alpha e(C_A, g)^{-w} e(\hat{g}, g)^{-\rho_a}, \tag{2}$$

$$C_{\rho_S} = g^{\rho_S}\hat{g}^{\rho'}, 1 = C_{\rho_S}^{\rho_a}g^{-\zeta}\hat{g}^{-\rho_\zeta}, 1 = C_{\rho_S}^{\rho_T}g^{-\xi}\hat{g}^{-\rho_\xi}, \tag{3}$$

$$e(C_S, \tilde{Y}C_aC_T)e(g, g)^{-1} = e(\hat{g}, \tilde{Y}C_aC_T)^{\rho_S}e(C_S, \hat{g})^{\rho_a+\rho_T}e(\hat{g}, \hat{g})^{-\zeta-\xi}, \tag{4}$$

$$e(\tilde{g}, C_T)e(C_U, \hat{Y})^{-1} = e(\tilde{g}, \hat{g})^{\rho_T}e(\hat{g}, \hat{Y})^{-\rho_U}, \tag{5}$$

$$e(\tilde{g}, C_a)e(C_F, g)^{-1} = e(\tilde{g}, \hat{g})^{\rho_a}e(\hat{g}, g)^{-\rho_F}, \tag{6}$$

$$e(D, C_a)e(g, C_W)^{-1}z^{-k} = e(D, \hat{g})^{\rho_a}e(g, \hat{g})^{-\rho_W}. \tag{7}$$

Proving OR Relation. For TFA $= \{a_1, \ldots, a_k\}$, the prover shows his possession of the certificate which includes one of the attributes, i.e., $a_1 \vee a_2 \vee \ldots \vee a_k$. Assume that $\tilde{a}$ is the proved attribute.

Before the protocol, the prover and the verifier prepare another accumulator $acc' = \prod_{a_j\in\text{TFA}} g_{n+1-a_j}$. This protocol is obtained by modifying that of the AND relation, as follows.

1. Similarly, the prover computes $W = \prod_{a\in\text{FA}}^{a\ne\tilde{a}} g_{n+1-a+\tilde{a}}$ for acc. Furthermore, the prover computes the new witness $W' = \prod_{a_j\in\text{TFA}}^{a_j\ne\tilde{a}} g_{n+1-a_j+\tilde{a}}$ for acc'.
2. In addition to step 2 in AND relation, the prover selects $\rho_g, \rho_{W'}, \rho_{\tilde{S}}, \rho_{\tilde{T}}, \rho_{\tilde{U}}$, $\rho_{\tilde{F}} \in_R \mathbb{Z}_p^*$, and compute the new commitment $C_g = g_{\tilde{a}}\hat{g}^{\rho_g}$, $C_{W'} = W'\hat{g}^{\rho_{W'}}$, $C_{\tilde{S}} = \tilde{S}_{\tilde{a}}\hat{g}^{\rho_{\tilde{S}}}$, $C_{\tilde{T}} = \tilde{T}_{\tilde{a}}\hat{g}^{\rho_{\tilde{T}}}$, $C_{\tilde{U}} = \tilde{U}_{\tilde{a}}\hat{g}^{\rho_{\tilde{U}}}$, and $C_{\tilde{F}} = \tilde{F}_{\tilde{a}}\hat{g}^{\rho_{\tilde{F}}}$.
3. In addition to step 3 in AND relation, the prover selects $\tilde{\rho}, \tilde{\rho}' \in_R Z_p^*$, sets $\delta = \rho_g\rho_a$, $\tilde{\zeta} = \rho_{\tilde{S}}\rho_g$ and $\tilde{\xi} = \rho_{\tilde{S}}\rho_{\tilde{T}}$. The prover computes auxiliary commitments $C_{\rho_g} = g^{\rho_g}\hat{g}^{\tilde{\rho}}$ and $C_{\rho_{\tilde{S}}} = g^{\rho_{\tilde{S}}}\hat{g}^{\tilde{\rho}'}$. Then, the prover sets $\rho_\delta = \tilde{\rho}\rho_a$, $\rho_{\tilde{\zeta}} = \tilde{\rho}'\rho_g$, and $\rho_{\tilde{\xi}} = \tilde{\rho}'\rho_{\tilde{T}}$.
4. The prover sends the commitments $(C_A, C_S, C_T, C_U, C_F, C_g, C_a, C_W, C_{W'}, C_{\tilde{S}}, C_{\tilde{T}}, C_{\tilde{U}}, C_{\tilde{F}}, C_w, C_{\rho_S}, C_{\rho_g}, C_{\rho_{\tilde{S}}})$ to the verifier.
5. Similarly to the AND relation, the prover conducts the PK, where the equation (7) is replaced by

$$C_{\rho_g} = g^{\rho_g}\hat{g}^{\tilde{\rho}}, 1 = C_{\rho_g}^{\rho_a}g^{-\delta}\hat{g}^{-\rho_\delta}, \tag{8}$$

$$e(C_g, C_a)e(g, C_W)^{-1}z^{-1} = e(C_g, \hat{g})^{\rho_a}e(\hat{g}, C_a)^{\rho_g}e(\hat{g}, \hat{g})^{-\delta}e(g, \hat{g})^{-\rho_W}, \tag{9}$$

and the following equations are added:

$$C_{\rho_{\tilde{S}}} = g^{\rho_{\tilde{S}}} \hat{g}^{\tilde{\rho}'}, 1 = C_{\rho_{\tilde{S}}}^{\rho_g} g^{-\tilde{\zeta}} \hat{g}^{-\rho_{\tilde{\xi}}}, 1 = C_{\rho_{\tilde{S}}}^{\rho_{\tilde{T}}} g^{-\tilde{\xi}} \hat{g}^{-\rho_{\tilde{\xi}}}, \tag{10}$$

$$e(C_{\tilde{S}}, \tilde{Y}'C_g C_{\tilde{T}})e(g,g)^{-1} = e(\hat{g}, \tilde{Y}'C_g C_{\tilde{T}})^{\rho_{\tilde{S}}} e(C_{\tilde{S}}, \hat{g})^{\rho_g + \rho_{\tilde{T}}} e(\hat{g}, \hat{g})^{-\tilde{\zeta}-\tilde{\xi}} \tag{11}$$

$$e(\tilde{g}, C_{\tilde{T}})e(C_{\tilde{U}}, \hat{Y}')^{-1} = e(\tilde{g}, \hat{g})^{\rho_{\tilde{T}}} e(\hat{g}, \hat{Y}')^{-\rho_{\tilde{U}}}, \tag{12}$$

$$e(\tilde{g}, C_g)e(C_{\tilde{F}}, g)^{-1} = e(\tilde{g}, \hat{g})^{\rho_g} e(\hat{g}, g)^{-\rho_{\tilde{F}}}, \tag{13}$$

$$e(C_g, acc')e(g, C_{W'})^{-1} z^{-1} = e(\hat{g}, acc')^{\rho_g} e(g, \hat{g})^{-\rho_{W'}}. \tag{14}$$

4   Security

Here, we show the proposed protocols are the PKs for AND and OR relations on the finite-set attributes. The security on the string attributes can be proved in the similar way to the underlying protocols.

Theorem 3. *The protocol of AND relation is a proof of knowledge of a modified BBS+ signature (A, w, r) on secret x, the string type of attributes $M_1, \ldots, M_L$, and the finite-set type of attributes indicated by accumulator acc, s.t. all attributes in* TFA *are accumulated to* acc.

Proof. From the PK, we have an extractor of knowledge satisfying the equations. Using the equations (1), we obtain $1 = (g^w \hat{g}^{\rho_w})^{\rho_A} g^{-\alpha} \hat{g}^{-\rho_\alpha}$, and thus $1 = g^{w\rho_A - \alpha} \hat{g}^{\rho_w \rho_A - \rho_\alpha}$. Since the discrete log of $\hat{g}$ to base g is unknown under the DL assumption (due to q-SDH assumption), this means $\alpha = w\rho_A$. By substituting this to equation (2), we have

$$e(C_A, Y)e(C_a(\prod_{1 \leq j \leq L, M_j \in \text{TSA}} h_j^{M_j})g, g)^{-1} = (\prod_{1 \leq j \leq L, M_j \notin \text{TSA}} e(h_j, g)^{M_j})e(h_{L+1}, g)^{x}$$

$$\cdot e(g_0, g)^r e(\hat{g}, Y)^{\rho_A} e(\hat{g}, g)^{w\rho_A} e(C_A, g)^{-w} e(\hat{g}, g)^{-\rho_a}$$

$$e(C_A, Y)e(\hat{g}^{-\rho_A}, Y)e(\hat{g}^{-\rho_A}, g^w)e(C_A, g^w) = e(C_a(\prod_{1 \leq j \leq L} h_j^{M_j})g, g)e(h_{L+1}^x, g)$$

$$\cdot e(g_0^r, g)e(\hat{g}^{-\rho_a}, g)$$

$$e(C_A \hat{g}^{-\rho_A}, Yg^w) = e(C_a \hat{g}^{-\rho_a}(\prod_{1 \leq j \leq L} h_j^{M_j})h_{L+1}^x g_0^r g, g)$$

Thus, we can extract $A = C_A \hat{g}^{-\rho_A}$ and $acc = C_a \hat{g}^{-\rho_a}$ s.t.

$$e(A, Yg^w) = e(acc(\prod_{1 \leq j \leq L} h_j^{M_j})h_{L+1}^x g_0^r g, g).$$

Similarly, using equations (3), we have $\zeta = \rho_S \rho_a$ and $\xi = \rho_S \rho_T$. By substituting them to equation (4), we have

$$e(C_S, \tilde{Y}C_a C_T)e(g,g)^{-1} = e(\hat{g}, \tilde{Y}C_a C_T)^{\rho_S} e(C_S, \hat{g})^{\rho_a + \rho_T} e(\hat{g}, \hat{g})^{-\rho_S \cdot \rho_a - \rho_S \cdot \rho_T}$$

$$e(C_S, \tilde{Y}C_a C_T)e(\hat{g}^{-\rho_S}, \tilde{Y}C_a C_T)e(C_S, \hat{g}^{-\rho_a - \rho_T})e(\hat{g}^{-\rho_S}, \hat{g}^{-\rho_a - \rho_T}) = e(g, g)$$

$$e(C_S \hat{g}^{-\rho_S}, \tilde{Y}C_a \hat{g}^{-\rho_a} C_T \hat{g}^{-\rho_T}) = e(g, g)$$

Thus, for the extracted $acc = C_a \hat{g}^{-\rho_a}$, we can extract $S = C_S \hat{g}^{-\rho_S}$ and $T = C_T \hat{g}^{-\rho_T}$ s.t. $e(S, \tilde{Y} \cdot acc \cdot T) = e(g, g)$. Similarly, using equations (5), (6), we obtain $U = C_F \hat{g}^{-\rho_F}$ and $F = C_F \hat{g}^{-\rho_F}$ s.t. $e(\tilde{g}, T) = e(U, \hat{Y})$ and $e(\tilde{g}, acc) = e(F, g)$. Since F-secure BB signatures w.r.t. the public key $\tilde{Y}, \hat{Y}$ is issued on only accumulators, it means $acc = \prod_{a \in \mathrm{FA}} g_{n+1-a}$ for FA of a user (otherwise, the signature is forgeable).

On the other hand, using equation (7), we can similarly extract $W = C_W \hat{g}^{-\rho_W}$ s.t. $e(D, acc)e(g, W)^{-1} = z^k$ for $D = \prod_{1 \leq j \leq k} g_{a_j}$. From the security of the extended accumulator, all values $a_1, \ldots, a_k$ are accumulated into acc. □

Theorem 4. *The protocol of OR relation is a proof of knowledge of a modified BBS+ signature (A, w, r) on secret x, the string type of attributes $M_1, \ldots, M_L$, and the finite-set type of attributes indicated by accumulator acc, s.t. one of attributes in TFA is accumulated to acc.*

Proof. From the PK, we have an extractor of knowledge satisfying the equations. Similarly to AND relation, we can extract a modified BBS+ signature (A, w, r) as the certificate including $acc = \prod_{a \in \mathrm{FA}} g_{n+1-a}$.

Similarly to the extraction of F-secure BB signature in the AND relation, using equations (10) – (13), we can extract the F-secure BB signature $(\tilde{S}, \tilde{T}, \tilde{U})$ on $R = C_g \hat{g}^{-\rho_g}$ and $\tilde{F}$ s.t. $e(\tilde{S}, \tilde{Y}' R \tilde{T}) = e(g, g), e(\tilde{g}, \tilde{T}) = e(\tilde{U}, \hat{Y}')$ and $e(\tilde{F}, g) = e(\tilde{F}, g)$. Since F-secure BB signatures w.r.t. the public key $\tilde{Y}', \hat{Y}'$ is issued on only g_j's, it means $R \in \{g_1, \ldots, g_n\}$ (otherwise, the signature is forgeable), and we can set $R = g_{\tilde{a}}$.

Using equations (8), we can obtain $\delta = \rho_a \rho_g$. By substituting this into equation (9), we can extract $W = C_W \hat{g}^{-\rho_W}$ s.t. $e(g_{\tilde{a}}, acc)e(g, W)^{-1} = z$ for the extracted $g_{\tilde{a}}$. This means that attribute $\tilde{a}$ is accumulated into acc. Using equation (14), we can extract $W' = C_{W'} \hat{g}^{-\rho_{W'}}$ s.t. $e(g_{\tilde{a}}, acc')e(g, W')^{-1} = z$ for $g_{\tilde{a}}$. This means that attribute $\tilde{a}$ is also accumulated into acc', that is, attribute $\tilde{a}$ is one of attributes $a_1, \ldots, a_k$. □

5 Efficiency

We compare the efficiency between our system and the conventional pairing-based system using the BBS+ signatures. Similarly to the conventional RSA-based systems described in [10], we can construct the conventional PKs for AND and OR relations, which are described in Appendix A.

We introduce the following parameters.

- L: the total number of string attribute types
- $\tilde{L}$: the total number of finite-set attribute types (e.g., gender, profession)
- n: the total number of finite-set attribute values (e.g., male, female, student, teacher)
- k: the number of attributes referenced in a proof.

Table 1. Asymptotic computational complexity of proof

Relation	Conventional system	Our system
AND	$O(L + \tilde{L})$	$O(L)$
OR	$O(L + \tilde{L} + k)$	$O(L)$

Table 2. Concrete number of exponentiations in proof generation ($E(\mathcal{T})$: exponentiations on $\mathcal{T}$, $E(\mathcal{G})$: exponentiations on $\mathcal{G}$)

Relation	Conventional system	Our system
AND	$(L + \tilde{L} + 5)E(\mathcal{T}) + 8E(\mathcal{G})$	$(L + 15)E(\mathcal{T}) + 24E(\mathcal{G})$
OR	$(L + \tilde{L} + 5)E(\mathcal{T}) + (5k + 8)E(\mathcal{G})$	$(L + 26)E(\mathcal{T}) + 47E(\mathcal{G})$

In the following comparisons, we consider the computational complexity based on the number of exponentiations and pairings. Namely, we ignore the number of multiplications, since the cost is much smaller than the others' costs.

Table 1 shows the comparison of asymptotic computational complexity for the proof generation and verification. In the both cases of AND and OR relations, we can see that the complexity in finite-set attributes becomes constant. This is because our scheme uses the accumulator verification with constant complexity. The demerit of our system is the length of public key. Our system needs $O(n+L)$ size, while the conventional system needs $O(\tilde{L}+L)$, where n is much larger than $\tilde{L}$.

Next, compare the concrete computational costs. We suppose that mobile devices such as smartphones manage the proof generation, and thus we concentrate in the computation complexity of the proof generation. Table 2 shows the comparison of the concrete costs. Using the pre-computation of pairings, we can omit any pairing computation with adding some slight exponentiations. In this table, we shows the number of the exponentiations needed for the proof generation after the omission. Note that the exponentiation cost on $\mathcal{T}$ is larger than that on $\mathcal{G}$. The results of this table mean that our system has constant but extra costs. Using an example of eID as in [10], we demonstrate that our scheme is effective in spite of the extra costs. Table 3 shows the example of attributes in eID. Generally, the number of string attribute types, L, is much less than the number of finite-set attribute types, $\tilde{L}$. In the conventional system, if a user may own multiple attribute values from an attribute type, we have to prepare bases for the possible multiple values, namely $\tilde{L}$ increases by the number of possible multiple values. For example, a user can have multiple profession attributes such as student and technician in a company, and a user may own 5 or more language ability. As the results, $\tilde{L}$ becomes relatively large. Therefore, from Table2, in the general case that $\tilde{L}$ amounts to about 30–40 and $L \leq 5$, proving AND relation in our system has more efficiency.

Table 3. Example of string and finite-set attributes

String	Finite-set	Example Values
1) name	3) day of issuance	1–31
2) identity number	4) month of issuance	1–12
	5) year of issuance	2000–2011
	6) day of expiration	1–31
	7) month of expiration	1–12
	8) year of expiration	2000–2011
	9) gender	male,female
	10) day of birth	1–31
	11) month of birth	1–12
	12) year of birth	1930–2005
	13) marital status	single,marriage
	14-16) nationality	193 recognized states
	17) hometown	200 allocated cities
	18) city living	200 allocated cities
	19) residence status	citizen,immigrant,...
	20) religion	Moslem,Christian,...
	21) blood type	A,B,O,AB
	22-27) profession	student,teacher,...
	28-30) academic degree	B.S.,M.S,Ph.D.,...
	31-35) major	science,economic,...
	36-45) language	100 allocated lang.
	46-48) social benefit status	none, unemployed, ...
	49-51) eye and hair color	6 hair colors, 8 eye colors
	52-54) minority status	blind, deaf, ...
	...	

In case of OR relation, since the efficiency of the conventional system is influenced by parameter k, our system is more efficient. In [10], an example of OR relation is shown:

$$minority \in \{blind, deaf, ...\} \vee social\_benefit \in \{unemployed, social\_benefit\}$$

$$profession \in \{student, teacher, civil\_servant\} \vee type = kids\_card$$

This example considers that countries grant subsidies for access to cultural institutions to particular groups such children, students, handicapped persons, etc. In this case, $k = 10$ in addition to $L \geq 5$ and $\tilde{L} = 40$, and then our system is more efficient than the conventional one.

Finally, we discuss the concrete values of the public key size. We assume that an element of $\mathcal{G}$ is represented by 256 bits to obtain 256-bit ECC security. We set $L + \tilde{L} = 50$ and $n = 1,000$ to $n = 10,000$. In the conventional system, the public key size is less than 2KBytes. In our system, it becomes about 200KBytes to 2MBytes. In the current mobile environments, the data size is sufficiently practical, since the public key is not changed after it is distributed.

6   Conclusion

In this paper, for a pairing-based anonymous credential system, we have showed how to prove AND and OR relations on his attributes with constant complexity in the number of finite-set attributes. The compensation is the increase of the public key size, although the public key is not changed after it is distributed.

Our future works include the evaluation based on the implementation, and the application to authentications in the mobile environments.

Acknowledgments

This work was supported by Grant-in-Aid for Scientific Research (21300004) from Japan Society for the Promotion of Science (JSPS). We would like to thank the anonymous reviewers.

References

1. Au, M.H., Susilo, W., Mu, Y.: Constant-size dynamic k-TAA. In: De Prisco, R., Yung, M. (eds.) SCN 2006. LNCS, vol. 4116, pp. 111–125. Springer, Heidelberg (2006)
2. Au, M.H., Susilo, W., Mu, Y.: Constant-size dynamic k-TAA. Cryptology ePrint Archive: Report 2008/136 (2008); This is the extended version of [1]
3. Belenkiy, M., Chase, M., Kohlweiss, M., Lysyanskaya, A.: Non-interactive anonymous credentials. Cryptology ePrint Archive: Report 2007/384 (2007)
4. Belenkiy, M., Chase, M., Kohlweiss, M., Lysyanskaya, A.: P-signatures and noninteractive anonymous credentials. In: Canetti, R. (ed.) TCC 2008. LNCS, vol. 4948, pp. 356–374. Springer, Heidelberg (2008)
5. Bichsel, P., Camenisch, J., Groß, T., Shoup, V.: Anonymous credentials on a standard java card. In: Proc. ACM Conference on Computer and Communications Security 2009 (ACM-CCS 2009), pp. 600–610 (2009)
6. Boneh, D., Boyen, X.: Short signatures without random oracles. In: Cachin, C., Camenisch, J.L. (eds.) EUROCRYPT 2004. LNCS, vol. 3027, pp. 56–73. Springer, Heidelberg (2004)
7. Boneh, D., Boyen, X., Shacham, H.: Short group signatures. In: Franklin, M. (ed.) CRYPTO 2004. LNCS, vol. 3152, pp. 41–55. Springer, Heidelberg (2004)
8. Boneh, D., Shacham, H.: Group signatures with verifier-local revocation. In: Proc. 11th ACM Conference on Computer and Communications Security (ACM-CCS 2004), pp. 168–177 (2004)
9. Boyen, X., Waters, B.: Full-domain subgroup hiding and constant-size group signatures. In: Okamoto, T., Wang, X. (eds.) PKC 2007. LNCS, vol. 4450, pp. 1–15. Springer, Heidelberg (2007)
10. Camenisch, J., Groß, T.: Efficient attributes for anonymous credentials. In: Proc. ACM Conference on Computer and Communications Security 2008 (ACM-CCS 2008), pp. 345–356 (2008)
11. Camenisch, J., Kiayias, A., Yung, M.: On the portability of generalized schnorr proofs. In: Joux, A. (ed.) EUROCRYPT 2009. LNCS, vol. 5479, pp. 425–442. Springer, Heidelberg (2009)
12. Camenisch, J., Kohlweiss, M., Soriente, C.: An accumulator based on bilinear maps and efficient revocation for anonymous credentials. In: Jarecki, S., Tsudik, G. (eds.) PKC 2009. LNCS, vol. 5443, pp. 481–500. Springer, Heidelberg (2009)

13. Camenisch, J., Lysyanskaya, A.: Dynamic accumulators and application to efficient revocation of anonymous credentials. In: Yung, M. (ed.) CRYPTO 2002. LNCS, vol. 2442, pp. 61–76. Springer, Heidelberg (2002)
14. Cramer, R., Damgård, I.B., Schoenmakers, B.: Proof of partial knowledge and simplified design of witness hiding protocols. In: Desmedt, Y.G. (ed.) CRYPTO 1994. LNCS, vol. 839, pp. 174–187. Springer, Heidelberg (1994)
15. Furukawa, J., Imai, H.: An efficient group signature scheme from bilinear maps. In: Boyd, C., González Nieto, J.M. (eds.) ACISP 2005. LNCS, vol. 3574, pp. 455–467. Springer, Heidelberg (2005)

A Proving AND and OR Relations in Conventional System

For the reference, we describe proving AND and OR relations in the conventional system.

Certificate. Let L' be the total number of attribute types. Then, the certificate is as follows.

$$A = ((\prod_{1 \le j \le L'} h_j^{M_j}) h_{L'+1}^x g_0^r g)^{1/(X+w)}.$$

Proving AND relation. Let TA be the set of attributes referenced in the proof. Similarly to the proposed system, compute C_A, C_w. Then, prove the knowledge of $x, w, r, \rho_A, \rho_w, \alpha, \rho_\alpha$ and M_j for $M_j \notin$ TA s.t.

$$C_w = g^w \hat{g}^{\rho_w}, 1 = C_w^{\rho_A} g^{-\alpha} \hat{g}^{-\rho_\alpha},$$

$$e(C_A, Y)e((\prod_{1 \le j \le L', M_j \in \text{TA}} h_j^{M_j})g, g)^{-1} = (\prod_{1 \le j \le L', M_j \notin \text{TA}} e(h_j, g)^{M_j})e(h_{L'+1}, g)^x$$

$$\cdot e(g_0, g)^r e(\hat{g}, Y)^{\rho_A} e(\hat{g}, g)^\alpha e(C_A, g)^{-w}.$$

Proving OR relation. Let TA$= \{M'_{j_1}, \ldots, M'_{j_k}\}$ be the set of attributes referenced in the proof, where j_i means the j_i-th attribute types. Let STA be the set of j_i. Similarly to the proposed system, compute C_A, C_w, and additionally $C_j = g^{M_j} \hat{g}^{\rho_j}$ for $\rho_j \in_R Z_p^*$ with $j \in$ STA. Then, prove the knowledge of $x, w, r, \rho_A, \rho_w, \alpha, \rho_\alpha$, all M_j, and $\rho_{j'}$ for $j' \in$ STA s.t.

$$C_w = g^w \hat{g}^{\rho_w}, 1 = C_w^{\rho_A} g^{-\alpha} \hat{g}^{-\rho_\alpha},$$

$$e(C_A, Y)e(g, g)^{-1} = (\prod_{1 \le j \le L', j \in \text{STA}} e(h_j, g)^{M_j})(\prod_{1 \le j \le L', j \notin \text{STA}} e(h_j, g)^{M_j})$$

$$\cdot e(h_{L'+1}, g)^x e(g_0, g)^r e(\hat{g}, Y)^{\rho_A} e(\hat{g}, g)^\alpha e(C_A, g)^{-w},$$

$$C_j = g^{M_j} \hat{g}^{\rho_j} \text{(for } j \in \text{STA)},$$

Additionally, prove

$$C_{j_1}/g^{M'_{j_1}} = \hat{g}^{\rho_{j_1}} \vee \cdots \vee C_{j_k}/g^{M'_{j_k}} = \hat{g}^{\rho_{j_k}}.$$

This *PK* for OR relation on representations is described in [14].

Broker-Based Private Matching

Abdullatif Shikfa[1], Melek Önen[2], and Refik Molva[2]

[1] Alcatel-Lucent Bell Labs,
Route de Villejust, 91620 Nozay, France
[2] EURECOM,
2229, route des crêtes, 06560 Sophia Antipolis cedex, France

Abstract. Private matching solutions allow two parties to find common data elements over their own datasets without revealing any additional private information. We propose a new concept involving an intermediate entity in the private matching process: we consider the problem of broker-based private matching where end-entities do not interact with each other but communicate through a third entity, namely the Broker, which only discovers the number of matching elements. Although introducing this third entity enables a complete decoupling between end-entities (which may even not know each other), this advantage comes at the cost of higher exposure in terms of privacy and security. After defining the security requirements dedicated to this new concept, we propose a complete solution which combines searchable encryption techniques together with counting Bloom filters to preserve the privacy of end-entities and provide the proof of the matching correctness, respectively.

1 Introduction

Imagine that a company has an opening for a new position. The posting for new position consists mainly of requirements in terms of education, professional experience and skills. So the company has many selection criteria and is looking for the best suited candidate. Since the company does not want to take care of all the recruitment process itself, it delegates the search phase to a recruitment agency, which is more capable in terms of publishing the posting for new position on a large scale. Candidates are characterized first by their resume and they apply through the recruiting agency if they think they are fit for the job. The recruitment agency upon receiving a resume, looks at the matching ratio between the candidate characteristics and the posting's criteria and calls the best suited candidates for an interview at the company. The best suited candidates are either all candidates above a certain matching ratio threshold, or the top ten candidates for example. In order to prevent resume fraud, candidates should be able to prove the correctness of their resume, with diplomas from a university or validation of experience from a governmental agency.

This interesting scenario raises many security issues. First of all, both company and candidates' privacy should be preserved. The company does indeed not want that competitors learn about the posting, especially if it concerns an

S. Fischer-Hübner and N. Hopper (Eds.): PETS 2011, LNCS 6794, pp. 264–284, 2011.

important position because that would give a hint about the company's strategy. So the posting and more specifically the criteria expressed by the company should remain secret from other companies, including the recruitment agency. Candidates' privacy should also be preserved, to enforce equal opportunities among candidates. Therefore resumes should be confidential and anonymous to prevent the recruiting agency from discriminating between candidates on a non-professional basis. The problem is therefore to be able to compute the matching ratio between the posting's criteria and the candidates' resumes while both are encrypted. Furthermore it is important that candidates cannot forge their resume to obtain a higher matching ratio. This problem is especially hard since resumes cannot be checked directly in the case where they are encrypted: privacy and verification present conflicting requirements.

At first glance this problem has a flavor of private matching or private set intersection, whereby two parties want to learn only shared attributes without learning any information about the remaining ones. There is yet an important difference in the presented scenario which makes the problem more complex: the parties owning the private data (the company and the candidates) do not directly interact with each other, but they forward their secret data to a third party. This third party has to take a decision on the matching ratio without having any control or knowledge on the private data it received, and it should not be able to learn anything about the private data of either party in the process: it should just be able to securely compute the matching ratio (it should not even be able to tell which of the encrypted data matched or not). This paper therefore tackles with a new requirement for parties not to interact directly to achieve the matching result thus calling for a non-interactive solution.

In this paper, we analyze the requirements for the non-interactive and private computation of matching ratio and present a complete solution to address this issue. The solution is based on a searchable encryption scheme introduced by Boneh et al. in [3] used in a new mode of operation to allow the company to issue a unique query for all potential (and unknown) candidates. The solution further makes use of counting Bloom filters introduced by Fan et al. in [11], but in a radically new approach: those counting Bloom filters are not used as usual to prove the belonging of an element to a set but to compute the matching ratio without leaking privacy and to provide evidence of the correctness of the matching ratio computation. This solution presents the following advantages:

- it addresses the non-interactive scenario as it does not require the parties owning the private data to interact with each other (such as setting up keys prior to the matching process for example) or even to know each other,
- it allows a third party to compute the matching ratio and to get evidence of its correctness,
- it preserves the privacy of data, because the third party processes encrypted data blindly (in the sense that it handles encrypted data and does not learn any information about it),

- it is efficient, because the third party, which has to process a lot of data from several users, only needs to perform few and non-costly operations for the computation of each matching ratio.

The rest of the paper is structured as follows. Section 2 motivates the need for a broker-based private matching protocol comparing it with the classical two-party mechanisms, defines the security requirements and describes the underlying mechanisms. In section 3, the overall protocol and its security primitives are described in detail. The security and performance of the proposed protocol are evaluated in section 4. Finally, section 5 discusses relevant related work.

2 Problem Statement

2.1 Private Matching: Introducing a Third Party

The classical private matching scheme is a two-party protocol that enables both parties P_1 and P_2 to discover common data elements over their own datasets without revealing any additional private information. Assuming that P_1 and P_2 respectively own datasets X_1 and X_2, at the end of the private matching protocol P_1 and P_2 only learn $X_1 \cap X_2$.

In this paper, we propose a complete decoupling between these two parties in order to perform the same operation when the two parties do not interact and are even not aware of each other. The new protocol involves a third party, the Broker, which is in charge of computing the cardinality of the matching set without discovering any of its elements. Private and correct evaluation of the cardinality of the matching set by a third party has many applications, in particular for ranking, or finding friends in social networks or simply in dating sites, and compelling new applications are envisioned in the broad field of cloud computing. All these applications require a third party to take decisions while remaining oblivious to the matched information. This new broker-based private matching protocol consists of three entities, namely the **Query Issuer**, the **Subject** and the **Broker**, where the latter's main role is to discover the cardinality of the matching set originating from the other two entities' datasets. Each entity's role in the new protocol is formally defined as follows:

- the **Query Issuer** $\mathcal{QI}$ issues a query $Q_i = \langle q_{i,1}, ..., q_{i,n} \rangle$ consisting of n selection criteria which are elements of D, the global dataset. In the recruitment example, the company is the Query Issuer and an example of selection criterion could be "Degree = MSc".
- **Subjects** $\mathcal{S}^l$ ($1 \leq l \leq c$), answers a query Q_i with a matching proof $mp_{i,l}$ based on its profile. Each Subject is indeed characterized by a profile $P^l = \langle p_1^l, ..., p_m^l \rangle$ composed of m attributes which are elements of the same dataset D. These attributes are evaluated with respect to the query defined by the Query Issuer. In the aforementioned scenario, Subjects correspond to the candidates in the recruitment process.

– the additional party, namely the **Broker** $\mathcal{B}$, first publishes the query of $\mathcal{QI}$ to Subjects and collects their answers. The Broker then selects the best suited Subjects: $\mathcal{B}$ computes a matching ratio $\rho_{i,l}$ between a query Q_i and the Subject's answer $mp_{i,l}$ defined as the cardinality of the matching set between the selection criteria and the attributes over the cardinality of the selection criteria. In the example, the Broker is the recruiting agency.

In summary, the major difference between classical private matching and the broker-based private matching protocol is the fact that there is no direct interaction between the Query Issuer $\mathcal{QI}$ and Subjects $\mathcal{S}^l$. All messages go through the Broker $\mathcal{B}$, which is an active entity in the protocol and not a simple relay: the query Q_i of $\mathcal{QI}$ is sent to $\mathcal{B}$ which then publishes it to $\{\mathcal{S}^l\}_{1\le l\le c}$; each Subject $\mathcal{S}^l$ sends its answer $mp_{i,l}$ to $\mathcal{B}$ which decides which Subjects correspond to the query the best. Therefore, $\mathcal{QI}$ should be able to send a query without even knowing the Subjects $\{\mathcal{S}^l\}_{1\le l\le c}$: there is a complete decoupling between these two entities, and $\mathcal{B}$ is in charge of gathering the necessary data and taking the appropriate decision. Finally $\mathcal{QI}$ should be able to send a query with any selection criteria and is not limited to a set that it owns.

2.2   Security Requirements

The introduction of a third party in the private matching protocol requires to revisit all security requirements defined for the two-party protocol.

First of all, we assume that the Query Issuer is interested in getting the best suited Subjects; therefore $\mathcal{QI}$ is assumed to be honest. On the contrary, Subjects are considered to be potentially malicious, because it is in their interest to exhibit a high matching ratio in order to be selected by the Broker. Therefore Subjects might attempt to cheat on their attributes or more generally in the answer they send to $\mathcal{B}$ in order to lure $\mathcal{B}$ into computing a matching ratio higher than their real matching ratio. However we consider that nodes are selfish and that they do not collude with each other.

Concerning the Broker $\mathcal{B}$, we assume it to be honest but curious: $\mathcal{B}$ correctly executes the protocol and computes the matching ratio according to the data it receives, and finally sends to $\mathcal{QI}$ the truly best suited Subjects according to the matching ratio rankings. Yet, $\mathcal{B}$ is curious in the sense that it is interested in unveiling information from the private data it receives, whether being the selection criteria of the query of $\mathcal{QI}$ or the attributes of Subjects.

There are thus two main attacks to be considered:

– attacks by the Broker in an attempt to break the privacy of the other two entities: $\mathcal{B}$ tries to discover and reveal the content of the query of $\mathcal{QI}$, or to discover the attributes of one or many Subjects,
– attacks by Subjects aiming at illegitimately increasing their matching ratio with a given query.

This leads to the following two security requirements:

– **Preserving the privacy of the end entities $\mathcal{QI}$ and $\mathcal{S}^l$**: queries issued by $\mathcal{QI}$ and answers of Subjects are confidential and therefore encrypted. The

Broker should be able to compute the matching ratio using these two encrypted values without discovering any information about either the criteria of $\mathcal{QI}$ or the Subject's attributes: the protocol should be semantically secure. Furthermore, as for classical private matching protocol, since the query is forwarded by $\mathcal{B}$ to Subjects, these entities should not be able to derive information about non-matching criteria. These privacy properties can also be formally defined by comparing the real situation in our protocol with an ideal situation where the protocol is run by a trusted external entity, but we do not add this formalization in this article for the sake of clarity.

– **Guaranteeing the correctness of the matching ratio**: the answer $mp_{i,l}$ of a Subject $\mathcal{S}^l$ should enable the Broker to correctly compute the matching ratio between the query Q_i and the attributes of $\mathcal{S}^l$. This requirement is very different from the privacy one, but the latter hardens the task of verifying the correctness of the matching ratio. Indeed, a simple solution to this provably correct matching ratio computation would consist in the Subjects sending their attributes to the Broker, but this solution blatantly exposes the privacy of the Subjects. The challenge for the Broker is to be able to compute the matching ratio corresponding to a set of attributes while verifying their correctness without having access to their content.

2.3 Security Primitives

Based on the security requirements of the broker-based private matching protocol, we define the following security primitives:

– SQE (Secure Query Encoding): in order to ensure the confidentiality of the query Q_i, this primitive, used by the Query Issuer $\mathcal{QI}$, securely encodes Q_i and returns Q_i'. $\mathcal{QI}$ can express its queries on any selection criteria in the global dataset D, hence SQE should be a public function in that it should not require any secret information on input. Furthermore, this function should be randomized to prevent dictionary attacks.
– SLU (Secure Look-up): A Subject $\mathcal{S}^l$ uses this primitive to look-up its attributes against an encoded query, and outputs the corresponding answer $mp_{i,l}$. This function should be public but requires secret information (credentials) to be processed.
– SMRC (Secure Matching Ratio Computation): on input of a Q_i' and a corresponding $mp_{i,l}$, this primitive first verifies the correctness of $mp_{i,l}$:
  1. if $mp_{i,l}$ is invalid ($\mathcal{S}^l$ attempted to cheat), the process breaks;
  2. otherwise, the primitive outputs the correct matching ratio $\rho_{i,l}$.

In the next section, these three primitives are formally described based on a combination of different cryptographic mechanisms: searchable encryption and counting Bloom filters.

3   Solution

We now present our solution by first introducing the underlying mechanisms and further by formally describing the overall protocol divided into two phases.

3.1   Overview

In order to allow the correct execution of the new protocol, Subjects first need to retrieve their credentials (private information corresponding to their profile) from a certain authority that approves their validity. Therefore, a trusted authority is initially available during a setup phase. This authority does not play any role during the execution of the matching protocol, namely the runtime phase.

In this second phase, the broker-based private matching protocol actually takes place, and it features four main steps:

1. Query: The Query Issuer $\mathcal{QI}$ issues a query Q_i. It encodes this query using the SQE primitive and sends the result Q'_i to the Broker. Based on the query Q_i, $\mathcal{QI}$ also constructs a counting Bloom filter CBF_i, called a matching reference and sends it to the Broker along with the encoded query.
2. Publish: The Broker publishes the encoded query $Q'i$ to all Subjects. The matching reference is not forwarded.
3. Look-up: Each subject $\mathcal{S}^l$ looks-up its credentials in the encoded query Q'_i to determine which conditions $\mathcal{S}^l$ matches. Based on these matched conditions, $\mathcal{S}^l$ constructs another counting Bloom filter $CBF_{i,l}$, called a matching proof. This matching proof $mp_{i,l}$ is sent to the Broker.
4. Verify: The Broker compares the matching reference and the matching proof to assess first whether the matching proof is valid or not, and then to compute the matching ratio $\rho_{i,l}$. Finally, the Broker informs $\mathcal{QI}$ about the Subjects best suited to its query Q_i.

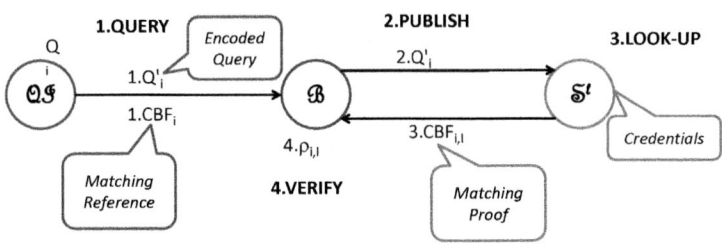

Fig. 1. High level description of the protocol

The protocol is summarized in figure 1. A major advantage of our solution is that it enables some computation on encrypted data to preserve end-entities privacy: the Broker is able to compute the matching ratio based on two encrypted data structures, the matching reference and the matching proof. This computation on encrypted data is achieved thanks to an extension of a searchable encryption mechanism that allows a third node to verify whether an encrypted keyword is included in a database or not. This mechanism is also combined with counting Bloom filters in order to prove the correctness of the computation of the matching ratio. Before formally describing the new protocol, these two mechanisms are briefly presented in the next section.

3.2   Background-Tools

Searchable encryption. Searchable encryption is a general concept which enables a third entity to store an encrypted list destined to a certain party and to look-up encrypted keywords on behalf of this party without learning additional information both on the keyword and the encrypted list.

One of the main searchable encryption approaches was proposed by Boneh et al. in [3] and it uses three main operations:

- SE-Encrypt: a public encryption function used to encrypt the list that is stored by the third party. This function requires the knowledge of the public key of the destination.
- SE-Trapdoor: a private function which gives the capability of looking-up a specific keyword, called a trapdoor. This function requires the private key of the recipient and hence can only be computed by the recipient.
- SE-Test: on input of a trapdoor and an encrypted keyword, the third party uses this operation to verify whether the private keyword is included in the list or not. Hence, this function returns 1 if the trapdoor corresponds to the encrypted keyword and 0 otherwise.

Due to its non-interactivity this searchable encryption proposal looks appropriate for the new broker-based private matching scenario, where the SE-Test operation can be implemented by the Broker while Query Issuers may encrypt some keywords with SE-Encrypt and the Subjects run the SE-Trapdoor. Unfortunately, the use of this mechanism is not straightforward because:

- As opposed to the SE-Test operation, the Broker should only be able to compute the global matching ratio and not individual matching attributes;
- The Query Issuer does not know the Subjects in advance, hence it does not have knowledge of their public keys and cannot use SE-Encrypt easily.

To circumvent these two main constraints, we propose to introduce a Trusted Third Party which alleviates the requirement of the knowledge of the (unknown) recipient's public key in our scheme (see section 3.3).

Bloom filters. A Bloom filter is a probabilistic data structure which was first introduced by Burton Bloom ([5]). The classical use of Bloom filters is to test whether an element is a member of a set in a space-efficient way. We focus on an extension of Bloom filters called counting Bloom filters that were proposed by Fan et al. in [11] to support the dynamic deletion of an element.

A counting Bloom filter. CBF is an array of ϕ positions (also called buckets) used to represent a set $\mathcal{X}$ with the aid of u hash functions $\{h_1, .., h_u\}$ mapping an element of $\mathcal{X}$ to one of the ϕ array positions. Counting Bloom filters implement the following three functions:

- Insert(x, CBF): on input of an element x, the digest of this element is computed using each of the u hash functions. The values of the filter CBF at these positions are incremented by 1.
- Query(x, CBF): this function verifies with a certain probability whether x is an element of the filter or not.

– Delete(x, CBF): this operation consists of decrementing the value at each of the u positions resulting from the hash functions evaluated over x, by 1.

In the sequel of this article, we denote by CBF($x_1, ..., x_n$) the counting Bloom filter obtained by inserting the elements x_i for $1 \leq i \leq n$.

The weight w_{CBF} of a counting Bloom filter CBF is defined as the sum of the values of all positions: $w_{CBF} = \sum_{0 \leq i \leq \phi - 1} CBF[i]$. An important property of counting Bloom filters is that the weight w_{CBF} of a counting Bloom filter CBF is linearly dependent on the number of elements inserted in it:

$$w_{\text{CBF}(x_1, ..., x_n)} = n \cdot u.$$

Hence, counting Bloom filters are useful for our broker-based private matching as they enable computing the cardinality of a set without revealing the elements of the set (see section 3.3).

3.3   Construction

As mentioned in section 3.1, the solution features two phases: a setup phase where Subjects retrieve their credentials, and a runtime phase where the private matching protocol is executed.

Setup phase. Contrary to $\mathcal{QI}$ which can choose any selection criteria in Q_i, $\mathcal{S}^l$ should answer Q'_i correctly based on their profile. Since the correctness of private matching operations depends on the correctness of these profiles, the latter should be certified, and we refer to the certified attributes as credentials. These credentials are retrieved during a setup phase which features a fourth entity, called the **Authority** $\mathcal{A}$. This Authority is required to define general parameters of the system and to provide Subjects with their matching credentials.

The general parameters are generated according to a security parameter which impacts the size of the groups that are used, as well as the size of keys. In particular, the Authority generates a private and public key pair $sk_\mathcal{A}/pk_\mathcal{A}$. In the recruitment example, universities delivering a diploma or governmental agencies can be considered as authorities.

In addition to the three security primitives defined in section 2.3, we define a fourth one, SCE (Secure Credential Extraction), which is used by $\mathcal{A}$ to provide $\mathcal{S}^l$ with the credentials corresponding to its profile (this primitive is similar to the private key extraction primitive in Identity-Based Encryption). On input of a Subject's profile, SCE returns a set of credentials. These credentials are used as matching capabilities and correspond to trapdoors in searchable encryption.

To be more precise, Subjects $\mathcal{S}^l$ first contact the Authority $\mathcal{A}$ and show their profile $P^l = \langle p_1^l, ... p_m^l \rangle$. $\mathcal{A}$ verifies the validity of P^l (this verification step is out of the scope of this paper), and then provides $\mathcal{S}^l$ with the corresponding credentials T^l which are computed using the SE-Trapdoor function applied over the Subject's attributes and the secret key of $\mathcal{A}$. Hence, at the end of the setup phase, each $\mathcal{S}^l$ receives the following set of credentials:

$$T^l = \langle t_1^l, ..., t_m^l \rangle = \langle \text{SE-Trapdoor}(p_1^l, sk_\mathcal{A}), ..., \text{SE-Trapdoor}(p_m^l, sk_\mathcal{A}) \rangle.$$

Runtime phase. As described in section 3.1, the runtime phase consists of four main steps that we describe formally in the following:

1. **Query:** During this step, $\mathcal{QI}$ expresses a query Q_i by choosing a set of selection criteria and performs a secure encoding of the query using the SQE primitive. The output of this primitive are the encoded query Q_i' and the matching reference mr_i: $\mathtt{SQE}(Q_i, pk_A) = (Q_i', mr_i)$.

   As previously introduced, the SQE primitive should be a randomized public cryptographic function, such as SE-Encrypt. However, SE-Encrypt requires the public key of the recipient and this key is unknown to $\mathcal{QI}$, hence we propose a new configuration where the public key of $\mathcal{A}$ is used instead. Therefore, the encoded query is computed as follows:
   $$Q_i' = \langle q_{i,1}', ..., q_{i,n}' \rangle = \langle \mathtt{SE\text{-}Encrypt}(q_{i,1}, pk_A), ..., \mathtt{SE\text{-}Encrypt}(q_{i,n}, pk_A) \rangle.$$
   On the other hand, the matching reference should help the Broker to compute the matching ratio correctly. To this extent, during the execution of the SE-Encrypt algorithm, $\mathcal{QI}$ also retrieves some intermediate values which can only be computed by itself or by the nodes that own the corresponding trapdoors. Indeed, the SE-Encrypt primitive makes use of a cryptographic hash function H at the last step of the computation[1]. For $1 \leq j \leq n$, we denote the preimage of $q_{i,j}'$ by $x_{i,j}$:
   $$q_{i,j}' = \mathtt{SE\text{-}Encrypt}(q_{i,j}, pk_A) = H(x_{i,j}).$$
   Thanks to the inherent security of the hash functions with pseudorandom inputs, a malicious user cannot compute $x_{i,j}$ based on the knowledge of $q_{i,j}'$. Hence, $\mathcal{QI}$ constructs the matching reference mr_i as a counting Bloom filter CBF_i, in which it inserts the elements $x_{i,j}$ for $1 \leq j \leq n$:
   $$mr_i = CBF_i = \mathtt{CBF}(x_{i,1}, ..., x_{i,n}).$$
   At the end of this first step, $\mathcal{QI}$ sends mr_i and Q_i' to the Broker.

2. **Publish:** The Broker forwards the encoded query Q_i' to all Subjects but keeps the matching reference mr_i.

3. **Look-up:** On input of an encoded query Q_i' and a set of credentials T^l, the SLU primitive returns a matching proof $mp_{i,l}$:
   $$\mathtt{SLU}(Q_i', T^l) = mp_{i,l}.$$
   By using the SE-Test function, Subjects can indeed detect selection criteria corresponding to their profile: for $1 \leq j \leq n, 1 \leq k \leq m$ $\mathtt{SE\text{-}Test}(q_{i,j}', t_k^l)$ returns 1 for matching elements and 0 for the others. Moreover, the Subject can compute the corresponding preimage $x_{i,j}$ for matching criteria. Hence S^l can construct a counting Bloom filter $CBF_{i,l}$ in which it includes all the preimages that it managed to compute and which is used as matching proof $mp_{i,l} = CBF_{i,l}$ and sent to the Broker.

4. **Verify:** On input of a matching reference mr_i and a matching proof $mp_{i,l}$ the primitive SMRC returns a matching ratio $\rho_{i,l}$.

   The Broker first compares the counting Bloom filters CBF_i and $CBF_{i,l}$ to assess the validity of the latter. To this extent, the Broker checks whether:

---

[1] See [3] for the detailed construction of PEKS. We roughly have $x_{i,j} = \hat{e}(H_1(q_{i,j}), r \cdot pk_A)$, and $q_{i,j}' = \langle rP, H(x_{i,j}) \rangle$, where $\hat{e}$ is a bilinear map, r a random scalar, and P a point on an elliptic curve.

- $\forall 0 \leq i_1 \leq \phi - 1, CBF_{i,l}[i_1] \prec CBF_i[i_1]$ denoted as $CBF_{i,l} \prec CBF_i$, otherwise it means that $CBF_{i,l}$ was not constructed only with (a subset of) $x_{i,1}, ...x_{i,n}$,
- the weight $w_{CBF_{i,l}}$ of $CBF_{i,l}$ is a multiple of u, because each inserted element leads to an increase of the weight by u.

If one of the verifications fails, the protocol aborts (the Subject attempted to cheat), otherwise the Broker accepts the answer of $\mathcal{S}^l$ as being valid and computes the matching ratio as follows:

$$\mathsf{SMRC}(mr_i, mp_{i,l}) = \frac{w_{CBF_{i,l}}}{w_{CBF_i}}.$$

The protocol is consistent in that:

Proposition 1. *If $CBF_{i,l}$ is generated as specified in the protocol, then the matching ratio between the query and the attributes of a Subject corresponds to the output of SMRC:*

$$\rho_{i,l} = \mathsf{SMRC}(mr_i, mp_{i,l}).$$

This proposition is a direct consequence of the fact that the weight of a counting Bloom filter is linearly dependent with the number of its elements.

This concludes the presentation of our solution, and we now evaluate its security and performance.

4   Evaluation

The security of the new broker-based private matching protocol is analyzed based on the attacker model and the security requirements defined in section 2.2. We assume that the communication channels between $\mathcal{QI}$ and $\mathcal{B}$ and between $\mathcal{B}$ and $\mathcal{S}^l$ are secured, hence eavesdroppers cannot access the messages exchanged in the protocol in clear. They thus have less information than any of the entities running the protocol, and we do not further take them into account.

4.1   Privacy

Privacy is the most important requirement in classical private matching. In this section, we assume that entities are curious and try to discover information that they should not access. We first show that our solution preserves the privacy of end-entities and we further prove that the introduction of a third party (the Broker) does not threaten the Query Issuer's and Subjects' privacy.

First, the privacy of the $\mathcal{QI}$ is preserved with respect to $\mathcal{S}^l$. Indeed, in [3], Boneh et al. proved that their construction is semantically secure against a chosen keyword attack in the random oracle model, assuming that the Bilinear Diffie-Hellman problem is hard. It is thus unfeasible for an entity to discover the value of an encoded selection criteria unless it knows the corresponding trapdoor, in other words $\mathcal{S}^l$ can only discover the matching selection criteria.

Furthermore, since only the Authority $\mathcal{A}$ knows the private key $sk_{\mathcal{A}}$, nodes cannot forge trapdoors. Recovering the private key $sk_{\mathcal{A}}$ amounts to a discrete logarithm computation which is assumed to be hard.

Second, we prove that the introduction of $\mathcal{B}$ does not threaten the privacy of end-entities. On one hand, as an intermediate node, $\mathcal{B}$ receives the same encoded queries that $\mathcal{S}^l$ receives, but $\mathcal{B}$ has no trapdoors and thus cannot discover the value of the encoded queries. Furthermore, $\mathcal{B}$ cannot link successive queries even if they correspond to the same selection criteria because the encoding mechanism is inherently randomized. On the other hand, in addition to the queries, $\mathcal{B}$ receives matching reference and matching proofs from $\mathcal{QI}$ and $\mathcal{S}^l$ respectively. As proven in the following theorem, the knowledge of a counting Bloom filter does not enable the Broker to recover the elements $x_{i,j}$ inserted in it.

Theorem 1. *Let $x_1, ..., x_n$ be n elements randomly chosen from a group G of order q. Let CBF be a counting Bloom filter of size ϕ in which the n elements $x_1, ..., x_n$ were inserted using u hash functions $h_1, ..., h_u$. Then, there are more than $\frac{q}{\phi^u}$ possible sets of elements of G^n leading to the same counting Bloom filter:*

$$|\{(x'_1, ..., x'_n) \in G^n | CBF(x'_1, ..., x'_n) = CBF(x_1, ..., x_n)\}| > \frac{q}{\phi^u}$$

The proof is given in section 7.1. This result is a lower bound on the set of preimages but the actual result can be multiplied by a factor of up to $u!$ depending on the outputs of the hash functions, and is multiplied even further if more elements are inserted. Note that this result does not even take into account the complexity required to find the corresponding set of preimages.

From the perspective of an attacker, being able to solve the equations would lead to an advantage as it reduces the size of the space of possibilities from q down to $\frac{q}{\phi^u}$. However, careful setting of the parameters q, ϕ and u, makes the size of this set large enough to prevent brute force guessing (see section 7.3).

In summary, the counting Bloom filter cannot be reversed to obtain the entries that were inserted in it, which guarantees the privacy of the Query Issuer and Subjects. We now focus on the security of the matching ratio computation.

4.2   Correctness of the Matching Ratio

Concerning the security of the matching ratio computation, we consider now a malicious $\mathcal{S}^l$ trying to convince $\mathcal{B}$ that its matching ratio is higher than its actual value, and we show that the probability of success of such an attack is negligible.

To be more precise, we assume that $\mathcal{S}^l$ does not know the matching reference mr_i, thus the only information known by $\mathcal{S}^l$ on CBF_i are the global parameters: the hash functions used $h_1, ..., h_u$ and the size ϕ. $\mathcal{S}^l$ also knows Q'_i and therefore the number n of elements $x_{i,j}$ inserted in CBF_i.

The goal of the malicious $\mathcal{S}^l$ is to claim a matching ratio $\rho_{i,l}^{claim}$ higher than the actual ratio $\rho_{i,l}$. To this extent, $\mathcal{S}^l$ needs to claim a corresponding counting Bloom filter $CBF_{i,l}^{claim}$. For $\mathcal{S}^l$ to be successful, $CBF_{i,l}^{claim}$ has to verify the following conditions:

1. it should be considered valid by $\mathcal{B}$, as required by the last step of the protocol described in section 3.3, which implies that:
   - $CBF_{i,l}^{claim} \prec CBF_i$,
   - the weight $w_{CBF_{i,l}^{claim}}$ of $CBF_{i,l}^{claim}$ is a multiple of u,
2. it should lead to $\rho_{i,l}^{claim} > \rho_{i,l}$, hence the weight of $CBF_{i,l}^{claim}$ needs to verify $w_{CBF_{i,l}^{claim}} > w_{CBF_i}$.

The probability of success of $\mathcal{S}^l$ is exponentially decreasing in the malicious ratio increment $\rho_{i,l}^{claim} - \rho_{i,l}$, as shown in the following theorem.

Theorem 2. *Let Q_i' be an encoded query concerning n selection criteria. Let CBF_i be the corresponding matching reference.*

The probability of success $\mathcal{P}_{adv}[\rho_{i,l} \to \rho_{i,l}^{claim}]$ of an adversary $\mathcal{S}^l$ in generating an array $CBF_{i,l}^{claim}$ which is accepted by $\mathcal{B}$ and results in an increase of the matching ratio from $\rho_{i,l}$ to $\rho_{i,l}^{claim}$ is upper bounded by:

$$\mathcal{P}_{adv}[\rho_{i,l} \to \rho_{i,l}^{claim}] \leq \left(1 - e^{-\frac{(1-\rho_{i,l})n \cdot u}{\phi}}\right)^{(\rho_{i,l}^{claim} - \rho_{i,l})n \cdot u}$$

The proof is given in section 7.2. The formula of $\mathcal{P}_{adv}[\rho_{i,l} \to \rho_{i,l}^{claim}]$ shows that the probability of success of an adversary decreases exponentially with the malicious ratio increase $(\rho_{i,l}^{claim} - \rho_{i,l})$ and, decreases also depending on the value of the legitimate matching ratio $\rho_{i,l}$.

It is possible to go further and bound $\mathcal{P}_{adv}[\rho_{i,l} \to \rho_{i,l}^{claim}]$ independently of $\rho_{i,l}$ and $\rho_{i,l}^{claim}$, by observing that:

- the function $x \mapsto \alpha^x$ decreases with x for $0 < \alpha < 1$,
- $0 < \left(1 - e^{-\frac{(1-\rho_{i,l})n \cdot u}{\phi}}\right) < \left(1 - e^{-\frac{n \cdot u}{\phi}}\right) < 1$,
- $u < (\rho_{i,l}^{claim} - \rho_{i,l})n \cdot u$.

Hence, the probability of success of the adversary is bounded by $\mathcal{P}_{adv}$:

$$\mathcal{P}_{adv} = \left(1 - e^{-\frac{n \cdot u}{\phi}}\right)^u.$$

The security of the scheme hence depends on the general parameters of the counting Bloom filter and we now show how to optimize these settings.

First of all, we assume that the maximum number of selection criteria in a query is bounded and known in advance; we designate it as n_{max}. For all queries, the probability of success of the adversary is thus bounded by

$$\mathcal{P}_{adv} \leq \left(1 - e^{-\frac{n_{max}u}{\phi}}\right)^u.$$

If we fix ϕ, then the function $p_{max} : u \mapsto \left(1 - e^{-\frac{n_{max}u}{\phi}}\right)^u$ is C^∞ on $[1, +\infty[$, and it reaches its minimum in $u_0 = \frac{\phi}{n_{max}}ln(2)$ and $p_{max}(u_0) = 2^{-u_0}$. Therefore, for a fixed n_{max}, increasing u and ϕ exponentially increases the security, but increasing ϕ linearly impacts on the performance of the scheme. We propose the following strategy to optimize the trade-off between security and performance:

1. Set n_{max} the maximum number of criteria per query,
2. Choose a security parameter u: $\mathcal{P}_{adv}$ is then bounded by 2^{-u},
3. Set the size ϕ of the counting Bloom filter as $\phi = \left\lceil \frac{n_{max}u}{\ln(2)} \right\rceil$.

This strategy prioritizes security over performance: it defines the desired security level ($\mathcal{P}_{adv} \leq 2^{-u}$) and then sets the minimal size ϕ to achieve this security level. Note that u does not need to be very large, because $\mathcal{P}_{adv}$ is an upper bound and is obtained with very restrictive conditions:

- $n = n_{max}$, which means that $\mathcal{QI}$ uses n_{max} selection criteria,
- $\mathcal{S}^l$ has a legitimate matching ratio of 0 ($\rho_{i,l} = 0$).

With these conditions, $\mathcal{S}^l$ has a probability less than 2^{-u} of success in making $\mathcal{B}$ believe that its matching ratio is $1/n_{max}$ instead of 0. In many cases, this would not be of any use to the attacker, because the attacker needs to claim the highest matching ratio among the Subjects in order to take advantage of its attack. The attacker does not even know the matching ratio of the other Subjects, so the only way for the malicious $\mathcal{S}^l$ to be sure to benefit from its attack is to claim a matching ratio of 1, and the probability of $\mathcal{S}^l$ succeeding falls down to $2^{-u \cdot n_{max}}$.

4.3   Performance Evaluation

Following the analysis of the trade-off between security and performance in the previous section, we now evaluate the overall communication and computational overhead resulting from the proposed protocol.

Communication overhead. We consider that the cost originating from the setup phase is negligible given that it takes place offline. We only evaluate the communication overhead during the runtime phase.

The size of encoded queries is linear in the number of selection criteria that it includes. Each encoded criterion is the output of the SE-Encrypt primitive and thus has size $2q$ bits, where q is the size of the group used in the searchable encryption scheme.

Concerning the size of counting Bloom filters, they are arrays containing ϕ buckets. According to [11], we choose $\beta = 4$ bits for the size of each bucket to keep a negligible probability of overflow, thus the communication overhead incurred by the matching reference or the matching proof is 4ϕ bits.

Computational overhead. The primitives of searchable encryption rely on elliptic curve operations which cost is of the same order of magnitude as classical asymmetric cryptography [18]. The most costly operation is the pairing computation: our mechanism requires one pairing computation per encoding and one per SE-Test evaluation, the cost is thus linear in the number of selection criteria used in the queries. In comparison, the cost of generating the counting Bloom filters which amounts to $n \cdot u$ hash computations is negligible.

The aforementioned computations are performed by the end-entities, but the Broker only carries on simple operations to compute the matching ratio:

- $\mathcal{B}$ verifies that the matching proof is smaller than the matching reference which requires ϕ integers inequality checks,
- $\mathcal{B}$ computes the weight of the matching proof and reference (a sum of ϕ integers) and performs a division.

The overhead on $\mathcal{B}$ is thus very small which shows that our scheme is scalable and efficient to disseminate a query to multiple Subjects.

5   Related work

Several previously studied problems in the literature show similarities with broker-based private matching. We list them in two main categories and show how they differ from our problem.

5.1   Private Matching and Private Set Intersection

Private matching came up as a generalization of private equality tests. A first approach introduced a Trusted Third Party (TTP) as proposed in [2] and [15]. In theses proposals, the TTP is completely trusted, computes $X_1 \cap X_2$ and sends the result back to P_1 and P_2. This solution is not satisfying from a privacy perspective as it is fully dependent on the honesty of the TTP which has full access to the parties' sets. This three-party protocol is thus very different from our broker-based private matching solution.

In [1], Agrawal et al. propose a protocol performing private matching without a TTP, building on a previous work by Huberman et al. [14] by using a pair of commutative encryption schemes. Building on this work, Li et al. formalize in [17] the security requirements of private matching and identify the issue of spoofing, which consists in one of the entities claiming elements that it does not own. The issue of spoofing is similar to Subjects cheating in their matching proof (however this issue is not relevant for the Query Issuer). To solve this issue, Li et al. further introduce a Trusted Third Party which provides Data Ownership Certificates (similar to the Authority providing credentials) and propose a modified version of the Agrawal protocol.

A different approach was investigated by Freedman et al. in [12]: they propose a solution derived from secret sharing protocols based on Oblivious Polynomial Evaluation. They also study some variants of private matching, among which the private cardinality matching, which is very close to our matching ratio computation. The solution for the latter is only proposed for semi-honest parties but the case of malicious entities is not considered. Kissner and Song [16] proposed multi-party protocols that apply to several set operations (including set intersection) and that are secure in the presence of honest-but-curious adversaries. They also propose a construction secure in the presence of malicious adversaries based on zero-knowledge proofs. For the same problem, Dachman-Sold et al. propose a more efficient solution in [10].

In [8], Camenisch and Zaverucha introduce the notion of certified sets: a trusted third party provides credentials to users prior to the private set intersection protocol. This trusted third party plays the same role as $\mathcal{A}$ in our solution.

Finally, we note the recent work of De Cristofario and Tsudik, who propose in [9] more efficient protocols to various flavors of private set intersection.

All these protocols cannot readily be applied to our scenario, because they are interactive protocols between two entities (a client and a server) that interact directly (possibly in several rounds), and there is no clear translation of this two-party setting to our problem. The presence of an active Broker indeed introduces different privacy threats while enabling a decoupling between Query Issuer and Subjects. Furthermore, one of the entities in our scenario, namely the Query Issuer, can express queries on any selection criteria and is not limited to a predefined set contrary to P_1 limited to X_1 in classical private matching.

5.2   Oblivious Keyword Search

Oblivious Keyword Search is a generalization of Oblivious Transfer [21,4,7,13] where the client receives all messages related to a given private keyword instead of requesting a message at a particular position. It was proposed by Ogata and Kurosawa in [20] who showed the relationships between both notions and presented two efficient methods to achieve oblivious keyword search.

Oblivious Keyword Search is relevant to our problem because it can be used to construct private set intersection protocols [12], and more importantly they can be combined with Public Encryption with Keyword Search (PEKS) to offer additional properties as presented in [6]. The latter scheme, that we refer to as PEOKS, enhances PEKS by introducing the notion of committed blind anonymous identity-based encryption, which allow Subjects S^l to privately request trapdoors for attributes without revealing the attributes to the Authority $\mathcal{A}$: S^l commit to their attributes which allows $\mathcal{A}$ to request proofs of statement from users later on. Furthermore, the trapdoors are unique to each subject (even for the same attribute), making the scheme robust and **secure against colluding attackers**. Those properties make PEOKS more suitable to our scenario than PEKS but it is also more difficult to expose briefly and could stray the focus from our contributions and in particular the main novelty of our scheme, which is the introduction of counting Bloom filters and their use in an original way. We keep the advanced version of our scheme based on PEOKS for the extended version of the article.

6   Conclusion

In this paper, we have presented a new private matching protocol which involves an intermediate node that performs some of the matching operations on behalf of the end-entities. Contrary to classical private matching settings, where the client and the server interact directly in the process, in our new scenario the Query Issuer and the Subjects do not interact at all, and do not even need to know each others' identity. The new protocol is based on the combination of searchable encryption mechanisms and counting Bloom filters used in a radically different mindset and allows a third entity, namely the Broker, to correctly compute the matching ratio based on encrypted information only. While introducing this third entity allows a decoupling between the end-entities, it raises new privacy and security issues. We have proved that the proposed protocol preserves the privacy of end-entities thanks to the semantic security of the underlying searchable encryption mechanisms. The security against malicious Subjects cheating on the matching ratio has been analyzed and proved by bounding the probability of the success of the malicious Subject. Finally we have identified an interesting trade-off between security and performance, and we have computed the optimal parameters for an efficient execution of the protocol under a certain security level.

As future work, we plan to implement this mechanism with a PEOKS scheme to mitigate the impact of colluding attackers. We also envision to introduce multiple authorities to reduce the importance and the capabilities of $\mathcal{A}$.

References

1. Agrawal, R., Evfimievski, A., Srikant, R.: Information sharing across private databases. In: SIGMOD 2003: Proceedings of the 2003 ACM SIGMOD international conference on Management of data, pp. 86–97. ACM, New York (2003)
2. Ajmani, S., Morris, R., Liskov, B.: A trusted third-party computation service. Tech. Rep. MIT-LCS-TR-847, MIT, May 2001),
   http://www.pmg.csail.mit.edu/ajmani/papers/tep.pdf
3. Boneh, D., Di Crescenzo, G., Ostrovsky, R., Persiano, G.: Public Key Encryption with Keyword Search. In: Cachin, C., Camenisch, J.L. (eds.) EUROCRYPT 2004. LNCS, vol. 3027, pp. 506–522. Springer, Heidelberg (2004)
4. Brassard, G., Crépeau, C., Robert, J.M.: All-or-Nothing Disclosure of Secrets. In: Odlyzko, A.M. (ed.) CRYPTO 1986. LNCS, vol. 263, pp. 234–238. Springer, Heidelberg (1987)
5. Broder, A., Mitzenmacher, M.: Network applications of bloom filters: A survey. Internet Mathematics, 636–646 (2002)
6. Camenisch, J., Kohlweiss, M., Rial, A., Sheedy, C.: Blind and Anonymous Identity-Based Encryption and Authorised Private Searches on Public Key Encrypted Data. In: Jarecki, S., Tsudik, G. (eds.) PKC 2009. LNCS, vol. 5443, pp. 196–214. Springer, Heidelberg (2009)
7. Camenisch, J.L., Neven, G., Shelat, A.: Simulatable Adaptive Oblivious Transfer. In: Naor, M. (ed.) EUROCRYPT 2007. LNCS, vol. 4515, pp. 573–590. Springer, Heidelberg (2007)
8. Camenisch, J., Zaverucha, G.M.: Private intersection of certified sets. In: Dingledine, R., Golle, P. (eds.) FC 2009. LNCS, vol. 5628, pp. 108–127. Springer, Heidelberg (2009)
9. Cristofaro, E. D., and Tsudik, G.: Practical private set intersection protocols with linear complexity. In: Financial Cryptography 2010, pp. 143–159 (2010)
10. Dachman-Soled, D., Malkin, T., Raykova, M., Yung, M.: Efficient Robust Private Set Intersection. In: Abdalla, M., Pointcheval, D., Fouque, P.-A., Vergnaud, D. (eds.) ACNS 2009. LNCS, vol. 5536, pp. 125–142. Springer, Heidelberg (2009)
11. Fan, L., Cao, P., Almeida, J., Broder, A.Z.: Summary cache: a scalable wide-area web cache sharing protocol. IEEE/ACM Transactions on Networking 8(3), 281–293 (2000)
12. Freedman, M.J., Nissim, K., Pinkas, B.: Efficient private matching and set intersection. In: Cachin, C., Camenisch, J.L. (eds.) EUROCRYPT 2004. LNCS, vol. 3027, pp. 1–19. Springer, Heidelberg (2004)

13. Green, M., Hohenberger, S.: Blind Identity-Based Encryption and Simulatable Oblivious Transfer. In: Kurosawa, K. (ed.) ASIACRYPT 2007. LNCS, vol. 4833, pp. 265–282. Springer, Heidelberg (2007)
14. Huberman, B.A., Franklin, M., Hogg, T.: Enhancing privacy and trust in electronic communities. In: EC 1999: Proceedings of the 1st ACM Conference on Electronic Commerce, pp. 78–86. ACM, New York (1999)
15. Jefferies, N., Mitchell, C.J., Walker, M.: A proposed architecture for trusted third party services. In: Proceedings of the International Conference on Cryptography: Policy and Algorithms, pp. 98–104. Springer-Verlag, Heidelberg (1995)
16. Kissner, L., Song, D.: Privacy-preserving set operations. In: Shoup, V. (ed.) CRYPTO 2005. LNCS, vol. 3621, Springer, Heidelberg (2005)
17. Li, Y., Tygar, D., Hellerstein, J.M.: Private matching. Tech. Rep. IRB-TR-04-005, Intel Research Laboratory Berkeley (2004), http://www.eecs.berkeley.edu/~tygar/papers/Private_matching.pdf
18. Lynn, B. The pairing-based cryptography library (2006), http://crypto.stanford.edu/pbc/
19. Menezes, A., Vanstone, S., Okamoto, T.: Reducing elliptic curve logarithms to logarithms in a finite field. In: STOC 1991: Proceedings of the Twenty-third Annual ACM Symposium on Theory of Computing, pp. 80–89 (1991)
20. Ogata, W., Kurosawa, K.: Oblivious keyword search. Journal of Complexity - Special Issue on Coding and Cryptography 20, 356–371 (2004)
21. Rabin, M.O. How to exchange secrets with oblivious transfer, Harvard University Technical Report (1981)

7   Appendix: Proofs and Example

7.1   Proof of Theorem 1

Theorem. *Let $x_1, ..., x_n$ be n elements randomly chosen from a group G of order q. Let CBF be a counting Bloom filter of size ϕ in which the n elements $x_1, ..., x_n$ were inserted using u hash functions $h_1, ..., h_u$. Then, there are more than $\frac{q}{\phi^u}$ possible sets of elements of G^n leading to the same counting Bloom filter:*

$$|\{(x'_1, ..., x'_n) \in G^n | CBF(x'_1, ..., x'_n) = CBF(x_1, ..., x_n)\}| > \frac{q}{\phi^u}$$

Proof. Let us examine the simplest case of $n = 1$ and $CBF = \text{CBF}(x_1)$. In that case the positions $h_1(x_1); ...; h_u(x_1)$ are incremented in CBF. The security argument is based on two main observations:

- The first observation is that the hash functions $h_1, ..., h_u$ are not invertible, even though they are not necessarily cryptographic hash functions. Indeed, these functions map elements of G (a group of order q) to a small set (the integers smaller than ϕ). Therefore, if the hash functions have a uniformly distributed output then each output has $\frac{q}{\phi}$ preimages. If we combine the u equations corresponding to the u hash functions, the number of inputs simultaneously verifying u conditions on their digests is $\frac{q}{\phi^u}$.

– The second observation is that there is an information loss in the construction of this structure: the order of the hash functions is lost once the element is inserted in the counting Bloom filter, and it is impossible to know which hash function resulted in the incrementation of a given position in the filter. This second fact further increases the size of the potential preimages by a factor of up to $u!$: it is possible to set many sets of equations for the same counting Bloom filter.

As a result, the set of possible preimages corresponding to a counting Bloom filter containing a single element is at least $\frac{q}{\phi^u}$. This set is even larger when considering several elements.   □

7.2   Proof of Theorem 2

Theorem. *Let Q'_i be an encoded query concerning n selection criteria. Let CBF_i be the corresponding matching reference.*

The probability of success $\mathcal{P}_{adv}[\rho_{i,l} \rightarrow \rho_{i,l}^{claim}]$ of an adversary $\mathcal{S}^l$ in generating an array $CBF_{i,l}^{claim}$ which is accepted by $\mathcal{B}$ and results in an increase of the matching ratio from $\rho_{i,l}$ to $\rho_{i,l}^{claim}$ is upperly bounded by:

$$\mathcal{P}_{adv}[\rho_{i,l} \rightarrow \rho_{i,l}^{claim}] \leq \left(1 - e^{-\frac{(1-\rho_{i,l})n \cdot u}{\phi}}\right)^{(\rho_{i,l}^{claim} - \rho_{i,l})n \cdot u}$$

Proof. We first observe that $\mathcal{S}^l$ cannot know whether the first property (that is $CBF_{i,l}^{claim} \prec CBF_i$) is met or not as $\mathcal{S}^l$ does not know CBF_i. $\mathcal{S}^l$ can only make guesses based on the general parameters of CBF_i. We thus first establish a probabilistic model of counting Bloom filters in order to evaluate the probability of having the three aforementioned properties validated without the knowledge of CBF_i.

We consider a counting Bloom filter CBF of length ϕ containing n unknown elements which were inserted using u hash functions. Given that the probability distribution of the values in CBF_i follows a binomial distribution at each position, the probability $\mathcal{P}'(i_2)$ that the value $CBF[i_1]$ at position i_1 is greater than a given i_2 can be computed as follows: $\forall 0 \leq i_1 \leq \phi - 1, \forall 1 \leq i_2 \leq n \cdot u$,

$$\mathcal{P}'(i_2) = P[CBF[i_1] \geq i_2] = 1 - \sum_{i_3=0}^{i_2-1} \binom{n \cdot u}{i_3} \left(1 - \frac{1}{\phi}\right)^{n \cdot u - i_3} \left(\frac{1}{\phi}\right)^{i_3}.$$

Based on this result, we then prove by induction[2] that the probability $\mathcal{P}'(i_2)$ decreases faster than a geometric series of ratio $\mathcal{P}'(1)$, or to be more precise that, for $1 \leq i_2 \leq n \cdot u$,

$$\mathcal{P}'(i_2) \leq (\mathcal{P}'(1))^{i_2} \tag{1}$$

assuming that $n \cdot u \leq \phi - 1$.

---

[2] The (long) details of this proof are not included due to page constraints.

We then consider ARR to be an array of size ϕ (the matching proof). The probability $\mathcal{P}[ARR \prec CBF]$ that ARR is smaller than CBF can be computed as follows:

$$\mathcal{P}[ARR \prec CBF] = \prod_{i_1=0}^{\phi-1} \mathcal{P}'(ARR[i_1]).$$

Following the result in inequation 1, this probability can be upperly bounded as follows:

$$\mathcal{P}[ARR \prec CBF] \leq \prod_{i_1=0}^{\phi-1} \mathcal{P}'(1)^{ARR[i_1]}$$

Finally, based on the approximation of the Taylor series development of $\mathcal{P}'(1)$ we obtain the following upper bound:

$$\mathcal{P}[ARR \prec CBF] \leq \left(1 - e^{-\frac{n \cdot u}{\phi}}\right)^{w_{ARR}} \tag{2}$$

The last step of the demonstration consists in applying this important result to the matching reference CBF_i and the matching proof $CBF_{i,l}$ where the parameters CBF and ARR are replaced by the challenging reference counting Bloom filter CBF_i and the malicious matching proof $CBF_{i,l}$, respectively. However, this modification is not straightforward because while CBF was assumed to contain n random elements, a malicious Subject $\mathcal{S}^l$ knows some of the elements, that are the ones corresponding to the selection criteria that $\mathcal{S}^l$ matches. Thus, the following modifications have to be performed to evaluate the probability $\mathcal{P}_{adv}[\rho_{i,l} \to \rho_{i,l}^{claim}]$ of success of a Subject in increasing its matching ratio from $\rho_{i,l}$ to $\rho_{i,l}^{claim}$:

- We first define by $CBF_i^{chal} = CBF_i - CBF_{i,l}$ the challenging reference counting Bloom filter, that is the part of the counting Bloom filter unknown to $\mathcal{S}^l$. The weight of CBF_i^{chal} is $w_{CBF_i^{chal}} = n(1 - \rho_{i,l}) \cdot u$
- Moreover, $CBF_{i,l}^{mal} = CBF_{i,l}^{claim} - CBF_{i,l}$ defines the part of the matching proof which is malicious which weight is denoted by $w_{CBF_{i,l}^{mal}}$ which is computed as follows: $w_{CBF_{i,l}^{mal}} = w_{CBF_{i,l}^{claim}} - w_{CBF_{i,l}} = (\rho_{i,l}^{claim} - \rho_{i,l})n \cdot u$

We therefore obtain the following inequality:

$$\mathcal{P}[CBF_{i,l}^{mal} \prec CBF_i^{chal}] \leq (1 - e^{\frac{n(1-\rho_{i,l}) \cdot u}{\phi}})^{(\rho_{i,l}^{claim} - \rho_{i,l})n \cdot u} \tag{3}$$

which corresponds to $\mathcal{P}_{adv}[\rho_{i,l} \to \rho_{i,l}^{claim}]$ if $\rho_{i,l}^{claim} - \rho_{i,l}$ is a multiple of $\frac{1}{n}$ (if $w_{CBF_{i,l}^{mal}}$ is a multiple of u) to satisfy the second of the aforementioned conditions (otherwise the claimed counting Bloom filter would be rejected). $\square$

7.3 Typical Figures

To illustrate the performance of the global solution more concretely, we provide some figures of a typical scenario.

First of all, the maximum number of selection criteria that can be used in each query should be reasonably small as it directly leads to an increase in the communication and computation complexity. We therefore set this maximum number to $n_{max} = 20$.

The level of security in groups over elliptic curves depends on a security parameter called the MOV degree [19]: by carefully choosing the elliptic curve it is possible to adjust the trade-off between key size and computation time, while maintaining a given level of security. We choose a curve with a small MOV degree of 2 and a group of order q of 512 bits length to have a security equivalent to 1024 bits RSA.

The size of an encoded query is then less than $2q \cdot n_{max} \approx 20$ Kbits. To put this size into perspective, note that in the case where there is no privacy protection (where queries and replies are sent in clear) and where each selection criteria is stored in a string with 16 8bits-characters, the size of queries is approximately 2.5 Kbits. The size of encoded queries is therefore 8 times larger than their queries in clear, but this is a deliberate choice to optimize the computation performance. If the communication overhead is considered as more important, it is possible to use curves with a higher MOV degree of 6: in that case it is possible to consider groups of smaller order and the overhead would be reduced to 2.5 times.

Concerning the parameters of counting Bloom filters, in addition to n_{max}, we need to define ϕ and u.

First of all, u is used as a security parameter, since the probability of success of an adversary can be bounded by 2^{-u}. As explained in section 4.2, it is not necessary to choose a very high value for u as it does not lead to revealing a secret but only to being able to cheat on the matching ratio. By choosing $u = 10$ for example, the probability of success of an attacker would still be bounded by 10^{-3} in the most favorable case. Other probabilities of success are presented in table 1. This table shows that the probability of success for significant attacks is very low (for reference the typical security margin for symmetric encryption is $2^{-80} \approx 10^{-24}$). It is of course possible to choose a higher value for u to make sure that even in the most favorable case the attacker would not succeed with probability more than 2^{-80} but u impacts first on the construction of counting Bloom filter (each element requires the computation of u hash values) and second and more importantly on the size of counting Bloom filters. We therefore believe that choosing a smaller value for u (as we did) is a better trade-off.

The number of positions ϕ of the counting Bloom filter according to the strategy explained in section 4.2 should be $\phi = \left\lceil \frac{n_{max} \cdot u}{\ln(2)} \right\rceil$ which is equal to 289 when $n_{max} = 20$ and $u = 10$. We choose to allocate 4 bits for each position in the counting Bloom filter, thus the total size of the filter is slightly more than 1 Kbit while the probability of a bucket overflow to happen would be less than 2.10^{-12}. The size of the counting Bloom filters is therefore really negligible in comparison with the size of the queries, thus the use of counting Bloom filters

Table 1. Probability $\mathcal{P}_{adv}[\rho_{i,l} \rightarrow \rho_{i,l}^{claim}]$ of an adversary $\mathcal{S}^l$ with legitimate matching ratio $\rho_{i,l}$ to successfully claim a matching ratio of $\rho_{i,l}^{claim}$ with an encoded query Q_i' containing n selection criteria. The general parameters used for the counting Bloom filter are $n_{max} = 20$, $u = 10$, and $\phi = 289$.

n \ $\mathcal{P}_{adv}$	$0 \rightarrow \frac{1}{n}$	$0 \rightarrow \frac{2}{n}$	$0 \rightarrow \frac{1}{2}$	$0 \rightarrow 1$	$\frac{1}{2} \rightarrow \frac{1}{n} + \frac{1}{2}$	$\frac{1}{2} \rightarrow 1$	$1 - \frac{1}{n} \rightarrow 1$
6	5.10^{-8}	3.10^{-15}	1.10^{-22}	2.10^{-44}	9.10^{-11}	7.10^{-31}	2.10^{-15}
10	5.10^{-6}	2.10^{-11}	2.10^{-27}	4.10^{-54}	1.10^{-8}	1.10^{-40}	2.10^{-15}
20	1.10^{-3}	9.10^{-7}	7.10^{-31}	5.10^{-61}	5.10^{-6}	4.10^{-54}	2.10^{-15}

really offers a decisive advantage from a performance perspective on top of the advantage from a privacy point of view.

On this matter, we mentioned in section 4.1 that the size of the set of possible preimages that lead to a counting Bloom filter is around $\frac{q}{\phi^u} \approx 2^{448}$. This proves that a brute-force attack to break the privacy-preserving properties of the computation assurance solution is out of reach of current computing power.

Author Index